ʃ

ſ

ʃ

..

1.

2

1ʌ

Please
A fine

Pythagoras, Archytas, Plato and all the rest of the old philosophers hold that the motion of the whole world, together with the revolution of the stars, is not performed without music: for they teach that God framed all things by harmony.

Plutarch, *Moralia*, XLIV

Phaidon Press Limited
Regent's Wharf
All Saints Street
London N1 9PA

Phaidon Press Inc.
180 Varick Street
New York, NY 10014

www.phaidon.com

First published 2005
© 2005 Phaidon Press Limited

ISBN 0 7148 4351 2

A CIP catalogue record for
this book is available from
the British Library

Designed by Karl Shanahan
Printed in China

Cover: Detail of pl. 12,
Eustache Le Sueur, *The Music Party* (*Réunion d'Amis*), c.1640

The extracts from *The Divine Comedy* by Dante Alighieri quoted in
Chapter 3 were translated by John Ciardi, copyright 1954, 1957,
1959, 1960, 1961,1965, 1967, 1970 by the Ciardi Family Publishing
Trust. Used by permission of W. W. Norton & Company, Inc.

THAT DIVINE ORDER

Music and the Visual Arts from Antiquity to the Eighteenth Century

PETER VERGO

11   INTRODUCTION

Scope of this enquiry – Music as order or emotion – Music and
the visual arts – Advantages and disadvantages of music –
Aims and methods of the present study

25   I THE CRY OF THE PHOENIX

Origins of music and art – Music and mathematics – Music and
society in ancient China – The legacy of China – Ancient Chinese
theories of painting – Theories of music and art compared –
Art, music and ritual

57   II SPHERICAL MUSIC

Art and music in ancient Greece – The doctrine of the modes –
Moral effects of music – Harmonic theory and practice – Raphael
and Pythagoras – The Pythagorean consonances – Pythagoras
and Plato – Music in Plato's *Timaeus* – The Myth of Er – Celestial
harmonies from Cicero to Mozart – The power of music: Giovanni
de' Bardi and the Florentine *Intermedi* of 1589 – Monteverdi
and the beginnings of opera

95   III GOTHIC ARCHITECTURE AND POLYPHONY

Medieval learning and the theory of music – Builders and
scholars – Simson's theory of musical ratios criticized – Villard
de Honnecourt – Development of polyphony – Guido of Arezzo –
Musical space – The rise of the motet – Space in Gothic
architecture – Affinities between architecture and music –
The role of architecture in medieval musical theory – Music and
architecture in paradise

135   IV DIVINE HARMONIES

The liberal and the mechanical arts – The worth of painting –
Music as a model worthy of emulation – Leonardo and music –
Proportion in Renaissance music and architecture – Vitruvius,
Alberti and the principle of 'harmonic' ratios – Zorzi and Palladio
– Palladio's musical villas – Brunelleschi, Dufay and S. Maria
del Fiore – Music and architecture at St Mark's, Venice

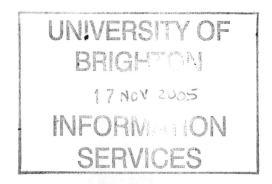

Acknowledgements

I am deeply indebted to many people who, in the course of my work, repeatedly, generously and way beyond the call of duty offered advice, commented on drafts of one or more chapters or were, at one point or another, a source of encouragement and support. I am grateful first of all to my extended academic 'family' – by which I mean my fellow-members of the Department of Art History and Theory at Essex University – who aided or inspired me in various ways. I would like to thank them all: Dawn Ades, Libby Armstrong, Neil Cox, Valerie Fraser, Michaela Giebelhausen, Margaret Iversen, Tim Laughton, Jules Lubbock, John Nash, Michael Podro, Deborah Povey, Thomas Puttfarken, Mickey Reid, Sarah Symmons-Goubert, Lisa Wade. Also at Essex, colleagues in other departments likewise expressed an interest, provided information or commented on sections of my text. I am especially grateful to Stephen Smith (History), Rodney Loudon (Electronic Systems Engineering) and Jonathan White (Literature) for assisting me in this way, also to Librarian Robert Butler and the staff of the Albert Sloman Library, who were unfailing in their helpfulness and patience – especially the members of the inter-library loans department, who dealt promptly and efficiently with my many requests.

Friends from my student days were another valuable source of assistance. Stephen Barber shared with me his lifelong love of antique myth and his fascination with Pythagoras. He also read and commented on large sections of my text. Richard Escritt, now a busy civil servant in Brussels, somehow found time to locate out-of-the-way publications, unavailable in the UK, that would otherwise have necessitated yet another costly and time-consuming trip abroad. Similar help was provided in Vienna, whose libraries proved to be an Aladdin's cave of hard-to-locate material, by Kathrin Nagel, Peter Klinger, Ioannis Bitzios and the late Hanna Egger. In Munich, the staff of the Zentralinstitut für Kunstgeschichte extended to me again that unique courtesy and hospitality that make it so enjoyable to work there.

Closer to home, Director Eric Fernie and the staff of the Courtauld Institute of Art were both prompt and generous with advice on various aspects of my research. I am especially grateful to Paul Crossley, who read and commented in detail on my Gothic architecture chapter and provided me with offprints or copies of material that would have been extremely hard to find otherwise. And there were other friends, now located in various university departments around the UK, who were likewise unstinting with help and advice. David Fallows, Professor of Music at Manchester and a recognized authority on Dufay, gave valuable guidance on the thorny question of Brunelleschi's dome and Dufay's dedicatory motet (see pp. 163–70). He also commented on the latter part of my chapter on Renaissance architecture and music. Deborah Howard at Cambridge read the same chapter and added or corrected several important points of detail.

I am grateful to her and her husband Malcolm Longair for their interest and for their advice both on Palladio and on Venetian music. At the University of Leicester, Phillip Lindley first guided me through the fabulous maze of Gothic art and architecture. At Birmingham, Andrew Barker was extremely generous in taking so much time and trouble over my chapter on Greek art and music. Having read it, he knows already how much I owe to his published writings on ancient musical theory. At the University of California at Los Angeles, Lothar von Falkenhausen kindly read my account of ancient Chinese art and music and made numerous corrections and comments. I am extremely grateful to him for his advice on many matters of detail.

I am especially indebted to Anthony King who, having read the entire manuscript, suggested many improvements in clarity and style, although he should not be held to account for any infelicities that remain. And I owe a particular kind of gratitude to John and Lesley Milner, whose encouragement knew no bounds, and to Kenneth Lindsay, Professor Emeritus at the State University of New York at Binghamton, who was in everything that matters the spiritus rector of this whole undertaking. I hope that this book will give them pleasure and that they will not consider their efforts on my behalf to have been wasted.

My research was only made possible by a Leverhulme Fellowship, which I held for two academic years from 1999–2001, when most of the reading and writing were done. I am grateful to the Leverhulme Trust for this welcome support and to my university for allowing me to take such a long period of study leave, also to Felicity Lunn, who carried the burden of much of my teaching while I was absent.

My children Oliver and Emilia showed remarkable patience with their absent-minded father when, deep in writing, I paid them less attention than I should have done. As for my wife Caroline, only she knows how much I owe to her support. Not only did she, too, read my text, making many suggestions that have saved me from embarrassment. She also provided a vital link with that real world to which, for a time, I must have seemed all too reluctant to return. I am very grateful to her for everything she did and for the many sacrifices she made.

Members of the editorial staff at Phaidon Press with whom I had contact were invariably patient, helpful and supportive. I am indebted to David Anfam, who encouraged me to submit my text to Phaidon in the first place, to Bernard Dod, who began editing it, and to Beulah Davies, who completed the task; likewise to picture researchers Holly Barton and Emmanuelle Peri, and designers Karl Shanahan and Lucy Newell. I am also grateful to Phaidon's Editorial Director, Amanda Renshaw, who believed in my book and ensured its smooth progress through the various stages of the editorial process.

Peter Vergo, Spring 2004

Author's Note

For reasons of space, the bibliography printed at the end of this volume lists only publications actually cited in my text. I hope that other authors who have written on related topics will not feel offended if they discover that I have not referred specifically to their work. This does not mean that I have not read it or that I am not interested in it – merely that I did not, in the end, need to draw on it as a source of ideas or for specific pieces of information.

Also missing from the bibliography are most of the classics – everything from Plato and Aristotle via Cicero and Seneca to St Augustine and Vasari – which exist, of course, in numerous editions. In most cases I prefer the editions and translations of Greek and Latin texts published in the Loeb Classical Library series. However, there seemed no good reason to list in the bibliography one edition rather than another, since different editions obviously have different merits. They may include notes or appendices that provide additional (and useful) information. Where I have drawn on such information, I have indicated in a footnote which edition I have been using. But if it is just a question of looking up an extract from a well-known text such as Plato's *Republic* or Aristotle's *Poetics*, the reader should be able to find without difficulty the relevant passage in any edition, simply by following the indications (book, chapter or running number) that are, once again, given in the footnotes.

Two major and invaluable works of reference I have frequently cited are *The Dictionary of Art* (1996, 34 vols) and *The New Grove Dictionary of Music and Musicians* (1980, 20 vols), both published by Macmillan in Great Britain and by Grove Dictionaries in the United States of America. Somewhat frustratingly, a new edition of Grove (Stanley Sadie, ed., *The New Grove Dictionary of Music and Musicians*, 2nd edn, 2001) appeared at a moment when research for my book was already at an advanced stage. After some thought, I decided that I would stick to the old *Grove* not only for the sake of consistency and in order to avoid confusion but also because some of the information it contains does not appear in the new edition. Very occasionally, I have referred to the new *Grove* on account of recent discoveries or in order to incorporate more up-to-date references, but I have indicated clearly those few instances when I have done so. Otherwise, references simply to *Grove* should be taken to mean the 1980 edition.

As for the footnotes, when a book or catalogue, essay or article is mentioned for the first time, the corresponding reference is given in full. Thereafter, references are usually given in abbreviated form:

either author and title or author and date. Using this information, it should be possible easily to identify the item in question as it appears in the bibliography. Where the same author has published two or more items in the same year, I have followed the usual convention of '1993 (a)', '1993 (b)' and so on. German authors whose surnames are preceded by the aristocratic 'von' are (though not out of malice) stripped of their titles when they appear in alphabetical order in the bibliography: thus, Otto von Simson appears under S as 'Simson', not under V for 'von'. In all other cases, surnames are given exactly as they appear in the published sources: for example, Robert van Gulik will be found under V as 'Van Gulik,' not under G for 'Gulik'.

If all this appears relatively straightforward, there is nothing straightforward about the problem of Romanizing Chinese characters. I explain in Chapter 1 why I thought it important to begin with at least a brief account of ancient Chinese art and music, although I do not myself speak Chinese – to my considerable regret. For Oriental writings I have therefore been dependent in every case on translations and on secondary sources. These, however, are by no means consistent as regards which of the available systems of Romanization they use. By now, the convention known as Pin-yin (which gave us 'Beijing' instead of 'Peking') has found widespread acceptance; but it is very different from the older system, referred to as 'Wade-Giles'. One might well be forgiven for failing to realize that 'Hsün-tzǔ' and 'Xunzi' are the same person, likewise 'Hsieh-ho'and 'Xie-he'. I have therefore given both forms on the first occasion that a particular name (or title of a book or treatise) is mentioned; thereafter, I have consistently used the older form. This is not because of any innate conservatism on my part, simply because all but the most recent studies (in English, at least) likewise use the older Wade-Giles system. For this reason, I thought it would be merely confusing to allude to 'Zong Bing's' essay on landscape when several older accounts of this venerable painter – for example, that by leading Sinologist Susan Bush – refer to him as 'Tsung Ping'. However, I am well aware that there is no ideal solution to this problem and can only hope that the reader will be suitably patient, at least for the duration of Chapter 1.

INTRODUCTION

It may be as well to explain in advance what kind of study this is, so that knowing beforehand the road, as it were, on which we are to travel, and understanding which part of it we are on, we may walk more easily, and not adopt unwittingly a misconception of the project. This, as Aristotle used to recount, was what happened to most of those who heard Plato's lecture on the good. They all came, he said, supposing that they were going to acquire one of the things people commonly consider good, such as wealth, health, strength – in general, some astounding happiness or other. But when the discourse turned out to be about the mathematical sciences, about numbers and geometry and astronomy ... it seemed to them, I imagine, altogether contrary to their expectations, so that some of them belittled it while others found fault. And why? Because they did not know in advance what the subject was ... But I take it that, if an overall account of the subject had been presented in advance, the prospective listener could either have abandoned it or, if he found it attractive, he could have continued to hold the conception of it which he had acquired. Aristotle himself, so he said, used to give introductions for just these reasons.

Aristoxenus, *Elementa Harmonica*[1]

This is not the first book to explore the relationship between music and the visual arts. Other writers – Rudolf Wittkower, for example – have already staked out parts of the same terrain and I have, at times, drawn gratefully upon their work. In his classic text *Architectural Principles in the Age of Humanism* (1949), Wittkower examined in detail the use of what he considered to be 'musical' proportions in certain works of Renaissance architecture. Although the significance he attributed to Platonic numerology and its supposed impact on actual building practice is now seen as exaggerated, it remains almost impossible to draw any kind of comparison between architecture and music without making some reference to his ideas. In the field of painting, Franzsepp Würtenberger's *Malerei und Musik* (1979) was, in its day, a quite remarkable achievement that covered a broad historical scope and has significantly influenced my own thinking as well as, no doubt, that of countless other people. Two other substantial publications,

---

1 The quotation is taken from the introduction to Book II of Aristoxenus' treatise on harmonics; see Andrew Barker (ed.), *Greek Musical Writings*, vol. 2 (*Harmonic and Acoustic Theory*), Cambridge (Cambridge U. P.) 1989, p. 148. Aristoxenus of Tarentum, a pupil of Aristotle, was one of the outstanding musical theorists of antiquity. He was also the principal source on which the Roman author Vitruvius, in his *Ten Books on Architecture*, based his account of Greek harmonic theory; see below, ch. 4, pp. 150–1.

Edward Lockspeiser's *Music and Painting* (1973) and Karin von Maur's *Vom Klang der Bilder* (1985) also dealt in sophisticated and interesting ways with comparisons and affinities between music and visual art, although the scope of both was limited to the modern period.[2] More recently Karl Schawelka, in his monograph *Quasi una Musica* (1993), approached the subject from a somewhat different angle but again concentrated mainly on the period since 1800 and mainly on painting.[3] Apart from these detailed studies, there have been one or two more general surveys, among them Tom Phillips' *Music in Art through the Ages* (1997),[4] and several catalogues of exhibitions devoted to topics such as representations of musical instruments in the painting of particular places or periods.[5]

My own book differs in several respects from those I have just cited. For one thing, it is as much about the history and theory of music as it is about the visual arts. For another, apart from a brief epilogue tracing the development of the colour organ, it stops at just the point where several other writers begin, in the late eighteenth century. I have also largely ignored one important subject that has been well covered in the existing literature, namely depictions of people making music. Drawn and painted images of singers, dancers and musicians are found at every period and in every culture: in Chinese scrolls, Greek vase paintings, stained-glass windows, the illuminations and miniatures that illustrate the psalters and books of hours of the Middle Ages and early Renaissance, the pastorales and mythological paintings of Titian and Giorgione, the tavern scenes and genre paintings of the Dutch seventeenth-century masters as well as the sublime works of Vermeer, the *fêtes galantes* and *fêtes champêtres* of Watteau ... the list is virtually endless. Apart from their other qualities as works of art, these images constitute an

---

2   There is a recent English translation of von Maur's book, published by Prestel (the original publishers) under the title *The Sound of Painting: Music in Modern Art* (Munich/London, 1999), but it is, alas, greatly truncated in comparison to the German edition.
3   Karl Schawelka, *Quasi una Musica. Untersuchungen zum Ideal des 'Musikalischen' in der Malerei ab 1800*, Munich (Mäander) 1993; compare also Helga de la Motte-Haber, *Musik und bildende Kunst. Von der Tonmalerei zur Klangskulptur*, Laaber (Laaber-Verlag) 1990; Elisabeth Schmierer et al. (eds), *Töne – Farben – Formen. Über Musik und die bildenden Künste*, Laaber (Laaber-Verlag) 1995; Monika Fink, *Musik nach Bildern. Programmbezogenes Komponieren im 19. und 20. Jahrhundert*, Innsbruck (Helbling) 1988.
4   Tom Phillips, *Music in Art through the Ages*, Munich/New York (Prestel) 1997. Other recent publications in English, which appear to show a growing interest in this field of enquiry, include Marsha L. Morton and Peter L. Schmunk (eds), *The Arts Entwined. Music and Painting in the Nineteenth Century*, New York (Garland) 2000; compare also James Leggio (ed.), *Music and Modern Art*, New York/London (Routledge) 2002.
5   See, for example, Edwin Buijsen and Louis Peter Grijp (eds), *The Hoogstedter Exhibition of Music and Painting in the Golden Age*, The Hague/Zwolle (Hoog & Hoog/Waanders) 1994. This catalogue of an exhibition that included mainly Dutch seventeenth-century artists provides a useful account of the emblematic, symbolic, historical and anecdotal uses of musical imagery in painting generally. A more recent exhibition on the theme of music in European paintings 1500–1700, *Dipingere la musica. Musik in der Malerei des 16. und 17. Jahrhunderts* (Vienna: Kunsthistorisches Museum, 2001) likewise concentrated on a relatively brief period; its catalogue, however, contains an extensive further bibliography on the subject of painting's relationship with music.

important part of the historical record. They often tell us about archaic instruments and how they were played; without such information, our understanding of these things would, in many cases, be scanty in the extreme. They also tell us about the social uses of music, the role it played in love and war and, more generally, about the preoccupations and manners of earlier times. But, while there are monographs devoted to precisely such questions, I have not dealt with these topics here.[6] Only occasionally – for example, in Chapter 5 – do I refer to paintings that show musical instruments or people making music. I do so, however, not primarily because of the subjects they depict but because of the background of ideas against which they should properly be seen.

Scope of this enquiry

Paintings and other works of art do, of course, feature prominently at various points in the following narrative. However, neither they nor particular pieces of music are, in the end, my main concern. What interests me more is how, over a very long time-scale and in quite different contexts, writers on a variety of subjects have persisted – obstinately, repeatedly and sometimes bafflingly – in *comparing* music with art. To any sane person, at least some of these comparisons must seem far-fetched to a degree. Take, for example, the notion that individual details of architectural decoration might correspond to different notes of the musical scale. This was an idea put forward, apparently in all seriousness, by the French eighteenth-century writer Camus de Mézières who, in his book *Le Génie de l'architecture* (1780), attempts to persuade us that, when we look at a classical building, 'the first *torus*, the *scotia*, and the second *torus* seem to produce for the eye what the notes *soh*, *ti* and *re* do for the ear. The beadings are like voice passages and glides.'[7] Clearly they are nothing of the sort. But the crucial question, to my mind, is not whether the particular analogy de Mézières draws is plausible or implausible, nor whether there might really be some other, equally precise resemblance or affinity between music and visual art. Instead, it seemed more important to ask *why*, in so many different periods, societies and cultures, resemblances or affinities of this kind were thought to exist. Why did medieval writers on music compare the relationship between ground plan and elevation that characterized the great Gothic cathedrals to the relationship

---

6 The most accessible study of this kind is that by Emanuel Winternitz, *Musical Instruments and Their Symbolism in Western Art: Studies in Musical Iconology*, New Haven/London (Yale U. P.) 2nd edn 1979.

7 Camus de Mézières, *Le Génie de l'architecture ou l'analogie de cet art avec nos sensations*, Paris, 1780, p. 32, quoted after H. James Jensen, *The Muses' Concord*, Bloomington, IN (Indiana U. P.) 1976, p. 74.

between tenor part and upper voices in polyphonic motets of the thirteenth and fourteenth centuries? Why did Alberti warn against altering the proportions of his proposed façade for the church of S. Francesco (c.1454–5) in Rimini lest 'all that music' be disturbed? Why did Poussin try to adapt Renaissance ideas about the musical modes of antiquity to the theory of painting? Why did an eighteenth-century French Jesuit named Louis-Bertrand Castel spend much of his life experimenting with designs for an 'ocular harpsichord', based on the imagined similarity between colours and musical tones – an idea mentioned approvingly even by an artist as down-to-earth as Hogarth? And why, faced with the scepticism of provincial audiences, did the Victorian painter Alexander Wallace Rimington persist in building gigantic and costly colour organs powered by electricity, claiming for what he called 'colour-music' the status of an entirely new form of art?

As so often, to each of the questions I have just posed there is both a long and a short answer. The long answers are the main business of the chapters that follow, which offer a detailed account of what I think were the reasons why such analogies between music and visual art were employed. However, it may be as well to give the gist of those answers here. In the systems of articulation upon which Gothic architecture depended, musical theorists who wrote about polyphony during the years after 1200 saw, at least in their imagination, solutions to problems similar to those confronting musicians at that time – problems that had to do, above all, with order and coherence. Alberti, writing in the fifteenth century, was anxious to prescribe principles of design that would enable him and his contemporaries to create a modern style of architecture to rival that of the ancients. Such principles could, he thought, be derived from a study of the mathematical rules by which musical consonances were determined. Thus, buildings designed according to these principles would embody 'musical' proportions, thereby creating 'harmonies for the eye'. Poussin, dazzled by his reading of the Venetian musical theorist Gioseffo Zarlino (1517–90), thought that ancient ideas about the modes of Greek music and the precise effects these were capable of producing upon the emotions of the listener could provide, if not a rationale or method for art, then at least a way of thinking about how one might attune the resources of painting to the emotional and moral character of the subject depicted. Castel, no less dazzled by his reading of Newton's *Opticks* (although he later rejected Newton's theories altogether), tried to elaborate a system of correspondences between the colours of the spectrum and the pitches of the musical scale in order to create 'colour melodies' that would enable even a deaf person to judge of the power and beauty of music. (Interestingly, almost two centuries later the German Expressionist painter August Macke speculated in very similar fashion about the 'undreamed-of power' painters would possess if only they could 'organize colours into a system, like notes'.)[8] And, when advances in lighting technology at last offered the possibility of actually creating 'colour-music', Rimington and his followers – artists such as Alexander László in Germany or Thomas Wilfred in the United States of America – set themselves the task of realizing the goal Castel had envisaged more than a century before, that of staging 'concerts for the eye', thereby creating a new form of public entertainment that, for a time at least, vied in popularity with the early cinema.

Music as order or emotion

Of course, Macke writing about 'organizing colours into a system, like notes' is very different from medieval musical theorists discussing the structural principles underlying Gothic architecture. And both are different again from Poussin reflecting upon the supposedly determined and systematic effects music could exert upon our emotions and wondering whether painting could be made to elicit equally precise responses on the part of the spectator. Yet the notion that music could, in one way or another, be equated with order or system is common to all the examples just cited – a view that persisted until well into the Romantic era and in some cases for even longer. Not only did this idea profoundly affect discussions about the relationship between music and the visual arts. It also had a very long pedigree. From antiquity onwards, musicians, writers and philosophers had pointed repeatedly to what they saw as music's inherent orderly aspect, even if what they meant by 'music' often had precious little to do with the business of actually making or enjoying those pleasant and melodious sounds that rejoice the human ear. On the contrary, singing and playing instruments were, at times, considered suspect activities, at least by some of the stuffier Greek philosophers, who tended to equate professional musicians with negligibly clad girls brought in at dinner parties to amuse guests.[9]

[handwritten marginal note: separation of music 'object' & musicking 'practice' (as in Small)]

---

8 August Macke, letter to his fiancée Elisabeth Gerhardt dated 14 July 1907, in Werner Frese and Ernst-Gerhard Güse (eds), *Briefe an Elisabeth und die Freunde. August Macke*, Munich (Bruckmann) 1987, pp. 137–8.

9 See Henry Chadwick, *Boethius. The Consolations of Music, Logic, Theology and Philosophy*, Oxford (Clarendon Press) 1981, p. 86. These attitudes first developed only during the latter part of the fourth century BC. Prior to this, practical music making was a major element in Greek culture. Andrew Barker points out that musical activities were as much a part of civic life as were political ones and as much a part of religious observance as was the act of sacrifice (letter to the author, September 2001).

Aristotle, for example, dismissed such vulgar pursuits as unworthy of an educated person, remarking acidly that the poets 'never describe Zeus as singing or playing the *kithara*; rather, we say that such practitioners are vulgar artisans and that what they do is not for real men, unless they are drunk or joking'.[10] Similarly, the Latin author Boethius, who based his influential treatise *De institutione musica* principally on earlier Greek sources, considered the true musician or *musicus* to be someone whose superior understanding rendered him capable of *judging* music – by contrast with composers and performers (often referred to slightly by medieval writers as *cantores*) who merely produced it on demand.[11] What Boethius and most of his followers meant by 'music' was, first and foremost, the abstract science of harmonics, which showed (or so it seemed) the patterns of musical consonances to be a manifestation of the same mathematical laws that gave order to the cosmos and governed the movements of the heavenly bodies. This intimate relationship with mathematics and astronomy allowed music (that is, music conceived by the intellect) to claim a special kind of respect that, prior to the Renaissance, was accorded to no other form of art.

Just how forcibly antique notions of this kind impressed themselves upon the European mind can be gauged from the writings of Isidore, Bishop of Seville, who, as late as the seventh century AD, could still announce in rhapsodic tones that, 'without music, no discipline can be perfect, for there is nothing without it. The very universe, it is said, is held together by a certain harmony of sounds, and the heavens themselves are made to revolve by the modulation of harmony. Music moves the feelings and changes the emotions.'[12] This brief quotation from Isidore's *Etymologies* neatly encapsulates two entirely contradictory definitions of music, both of which can be found in numerous classical sources. The first had to do with the notion of harmony, which in this context did not mean two or more notes sounded simultaneously: the modern sense of the term. Rather, 'harmony' referred to that orderly aspect of music just mentioned, which had its mysterious counterpart in the regular

---

10 *Politics*, 1339b–40a. However, musicians were objects of admiration in texts from Homer onwards; and although Aristotle is right in saying that Zeus didn't sing or play instruments, Apollo and the Muses did, and so on occasion did other gods – for example, at the wedding of Peleus and Thetis; see Andrew Barker (ed.), *Greek Musical Writings*, vol. 1 (*The Musician and his Art*), Cambridge (Cambridge U. P.) 1984, pp. 80, 172–3.

11 'That person is a musician who possesses the faculty of judging – according to speculation and reason that is appropriate and suitable to music – of modes and rhythms, of the classes of melodies and their combinations ... and of the songs of the poets.' (Boethius, *De institutione musica*, I, 34, quoted after James McKinnon, 'The Early Christian Period and the Latin Middle Ages', in Oliver Strunk, ed., *Source Readings in Music History*, rev. edn by Leo Treitler, New York (W. W. Norton) 1998, pp. 142–3, cited hereafter as Strunk II.)

12 *Isidori Hispalensis Episcopi Etymologiarum sive Originum libri XX*, III, 17, quoted after Strunk II, p. 150.

motions of the stars and planets and in the harmonious ordering or 'pattern of attunement' of the human soul.[13] Many antique theorists who wrote about music singled out this orderliness as particularly worthy of praise. By contrast, the other aspect of music Isidore mentions, its power to 'move the feelings and change the emotions', was anything but orderly. One of its most striking attributes – now, of course, we are talking about music heard by the sensual ear, not the abstract theory of music – was its capacity to influence our emotions and thereby affect our behaviour. The fact that this influence could be not only for good but also, worryingly, for evil had, as far back as Plato's time, occasioned serious misgivings. At its noblest, music could call forth courageous and patriotic feelings, stiffen the resolve and inspire young men to deeds of valour. (Whatever we may think, these were all considered to be good things, at least according to Plato's account of them.) At its most debased, it acted as an encouragement to licentiousness and debauchery, weakened men's moral fibre and could thereby bring about the downfall not just of the individual but, ultimately, of the state. Plato's *Republic* is full of dire warnings about the fateful consequences for society should the proper rules of music be flouted to even the smallest degree.

Music and the visual arts

Again, it does not really matter whether we consider ideas like these to be true or false, plausible or implausible. What matters is the impact they had on both thinking about music and the theory and practice of other forms of art. In the case of the visual arts, the marks of that impact can be discovered at almost every turn. Sometimes both aspects of music – on the one hand, as a metaphor for order and the proper regulation of society and its institutions, on the other, as an incitement to licence and impropriety – are alluded to in a single picture, as in the case of Jan Miense Molenaer's *A Music Party* (*Allegory of Fidelity in Marriage*) of 1633 (pl. 1). This is a work discussed in detail by Richard Leppert in his monograph *The Sight of Sound* (1993), albeit from a standpoint rather different from my own.[14] Leppert interprets the music making depicted in the painting as an attribute or pursuit of different social classes. It therefore stands simultaneously for both the 'wrong' and the 'right' kind of music: disruptive and bawdy in the case of the lower orders, an

---

13 Compare, again, Aristotle who observes without specifying whom he has in mind that 'many of the wise say, some of them that the soul is a *harmonia*, others that it contains a *harmonia*' (*Politics* 1340b18).

14 See Richard Leppert, *The Sight of Sound. Music, Representation and the History of the Body*, Berkeley/Los Angeles/London (California U. P.) 1993, p. 2 and fig. 3, also pp. 6ff.

image of harmony and orderly social relations in the case of the middle class. At other times, artists clearly had in mind only one of these conflicting aspects of music. For example, its association with debauchery – and hence with death and perdition – often finds allegorical expression in the sculptures of music-making demons who play out their grisly role in many Romanesque and Gothic Last Judgement portals (fig. 1).[15] The use of such imagery has been analysed by Kathi Meyer-Baer in her classic study *Music of the*

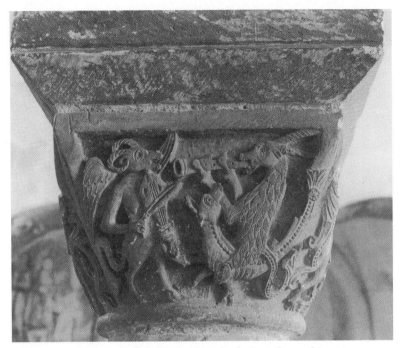

Figure 1. Romanesque capital showing demons playing rebec and cornet, from St Gabriel's chapel, Canterbury cathedral, *c.*1100

Spheres and the Dance of Death. Four centuries later, those innumerable tavern scenes that were the stock-in-trade of Dutch and Flemish seventeenth-century genre painters repeatedly link music with amorous exploits, drunkenness and the singing of bawdy songs – one of several reasons why music in general was frowned on by Calvinist writers, given that the language and content of such songs was usually coarse and often sexually explicit.

---

15 Such demons have their celestial counterpart in the sculpted figures of cheerily smiling musical angels who guide the souls of the blessed towards heaven; on this most interesting topic see Paul Binski, 'The Angel Choir at Lincoln and the Poetics of the Gothic Smile', *Art History*, vol. 20, no. 3 (September 1997), pp. 350–74.

In contrast to these lewd images, that subject popular with eighteenth- and nineteenth-century painters, a music lesson given by an invariably male teacher to an invariably female pupil, does not usually involve any blatant act of impropriety. These seemingly everyday scenes evoke in subtler ways the possibility of an illicit sexual liaison or, at the very least, snatched moments of intimacy.[16] In Fragonard's *The Music Lesson* (1765–72; pl. 2) we are merely left to imagine that the man shown gazing distractedly at the young woman's cleavage as she runs her fingers over the keyboard is waiting for a chance to start running his fingers over her.[17]

Advantages and disadvantages of music

Apart from its association with lasciviousness and dissolute behaviour, music – real music, that is – was thought to exhibit a number of other flaws or failings. One of the most glaring of these was its essentially transitory nature. Musical sounds are, by their nature, short-lived. A musical performance is soon over. No matter what feelings it may have produced in the listener, nothing remains other than a relatively imprecise memory and perhaps a lingering sense of excitement or sadness or nostalgia. This was what Leonardo da Vinci called music's 'mortal sickness', which he contrasted with the 'durability' of painting, an art capable of immortalizing the beauty of a face that would soon forfeit its youthful grace. Moreover, the unfolding of time was necessary for the structure, the organizational logic of a piece of music, to become apparent. A further advantage of pictures was that their content and structure could be grasped in a single, concentrated moment. Or so it was often said. In reality, no serious account of how we actually attend to pictures would lead us to think that this was true. Few works of visual art, if any, reveal their underlying structure all at once. In most cases, it needs to be discovered and analysed in a variety of ways – a complex process demanding considerable expenditure of time, effort and attention. Nevertheless, in many of those discussions in which the qualities of music and of painting were compared, this time-consuming aspect of looking at pictures was conveniently ignored. For whatever reason, writers on music insisted on pointing

---

16 Phillips points out that the ease with which the male music teacher could gain access to the 'young wife and even younger daughters' of an otherwise well-regulated household provided ample material for the intrigues that characterize the plots of many eighteenth- and nineteenth-century operas (*Music and Art*, p. 12).

17 Such thoughts were by no means confined to painting nor to the eighteenth and nineteenth centuries. A similar idea had already occurred to Shakespeare who, in Sonnet 128, portrays the lover standing alongside his mistress, envying the keyboard as her fingers explore '... those jacks [that is, keys] that nimble leap / To kiss the tender inward of thy hand.' The final couplet reads, 'Since saucy jacks so happy are in this / Give them thy fingers, me thy lips to kiss.'

to what they considered to be one of the particular strengths of pictorial art, namely that its entire content did not need to be viewed sequentially but could be assimilated more or less in one go.

Another shortcoming frequently ascribed to music was a matter for more serious concern. Painting could depict in vivid and affecting ways subjects that were deemed noble or elevating – an attribute on which its claim to moral value was largely based. But what did music represent? Could it deal in concrete representations at all, as did painting, or only in abstract evocations? Was it capable of imitating nature or the human passions? And if it did imitate the passions, what value might such imitations possess? The specific problem of morality could, of course, be alleviated by joining music to words that served as the principal vehicle for meaning, music being relegated to the subsidiary though important task of reinforcing that same meaning. But what of purely instrumental music? Was music without words devoid of significance, as some writers thought? Or were the tones of music expressive in themselves? If so, expressive of what? As the seventeenth century gave way to the eighteenth, critics of the arts and also philosophers began to direct more and more of their attention to just such questions.[18]

Meanwhile, music itself did not wait for an answer. By now, it had begun to cast aside its auxiliary role, no longer content to be regarded merely as a backing for the words. The second half of the eighteenth century would witness the dawn of a new golden age of purely orchestral and instrumental music: the age of the symphony, the sonata and the string quartet. By the early Romantic era, extravagant claims were already being made regarding the value and significance of these kinds of 'abstract' compositions. The poet Goethe, for example, thought that music owed 'its particular worth to the fact that it has no *Stoff* that needs to be discounted'.[19] The German word *Stoff* has two meanings: it can refer either to the subject-matter of a story or drama or simply to 'material' (the fabric covering an armchair is also *Stoff*). The fact that music was not burdened by any material substance, of the kind that weighed heavily upon both architecture and sculpture, was held to confer on it a certain advantage by comparison with other forms of art. But the principal advantage of music was that it had no need of narrative in order to make its point. The stories on which operas were based and the texts and poems set to music by composers of *Lieder* were merely coincidental.[20] Even when deprived of words or stories, audiences

---

18 For discussion of Descartes' surprisingly early reflections on non-vocal music, see below, ch. 5, pp. 192ff.
19 Quoted after Jutta Hecker (ed.), *J. W. von Goethe. Maximen und Reflexionen* (Leipzig, 1941), no. 486.

still had no difficulty in responding intuitively to purely 'abstract' music, which was clearly neither illogical nor devoid of meaning. On the contrary, composers of instrumental music were preoccupied with meanings that were, as Mendelssohn observed, 'too precise' for words.[21] As the nineteenth century drew to a close, artists and critics anxious to explore the communicative potential of painting as a means of expression in its own right – that is, independent of subject-matter or any kind of representation – looked increasingly to music as a model for what would eventually become an entirely non-narrative, even 'non-objective' form of visual art.

→ Could inform film / video work to these ends, in an entirely different way?

Aims and methods of the present study

In Volume Two, which traces the continuing story of music's relationship to the visual arts as it unfolded in the course of the nineteenth and twentieth centuries,[22] I shall consider in some detail how modern writers came to view music as the paradigm of an abstract yet expressive art. The principal focus of this first volume, by contrast, is upon older ideas – ideas that have little to do with music's abstract qualities but a good deal to do with what people imagined to be the orderly nature not just of music itself but also of the cosmos and other forms of human experience. Today, some of those ideas must strike us as decidedly bizarre. Newton's account of the 'musical' division of the spectrum, which greatly influenced eighteenth-century discussion of the relationship between music and colour, is now regarded merely as a curiosity, as is the once widely held view that the heavens consisted of an interlocking system of crystalline spheres kept in constant motion by angels. As I have already stated, my main aim is not to explain why, in the past, people believed such things. That would be a quite different kind of enterprise. Instead, the purpose of this study is to examine how such beliefs influenced thinking about the resemblances or disparities between visual art and music. But in describing, for example, how the universe was thought to be arranged according to a musical system of proportions, it is necessary first to explain what musical proportions are, even though the mathematical division of the octave, on which the notion of 'harmonic' ratios was based, bore

---

20 Given his views cited above, it is ironic that Goethe, of all people, should have provided nineteenth-century composers with a seemingly limitless supply of poems that were, or so it appeared to them, just crying out to be set to music, from Schubert's spine-chilling 'Erlkönig' to Hugo Wolf's sublime setting of 'Kennst Du das Land'.

21 Felix Mendelssohn Bartholdy, letter to Marc-André Souchay dated 15 October 1842, quoted after Ruth A. Solie, *The Nineteenth Century*, in Oliver Strunk (ed.), *Source Readings in Music History*, rev. edn by Leo Treitler, New York (W. W. Norton) 1998, p. 1201.

22 *Visual Music: Music and the Visual Arts from the Enlightenment to the late Twentieth Century* is scheduled for publication by Phaidon Press in 2008.

little or no relation to the realities of musical perception.[23] Needless to say, the fact that I devote considerable space to analysing such ideas should not be construed as a wish to persuade people of their truth or suggest that they are relevant to thinking about art today. Describing and analysing are not the same as convincing or persuading – something I try to make clear when introducing a class of students to writers like Nietzsche, since I would not want them to think that I am a committed Nietzschean or that I consider his philosophy to be a useful adjunct to life. Far from it: I would be seriously alarmed if anyone thought either of these things were true.

The aims just outlined have largely determined the manner in which the following chapters are organized. Throughout much of the text, sections deploying the relevant critical and theoretical sources are deliberately interspersed with others whose principal focus is on individual pieces of music and works of art. These are, in most cases, discussed not for their own sake but in terms of their relation to each other and to the intellectual and creative traditions of which they are part. The exceptions to this general rule are Chapters 1 and 2, which, although they do contain a certain amount of analytical material, are aimed primarily at setting the scene. They therefore raise, if only briefly, various questions to be explored in more detail later on. In these early chapters I have also paused from time to time in order to explain specific aspects of musical theory – for example, the nature of the modes – that are essential to an understanding of that later discussion.

Although I have covered a good deal of ground, the following account of the relationship between music and art still omits far more than it includes, and many famous painters, architects and composers are missing from these pages. This does not mean that I do not like them; it is merely the case that, whatever their other achievements, they played little or no part in the story I am about to tell. Moreover, compared with its very long time-scale – from antiquity to the dawn of the modern era – that story has (as will quickly be seen) a relatively narrow geographical focus. It is concerned, for much of its course, with European 'high culture' – an essentially literate, urban culture – rather than with folk art and music or the indigenous arts. It would, however, have been perverse to ignore entirely the role played by other non-European civilizations. Some of the earliest evidence we have regarding the origins of music as an art form – meaning, in effect, ritual and

---

23 On the discrepancy between the mathematical division of the octave and 'just' intonation see below, ch. 1, pp. 32ff.

courtly music – comes from ancient China. In the next chapter, I take that evidence as a point of departure not just because of its great antiquity but also because the ancient Chinese authors invariably discuss music in terms of its cosmological, political or moral significance – the kinds of issues frequently addressed by later theorists. The principal object of this study remains, nevertheless, European art and music of the past two-and-a-half millennia, with – as we shall see – occasional detours and diversions along the way.

I THE CRY OF THE PHOENIX

The little and big drums are hung for beating;
The tambourines and stone chimes, the staff and clapper.
All is ready and they play.
Pan-pipes and flute are ready and begin.
Sweetly blend the tones,
Solemn the melody of their bird-music.
The ancestors are listening;
As our guests they have come,
To gaze long upon their victories.

Let bell and drum blend,
Stone chime and pipes echo,
That rich blessings may come down ...
Every act and posture has gone rightly,
We are quite drunk ...[1]

Origins of music and art

What we know about the beginnings of art has been dictated largely by chance. A considerable number of prehistoric images and artefacts have come down to us, many dating back as far as the Palaeolithic era: early examples of carving such as the steatopygian *Venus of Willendorf* (c.23,000 BC; fig. 2) or the vivid cave paintings

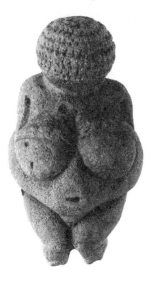

Figure 2. *Venus of Willendorf*, c.23,000 BC, carved limestone figurine, h. 11.1 cm, 4^3_8 in (Naturhistorisches Museum, Vienna)

1 *The Book of Songs*. Translated from the Chinese by Arthur Waley, London (George Allen & Unwin) 1937, pp. 218, 230.

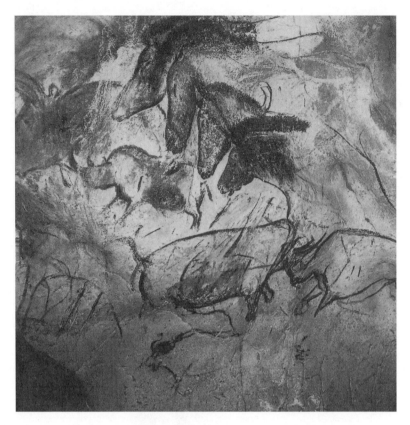

Figure 3. Depictions of animals, *c.*30,000 BC, from the Cave Chauvet, Ardèche

of Cosquer and Chauvet (fig. 3).[2] These, however, are not the oldest forms of sculpture or painting. They are simply among the oldest to have survived, because they were the most durable or because a fortuitous combination of circumstances ensured their preservation. There must have been earlier kinds of painting and carving on perishable materials like skin or wood. But, as one writer on ancient art and archaeology has remarked, the trouble with perishable objects is that they tend to perish.[3] As a consequence, we know next to nothing of them.

Nor do we know anything about the intentions of the earliest makers of art. Whether they themselves considered any of the

2 Radio-carbon analysis of some of the animals depicted in the Cave Chauvet (Ardèche) suggests a date before 30,000 BC, making these some of the oldest known images drawn and painted by early humans; for discussion of dating and style see Jean Clottes, 'The "Three Cs": fresh avenues towards European Palaeolithic Art', in C. Chippindale and P. Taçon (eds), *The Archaeology of Rock Art*, Cambridge (Cambridge U. P.) 1998, pp. 117ff.

3 See Jeffrey M. Hurwit, *The Athenian Acropolis. History, Mythology and Archaeology from the Neolithic Era to the Present*, Cambridge (Cambridge U. P.) 1999, p. 62.

objects they made to be 'art' – a distinctively modern concept – seems highly unlikely. If they thought about them at all, they probably thought in the first instance about the uses to which such objects were put; and we, too, faced with their mute intractability, may find ourselves wondering about their ritual or symbolic or practical functions.[4] For example, it is tempting to interpret the lively images fashioned by the cave-dwellers of France and Northern Spain as proof of their desire to lay hold of the visible world, to 'pin down' the rhinoceros and bison and other fauna that were almost certainly a source of danger and that must have been objects of the chase, but which may also have had other kinds of mythic or magical significance. Making such images may even have been, for their creators, a way of exerting magical power over their four-footed quarry: part of some rite to ensure successful hunting. If this were true, it would perhaps indicate the earliest point of connection between making images and making music, since one theory about the totemistic character of song sees its origin in the imitation of animal cries that primitive hunting peoples uttered in order to assert power over their prey by means of sympathetic magic.[5]

But if early music and early art were similar in this respect, there is an important difference between them. We cannot compare cave paintings or rock carvings with the tunes once played or sung by our human ancestors who fashioned these things because their tunes, unlike their paintings and carvings, have not survived. More surprisingly, the same is true of civilizations and societies far closer in time to our own. We know next to nothing about the melodies devised by the inhabitants of ancient Egypt or even ancient Rome. In fact, we are woefully ignorant about the music of anything other than our most recent past. An abundance of material evidence in the form of painting and sculpture, architecture and decoration testifies to the aesthetic impulses that characterized earlier peoples and cultures. By contrast, their music – one of the most vivid expressions of mankind's instinctive urge to create – is, in almost every case, entirely lacking.

Whether fragments of folk song or the teasing chants that accompany children's games and that seem to transcend all

---

4 A concise, thought-provoking article by Thomas Heyd, 'Rock Art Aesthetics: Trace on Rock, Mark of Spirit, Window on Land' highlights the problem of bringing aesthetic criteria to bear on examples of primitive art (including cave art); see *Journal of Aesthetics and Art Criticism*, vol. 57, no. 4 (Fall 1999), pp. 451–8. Heyd neatly summarizes the debate among anthropologists over the various functions attributable, for example, to petraglyphs and other examples of rock art and discusses whether purely aesthetic aims may plausibly be ascribed to prehistoric 'artists'. See also John Halverson, 'Art for Art's Sake in the Paleolithic', *Current Anthropology*, 28 (1987), pp. 63–89.
5 Marius Schneider, 'Primitive Music', in Egon Wellesz (ed.), *The New Oxford History of Music*, vol. 1 (*Ancient and Oriental Music*), London (Oxford U. P.) 1957, esp. pp. 5ff.

geographical and cultural boundaries might still incorporate vestiges of these lost melodies of the past is a matter more of speculation than of proof. Likewise, it has been suggested that the music of tribal peoples, especially that used in ritual and ceremonial as well as social contexts (that is, not only tribal chants and war dances and incantations but also working songs that enliven rhythmically repetitive tasks such as lifting and carrying) may also bear the marks of older melodic forms.[6] But, in reality, we have no way of knowing. The magical, evanescent tones of music have faded, frustratingly, almost as soon as they have been played or sung, continuing to exist only in the minds of the performer and of those who happen to be listening. The only way of preserving them, other than by recourse to purely oral tradition, is by means of a generally accepted system of notation – or, in our own day, through the mechanical medium of sound recording. However, the invention of musical notation was an unconscionable time in coming. As late as the seventh century AD Isidore of Seville could still declare in his *Etymologies* that 'unless sounds are remembered by man, they perish, for they cannot be written down'.[7] In other words, as far as he knew, there existed in Western Europe at that date no way of accurately reproducing a piece of music that had not previously been heard. Although several major civilizations of the ancient world developed notational systems of one kind or another (the Greeks even had two: one for vocal, the other for instrumental music), the handing down of any kind of music from one generation to another remained a matter primarily of aural rather than written transmission. Once that chain of transmission was broken, the music itself was effectively lost.

The more we reflect on this contrast between music and other forms of art, the more disconcerting it seems. We may find our-selves inexpressibly moved by the scale and grandeur of the temples of the Acropolis or the sculptures of the Parthenon, just as we may be moved by reading about the sack of Troy or by a spir-ited rendition of the *Oresteia*: the verbal arts of poetry and drama, too, have survived, no matter in how corrupted a form, better than music. But we cannot be similarly moved by hearing the music of these different periods because, save for a few brief fragments, it no longer exists. Writing about the music of Greek antiquity,

---

6 See, for example, Alan P. Merriam, *The Anthropology of Music*, Evanston, IL (Northwestern U. P.) 1964, ch. 11, 'Uses and Functions', esp. pp. 217ff.; also Melville J. Herskovits, *Man and His Works*, New York (Alfred A. Knopf) 1948, pp. 238–40.
7 *Isidori Hispalensis Episcopi Etymologiarium sive Originum libri XX*, III, 15, quoted after Strunk II, p. 39. On the beginnings of Western musical notation see below, ch. 3, pp. 109ff.

Isobel Henderson has emphasized the 'great and obvious divergence between the fates of language and of music among Greeks, who could quote their Homer for two millennia but who ceased, after a certain point, to know their musical past except as they knew the names of dead athletes'.[8] When the classical Greek language and its literature began to grow unintelligible, they were saved by the labour of ancient scholars. It seems that no such labour was undertaken on behalf of music and the 'insatiable scholarship' of Alexandria shows scant awareness of musical palaeography.[9] Only a few dozen examples of any kind of ancient Greek musical notation now survive, almost none of them predating the late classical or Hellenistic periods.[10] Among these are, as it hap-

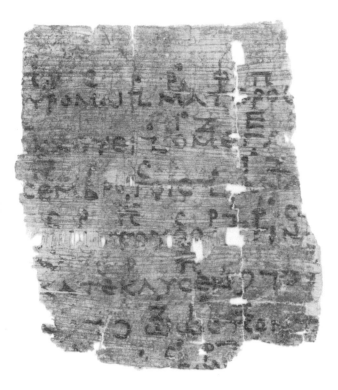

Figure 4. Fragment of papyrus containing lines from Euripides' *Orestes* accompanied by musical notation, *c.*200 BC (Österreichische Nationalbibliothek, Vienna, Papyrussammlung, Inv. no. G2315)

8 Isobel Henderson, 'Ancient Greek Music', in Wellesz, op. cit. (as n. [5] above), p. 336.
9 Ibid., pp. 337ff.
10 The most recent (and exhaustive) study lists 61 such examples: see Egert Pöhlmann and Martin L. West (eds),
   Documents of Ancient Greek Music. The Extant Melodies and Fragments, Oxford (Clarendon Press) 2001.

pens, two scraps of melody associated with the tragedies of Euripides– *Orestes* (fig. 4) and *Iphigenia in Aulis* – although the latter consists of only a few bars of melody. The most substantial of these musical fragments are the famous paeans in praise of Apollo (dated by most sources to 128/127 BC), inscribed on the wall of the Athenian treasury at Delphi.[11] Their reconstruction remains, even so, to some extent conjectural.[12]

Certain types of very early musical instruments have also been preserved. These include bone flutes and whistles, some perhaps as old as the Aurignacian period (*c.*35,000–20,000 BC).[13] It is thought that wind instruments generally may be among the oldest artefacts of all, because ancient peoples were inspired by natural sounds occasioned by the friction of air moving across surfaces or because hollow materials such as bamboo, reed and animal bones that can produce sounds were readily available.[14] These primitive instruments were followed in less distant times by bronze bells, stone chimes and the globular clay ocarinas characteristic of early Chinese cultures.[15] Depictions of performing musicians together with the physical composition of the artefacts themselves provide clues as to how such instruments were played; but they do not tell us how the *music* was played. We know, too, from contemporary descriptions a good deal about the social uses of ancient music, especially for religious and ceremonial and military purposes. Some of the earliest Chinese sources refer to weddings and funerals and – repeatedly – to rites and ceremonials. From them we can deduce that, in pre-modern China, music played an essential part not only in ritual worship but also at state banquets and in entertaining prestigious guests, rulers and ministers.[16] The so-called Five Classics of the Chou (Zhou) Dynasty (*c.*1122–249 BC) include many references to musical performances of this kind, particularly at court activities.[17] The *Shih-ching* (*Shi jing*, 'Odes' or

---

11 Ibid., pp. 62–85; see also Solon Michaelides, *The Music of Ancient Greece: An Encyclopedia*, London (Faber) 1978, p. 286; M. L. West, *Ancient Greek Music*, Oxford (Clarendon Press) 1992, ch. 10, 'The Musical Documents', pp. 277ff. and esp. pp. 284–7. For a dissenting view of the dating and attribution of these fragments, compare Thomas J. Mathiesen, *Apollo's Lyre. Greek Music and Music Theory in Antiquity and the Early Middle Ages*, Lincoln/London (Nebraska U. P.) 2000, pp. 39ff., 44.

12 Some of the surviving fragments of ancient Greek music, including the two Delphic paeans, have been recorded in a (hypothetical) performing edition by Gregorio Paniagua and the Atrium Musicae de Madrid, on Harmonia Mundi, CD HMA 1951015 (HM 31) under the title *Musique de la Grèce antique*.

13 *Aurignacian*: Western European culture of the Upper Palaeolithic era, from Aurignac, village in southwest France, site of numerous finds of bone and stone implements.

14 See Feng Guangsheng, 'Winds', in the catalogue *Music in the Age of Confucius* (as n. [24] below), p. 88.

15 On the archaeological evidence pertaining to the earliest Chinese instruments see Keith Pratt, 'The Evidence for Music in the Shang Dynasty: a Reappraisal', *Bulletin of the British Association for Chinese Studies*, September 1986, pp. 22–50. For a brief but useful account of prehistoric instruments generally see R. Bragard and Ferd. J. De Hen, *Les Instruments de musique*, Rhode-St-Genèse (Albert De Visscher) 1967, esp. pp. 11ff.

16 Feng Guangsheng, loc. cit. (as n. [14] above).

'Book of Poetry') also contains the words of over three hundred songs dating mainly from the tenth to the seventh centuries BC. Despite the intervening chasm of time, their content is still capable of calling forth a pang of almost uncanny familiarity, since they deal with topics as easily understood today as they must have been by contemporary audiences: topics such as love, ritual and political satire. And yet, as to what the music consisted of, we know – and can imagine – next to nothing.

Music and mathematics

Doubtless the origins of music itself were considerably older than the making of bells or tambourines, stone chimes or pipes. Long before anyone thought of stretching animal skin across a hollow gourd or carving a fragment of bone into a simple whistle, the ache of hunger, the craving for love or the need to comfort a fretful child must have caused men and women instinctively to utilize the one musical instrument that did not need to be fashioned: the human voice.[18] This instinctive character of song and its role in expressing thoughts and feelings were acknowledged by some of the earliest sages and philosophers. 'When feelings are stirred within', we read in the so-called 'Great Preface' to the Chinese *Odes*, 'their external form is in words. When words are not enough, feelings are expressed with exclamations. When exclamations are not enough, feelings are extended in song.'[19]

But there was one aspect of musical sound that the human voice, for all its expressive qualities, could not reveal. Music, it soon transpired, was inextricably linked with number – something readily apparent from even the crudest attempts at playing any kind of wind or, especially, stringed instrument. 'Stopping' a string at the halfway point resulted in a tone precisely one octave higher than

---

17 The 'five classics' were the *I-ching* (*Yi jing*, 'Book of Changes'), *Shu-ching* (*Shu jing*, 'Book of Documents'), the *Shih-ching* (*Shi jing*, 'Odes' or 'Book of Poetry'), the *San li* (*Sanli*, 'Three Compendia on Ritual') and the *Ch'un-ch'iu* (*Chunqiu*, 'Spring and Autumn [Annals]'). These canonical texts were held to contain the truth 'upon the highest subjects from the sages of China, which should be received as law by all generations' (James Legge, *The Chinese Classics*, Prolegomena to vol. 1, London 1861, p. 1). To this list is sometimes added the *Yüeh-ching* (*Yue jing*, 'Classic of Music'), which, if it ever existed, had been lost by the time the fragmentary remains of the ancient writings were reassembled by scholars of the Han dynasty. What may have been parts of this semi-mythical text were incorporated in the *Li-chi* (*Li ji*, 'Record of Rites') under the title 'Yüeh Chi' ('Yue ji', 'Annotations on Music').
18 Some philosophers have considered the human voice to be the origin both of all music and of all language. Rousseau, for example, wrote: 'With the first voices came the first articulations or sounds, which were shaped by the nature of the passions that dictated them ... All voices speak under the influence of passion: thus verse, singing and speech have a common origin.' See Jean-Jacques Rousseau, *Essai sur l'origine des langues, où il est parlé de la mélodie et de l'imitation musicale*. Édition critique. Avertissement et notes par Charles Porset, Bordeaux (Guy Ducros) 1970, p. 139.
19 Attributed to Wei Hung, *c*.25 AD. I have followed the translation given in Kenneth J. DeWoskin, *A Song for One or Two. Music and the Concept of Art in Early China*, Ann Arbor (Michigan U. P.) 1982, p. 20; see also Susan Bush and Hsio-yen Shih (eds), *Early Chinese Texts on Painting*, Cambridge, MA (Harvard U. P./Harvard-Yenching Institute) 1985, p. 6.

the note produced when the whole length of the string was left to vibrate. Stop the same string exactly one third of the way along, leaving two-thirds free to vibrate, and what we would describe as the 'fifth' note of the scale is sounded. In other words, these different pitches, which the untrained listener can recognize as easily as the trained musician, and which are often used as the primary building blocks of musical composition, were neither random nor arbitrary. On the contrary, they stood in a precise and determined relationship to one another: a relationship that could be expressed in simple mathematical terms.

Exactly the same principle applied to wind instruments. Holes could be cut in a bamboo pipe in such a way that, depending on where the fingers were placed, the column of air within resonated not along the whole of the pipe but over half or two-thirds or three-quarters of its length, again resulting in intervals of an octave, a fifth and a fourth. These particular intervals, often referred to as the 'primary consonances', eventually came to play an important, indeed unique role both in harmonic theory and in actual musical practice. Many cultures consider the primary *datum* of musical experience to be the octave, which is frequently employed as the first and most important unit of musical organization, while two notes an octave (or several octaves) apart are usually regarded as the 'same' note and are given the 'same' name – thus: C–c–c', and so forth.[20]

By contrast, the fourth and fifth notes of the scale are harmonically just as important but in a different way. As already remarked, the note we hear if the length of a string or pipe is multiplied by two-thirds is the 'dominant' or fifth above the fundamental ('fundamental' meaning the pitch from which we started, produced by not stopping the string or pipe at all). If, however, the length of the same string or pipe is multiplied by four-thirds, the resulting note will be a 'perfect' fourth lower, which is actually the *same* note as the dominant but in a lower register: low g as opposed to high g'. Multiply the length of that G string by two-thirds and the next fifth (d') above resounds; multiply the length of the new D string by four-thirds and you will hear the fourth below, which is identical with the *next* fifth above, only an octave lower (fig. 5). Rearranging this succession of perfect fifths into an ascending sequence – repeatedly building a fifth upon a fifth, so to speak (thus: C–G–d–a–e'–b') – produces in the end all twelve semitones of the chromatic scale (fig. 6).

---

20 Throughout this book, I have followed the convention of indicating musical pitches by lower or upper case letters. According to this convention, the octave from C to B is the octave below the one below middle C, while c to b is the octave below middle C. c' to b' is the octave from middle C upwards; c" to b" is the octave above that.

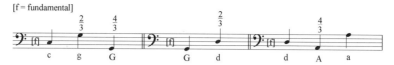

Figure 5. The relationship between the primary consonances and the ratios of the smallest whole numbers

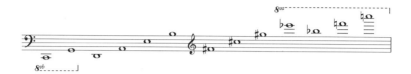

Figure 6. Showing how all twelve semitones of the chromatic scale are produced by the 'great cycle of fifths'

Moreover, this 'great cycle of fifths', as it is sometimes called, ultimately returns (albeit at a higher pitch) to the note from which it started, like a serpent biting its own tail, that ubiquitous symbol of eternity and of perpetual rebirth. The fact that some of the higher notes were slightly out of tune by a fraction known as the 'Pythagorean comma' was also noticed, but was not found particularly bothersome – at least, not by singers or players of stringed instruments that could be intuitively tuned to the correct pitch. It did, on the other hand, represent a major obstacle for fixed-pitch instruments like bells – or, at a later date, keyboard instruments such as the harpsichord or organ – which, unless they were retuned, could be played in only a limited number of keys if they were not to sound horribly cacophonous. This problem was eventually solved by the introduction of equal temperament: the system of slightly but permanently adjusted tuning that was celebrated, for example, by Johann Sebastian Bach in his great cycle of forty-eight preludes and fugues in every major and minor key, to which he gave the name 'The Well-Tempered Clavier'.[21]

In time, the discovery that the octave, the fifth and the fourth corresponded to simple numerical ratios came to be associated with the Greek philosopher Pythagoras (*c*.550 BC). Miraculously (or so it must have seemed to him and his followers) it was these, the most

---

21 In Europe, the possibility of equal temperament had been widely discussed from the sixteenth century onwards. Long before Bach, Vincenzo Galilei included in a codex of 1584 *passamezzos*, *romanescas* and *saltarellos* in all twenty-four major and minor keys; see *Grove*, vol. 7, p. 96. For a more detailed account of the problem of tuning, see the essay by D. P. Walker, 'Seventeenth-Century Scientists' Views on Intonation', ch. 7 of his *Studies in Musical Science in the Late Renaissance*, London and Leiden (Warburg Institute, University of London/E. J. Brill) 1978, pp. 111–22.

'consonant' intervals – that is, the smoothest or most pleasing – that were found to correspond to the ratios between the smallest whole numbers: 1:2, 2:3, 3:4. The Pythagoreans stopped at this point, perhaps because these smallest integers, if added together, came to ten: the mystical tetraktys that, in their philosophy, was the basis of everything.[22] Or it may have been that they were not greatly interested in applying all this abstract theory – so beautiful in its apparently symmetrical sets of relations – to actual musical practice.[23] But Pythagoras cannot really have been the only person in the world to have noticed this obvious relationship between sounds and numbers. The same phenomenon was probably observed at much the same time by several geographically remote

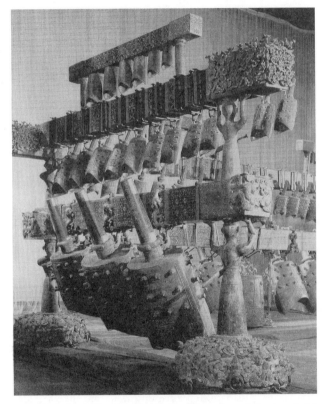

Figure 7. Bronze chime bells of the Marquis of Zeng, from Leigudun, Suizhou, China, *c*.433 BC (Hubei Provincial Museum, Wuhan, China)

22 For more on Pythagoras and 'his' system of musical consonances, see below, ch. 2, pp. 69ff.
23 For a more detailed account of these symmetries, how they are formed, and on what they are based, see Julius Schwabe, 'Hans Kaysers letzte Entdeckung: Die pythagorische Tetraktys auf Raffaels "Schule von Athen"', *Symbolon*, vol. 5 (1966), pp. 92–102 (also in relation to the discussion of Raphael's *School of Athens* to be found in ch. 2: see below, pp. 72–5).

cultures having little or no direct contact with each other. An astonishing (and astonishingly well-preserved) set of sixty-five accurately tuned bronze bells, excavated in north-eastern Hupei province from the tomb of the Marquis of Tseng (Zenghou Yi, d.c.433 BC; fig. 7),[24] has been interpreted as evidence that the 'Pythagorean' system of pitch determination was known in China as early as the fifth century BC.[25] Several centuries later, the 'Lü Shu' chapter of the *Shih-chi* (*Shi ji*, 'Records of the Historian') by Ssu-ma Chien (Sima Qian; second–first century BC) also defines the lengths of the various pitch pipes used to determine the tonal frequencies of ancient Chinese music in terms of their mathematical proportions (fig. 8):[26]

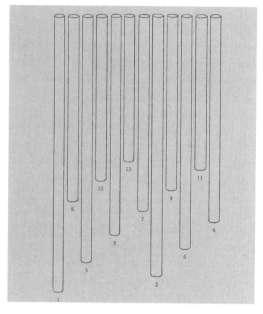

Figure 8. Showing Chinese pitch pipes arranged according to the 'Pythagorean' ratios, after Needham, *Science and Civilisation* (1962)

---

24 Photographs of the bells and a detailed study of their history and construction can be found in Lothar von Falkenhausen, *Suspended Music. Chime-Bells in the Culture of Bronze Age China*, Berkeley (California U. P.) 1993, and in Jenny F. So (ed.), *Music in the Age of Confucius*, Washington, DC (Smithsonian Institution/Freer Gallery of Art/Arthur M. Sackler Gallery) 2000.

25 In a recent discussion of the significance of these bells, Robert Bagley has remarked that while we 'cannot be certain that the relationships we associate with Pythagoras were known at Marquis Yi's court, the theoretical sophistication of his musicians taken together with their experience of highly developed string instruments would seem to make it likely'; see his essay 'Percussion' in *Music in the Age of Confucius* (as preceding note), p. 61. Compare also Ernest G. McClain, 'The bronze chime bells of the Marquis of Zeng: Babylonian Biophysics in Ancient China', *Journal of Social and Biological Structures*, 8 (1985), pp. 147–73 and especially pp. 154ff.

26 In specifying the length of the standard pitch pipes, a much older text, the *Shih-ching* defines the *lin-chung* pipe, for example, as two-thirds of the length of the *huan-chung* pipe that produces the fundamental – quite correctly, since the pitch of *lin-chung* is a fifth higher: see Falkenhausen, *Suspended Music*, p. 311.

Nevertheless, in Western writing about music the octave, fifth and fourth are still referred to, even today, as the 'Pythagorean consonances'.

For some societies, the 'Pythagorean' system just described can have held only passing interest. Not all kinds of music depend on sustaining a definite pitch or on the alternation of tones and semitones characteristic of the Western scale. This is true, for example, of a number of Asiatic musical cultures: 'Japanese *shakuhachi* music and the *sanjo* music of Korea ... fluctuate constantly around the notional pitches in terms of which the music is organized. And there is other music in which discrete pitches do not even have a notional role – African percussion music, say.'[27] But for the ancient civilizations of both East and West, these simple facts of acoustics often provided the foundation for a vast and imposing edifice of philosophical, numerological and even cosmological speculation. Because of music's evident relationship with mathematics – and thus with other exact sciences such as geometry and astronomy – it was accorded a privileged, even unique place not only within society but also within nature and the cosmos. Musical order, mathematical order, the order of the cosmos and the ethical and social order were one. For the Pythagoreans, observations of the regular movements in the sky led to the concept of a beautifully ordered 'harmony' of the spheres, that *musica coelestis* that is inaudible to the human ear, but which was nevertheless thought to exist. The mathematical ratios that governed musical harmony were deemed part of a mysterious system of relationships with the stars and other natural phenomena, the rising and setting of the sun and the phases of the moon, those 'signs in the great book of nature that serve to measure human life'.[28] For the ancient Chinese, music not only existed in harmony with nature but was also part of nature. Therefore, a society ordered according to 'musical' principles as regards its government, its educational system and its administration would be 'in tune' with nature and the cosmos. 'Rites regulate [people's] minds, music harmonizes their emotions, government directs them, punishments restrain them; when these four spread uninterruptedly in all directions, the kingly way is complete', it is written in the 'Yüeh-chi'.[29]

---

27 Nicholas Cook, *Music, Imagination and Culture*, Oxford (Clarendon Press) 1990, p. 7.
28 Annemarie Schimmel, *The Mystery of Numbers*, New York/Oxford (Oxford U. P.) 1993, p. vi.
29 Quoted after Pratt, 'Evidence for Music', p. 44.

How music might be thought to pervade all aspects of life and human society is demonstrated by one of the oldest Chinese legends, which chronicles the deeds of the 'Yellow' Emperor Huang-ti (Huangdi), one of the mythical Chinese emperors who supposedly ruled in or about the third millennium BC. It tells of the scholar Ling Lun, sent by the emperor to the mountainous border region on the western margins of China. His mission was to cut bamboo pipes capable of emitting sounds that emulated the cry of the phoenix. The music of the imperial court could then be properly pitched, ensuring harmony between the emperor's reign and the universe:

In ancient times, the Yellow Emperor ordered Ling Lun to make pitch standards ... He gathered bamboo from the valleys of Hsieh-ch'i and, selecting those pieces with chambers and walls of uniform thickness, he cut a section from between the two nodes. The length of a section was 3.9 inches [9.9 cm] and he blew it. That sound he took to be the kung *tone at the yellow-bell pitch. Blowing it, he said 'That is good!' and proceeded to make shortened sections in a series, creating twelve pipes.*

He carried them back to the foot of the Juan-yü Mountain where he listened to the songs of the male and female phoenix in order to divide the twelve pitches. The male calls numbered six and the female calls numbered six. Proper concord was achieved by their relation to the kung *tone at the yellow-bell pitch ... Therefore, Ling Lun said that the* kung *tone at the yellow-bell pitch was the origin of all the* yang *and all the* yin *pitches.*

The Yellow Emperor subsequently ordered Ling Lun ... to cast twelve bronze bells. These would provide harmonious placements of the five tones and allow the harmonious symphony to be performed. In the middle of spring, on the twelfth day of the cycle of sixty ... it was performed for the first time.[30]

Like most legends, this enchanting tale has several layers of significance. The fact that it describes the new pitch standards as being brought back from the West may, according to one theory,

---

30 This story is alluded to in a variety of sources. The version given here is taken from the *Lü-shih ch'un-ch'iu* (*Lüshi Chunqiu*, 'Spring and Autumn Annals of Lü Pu-wei', § 5), the preface to which is dated 245 BC; I have followed the translation given in DeWoskin 1982, pp. 59–60.

evoke faint memories of the arrival of Babylonian science in China – science that could have been transmitted via Vedic India, complete with the mathematical knowledge necessary for calculating the precise ratios of all twelve semitones of the chromatic scale.[31] The story of Ling Lun's quest also underlines the ancient conviction that the establishment of musically precise pitches – the primary purpose of his journey – was not something to be invented arbitrarily by the sage or scholar but to be 'found' in nature. In order to reconcile music with the natural order of things, the first and most important task was to determine the basic pitch from which all others were derived. This was traditionally expressed in terms of a particular bell, known as *huang-chung* or 'yellow bell'. The exact meaning of the vivid and evocative names given to the various pitches is still obscure and has been a matter of controversy. Although the names themselves often allude to bells – 'new bell' (*lin-chung*), 'forest bell' and so on – it is clear that the Chinese thought first of strings or pipes, rather than bells, as representing the basic units of musical measurement. (Note that Ling Lun's first act was to cut a set of bamboo *pipes* whose tones he compared with the calls of the phoenix.)[32]

The 'five tones' mentioned in the legend, on the other hand, corresponding to the five notes of the Chinese pentatonic scale, were initially an abstract concept: merely a set of numerical relationships. They were without sound until the fundamental tone had been fixed - the '*kung* tone at the yellow-bell pitch', which 'could generate all the rest'. Hence the importance of Ling Lun's mission, since only the establishment of the yellow-bell tone could enable the remaining notes of the scale to be properly pitched. However, these pitches were not immutable: they could be changed by the work of acousticians or astrologers on behalf of a new emperor in order that his kingdom should remain in tune with the cosmos. Several histories of music in China record in excess of thirty pitch reforms between the late Chou period (mid-third century BC) and the Ch'ing dynasty (1644–1911 AD), with the pitch of the 'yellow-bell pipe' varying between our middle c' and the f' or even the a' above.[33] This constant tinkering with pitch standards may reflect a growing uncertainty among Chinese musicians and theorists of music as to

---

31 McClain, loc. cit. (as n. [25] above).
32 Lothar von Falkenhausen points out that one reason why bell tones were taken as reference points in musical theory was, almost certainly, their relative immutability. While tone calculations may indeed have been performed on strings, it is likely that, in order to be considered 'fixed', they were thereafter correlated to bell tones (letter to the author, November 2001).
33 Falkenhausen, *Suspended Music*, pp. 317–8 and n. 30.

the extent of the knowledge that had been lost during the war-torn years of the late Chou and also as a consequence of the 'burning of the books and burying of the scholars' that occurred under the first Ch'in emperor (Ch'in Shih huang-ti; r.221–10 BC).

The verification of precise pitches was also important in other ways. On a purely practical level, one consequence of the fact that pitch could be directly related to string and pipe length was that the 'yellow-bell pipe' seems to have become a standard measure, like a metre. Perhaps for this reason, it is said that the pipe itself ultimately became the property not of the imperial music department but of the office of weights and measures, the pitch standard that it represented being used to determine not only length but also weight and volume.[34] The legend of Ling Lun also records that the set of twelve bells cast at the behest of the Yellow Emperor was inaugurated in the middle of spring 'on the twelfth day of the cycle of sixty', implying that a complex system of musical relationships was used as a basis for setting the dates of festivals, performing certain rites and making calendric observations. Later writers, preoccupied with this kind of 'correlative cosmology', specifically related the five tones, twelve pitches and sixty mode-scales both to the lunar phases and to the months and seasons. In the *Record of Rites of the Elder Tai*, for example, we read:

the sages invented the twelve musical tones, so as to provide
standards for the eight notes ... These are called the 'pitch
pipes' (lü)... the pitch pipes and the calendar give each other
a mutual order, so closely that one could not insert a hair
between them.[35]

Equally significant was the fact that, according to legend, the emperor's first act after Ling Lun returned from his journey was to order the casting of bells. The possession of accurately tuned instruments – whether bells or flutes or stone chimes – was interpreted as a metaphor for good government, since the orderly arrangement of music and its correct performance in accordance with ancient precepts was thought to mirror and also to influence proper social organization and the effective regulation of the state:

---

34 Needham remarks that the ancient Chinese were apparently unique in considering pitch measure as not merely on a par with linear measure, capacity and weight but as the basis of the other three; see Needham 1962, pp. 199, 200ff.

35 *Ta Tai li-chi*; quoted after Joseph Needham, *Science and Civilisation in China*, vol. 2 (*History of Scientific Thought*), Cambridge (Cambridge U. P.) 1956, pp. 269ff. The text is dated by Needham to *c*.80–105 AD.

music the Holy Sages took delight, because music can improve the heart of the people. Music has a profound influence on man, it can improve customs and ameliorate morals ... therefore, when music flourishes, human relations are clarified, eyes and ears are made more susceptive, body and mind are in balanced harmony, good customs prosper and morals are improved, and peace reigns everywhere under Heaven.[36]

By the early Han period, this association between music and morals had become a *locus classicus* of post-Confucian commentary. The 'Annotations on Music', which were incorporated into the *Record of Rites* and which probably contain a digest of older musical theory, repeatedly equate the harmonies of music with public morality and with the settled nature of the relationship between ruler and ruled. But it had to be the right kind of music. 'Improper' music – music that was licentious or seductive or depraved – was symptomatic of misrule and of the decline of the state. The Confucian philosopher Hsün-Tzǔ (Xunzi) warned:

Then the people will become abandoned and mean-mannered. Those who are abandoned will fall into disorder; those who are mean-mannered will fall to quarrelling; and where there is disorder and quarrelling, the troops will be weak, the cities will revolt, and the state will be menaced by foreign enemies ... The common people will find no safety in their dwellings and no delight in their communities, and they will feel only dissatisfaction towards their superiors ... For this reason, the former kings honoured the proper rites and music, and despised evil music.[37]

In fact, the tussle between what Hsün-Tzǔ here terms the 'elegant classical modes' and 'barbaric' or 'evil' music occupied a good deal of time and energy among the *literati*, that élite circle of highly educated court officials, writers and philosophers who, during the first and second centuries BC, exerted considerable influence on Chinese society and on thinking about the nature and functions of

---

36 *Lü-shih ch'un-ch'iu* (see n. [30] above), §§ 7–8; quoted after R. H. van Gulik, *The Lore of the Chinese Lute. An Essay in Ch'in Ideology*, Tokyo (Sophia University: Monumenta Nipponica) 1940, p. 24.
37 *Hsün Tzǔ. Basic Writings*, translated by Burton Watson, New York (Columbia U. P.) 1963, pp. 114–15. Other sources also stress the politically disastrous consequences of improper music. The *Shih-chi*, for example, records the legend of the downfall of the Shang dynasty, brought about because its last king Zhouxin 'altered and changed proper sound' (*ie* ordered erotic music and dances) in order to please his wife; thereafter, 'he himself perished and his kingdom was destroyed'; quoted after Pratt, 'Evidence for Music', p. 46.

that society. For those concerned with upholding the Confucian tradition, 'proper' as opposed to 'improper' music was almost exclusively ceremonial in character, the music of rites and religious festivals. In private performance, the only instruments capable of transmitting the ennobling tones of antiquity were the *sê* and the *ch'in* (*qin*). The *sê* was an ancient instrument with twenty-five strings, each supported by a movable bridge, which the player plucked with the fingers of both hands. The *ch'in*, in its earliest form, was a kind of five-stringed lute or zither held on the lap or placed on a low table; without frets or bridge, it was played with the fingers of one hand. (The original five strings, corresponding to the gamut of the pentatonic scale, were later increased to seven, thus providing the possibility of two further half tones as well as the completion of the octave.)[38] By the early Han dynasty, the *ch'in* had become synonymous with the upholding of classical tradition (Confucius was said to have played the *ch'in*), even though, at this date, skilled performers were relatively few. This did not matter very much, since actually playing it was by no means the most important thing. Holding it or discussing it or writing poems in praise of it were just as important to the *literati*, many of whom prided themselves on owning antique and valuable instruments on which, in reality, they were incapable of performing.[39] Often mute and stringless, these instruments would be carefully placed on a writing desk or hung on the wall of a library to indicate, as did a chess set or an inkstand, that its owner was a man of letters. Numerous depictions of the scholar or wise man show him alone with his lute, not playing and without an audience. Or he may be found contemplating the beauties of nature – a waterfall, for example – while his servant follows closely behind carrying his instrument: an attribute appropriate to such a setting, no matter whether or not it was actually used.

But even among accomplished performers there existed a cult of *not* playing the lute, evoked in the lines written centuries later by the poet T'ao Ch'ien (Tao Qian; 372–427 AD): 'I have acquired the deeper significance of the lute. Why should I strive after the sound

---

38 By way of a simple demonstration, one version of the pentatonic scale (called 'anhemitonic') can be produced by playing only the black notes on the piano, thus (in ascending order): D flat, E flat, G flat, A flat, B flat. The two additional tones F and C, which in the Western post-classical tradition are sometimes called the 'gift of Orpheus', enable the full seven notes of the diatonic scale to be played. In Chinese, the original five notes of the pentatonic scale were called *kung* (*gong*), *shang*, *chüeh* (*jue*), *chih* (*zhi*) and *yü* (*yu*); see Van Gulik, pp. 80–1, 85ff.

39 As Bell N. Yung remarks, the *ch'in* was 'traditionally the instrument of the scholar; it was played in order to concentrate the mind and achieve a certain type of self-control. Virtuosity and acoustic gratification were disdained; what mattered was not the sound of what was played but the moral and intellectual qualities which it embodied.' ('Choreographic and Kinesthetic Elements in Performance on the Chinese Seven-String Zither', *Ethnomusicology*, 28, 1984, pp. 514–15.)

of its strings?'[40] It has also been pointed out that, in the case of the *ch'in* – an instrument capable of only a limited number of pitches and whose tradition centred rather on the correct manner of their production and on the numerous possible variations of timbre – silence (that is, the spaces between the notes) was as significant as the notes themselves. 'Skilful listening involves following a tone from audibility to inaudibility ... The climactic moment is that point in time which hangs between sound and silence. Ideally, the listener's mind (and the listener may be both the performer and the audience) is brought to tranquillity at that point. Skills for listening are no less essential than skills for performing.'[41] Half a world away, in the twentieth century the American composer John Cage, deeply affected by his own contemplation of the Chinese classics, would seek in a similar fashion to focus the minds of performers and audience alike on the musical significance of silence.[42]

The legacy of China

In pre-modern China, discussion of music's role in society was, of course, a question not just of public or even private morality. As in every age, personal taste also exerted a significant – some might say decisive – influence. In the last years of the Chou and during the early Han period, when the upper classes enjoyed an increasing variety of musical pursuits, some listeners openly relished the popular songs newly imported from other states and were prepared to admit that they found ancient ceremonial music mind-numbingly boring. 'When in full ceremonial dress', wrote Prince Wên of Wei (426–387 BC), 'I must listen to the Ancient Music [and] I think I shall fall asleep, but when I listen to the songs of Chêng and Wei, I never get tired.'[43] In this context, the specific reference to the 'songs of Chêng' is a provocative one, since traditionalists often mention the 'lewd music of Chêng' with something close to loathing. But it was not (as far as we know) considered 'lewd' and 'licentious' because it comprised ballads that dealt with salacious or risqué subjects.[44] One contemporary

---

40 Van Gulik, p. 18; also quoted in a slightly different version by DeWoskin, who notes that in the collected biographies of recluses in the *History of the Sung*, T'ao is described as 'owning one very plain *ch'in*, without any strings at all, which he would hold and stroke to express his feelings whenever he became drunk'. (*A Song for One or Two*, p. 144.)

41 Ibid., p. 162.

42 In 1949–50 Cage became deeply interested in Oriental philosophy. In 1950 he made a close study of the *I-ching*, a preoccupation reflected in his mammoth opus for piano, *Music of Changes*, written in 1951; see *Grove*, vol. 3, pp. 598ff. His preoccupation with silence is reflected in another piano work of the 1950s, *4' 33"*, in which the performer sits at the keyboard and opens and closes the lid of the instrument, but does not touch the keys.

43 Van Gulik, p. 37.

44 Waley in his edition of the *Analects* likewise notes that it was to the character of the music of Chêng that Confucius objected rather than to the words, which can in fact be found in books VII and IX of the *Songs* (ie the *Odes*). See also William R. B. Acker, *Some T'ang and Pre-T'ang Texts on Chinese Painting* (*Sinica Leidensia*, vol. 8), Leiden (E. J. Brill) 1954, p. 17 and n. 1 (hereafter Acker 1954), also (for a dissenting view) *Confucius, The Analects*. Translated with Introduction by D. C. Lau, London (Penguin) 1979, pp. 40–1.

commentator described it merely as 'excessively intricate'.[45] Rather, it was disdained because it departed from classical norms, in which alone virtue was held to reside. ('I detest the tunes of Chêng for corrupting classical music', the *Analects* record Confucius as saying.)[46] Above all, it was distrusted because of its immediate appeal to the senses. The purpose of the ancient melodies had been to give expression to cosmic and earthly harmony and, at the same time, to uplift and ennoble, since music 'belonged to heaven'. As such, its purpose was to assist man to regain his original heavenly nature, to help retrieve 'what was heavenly in man'. 'When the saints of old invented music', wrote the scholar Juan Chi, 'they made it to be in conformity with the structure of the universe and to bring to perfection the nature of the beings that inhabit it.'[47] They had certainly not intended it to divert or entertain.

The ancient Chinese writers thus bequeathed to posterity two notions that, as it happens, also dominated thinking about music in the West over a period of many centuries, from antiquity until late medieval times and beyond. The first was the idea that music, in a sense, signified or reflected something beyond itself, thereby transcending any value it might have merely as a form of entertainment or source of aesthetic pleasure. Its derivation from precise physical laws, expressible in mathematical terms, related it to those greater laws that governed the workings of the cosmos as well as to the patterns of the human mind. It was for this reason that music was later thought by many Christian writers and commentators to reflect divine law and the action of God's will upon the universe. This was the orderly side of music, which the ancients had ranked with mathematics and astronomy, thus distinguishing it from painting, sculpture and architecture, which they considered to be purely manual occupations.

But music also had its subjective, disorderly side, since it was capable not only of expressing but also of affecting human emotions. Its sensuous beauty could, even if unintentionally, seduce the mind and confuse the senses. It is said that the 'perfectly beautiful' music of the succession dance *Shao*, which Confucius acknowledged as the highest beauty and at the same time perfect goodness, so bewitched the philosopher's faculties that he was

---

45 The reference that occurs in the *Tso Commentary* to the *Spring and Autumn Annals* is to a performance of various forms of ancient music attended by Duke Cha, fourth son of the King of Wu, which allegedly took place in 543 BC. On hearing the airs of Chêng, Cha observed: 'In intricacy they have gone too far. The people will not be able to endure, so Chêng will be the first state to vanish.' (DeWoskin 1982, p. 22.)

46 XVII, 18.

47 DeWoskin 1982, p. 86.

unable to distinguish the taste of meat for three months.[48] And, if lewd or debased, music could distort the emotions and inflame the passions, thereby crippling its moral effect. Throughout antiquity, writers were openly distrustful of the sensuous appeal of music, and their misgivings were inherited and reinforced by philosophers and theologians of the Christian era. That deeply spiritual thinker St Augustine, Bishop of Hippo, while acknowledging that music afforded a powerful vehicle for the expression of spirituality and for singing the praises of the Most High, was tormented by what seemed to him the 'dangerous pleasure' to be had from music's all too earthly beauty. Finally, but only after an inner struggle, he endorsed the 'custom of singing in church so that weaker souls might rise to a state of devotion by indulging their ears', admitting that he himself felt the words 'stir my soul to greater religious fervour and to a more ardent piety if they are sung, than if not.'[49] That he came to this conclusion was fortunate not only for the subsequent development of music in the Western Church but also for us. Augustine's writings were held in high esteem, especially during the Middle Ages, and greatly influenced later thinking about both theological and ecclesiastical matters. Had he come out firmly against the use of music in church, some of the greatest works by European composers – the masses of Guillaume Dufay (c.1400–74), the sacred motets of Lassus and Palestrina (both choirmasters of the Church of St John Lateran in Rome during the mid-sixteenth century), Monteverdi's *Vespers*, the church cantatas of Bach and his *B-minor Mass*, Mozart's and Haydn's masses, Beethoven's *Missa Solemnis*, Verdi's *Requiem* – all these might never have been written.

Ancient Chinese theories of painting

In contrast to the 'lost' music of China's distant past, there are plenty of examples of early Chinese forms of image making, from wall paintings and tomb sculptures via the decoration found on bronze vessels and images painted on ceramics, through to the birth of painting on silk and other materials. But, as for the meaning of such images and what significance their makers attached to the act of depiction, these are, for the most part, matters of conjecture. Any attempt to reconstruct what the Chinese sages and philosophers of antiquity thought about the nature and purpose of visual art is hampered by the almost complete lack of any textual record. There exists no pre-Han or Han text on painting to compare with the *Classic*

---

48 *Analects*, VII, 14.
49 *Confessions*, X, 33, quoted after Strunk II, pp. 132–3.

of Poetry or the 'Annotations on Music'. Nor is it likely, given the absence of any mention by early writers, that such a text once existed, only to be lost in more recent times, like the lost *Classic of Music*.[50] We can search the first dictionaries and encyclopedias for references to any discussion of visual art, to be met only with a resounding silence, perhaps because the arts of depiction were not – initially, at least – considered to be 'art' at all.

In the *Shuo-wên chieh-tzŭ* (*Shuowen jiezi*, 'Explaining the Graphic Units and Analysing the Characters'; *c*.120 AD) the six 'arts' are defined as ritual, music, archery, charioteering, writing and mathematics.[51] In other early compilations, painting and calligraphy are sometimes accorded little more space than the better-known games such as chess.[52] Only during the Eastern Han period (25–220 AD) did the scholarly attributes of a gentleman begin slowly to extend from a knowledge of poetry and music (expressed by playing the lute) via calligraphy to landscape painting. Indeed, painting's claim to a more elevated status seems to have derived, at least in part, from its affinity with calligraphy, inasmuch as both utilized the same instrument, the brush, and depended upon similar techniques.[53] But even as late as the Northern Sung (Song; 960–1127 AD), when the term 'scholars' painting' was first coined, it is clear from a number of (occasionally deprecating) references that some painters were still considered little better than artisans and that painting itself was regarded as a primarily manual occupation involving merely the exercise of a certain level of skill.[54]

Precisely because of the belated appearance of any serious discussion of visual art in China, particular interest has centred on what are thought to be the first surviving treatises on painting, all dating from the period of the so-called 'Six Dynasties' (265–589 AD).[55]

---

50 See n. [17] above.
51 This ancient division corresponds to the 'six sciences' taught by the Protector to the sons of the Chou kings and of the nobility: 'the five ceremonials, the six kinds of music, the five ways of shooting arrows, the five ways of driving chariots, the six scripts, the nine kinds of reckoning'; see Acker 1954, p. 61 and n. 3.
52 *Dictionary of Art*: 'China', I, 7 ('Concept of art'). Significantly, the following section on the philosophy of the arts in China devotes far more space to the ritual and moral significance of music than to the 'arts' of painting and calligraphy.
53 William Acker, in the introduction to his edition of early texts on Chinese painting, finds it 'astonishing' that there should have been so little mention of painting in the literature of the Chou period: 'certainly nothing of a critical nature, and nothing in the way of praise of the art as a discipline worthy of the philosopher's serious consideration'. He ascribes the rise of art criticism in about the fifth century AD to changes in social conditions that had begun during the later Han, when 'painting came to be recognized as an end in itself, and a new form of society arose in which the individual painter could receive high honour for his work as the result of his skill or as the expression of his personality'; see Acker 1954, pp. ix–x.
54 Susan Bush, *The Chinese Literati on Painting. Su Shih (1037–1101) to Tung Ch'i-ch'ang (1555–1636)*, Cambridge, MA (Harvard-Yenching Institute Studies XXVII) 1971, pp. 3ff., 29–30.
55 Apart from the *Ku-hua p'in-lu* of Hsieh Ho (see following note) which was independently transmitted to posterity in the form of later editions, we would know little about the other early Chinese texts on painting mentioned here, were it not for the *Li-tai ming-hua chi* (*Lidai minghua ji*; 'Record of All the Famous Painters of All the Dynasties') by Chang Yen-yüan (Zhang Yanyuan; compiled *c*.847 AD), which quotes *in extenso* from essays by earlier painters; see Acker 1954, pp. 6ff., also Acker 1974 (*Some Pre-T'ang and T'ang Texts on Chinese Painting*, vol. 2), *passim*.

Among them are the 'Introduction to Painting Landscape' by Tsung Ping (Zong Bing; 375–443 AD), probably written about the beginning of the fifth century AD, the 'Discussion of Painting' by Wang Wei (415–443 AD) and the celebrated 'six laws' of painting by Hsieh Ho (Xie He; *fl.*500–535 AD).[56] Together with a small number of other (sometimes doubtfully attributed) texts, these early writings constitute the only significant theory of art prior to the mid-sixth century AD.[57] All pose considerable difficulties of interpretation. Tsung Ping, for example, was not only a painter but also a mountaineer and recluse whose thinking was in all probability influenced by Buddhist teachings. To what extent specifically Buddhist notions are reflected in his essay on landscape – sometimes held to be the earliest known philosophical treatise on painting – or whether it is more a mixture compounded of Buddhist, Taoist and straightforwardly Confucian ideas has been debated.[58] Nor can we be sure whether it was conceived as an abstract, philosophical enquiry or whether it was meant to reflect actual painting method and practice at that time. Some writers have interpreted it as primarily instructional in purpose, occupied with practical problems such as scale and the accurate representation of natural forms – above all, with achieving a convincing likeness.

More recently, however, a different and in many ways more persuasive reading has been proposed.[59] Kiyohiko Munakata has argued that Tsung's essay is not about practical considerations at all but about the communicative function of painting.[60] This does not mean that it deals with the problem of how to convey individual thoughts and feelings. As other writers have pointed out, only much later did an 'expressive' theory of this kind develop in China: the notion that the painter or poet might seize the brush or pen in order to express his thoughts or even that we may infer something about the artist's character or morals from the qualities of his work.[61]

---

56 The 'six laws' are not, strictly speaking, a text in their own right: they are enumerated in lapidary fashion in the introduction to Hsieh Ho's *Ku-hua p'in-lu* ('Old Record of the Classification of Painters'), which otherwise consists mainly of descriptions of painters ancient and modern together with their works; see Acker 1954, pp. 3ff.

57 Another early text, 'Painting the Cloud Terrace Mountain', is attributed to the painter Ku K'ai-chih (Gu Kaizhi, 344–407 AD) but is mainly descriptive rather than prescriptive in character; see Acker 1974, pp. 73–5, also Bush and Shih, pp. 34–6.

58 Munakata, p. 105 (see n. [60] below); also Susan Bush, 'Tsung Ping's Essay on Painting Landscape and the "Landscape Buddhism" of Mount Lu', in S. Bush and C. Murck (eds), *Theories of the Arts in China*, Princeton, NJ (Princeton U. P.) 1983, pp. 132ff.

59 More persuasive, because both the language and content of Tsung's essay on landscape contrast markedly with a text of obviously didactic intent such as Ku K'ai-chi's notes on copying, reproduced in the *Li-tai ming-hua chi* (see n. [55] above) under the somewhat misleading title 'Eulogies on the Superior Sort of Paintings of the Wei and Chin Periods'; see Acker 1974, pp. 68ff.

60 See Kiyohiko Munakata, 'Concepts of *Lei* and *Kan-lei* in Early Chinese Art Theory', in Bush and Murck 1983, pp. 105–31.

61 See, for example, Bush 1971, pp. 29ff.

Rather, Munakata suggests that Tsung was primarily concerned with how painting might succeed in communicating spiritual truths and the essential character of the depicted subject: a suggestion that seems highly plausible, given that the main topic of the 'Introduction to Painting Landscape' is not, in fact, landscape in general but the depiction of mountains – and not just any mountains but sacred or even mythical ones.[62] It is a mythical mountain, K'un-lun, that Tsung singles out in order to discuss in detail how it might be represented, not a real mountain such as Mount Lu, where he had studied as a young man under the Buddhist monk Hui-Yüan and which he knew well.[63] Thus, any question of verisimilitude, of fidelity to the appearance of an actual location, becomes irrelevant. Tsung is not writing about painting physical features or faithfully rendering every crag and gully but about conveying the sacred essence of the mountain. Even when painting a real mountain, nothing would be gained, to his way of thinking, by revisiting the place itself merely in order to ensure accuracy:

Though one might again seek out solitary cliffs, it would be futile, for what more could be added? The essence of spirit, being limitless, resides in forms and responds to species, and truth enters into reflections and traces. One who can truly describe with skill will also truly achieve this.[64]

Nor, according to his account, is the viewer likely to be disturbed by discrepancies of scale or inaccuracy of detail but only by awkwardness in the composition.

That Tsung was indeed writing about painting not from nature but from the imagination is borne out by a succession of further references – for example, allusions to 'reflecting from afar' that likewise occur in his essay on landscape. Elsewhere in the same essay, he describes how truths 'lost in antiquity' may be summoned up by an effort of memory 'a thousand years later' and how 'meaning subtler than the images of speech' can be conveyed by books and records. The implication is clear. If the mind is capable of being

---

62 From earliest times, mountains exercised an extraordinary hold on the Chinese imagination. Sacrifices to sacred mountains and rivers were regularly performed during the second millennium BC, and as late as the Han period the five holy mountains (*wu-yüeh*) were still the object of a state-sponsored cult; see K. Munakata, *Sacred Mountains in Chinese Art*, Urbana/Chicago (Illinois U. P.) 1991, esp. pp. 3ff.

63 Bush, 'Tsung Ping's Essay ...', loc. cit. On the various hypothetical locations suggested for the (non-existent) Mount K'un-lun and its symbolic function as spanning the gulf between heaven and earth see Munakata, *Sacred Mountains*, pp. 9ff.; also Deborah Porter, 'The Literary Function of K'un-lun Mountain', *Early China*, 18 (1993), pp. 73ff.

64 Tsung Ping's landscape essay has been translated in various anthologies. I have mainly followed the translation by Susan Bush, in Bush and Murck 1983, pp. 144–6, but I have ventured to make a few minor alterations for the sake of style.

moved and stimulated merely by word or memory, how much more powerful will be the effect of images that serve as a reminder of 'where the body has strolled and the eyes rested repeatedly', such places being reproduced 'form for form and colour for colour'? He also tells how, old and frail, he must now do his mountain climbing from his bed (that is, in his mind) 'for fear of limping amongst those at the Stone Gate'.[65] In old age, he too must rely upon the power of the painted image to summon up memory and stimulate the imagination:

Thus I live at leisure, brandishing my wine cup and sounding my lute. I unroll paintings and face them in solitude; seated, I plumb the four ends of the earth ... simply responding to the uninhabited wilderness, where grottoed peaks tower on high and cloudy forests mass in depth. The sages and virtuous men shed reflected light from the distant past and myriad delights are fused with their spirits and their thoughts. What should I then do? Freely expand my spirit, that is all. What should be placed higher than that which expands the spirit?[66]

Theories of music and art compared

Tsung's contemporaries would doubtless have recognized many of the allusions contained in this wonderfully evocative passage: for example, to drinking wine and playing the lute, which were both considered to be typically 'Taoist' pursuits.[67] The lute, moreover, by this date the unmistakable attribute of the poet or scholar was, as we saw earlier, the fitting accompaniment to the contemplation of landscape, whether natural or – as here – painted. In sounding the lute while unrolling his paintings, Tsung was therefore preparing himself for the act of looking by attuning his mind to the represented subject. But, to any educated person, the lute would also have been synonymous with ancient ceremonial music and with the 'correct' and harmonious tones that traditionally accompanied long-established rituals. This almost inevitable association would have suited Tsung's purpose perfectly. By symbolically harnessing landscape painting to tradition and

---

65 The 'Stone Gate' was a gorge in the vicinity of Hui-Yüan's Tung-lin monastery on Mount Lu. It is described in the preface to a collection of poetry composed by members of Hui-Yüan's community following an excursion there, which apparently took place in 400 AD; see Bush, 'Tsung Ping's Essay ...', pp. 146–7. In his younger days, Tsung Ping had also studied at the Tung-lin monastery, which taught elements of Buddhist doctrine as well as the classic rites of Confucianism.

66 'Tsung Ping's Essay ...', pp. 145–6.

67 Bush and Shih 1985, p. 21.

ritual, it was easier to argue for a more exalted function for painting generally: the task of revealing spiritual truth.[68] In his eyes, the aim of painting landscape was not to capture the chance appearances of nature. Instead, having contemplated its wonders, the artist should transmit the state of spiritual exaltation thus attained to the (one assumes) suitably attuned viewer. In this way, the cosmic force or spiritual essence that resided in the real-life subject would enter into the heart or soul of the beholder via the intermediary of the painted image.

As Munakata has pointed out, this account of how painting might affect its audience closely resembles Tsung's ideas concerning the affective power of music. In the *Ming fo lun* ('Discourses Illuminating the Buddha') Tsung writes that 'musical tones evoke sympathetic responses [in the listeners], in their hearts attaining mystical realization'.[69] The tones of music strike the ear just as the colours and forms of painting impinge on the eye, but it is in the heart that the mystical content of each is apprehended. Recognition of a depicted form or musical phrase and the physical mechanisms whereby these are perceived are unimportant. What is important is the communication of spiritual content by means of 'sympathetic vibration' – a notion frequently encountered in early Chinese musical theory, but which Tsung was seemingly the first to apply to painting.[70] The simple fact of acoustics that a particular tone vibrating at a given frequency is capable of calling forth a corresponding tone from another similarly pitched vessel or instrument was thought by the Chinese to have important ritual or even cosmic implications.[71] Indeed, this purely physical phenomenon not only matched but also appeared to substantiate more far-reaching theories as set forth, for example, in the *Li-chi*, about the reciprocity of forces acting upon and within the universe and how individual forms responded to and, at the same time, influenced one another:

---

68 Chang Yen-yüan (see n. [55] above) employs the same strategy by linking painting with calligraphy, acknowledged by the classical texts as belonging among the six arts. As Falkenhausen has observed, Chinese history – both cultural and political – shows numerous instances of the tendency rhetorically to express new ideas or innovations in terms of a 'return to hallowed antiquity'; see Lothar von Falkenhausen, 'Issues in Western Zhou Studies: A Review Article', *Early China*, 18 (1993), p. 214.

69 Munakata, 'Concepts of *Lei* and *Kan-lei*', p. 125.

70 Western writers have had some difficulty in translating the term *ch'i* (*qi*), nearly always used in this context, and which has been rendered variously as 'remote interaction' or 'configured energy'; see, for example, DeWoskin 1982, pp. 17, 37ff. In a purely musical context, however, it clearly refers to sound waves or, more specifically, the phenomenon of sympathetic vibration described here.

71 The first of Hsieh Ho's six 'laws' of painting, which scholars have generally acknowledged to be the most important, can also be construed as meaning 'resonance of the vital spirit', the task of painting being to cause the soul of the viewer to vibrate in sympathy with the vital force of the living being or object being depicted. For a comparison of several possible translations of the 'six laws' see Michael Sullivan, *The Birth of Landscape Painting in China*, Berkeley, CA (California U. P.), 1962, pp. 106–7; also the brief but useful article by Clay Lancaster, 'Keys to the Understanding of Indian and Chinese Painting: the "Six Limbs" of Yasodhara and the "Six Principles" of Hsieh Ho', *Journal of Aesthetics and Art Criticism*, XI, no. 2 (December 1952), esp. pp. 100ff.

The initiating cause and the result correspond to each other.
The round and the deflected, the crooked and the straight, have
each its own category; and such is the character of all things,
that they affect one another severally according to their class.[72]

Elsewhere in the same text, these reciprocal forces are specifically
associated with the seemingly magical properties of music:

Ceremonies and music resemble the nature of Heaven and
Earth, penetrate to the virtues of the spiritual Intelligences,
bring down the spirits from above, and raise up those whose
seat is below ... Then plants and trees will grow luxuriantly;
curling sprouts and buds will expand; the feathered and
winged tribes will be active ... and all will have to be
ascribed to the power of music.[73]

Art, music and ritual

Not only do ideas like these supply the context for Kiyohiko
Munakata's re-reading of Tsung's 'Introduction to Painting
Landscape'. They also open up a wealth of intriguing possibilities.
Tsung Ping himself was seemingly a traditionalist at heart.[74] Is it
possible that Tsung's essay, as well as providing us with clues about
the state of development of painting during the fifth century AD,
contains echoes of earlier theories of art, of which otherwise we
have no record? Certainly, one important strand in Chinese
historical and philosophical writing consisted of creating a kind of
amalgam of the author's own ideas and observations and, at the
same time, a commentary on and incorporation of previously
established notions.[75] Was Tsung really writing only about painting
and about his own era or was he formulating more ambitious claims
about the purposes of art generally: not only then but in earlier
periods as well? Can we, moreover, deduce from his remarks on
painting that the arts of depiction in former times fulfilled a dual

---

72 *Li Chi, The Book of Rites*, translated by James Legge, New York (University Books) 1967, vol. 2, p. 110.

73 Ibid., p. 115.

74 Munakata points out a number of other traditional ideas and allusions embedded in Tsung's essay on
landscape, which he describes as a '"last glory" of the pre-Han and Han theory of art'. He also notes that
some of the specific imagery employed derives from earlier sources. References to the 'four ends of the
earth', 'a host of supernatural forces' and the 'uninhabited wilderness' are virtually a paraphrase of a
passage which occurs in the *Shan-hai-ching (Shan hai jing, '*Classic of Mountains and Seas'), a pre-Han
compilation of fantastic descriptions of sacred mountains both beyond and within the borders of China.
('Concepts of *Lei* and *Kan-lei* ...', p. 128, also ibid., p. 125 and n. 59.)

75 Acker advances a very similar hypothesis in relation to Hsieh Ho's six laws, remarking that the casual way
in which the author introduces these six elements of painting suggests that he is quoting from some earlier
work and is not 'enunciating the Six Canons' for the first time. See Acker 1954, introduction p. xli, also p. 4
and n. 2; compare (in relation to the exigetic tradition concerning the *Odes* or *Book of Songs*) the excellent
study by Haun Saussy, *The Problem of a Chinese Aesthetic*, Stanford, CA (Stanford U. P.) 1993, esp. ch. 2, 'The
Other Side of Allegory', pp. 47ff.

function, as music undoubtedly did: a form of social intercourse or a source of aesthetic pleasure on the one hand, part of a system of religious belief and ritual enactment on the other?

In the absence of older documents relating to early Chinese art, any attempt to answer such questions must depend largely on the archaeological record. Inevitably, what archaeology has unearthed have been, for the most part, burial goods. While some of these were items of individual adornment or pieces intended for personal use, most of the objects that have been discovered were of primarily ritual significance.[76] But did their decoration likewise have a particular ritual or mythic meaning, therefore fulfilling (as did music) an essentially communicative function by serving as a vehicle for the transmission of spiritual messages?

This is a problem that has divided students of Chinese antiquity into two clearly defined camps. On the one side are those who identify the highly abstracted forms and motifs found, for example, on early bronze sacrificial vessels with real or fabled birds or beasts having a specific place in Chinese mythology. They have argued that these motifs would necessarily have corresponded to the nature and purpose of the ritual being enacted: part of an elaborate network of associations between symbolic animals, like tigers and dragons, and the elements of wind or water. Some scholars even think that, without some understanding of the symbolic connotations attached to such images, we cannot form a wider picture of the culture or patterns of thought of that era. Munakata is one such scholar who, when discussing the decoration consisting of dragon motifs found on a bronze sacrificial vessel, probably of the late Chou period (fig. 9), proposes that, since dragons were symbolically associated with clouds, they would have been appropriate to a rain-making ritual, and he quotes from the *Huai-nan-tzŭ* (3, 1b–2a): 'When a tiger roars, the wind from the gorge comes out, and when a dragon rises, the felicitous clouds gather around it ...'[77] Another expert on early China, Li Xueqin, in a paper entitled 'Liangzhu Culture and the Shang Dynasty *Taotie* Motif', has suggested that the *taotie* – an ancient form of ornament based on starkly abbreviated mouth and staring eyes that appear only vaguely zoomorphic in origin – had a specific religious and mythological meaning.[78] Even if we have not yet succeeded in defining that meaning, he argues, it is impossible

---

76 For a description and illustrations of the contents of the tomb, see Xiaoneng Yang (ed.), *The Golden Age of Chinese Archaeology. Celebrated Discoveries from the People's Republic of China*, New Haven/London (Yale U. P.) 1999, pp. 275ff. and further refs.

77 'Concepts of *Lei* and *Kan-lei* ...', pp. 108 and n. 11; compare also ibid., pp. 111ff. and figs 1a and 1b.

78 Falkenhausen ('Issues in Western Zhou Studies', pp. 223–4) dismisses *taotie* as 'an obscure antiquarian term', proposing as an alternative *shoumianwen* ('animal mask ornament'), a term also adopted by a number of Chinese and Japanese scholars.

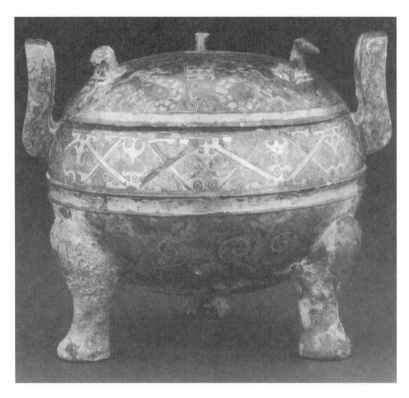

Figure 9. Chinese bronze sacrificial bowl (*ding*) showing dragon motifs,
inlaid with gold and silver, late Zhou Dynasty, 4th–3rd century BC
(Institute of Arts, Minneapolis)

to grasp the 'intentions of the ancients' unless one accepts that the transmission of such motifs also meant inheriting certain kinds of beliefs and myths.[79]

Arrayed against Li Xueqin and his colleagues who hold similar opinions are equally distinguished specialists who maintain that ornament of this kind is fundamentally devoid of any ascertainable 'meaning', whether religious, cosmological or mythological. Rather, it derives from a particular tradition of making and decorating such objects. It is thus, in a sense, self-referential: 'iconographically meaningless, or meaningful only as pure form'.[80] In a detailed study of the Chinese bronzes now in the Arthur M. Sackler Collection, one respected authority on the art of this period, Robert Bagley, devotes a lengthy and complex discussion to the evolution of the motifs with which they are decorated. He does not, however, advance any hypothesis whatever as to the (admittedly conjectural) meanings that have been attached to these motifs.[81] Elsewhere, he confesses that, even if the evidence were 'more promising', he would still begrudge the issue of symbolism any significant place in bronze studies and that to him, what he terms the 'explanatory power' of symbolic meanings appears greatly overrated.[82]

For my part, I am not a Sinologist, merely someone intrigued and often deeply moved by early Chinese art. But even to a non-specialist like myself, the very fact of this debate (to say nothing of the passion with which it has been conducted by leading archaeologists) is interesting for several reasons.[83] One is that there exists a strikingly similar divergence of opinion among his-

---

79 In Whitfield 1993 (see following note), pp. 56ff., 65; compare also Xiaoneng Yang, *Reflections of Early China. Decor, Pictographs, and Pictorial Inscriptions*, Kansas (Nelson-Atkins Museum of Art)/Seattle and Washington (University of Washington Press) 2000, esp. ch. 2, 'Review of Bronze Decor Studies' for an account of divergent opinions as to the symbolism and meaning of these kinds of decoration.

80 See Sarah Allen, 'Art and Meaning', in Roderick Whitfield (ed.), *The Problem of Meaning in Early Chinese Ritual Bronzes (Colloquies on Art and Archaeology in Asia*, no. 15), London (Percival David Foundation of Chinese Art) 1993, pp. 12–13. Allen is here summarizing the views of Max Loehr, among others, to which she is opposed.

81 Robert W. Bagley, *Shang Ritual Bronzes in the Arthur M. Sackler Collection*, Cambridge, MA (Arthur M. Sackler Museum/Harvard U. P.) 1987, pp. 19ff., also pp. 49–50 and n. 47. Bagley's views have been much criticized by recent scholars. See, for example, the article 'The *Taotie* Reconsidered: Meanings and Functions of Shang Theriomorphic Imagery' by Ladislav Kesner, who remarks that such attitudes 'block the way not only to an understanding of the stylistic development of this art form, but also to understanding the full cultural significance of these objects'. (*Artibus Asiae*, vol. 53 (1991), nos. 1–2, p. 36.)

82 Robert W. Bagley, 'Meaning and Explanation', in Whitfield 1993, pp. 34ff. Note that the views of Loehr, Bagley and others who consider the decorative forms found on Chinese bronzes to be devoid of symbolic meaning have, to some extent, been influenced by Suzanne Langer's classic account of the origins of ornament. Langer believes that the 'fundamental forms' that occur in the decorative arts of all ages and races, 'the circle, the triangle, the spiral, the parallel' precede any representational function, describing such forms as merely 'incentives to artistic creation'. For an account of the impact of Langer's ideas on the study of ancient Chinese artefacts, see Allen, 'Art and Meaning' (as n. [80] above), pp. 12ff.; compare Susanne K. Langer, *Feeling and Form*, London (Routledge) 1953, pp. 69ff.

83 Falkenhausen remarks that the question whether or not bronze ornamentation has concrete symbolic content has been 'for years the most hotly debated topic in the field'. ('Issues in Western Zhou Studies', p. 201.)

torians of modern Western painting – especially those concerned with the possible readings of twentieth-century art – many of whom believe that meaning resides primarily in such things as the gesture of the hand, the mark of the brush or the plasticity of form: that the 'meaning is in the making'. Others, no less persuasive, argue that a more far-reaching cultural, political, spiritual or religious significance attaches to the fabrication of images and to the making of art generally. It will be clear from other chapters of this book that, of these two views, I find the latter more compelling. But, given that music in ancient China was universally acknowledged to have a meaning 'beyond itself', like Li Xueqin and his colleagues I have also come to think it extremely unlikely that no such meaning was attributed to the arts of depiction. Both music and dance played a vital role in the ceremonial acts and religious rituals of Chinese antiquity: elaborate performances in which every component was assigned its preordained place and particular function.[84] Is it not probable that, just as the individual tones of music were required to 'correspond' to the specific character and historical associations of any given ceremony, the visual forms and motifs with which ritual objects were embellished would have been attuned no less precisely to the occasion and to the purpose of that ceremony?

Some historians have pointed out that the kind of grandiose ambition that would link not only rites and ceremonies but everything in the world and in the cosmos with everything else – the five tones of music with the five colours as well as the five elements (earth, wood, metal, fire and water), the five directions, and so on – may have been a preoccupation peculiar to writers of the Han era.[85] It may be to these writers, rather than to earlier sources, that we owe the notion that the constituent elements of music and of visual art were, by virtue of their orderly arrangement, related not only to the cosmos but also to each other.[86] Even so, those older fragments of evidence we possess, together with glosses and commentaries by later Chinese authors, likewise suggest that there had long existed an intimate relationship between ritual music and traditional forms of depiction. Both were seen as playing a similar and equally

---

84 'Liturgy, singing and ritual dance simultaneously contributed to this communication process: rituals were multi-media happenings'; see Falkenhausen (as preceding note), pp. 139ff., 147.

85 See, for example, John B. Henderson, *The Development and Decline of Chinese Cosmology*, New York (Columbia U. P.) 1984, pp. 24–5, 32ff.

86 In the *Ta Tai li-chi* ('Record of Rites of the Elder Tai') we read how 'the sages established the five rites ... they ordained the five degrees of mourning ... they made music for the five-holed pipe ... they established the proper places for the five colours, gave names to the five grains, and decided upon the relative standing of the five sacrificial animals'; quoted after Needham 1956, pp. 296ff.

important role: for example, in invoking the ancestral spirits and conjuring up cosmic forces. By giving expression to such forces, they could attune the mind of man to the spiritual aspect of nature and to the order and regularity manifested therein. They therefore functioned as essential constituents of that complex web of interrelations joining 'that which is above' – the domain of heaven and of the ancestors – to the sublunary sphere with its 'myriad things'. If this were the case, it seems probable that, at least in the context of ritual, music and depiction in ancient China can scarcely have counted as separate 'arts' at all. Instead, both would have been thought of as different aspects of the same vital process of communication between mankind and the supernatural powers.

II SPHERICAL MUSIC

Heard melodies are sweet, but those unheard
Are sweeter; therefore, ye soft pipes, play on;
Not the sensual ear, but, more endear'd,
Pipe to the spirit ditties of no tone.
                    Keats, *Ode to a Grecian Urn* (1819)

The sanguine enjoys pleasing and cheerful things, the
melancholic loves solitude, and the phlegmatic tranquillity
and quiet ... Therefore it is no wonder that our Sr. Giovanni,
altogether well proportioned in his soul and body, has
always had the greatest affection for the sweet and
delightful harmony of music, the art of the ancient Greeks,
among whom all the noble arts and virtues flourished to
such a degree that whoever was not expert and practised in
it was reputed to be uncouth and worthless.
                    Eulogy of Giovanni de' Bardi (1574)

Art and music in ancient Greece

We know the names of quite a number of Greek painters: Apelles, for example, or Polygnotus. But because no works by these artists have survived from antiquity, we have little notion of what their pictures – so highly praised and so often described – actually looked like. In order to form some idea of the evolution of Greek art, we must turn instead to sculpture, which has survived in quantity, or to the many thousands of drawn and painted images on pottery, from whose mute depictions much of our knowledge of the classical world derives. We also learn from Pliny and other ancient historians that there once existed numbers – perhaps even considerable numbers – of handbooks and treatises on both painting and sculpture, none of which has been preserved, except in the form of extracts or paraphrases by later authors.[1] We even know the names of some of them, like the celebrated *Canon* of Polyclitus: a text that seems to have propounded a system of proportions on which sculptural representations of the human figure might be based.[2] But from what we may surmise as to the content of these lost writings, they were probably concerned with materials and techniques or with

---

1 A useful account of the written sources from which our knowledge of ancient Greek theory and criticism of the visual arts derives can be found in J. J. Pollitt, *The Ancient View of Greek Art. Criticism, History and Terminology*, New Haven/London (Yale U. P.) 1974.
2 Pliny describes the *Canon* of Polyclitus as a statue but it is clear from Galen, *De Placitis Hippocratis et Platonis*, 5, that the name was given both to a sculpture and to a treatise. Two authors, Plutarch and Philo Mechanicus, preserve what appear to be direct quotations from the latter; see J. J. Pollitt, *The Art of Ancient Greece: Sources and Documents*, Cambridge (Cambridge U. P.) 1990, pp. 75ff., also idem, *Ancient View of Greek Art*, pp. 14ff.

solutions to purely formal problems – not with broader kinds of questions raised by the visual arts, on which, it appears, only a somewhat limited intellectual effort was expended.

If, moreover, we turn to the great philosophers of antiquity such as Plato or Aristotle, we may discover from passing references and from their discussions of other related topics what they thought about style and what 'excellence' in art might consist of. We may even gauge their opinion of some of the famous artists of their time. Yet neither devoted a treatise or dialogue to the fine arts as such. Instead, they addressed their analytical skills to the 'arts' of poetry or rhetoric or to entirely different areas of enquiry such as epistemology or ethics.[3] And while some recent commentators have interpreted Plato's ideas on imitation set out in his *Republic* as constituting a theory of visual representation, others have stressed that the primary object of his enquiry was in fact poetry and that the comparisons he draws with painting are useful to him only in order to illustrate poetry's particular defects.[4] Certainly, the visual arts were not the principal focus of Plato's attention, any more than they were of Aristotle's. The latter even expressed, on occasion, rather a low opinion of the utility of painting, acknowledging merely that it 'seems to be useful for improving our capacity to assess craftsmen's work'.[5]

Music, by comparison, not only pervaded every aspect of Greek life, as we learn from the writings of virtually all the major poets, dramatists and tragedians (whose works were, moreover, usually sung rather than recited). It also seems to have dominated Greek thinking about the nature of humankind, about our moral and emotional constitution and our relationship with the world and the cosmos. Not all Greek writers who speculated about the universe and its contents attempted to give a comprehensive account of music as such, nor did they necessarily describe its constituent elements in scientific terms. Again, neither Plato nor Aristotle made the scientific study of music a central part of his investigations. As already noted, their main concerns lay elsewhere: in the domains of ethics, or politics, or education. But, in considering these matters, they found it entirely natural to draw music into the argument,

---

3 Aristotle in various places writes at some length about art: for example, in the *Metaphysics* (98a ff.) and in the *Nicomachean Ethics* (VI, 4). But while he makes occasional reference to both painting and sculpture, it is clear that what he means by 'art' in general is very different from our use of the term, since his main concern is to distinguish between different kinds of knowledge (*Metaphysics*) or action (*Ethics*).

4 Notably E. A. Havelock, *Preface to Plato*, Oxford (Basil Blackwell) 1963, p. 32 and n. 28; compare Pollitt, who remarks that 'much of the extant evidence for the Greek view of Greek art occurs in the works of authors who, while discussing some other subject, make passing references to art for the purpose of analogy or illustration'. (*Ancient View of Greek Art*, p. 1.)

5 *Politics*, 1338a17.

sometimes discussing it at length and in considerable detail. Plato wrote emphatically and to great effect about various 'non-musical' aspects of music, about its relation to the ethical and social order, to the sciences and the other arts. We may be repelled by some of his more extreme prescriptions – for example, that only music and poetry beneficial to the state should be composed or that none but the elderly should be deemed capable of judging music properly.[6] Nevertheless, it is clear that, for him, music had a significant role to play as an instrument of educational and social policy, provided that its use – like everything else – was strictly controlled.

Aristotle, too, seemingly took it for granted that music can affect behaviour and shape men's character. 'It is clear', he writes in the *Politics*, 'that music is capable of creating a particular quality of character in the soul, and if it can do that, it is plain that it should be made use of and that young people should be educated in it.'[7] He also alludes to the discussion of music to be found in the *Republic*, where Plato, speaking this time in the person of Socrates, seeks to persuade his elder brother Glaucon that 'musical education is the most important, rhythm and attunement are what most penetrate the inner soul and grasp it most powerfully, bringing good order, and make a person well-regulated if he is educated correctly, and the opposite if he is not'.[8] If 'rhythm and attunement' could work such remarkable effects upon the mind or spirit, why not, it is tempting to ask, the constituent elements of other forms of art? What effects might they produce and how were these effects to be achieved – or avoided? Plato was in no doubt about the capacity of poetry and the visual arts, if misconceived or wrongly employed, to distract the mind or confuse the senses, just as music was capable of doing. But he does not stop to explore in detail the question of their affective potential, independent of their subject-matter, simply because, for much of the time, he is preoccupied with topics such as the role of narrative and imitation.

By contrast, Aristotle's more analytical turn of mind led him actually to compare the physical properties of colours with the

---

6 'Then we must give orders to our poets, and compel them to create in their poems only the image of good character.' (*Republic*, 401b; compare 801d, where Plato writes that the poet 'may not display his compositions to any private person until they have been displayed to those who are appointed as judges in these matters ... we have in fact appointed judges already'.) His requirement that those chosen to assess the quality of musical works should be 'not less than fifty years old' follows at 802b.
7 *Politics*, 1340a6–b19.
8 *Republic*, 401d. Plato's account of the role of music in education is complicated by the fact that he sometimes uses the term *mousike* in a wider sense to denote not music as we would understand it but that variety of disciplines presided over by the Muses, to which both history and poetry also belonged. In other instances, however, it is clear from the context that it is music itself he has in mind, as in the passage just quoted where 'music' is specifically linked with 'rhythm' and 'attunement'; for another example, see *Laws*, 812d.

tones of music – apparently the first time in Western culture that any such direct comparison was made. In *On the Senses*, he writes:

In this way, then, it is possible to accept that there are more colours than just white or black, and that they are many in ratio: for they may lie side by side in the ratio of three to two or that of three to four or in other relations of numbers ... Thus, they may be in the same condition as concords [symphoniai]: *the colours that depend on well-ratioed numbers, like concords in their domain, are taken to be the pleasantest of colours (purple and red and a few others of that kind – few for the same reason that the concords are few) ...*[9]

Notice that Aristotle here compares colours with musical consonances in terms of the mathematical relationships by which the latter are governed – or rather, he relates the effect of specific combinations of colours ('pleasant' or 'unpleasant') to the ratios that produce the fundamental concords in music.[10] He does not, however, seek to describe any particular aesthetic effect. Moreover, he compares the 'abstract' relationships between musical tones with colours likewise regarded solely in the abstract ('red', 'purple') – not with colours as they are employed by painters to describe form or capture the chance appearances of the natural world. In this context, questions of representation or description do not arise.

As for the music of his own time, Aristotle's tastes seem to have been largely conservative. He wrote scathingly about what he called the latest 'extravagances', by which he probably meant the works of composers such as Timotheus and Philoxenus. Certainly, he castigated the former's *The Persians* on the grounds of unseemly and inappropriate characterization.[11] Aristotle's pupil Aristoxenus went further, denouncing his contemporaries for succumbing to the 'muse of the concert-hall' and declaring that 'this vulgar music' had reached what he called 'an advanced state of corruption'. 'We few in isolation', he intoned smugly, 'recall what music used to be like.' But it was Plato who inveighed most vehemently against any form of musical innovation. In the *Republic* he cautioned against the

---

9 *De Sensu*, 439b19–440a4; Barker 1989, p. 74.
10 For an explanation of these ratios, see ch. 1, pp. 31ff.
11 Philoxenus's *Mysians*, by contrast, appears to have been criticized mainly on account of its more than usually frequent use of modulation. From Aristotle and from the Plutarchian *De Musica* we learn that it progressed from the Hypodorian via the Hypophrygian and Phrygian to the Dorian and Mixolydian modes, all within the same composition; see West, *Ancient Greek Music*, pp. 364ff. For a brief account of the Greek modes, see below, pp. 63ff.

'introduction of novel fashions in music' and quoted approvingly the opinion of his fellow Athenian Damon, who had warned that such changes endanger the 'whole fabric of society'.[12] He also provided a comprehensive account of the shortcomings of recent musical styles, pointing in particular to the endless quest for novel effects, the 'expressive' use of a wide range of variations of register and vocal timbre and the crass imitation of natural occurrences such as storms and thunder. It may have been Timotheus' *Niobe*, or *Semele*, or *Ajax's Madness* he had in mind when, again in the *Republic*, he pilloried music that mimics the bellowing of bulls and the crashing of seas, thunder and tempest, writing that, once such effects are excluded, there will be no need for 'polychordy or omnimodality ... for complex rhythms or instruments yielding excessive numbers of notes or scales'.[13] If this attack on 'excessive numbers of notes' seems vaguely familiar to the modern reader, it is surely because it reminds us of that keen observer of eighteenth-century musical life, Emperor Joseph II (r.1780–90), who criticized Mozart's *Die Entführung aus dem Serail* for precisely the same reason.[14]

The doctrine of the modes

Unfortunately, our own knowledge of ancient Greek music remains sketchy to a degree, frustrating any attempt to identify more precisely those works by his contemporaries that attracted Plato's particular censure. Although the last hundred years or so have been punctuated by discoveries of previously unknown fragments of antique musical notation, the total number of surviving examples is still lamentably small.[15] Some progress has been made in figuring out how these fragments might have been performed, but scholarly disagreements persist over their precise interpretation. Equally frustrating is the way in which antique musical theory turns out, with few exceptions, to be of little practical value when we come to examine what remains of the music. For much of the time, there seems to have been a marked discrepancy between that 'music' the theorists wrote about, about which scientists and philosophers speculated, and what people actually played and sang: the music

---

12 *Republic*, 424c. On what little is known of Damon see Barker 1984, pp. 168-9; also West, p. 246ff. Compare R. Wallace, 'Damone di Oa ed i suoi successori: un analisi delle fonti', in R. Wallace and B. MacLachlan (eds), *Harmonia Mundi*, Rome (Edizioni dell'Ateneo) 1991, pp. 30–53.
13 *Republic* 395d–400a; West, p. 369.
14 'Very many notes, my dear Mozart ...'; the anecdote has been repeated in nearly every account of the composer's life but probably goes back to the nearly contemporary biography by Franz Xaver Niemetschek, *Leben des k.k. Kapellmeisters Wolfgang Gottlieb Mozart* (Prague, 1798, rev. 2nd edn 1808).
15 See above, ch. 1, p. 29, n. [10].

heard by the physical ear rather than conceived by the intellect. The disciplines of acoustics and harmonics took little account of current musical styles, performing conventions or even the tuning systems employed for various instruments. Instead, both acoustics and harmonics tended to be thought of as subjects of investigation for their own sake, often giving rise to theoretical disputes of a highly rarefied kind. In the so-called 'Hibeh papyrus', one of the earliest surviving fragments of writing about any musical topic, the unknown author scathingly dismisses people who 'say they are "harmonicists" but who, on this subject with which they claim a special familiarity, have nothing articulate to say, but are carried away with enthusiasm'.[16] Moreover, remarks by later commentators who based themselves on earlier Greek sources sometimes betray only the shakiest grasp of the terminology employed by their predecessors. Unpicking the meaning of their writings, where musical terms are misused or patently misunderstood, has proved a Herculean task for even the most agile of modern musicologists.

We cannot follow the intricacies of these discussions here. For our purposes it is important merely to identify two main strands in Greek thinking about music, one represented by Pythagoras and his followers, the other by Aristoxenus. What we know of the Pythagoreans' account of music suggests that it was a highly abstract and in many ways speculative one, in which mathematical ideas, rather than the phenomena of musical experience, played a dominant role. It is to Aristoxenus, who tells us not only about the realities of contemporary musical life but also a certain amount about the historical development of Greek music, that we must turn for more practical information. From his writings it is evident that, by the late fourth century BC, a new, more varied and dramatic style of composition had begun to oust the older, simpler style associated with such revered figures of the past as the *kitharode* Terpander or Pindar. Elements of that older music were still preserved, especially in the form of the various *harmoniai* or 'modes'. However, the *harmoniai* of archaic Greek music were gradually being supplanted by the newer *tonoi*, which, confusingly, were given the same ancient names as the *harmoniai*: for example, Dorian or Phrygian.

---

16 Quoted after Barker 1984, pp. 184-5. The papyrus itself has been tentatively dated to the middle of the third century BC. The date of the passage quoted is uncertain but it was probably written in the first half of the fourth century. Otherwise, almost all our information about music theory in this period derives from later copies, commentaries or glosses; see Thomas J. Mathiesen, 'Hermes or Clio? The Transmission of Ancient Greek Musical Theory', in Nancy Kovaleff Baker and Barbara Russano Hanning (eds), *Musical Humanism and its Legacy. Essays in Honor of Claude V. Palisca*, Stuyvesant, NY (Pendragon Press) 1992, pp. 3ff., also idem, *Apollo's Lyre. Greek Music and Music Theory in Antiquity and the Middle Ages*, Lincoln/London (Nebraska U. P.) 1999, pp. 290ff.

It is difficult to define the difference between *harmoniai* and *tonoi* without resorting to technical language. Indeed, it is such a difficult subject altogether that one might be tempted to pass by rather rapidly, were it not for the fact that ideas about the 'modes' profoundly affected later thinking and writing about other forms of art. It is necessary, therefore, to explain that both *tonoi* and *harmoniai* consisted of a series of relationships between different musical notes. These were not necessarily notes of any predetermined pitch, although a subsequent development was to assign each *tonos* to a specific pitch range, at which point the *tonoi* became more like what we would call 'keys': A minor, C major and so on.[17] However, it would be mistaken to equate *tonoi* with anything resembling the key structures that we are accustomed to, since ancient Greek music was not tonal, at least not in our modern sense of the term. Nor, it seems, did the Greek 'modes' bear any resemblance to those employed in other European music, even though the names of the *harmoniai* were later applied to the medieval Church modes.[18] But the Greek *harmoniai* were not identical with the ecclesiastical modes; thus, to translate *harmoniai* as 'modes', as is often done, is likely to be misleading.[19]

What we do know – from Aristoxenus and from other sources – is that names such as Dorian and Lydian may once have conjured up neither a key structure nor a mode but types of melodies particular to different regions or peoples. Even in later times, Ionian, Phrygian, Lydian and Dorian music each seems to have retained its distinct regional character. Moreover, a number of writers – Plato, again, notable among them – associated the character of these *harmoniai* not just with particular kinds of regional melodies but with certain moods or emotions. Here, at last, we are on more familiar ground, since this idea was to cast a long shadow over subsequent discussion of the 'moral' effects of both music and art. It was also capable of being specifically applied to painting – at least, so thought the seventeenth-century artist Nicolas Poussin. In a

---

17 One way of explaining the arrangement of the different *harmoniai*, each of which consisted of an altered succession of tones and semitones, is by analogy with the scales produced on a modern keyboard by starting each time on a different note (and playing only the white notes). Following this system, a Mixolydian 'scale' would equate with that from our note b to the B below, Lydian with c - C, Phrygian with d - D, Dorian with e - E, Hypolydian with f - F, Ionian with g - G and Aeolian with a - A; see Michaelides, *Music of Ancient Greece*, p. 128. But only the *tonoi* were linked with specific pitches; the names of the *harmoniai* allude merely to the sequence of intervals within *any* chosen octave.

18 The misapplication of the names of the Greek *harmoniai* to the medieval Church modes may have been due to the detailed exposition of this subject found in the anonymous (*c*.tenth century) *Alia Musica*; see Strunk II, pp. 196ff.

19 I here follow Andrew Barker (see Barker 1989, pp. 14ff.), who advocates caution in the rendering of the term *harmonia*, which he himself usually translates as 'attunement' or 'pattern of attunement'. However, compare West 1992, pp. 177ff., where a whole section of his chapter 6 is devoted to what are termed the Greek 'modes'; the account given there of the relation between *harmoniai* and *tonoi* is admirably clear.

frequently cited letter dated 24 November 1647, sent from Rome to his patron Paul Fréart de Chantelou, he declared his intention to paint a picture 'in the Phrygian mode' and also discussed the character of the Dorian, Lydian, Hypolydian and Ionian modes in relation to painting. In the same letter, he described in detail his future plans, referring to those 'fine old Greeks, who invented everything that is beautiful', and in particular to the 'marvellous effects' they were able to produce by their use of the modes, which had:

the power to arouse the soul of the spectator to diverse emotions. Observing these effects, the wise ancients attributed to each a special character and they called the Dorian the Mode that was firm, grave, and severe, and they applied it to matters that were grave, severe and full of wisdom. And passing on from this to pleasant and joyous things they used the Phrygian Mode because its intervals were smaller than those of any other Mode and because its effect was sharper. These two manners and no others were praised and approved by Plato and Aristotle, who deemed the others useless; they held in high esteem this vehement, furious and highly severe Mode that strikes the spectator with awe. I hope within a year to paint something in this Phrygian Mode; frightful wars provide subjects suited to this manner.[20]

Moral effects of music

Poussin's admiring reference to 'those fine old Greeks' and the fact that he names both Plato and Aristotle make it clear that he was indeed alluding to the classical tradition of discussion about the 'modes' – a tradition that associated the various *harmoniai* with the evocation of certain emotional states and with specific moral values. Evidently, one of the questions occupying him is whether painting might also lay claim to moral value not only on account of the narrative depicted but also in terms of its capacity to call forth a variety of responses on the part of the viewer. Just what *kind* of responses is another matter. What Poussin may not have realized was that, even among the ancients, there had been only limited agreement as to what precisely the various *harmoniai* signified – or indeed, whether they signified anything at all. The unknown author

---

20 The text of this letter (original and translation) can be found in Anthony Blunt, *Nicolas Poussin*, London (Phaidon Press) 1967, pp. 367ff.; see also n. [61] on p. 199 regarding the translation.

of the Hibeh papyrus, mentioned earlier, poured scorn on the idea that 'some melodies make people self-disciplined, others prudent, others just, others brave ... The chromatic cannot make people cowardly, nor does the enharmonic ... make brave men of those who employ it.'[21] A small number of later writers, mainly of the Hellenistic and Roman periods, likewise resisted the idea that music could produce any particular ethical or moral effects on the listener. Principal among them were the Epicurean Philodemus (first century BC) and the Roman author Sextus Empiricus (c.200 AD), who argued that music consisted merely of an assemblage of audible tones, for which it might be claimed that they afforded an inessential source of pleasure but nothing more.[22]

Such voices were, however, in the minority. Among ancient Greek theorists there had been a more or less general acceptance of the notion that music, depending on its character, could significantly influence aspects of both mood and behaviour, albeit in a variety of ways. This belief finds expression in numerous legends: for example, that of Terpander whose singing, we are told, restored the city of Sparta to good order following a period of civil unrest.[23] Pythagoras is said to have employed music, as well as incantations and spells, in healing the sick.[24] He is also credited with preventing a jealous lover, inflamed by a combination of alcohol and Phrygian pipe-music, from burning down his mistress's front door by persuading the piper to play a more dignified melody.[25]

But it was Plato, both in the *Republic* and in several of his other dialogues, who set out in a systematic way to define the moral and emotive qualities of the various *harmoniai* and of particular types of melody. He also paid passing attention to the characteristics of certain instruments such as the *aulos* (fig. 10), which – like Aristotle – he considered 'orgiastic', being capable of reducing the hearer to a kind of frenzy.[26] So stern are the moral criteria Plato brings to his

---

21 Barker, loc. cit. (as n. [16]); for an explanation of 'chromatic' and 'enharmonic' see below, p. 69.
22 Empiricus, *Adversus musicos* (book 6 of *Adversus mathematicos*). For complete edition and translation, see Sextus Empiricus, *Against the Musicians*, new critical edition and translation by Denise Davidson Greaves (*Greek and Latin Music Theory*, vol. 3), Lincoln (University of Nebraska Press) 1986; also Strunk I, pp. 94ff.
23 West 1992, p. 31.
24 The notion of music's healing power seems to have been widespread. Boethius writes that 'Ismenias the Theban, when the torments of sciatica were troubling a number of Boeotians, is reported to have rid them of all their afflictions by his melodies'. (*De Institutione Musica*, quoted after Strunk II, pp. 139–40.) Athenaeus likewise records Aristotle's pupil Theophrastus as saying that persons subject to sciatica would 'always be free from its attacks if one played the *aulos* in the Phrygian *harmonia* over the part affected'. ('The Sophists at Dinner', quoted after Strunk I, p. 86.)
25 The principal source of such anecdotes is Iamblichus, *De Vita Pythagorica*. For an English version see *On the Pythagorean Life. Iamblichus*. Translated with notes and introduction by Gillian Clark, Liverpool (Liverpool U. P.) 1989. Compare also Porphyry, *Vita Pythagorae*, pp. 30, 32ff.; Boethius, *De Institutione Musica*, trans. McKinnon, in Strunk II, loc. cit. (as preceding note).
26 The *aulos* was a reed-blown pipe, often mistranslated as 'flute', yet in form and function more resembling the modern oboe. It is not certain whether it was a single or double-reed instrument: see West, op. cit., pp. 81ff; compare Kathleen Schlesinger, *The Greek Aulos*, London (Methuen) 1939, also Michaelides, pp. 42ff.

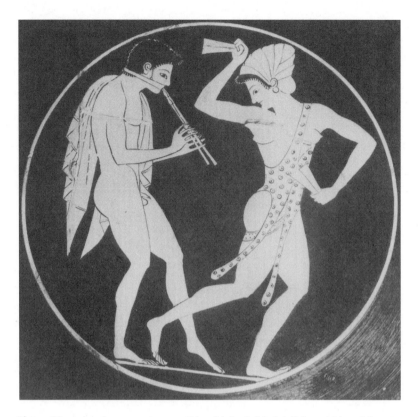

Figure 10. *Aulos* player wearing mouthband (*phorbeia*), detail from Attic red-figure amphora, *c*.480 BC (British Museum, London)

judgement of the *harmoniai* that finally (as Poussin stated) he is prepared to accept only two: the Dorian and, curiously, the Phrygian. Aristotle in fact chides him for allowing the latter, which was widely regarded as being dangerously inflammatory (sometimes literally so, as in the legend of the young man bent on arson!), describing it as 'exciting and emotional' and specifically associating it with the dithyramb and with 'Bacchic revelry and dancing'.[27]

The Dorian, by contrast, enjoyed almost universal approbation. Aristotle described it as 'steadfast' and 'manly',[28] while Plato considered it suitable for expressing 'the tones and accents of a brave man in warlike action or in any hard or dangerous task who, in the hour of defeat or when facing wounds and death, will meet every blow of fortune with steadfast endurance'.

---

27 *Politics*, 1342b2.
28 *Politics*, 1342b12.

The remaining *harmoniai* he dismisses with a succession of derogatory epithets: the Ionian and Lydian are 'soft' and 'sympotic', being associated with 'drunkenness, effeminacy and inactivity', while the Mixolydian and Hypolydian express sorrow and are suitable for 'dirges and laments' so that 'men, and even women of good standing, will have no use for them'.[29] Aristotle is less severe, describing the Lydian *harmonia*, disdained by Plato, as suitable for boys to learn since it is both 'decorous' and 'fun'. Another writer, summing up what Ionian music of former times was thought to have been like, characterized it as 'neither bright nor cheerful, but austere and hard, having a seriousness which is not ignoble, and so their *harmonia* is well adapted to tragedy'. That said, he conceded that 'today' the character of the Ionians themselves was 'much altered' and, therefore, so was their music.[30]

Equally divergent were opinions as to the respective merits of instrumental and vocal music. Aristotle thought music capable of producing certain effects (to his mind, largely beneficial ones, including the 'harmless' pleasures of amusement or relaxation) simply by virtue of its tones.[31] Plato disagreed; in his view, music derived its significance and its power to influence human emotion mainly from the conjunction of melody, rhythm and *logos* – words. Melody and rhythm did not in themselves express or evoke any particular emotion; instead, each was by its nature *appropriate* to the character of the ritual being enacted or the sentiment of the poetic narrative. For this reason, although melody and rhythm might be considered to have moral value, their 'meanings' were hard to identify without the help of words.[32] Music devoid of words was, Plato thought, 'confusing'. In the *Laws*, his last dialogue, which contains some of his most far-reaching pronouncements about the relationship between art and morality, he castigated those who:

tear rhythm and posture away from melody ... setting melody and rhythm without words and using the kithara and the aulos without the voice, a practice in which it is

---

29 *Republic*, 398e–399d.
30 Athenaeus (quoting Heraclides Ponticus), 'The Sophists at Dinner' (as n. [24] above), p. 88; West 1992, p. 182.
31 'The conduct of one's life ought to afford not only nobility but pleasure as well, since happiness comes from the combination of both. We say that music is one of the pleasantest things, whether it is purely instrumental or accompanied by song.' (*Politics*, 1339b.) Compare also the Aristotelian *Problemata* (a series of questions and propositions that clearly reflect Aristotelian ideas but that are not directly attributable to Aristotle), according to which 'even if there is a melody without words, it has moral character none the less'; quoted after Barker 1984, pp. 175–6, 197.
32 *Republic*, 399e–400a.

*extremely difficult – since rhythm and harmonia occur with
no words – to understand what is intended ... The use of
either by itself [for purposes other than the accompaniment
of dance and song] is characteristic of uncultured and
vulgar showmanship.*[33]

It is this kind of statement that supplies the context for a proper
understanding of Poussin's allusion to pictures painted in a
particular 'mode'. Later commentators have tended to place an
interpretation upon his 1647 letter that it was surely never intended
to bear. They have identified 'mode' with the abstract, expressive
forms of painting – colour, line and so on – as if Poussin were way
ahead of his time in formulating an apology for non-objective
art. But, as Thomas Puttfarken has pointed out, it would have
been extraordinary if any seventeenth-century artist had really
conceived of painting as producing its effect in purely 'musical'
terms – that is, solely by virtue of particular combinations of
colour, line and tone.[34] In that period, the colours and forms of
painting were not yet seen as ends in themselves. Instead, form and
colour, line and composition should be *in keeping* with the
represented subject, in just the same way that, according to Plato,
the skill of the *kitharode* lay in choosing the *harmonia* best
suited to the character of the emotions expressed in a particular
epic, verse or poem.[35]

Harmonic theory and practice

If we can no longer discover very much about Greek music and what
it actually sounded like, we do at least know a fair amount about
what was, by the fifth century BC at the latest (but probably earlier),
established harmonic practice. From Aristoxenus, as well as from
later theorists who paraphrased his works, we learn that, like many
musical cultures, the Greeks took as their starting point the octave.[36]
This, for much of their history, they divided not into two equal
segments but into two tetrachords (intervals of a fourth) separated
by a tone. Imagine playing C on the piano, then F above, then G,
followed by the c above that – except that, according to the Greek

---

33 *Laws* 669d–670; Barker 1984, p. 154.
34 See Thomas Puttfarken, *Roger de Piles' Theory of Art*, New Haven/London (Yale U. P.) 1985, pp. 29ff.
35 For a more detailed discussion of the analogy between painting and music as conceived by Poussin and his
    interpreters see below, ch. 5, pp. 199ff.
36 Even cultures that differ from one another in almost every other respect tend to regard the octave as one of
    the primary data of musical experience and to agree that two tones an octave (or several octaves) apart are,
    in effect, the 'same' note sounded at a higher or lower pitch. The article on pitch perception (under
    'Psychology of music', §II, 1) in *Grove* notes that the octave similarity in pitch perception is unlikely to be
    entirely culturally induced and that any theory of hearing that fails to account for it 'cannot be
    satisfactory'; see *Grove*, vol. 15, p. 398.

system, the names given to these 'fixed' notes did not indicate any particular pitch, as the names of our notes do, but only the distances separating them. Thus, the upper note bounding the lower of the two tetrachords was called *mese*, and the next note was *paramese* meaning 'beyond *mese*'. But *mese* was not necessarily 'F'; it could be any 'note', in our sense of the term, since the whole structure was not conceived as occupying any particular pitch-range.[37] According to this arrangement, the most important notes in any *harmonia* (system of pitch-relations) were the octave, the fifth and the fourth: precisely the same intervals that were produced by the 'Pythagorean' ratios of the smallest whole numbers.[38] The centre of the octave span was taken up by an interval of one whole tone that separated *mese* from the note beyond – *paramese* – corresponding to the mathematical ratio 9:8. The notes that marked the boundaries of the two tetrachords were fixed, but the interval of a fourth could be divided stepwise in a variety of ways using different combinations of tones and semitones and even quarter tones to produce what were called the three *genera*: diatonic, chromatic and enharmonic.[39] However, not until the time of Philolaus (late fifth century BC) were these remaining intervals accounted for in terms of (admittedly rather more complex) mathematical relationships.

Aristoxenus does not seem to have been very interested in the mathematical laws governing musical sound. Those were the kind of concerns more widely associated with Pythagoras and with the Pythagorean school of philosophy. However, by contrast with the historically well-documented Aristoxenus, Pythagoras himself remains a shadowy figure. What little we know about his life and career is derived entirely from the recollections of others and a good deal of what has been written about his ideas is based on conjecture.[40] At times his social and political beliefs, as recorded by his followers, seem to have aroused heated opposition and, to this

---

37 For a fuller account of the tetrachords and the 'fixed notes', see Barker 1989, pp. 11ff.; also *Grove*, vol. 7, pp. 663ff.

38 See ch. 1, pp. 33ff.

39 The diatonic *genus* used both tones and semitones, like our scale of C. In its commonest form, the chromatic *genus* divided the tetrachord into two semitones and a minor third. Least familiar to us is the enharmonic *genus*, which juxtaposed very wide intervals - ditones - with very small ones, approximating to a quarter tone. These are smaller than any intervals normally used in the West; such 'microtonal' intervals are, however, frequently encountered in various kinds of Oriental and Asiatic music.

40 On the problem of trying to document historically any of the doctrines popularly ascribed to Pythagoras, see Walter Burkert, *Lore and Science in Ancient Pythagoreanism*, Cambridge, MA (Harvard U. P.) 1972, esp. ch. 1, pp. 1ff.; also S. K. Heninger, Jr., *Touches of Sweet Harmony. Pythagorean Cosmology and Renaissance Poetics*, San Marino, CA (The Huntington Library) 1974, esp. ch. 3, pp. 45ff. For a more recent discussion of what distinguishes the teachings of Pythagoras from later Pythagoreanism compare Carl A. Huffman, 'The Pythagorean Tradition', in A. A. Long (ed.), *The Cambridge Companion to Early Greek Philosophy*, Cambridge (Cambridge U. P.) 1999, pp. 66–87.

day, lend themselves easily to ridicule.[41] He may have travelled to Egypt or Mesopotamia; if he did, he may well have been influenced by Egyptian or Babylonian theory of numbers.[42] His mathematical thinking evidently had a mystical tinge, reflected in the conviction held by the Pythagoreans that numbers and the relations between numbers formed the basis of all things. Particular numbers were also thought to have a special significance – ten, for example, being considered a 'perfect' number, since it is reached by adding together each of the smallest whole numbers (1 + 2 + 3 + 4). Aristotle wrote with undisguised irony about that kind of number mysticism, which he singled out for particular criticism:

The Pythagoreans thought to recognize in numbers many likenesses of what exists and what will be, such as the elements of fire, air, earth and water; they furthermore found the qualities and relations of musical notes in numbers, and thus considered the elements of numbers to be the elements of everything existing, as everything seemed to be formed according to numbers, which were regarded as the first things in all of nature, and they believed the entire vault of heaven to be harmony and numbers ... And they collected the correspondences between numbers and harmonies on the one hand and the qualities and parts of the sky and the whole world on the other hand and compared them. And if there was something missing, an artificial glue had to help produce relations everywhere in the system. For example, as the number 10 seems for them the most perfect thing and appears furthermore to embrace the whole realm of numbers, as a result there must also be 10 bodies circling in the sky as stars. But as there are only 9 visible ones, they invented a special tenth body, an invisible counter-earth ...[43]

Among his more positive achievements, Pythagoras is widely credited both with having founded Greek mathematics and, as we

41 An example is Russell's account of Pythagoras, which dwells at inordinate length on the Greek philosopher's seemingly irrational prohibition of a variety of mundane actions such as eating beans or stooping to pick up an object that has been dropped; see Bertrand Russell, *History of Western Philosophy*, London (George Allen & Unwin) 2nd edn 1961, pp. 49, 50ff. The ultimate source of the Pythagorean precepts, which also included putting on your right shoe first and helping a man to take up a burden but not to lay it down, is Iamblichus in the *Protrepticae orationes ad philosophiam* (xxi); all thirty-nine such precepts are quoted by Heninger, pp. 273–4 in the translation by Thomas Stanley.

42 For an up-to-date account of this vexed question, see Peter Kingsley, 'From Pythagoras to the *Turba Philosophorum*: Egypt and Pythagorean Tradition', *Journal of the Warburg and Courtauld Institutes*, vol. 57 (1994), pp. 1–13.

43 *Metaphysics*, 985b; a variant translation of this passage can be found in Barker 1989, pp. 32–3. On Aristotle's scepticism regarding Pythagorean number theory see Burkert, *Lore and Science*, pp. 28ff.

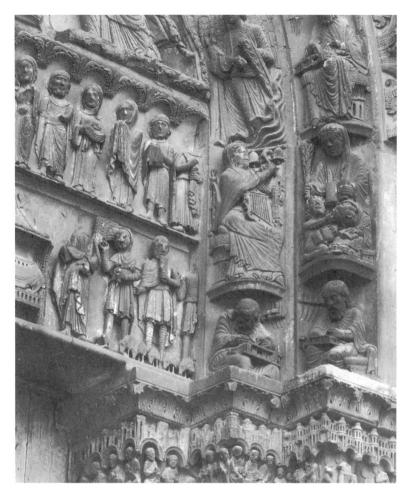

Figure 11. Royal Portal of Chartres cathedral, detail showing Pythagoras

saw in the preceding chapter, with the discovery of the simple numerical ratios (1:2, 2:3, 3:4) that correspond to the primary consonances in music.[44] The seemingly miraculous nature of that discovery exerted a remarkable hold on the imagination of later periods. For example, medieval depictions of Pythagoras often associate him with music or musical instruments (fig. 11). In the eyes of Renaissance artists, his reputation was specifically linked with both mathematics and musical theory – witness the fact that, on

---

44 'Pythagoras, so Xenocrates says, discovered also that the intervals in music do not come into being apart from number; for they are an interrelation of quantity with quantity. So he set out to investigate under what conditions concordant intervals come about, and discordant ones, and everything well-attuned and ill-attuned.' (Porphyry, *Commentary on Ptolemy's Harmonics*; Barker 1989, p. 30.)

various occasions, a number of them showed the philosopher demonstrating 'his' system of musical consonances.

Raphael and Pythagoras

Perhaps the most famous such depiction is to be found in Raphael's fresco the *School of Athens*, painted for the Papal apartments in the Vatican, where the great thinkers of antiquity are shown gathered together in something that looks rather like a hall of fame (pl. 3).[45] A bearded figure seated at the left foreground is transcribing something from a tablet held in front of him, on which can be made out a diagram and two sets of numbers together with inscriptions in Greek (pl. 4). Most commentators from the seventeenth century onwards have agreed that the bearded figure is Pythagoras and that what is drawn on the tablet must represent, one way or another, the ratios of the musical consonances.[46] Some writers have got into rather a muddle trying to analyse the diagram.[47] Others express bafflement as to where Raphael got it from, even suggesting he may have made it up himself, perhaps 'with the help of a humanist learned in musical theory'.[48] But it may be possible to pin down more precisely not only the intended meaning but also the likely source of this important detail. In the early sixteenth century, there were few printed treatises on music that circulated widely, of the kind that would have been well known among artists. Of these few, one of the most accessible would have been Franchino Gaffurio's *Theorica musice* (*Theory of Music*), published in Milan in 1492.[49] Gaffurio was choirmaster at Milan cathedral at the same time that Leonardo da Vinci was enjoying the patronage of the Milanese court. He had a considerable reputation as a teacher; more to the point, he was clearly well known in artistic circles. Both Bramante – who,

---

45 Several commentators have remarked on the disparity between the figures depicted and the architectural setting in which they are placed. See, for example, Ingrid D. Rowland, 'The Intellectual Background', in Marcia Hall (ed.), *Raphael's 'School of Athens' (Masterpieces of Western Painting)*, Cambridge (Cambridge U. P.) 1997, p. 149, who points out that Raphael has 'put Greek philosophers inside a Roman building'.

46 As early as 1879 an article by Emil Naumann entitled 'Erklärung der Musiktafel in Raffaels "Schule von Athen"' (*Zeitschrift für bildende Kunst*, vol. 14, pp. 1–14) explained in exhaustive detail the musical meaning of the diagram shown on Pythagoras's tablet. For a more manageable account of the Pythagorean intervals and their relation to Raphael's diagram, see Wolfgang Osthoff, 'Raffael und die Musik', in Volker Hoffmann (ed.), *Raffael in seiner Zeit*, Nuremberg (Hans Carl) 1987, pp. 161ff. Hall, in her introduction to *Raphael's 'School of Athens'* (see preceding note), provides a useful summary of earlier scholarly interpretations of Raphael's painting; this is followed by G. P. Bellori's article 'The Image of the Ancient *Gymnasium of Athens*, or, *Philosophy*', which is printed as the first of the 'critical views' included in the same volume (pp. 48ff.).

47 Wittkower (as n. [50] below) believes it to be an 'ingenious diagrammatic design of the four strings of the ancient lyra'. Rowland ('The Intellectual Background') describes the diagram merely as an 'ingenious composite illustration of Pythagorean numerical and musical theory' (*Raphael's 'School of Athens'*, p. 153).

48 Rowland, p. 169, n. 62.

49 For a modern edition and translation see Franchino Gaffurio, *The Theory of Music*. Translated, with Introduction and Notes, by Walter Kurt Kreyszig. Edited by Claude V. Palisca, New Haven/London (Yale U. P.) 1993.

Vasari tells us, was active as a musician – and Gaffurio were called upon to advise on the troubled design of Milan cathedral; Wittkower notes that Gaffurio was 'sent to Mantua to discuss with the architect Luca Fancelli the construction of the *tiburio*'.[50]

Architectural theorists, too, deferred to Gaffurio's authority, at least in musical matters. Cesare Cesariano, in the commentary to his edition of Vitruvius' *Ten Books on Architecture* (first century BC) refers specifically to the composer's theories in connection with Vitruvius' demand that the architect should understand elements of music.[51] He also appends to the Roman author's discussion of harmonic theory two diagrams that have clearly been 'adapted' from Gaffurio's treatises on music.[52] Several of these treatises, like Cesariano's own edition of Vitruvius' *Ten Books*, were published by Gottardo da Ponte, a Milanese who frequented the same musical and artistic circles in Milan to which figures such as Gaffurio, Luca Pacioli and Antonio Grifo belonged.[53]

All this makes it seem much less surprising when we discover that the diagram on Raphael's famous tablet looks for all the world like several of the illustrations in Gaffurio's *Theory of Music*: more precisely, those diagrams (5.3.1 and 5.5.1) based on Boethius's account of Greek musical theory (figs 12 a and b).[54] These show the mathematical ratios by which, according to Pythagorean doctrine, the octave may be divided harmoniously into two intervals of a fourth plus a single tone and the relationship within the octave between the consonances of the fourth and fifth.[55] Although his diagram is not identical to any that appears in Gaffurio's writings (it would be surprising if it were), what Raphael shows us is, in effect, the same thing. At the bottom of the tablet are the numbers one to four, added together to make ten: the Pythagorean *tetraktys*, from whose ratios the consonances are derived. At the top are the

50 Rudolf Wittkower, *Architectural Principles in the Age of Humanism*, London (Alec Tiranti) 3rd rev. edn 1962, p. 125. It is worth noting that Bramante, a relative of Raphael, helped to ease the younger artist's entrée into the world of papal patronage. He may also have drawn his attention to Gaffurio's teachings.

51 'Anchora quello che'l venerabile franchino gaffuro in la sua musicale commentatione ha dicto ...' ('Just as the venerable Franchino Gaffurio has said in his commentary on music ...'); see *Di Lucio Vitruvio Pollione De Architectura Libri Dece*, Como (Gotardus de Ponte) 1521, commentary to Book I, ch. i.

52 Ibid., Book V, ch. iv.

53 Among these treatises were Gaffurio's *De harmonia musicorum instrumentorum opus*, published in Milan by da Ponte in 1518. Concerning formative influences on Cesariano see the modern commentary to the facsimile edition of his 1521 Vitruvius: *Vitruvio, De Architectura. Translato commentato et affigurato da Cesare Cesariano (1521), a cura di Arnaldo Bruschi, Adriano Carugo e Francesco Paolo Fiore*, Milan (Edizioni Il Polifilo) 1981, p. lxxii. On Pacioli see below, pp. 136, 141–2.

54 Gaffurio (as n. [49] above), pp. 159, 170. It is Gaffurio's figure 5.3.1 that is closest to Raphael's diagram; the principal difference is merely that the former is based on the division of the double octave (*bisdiapason*), whereas Raphael's painting shows only a single octave.

55 In his *Art et humanisme à Florence au temps de Laurent le Magnifique* (Paris, Presses Universitaires de France, 1961, p. 479 and n. 5) André Chastel, in discussing Pythagoras' tablet, refers in passing to Gaffurio, but to the *Practica musice* rather than the *Theorica*; he makes no mention of Gaffurio's diagrams.

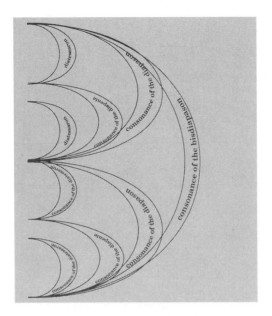

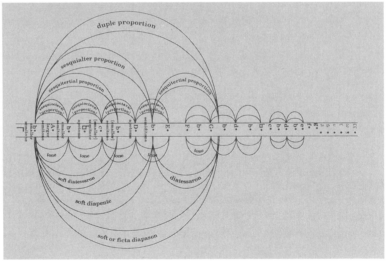

Figures 12 (a) and (b). Showing harmonic division of the consonances, from Franchino Gaffurio, *Theorica musice,* Milan (F. Mantegazza) 1492, figs 5.3.1 and 5.5.1

numbers six and twelve, divided by both the arithmetic and harmonic mean: 8 and 9.[56] Between these two sets of numbers, the diagram itself, like those in Gaffurio's treatise, shows how the octave (marked *diapason*), corresponding to the ratio 6:12, can

---

56 For a definition of these terms, see below, ch. 4, pp. 152–3.

be divided unequally into the fifth (*diapente*) and the fourth (*diatesseron*) or into two-fourths with an interval of a whole tone in between – that is, two disjoined tetrachords, the basis of one species of the ancient Greek musical scale. The numbers required to form the ratios of the consonances and of the interval separating *mese* from *paramese* (see above, p. 69) are all clearly shown.

The Pythagorean consonances

How Pythagoras' famous discovery of these musical ratios came about is another story – quite literally. His biographer Nichomacus of Gerasa tells us (and the same legend is repeated endlessly by other writers including, once again, Boethius) that the philosopher, happening:

> by some heaven-sent chance to walk by a blacksmith's work-shop, heard the hammers beating iron on the anvil and giving out sounds fully concordant in combination with one another ... and he recognized among them the consonance of the octave and those of the fifth and the fourth ... He ran into the smithy, and through a great variety of experiments he discovered that what stood in direct relation to the difference in the sound was the weight of the hammers.[57]

Although it seems a pity to spoil such a delightful tale, it is essential to point out (as many previous commentators have done) that it cannot possibly be true. For one thing, from the point of view of acoustics it is complete nonsense. By Nicomachus' time, the acoustic properties of physical objects had long since been subjected to exhaustive tests. The notion that the weight of the hammers could have determined their pitch was, even then, no more plausible than the belief that the proportional relationship between the length of the sides of Chinese stone chimes was a factor in their tuning.[58] Even so, the legend of Pythagoras and the hammers was repeated, seemingly without demur, by almost everyone who wrote about the origins of music, from late antiquity right up to the Renaissance. It was also frequently alluded to in visual form. For example, the frontispiece of Marcin Kromer's *Musicae elementa* (1542) depicts four blacksmiths busily plying their trade (fig. 13). This visual allusion would be wholly

---

57 Nicomachus, *Enchiridion*, ch. 6; Barker 1989, pp. 256ff. Compare Boethius, *De institutione musica*, I, 10; see also Jeremy Yudkin, *Music in Medieval Europe*, Englewood Cliffs, NJ (Prentice Hall) 1989, pp. 22ff. for the medieval reception of Pythagorean musical theory.

58 See Needham 1962, pp. 180–1. A similar experiment could, however, be made to give the desired result by using bronze discs of equal diameter but different thicknesses, as allegedly demonstrated by the early Pythagorean Hippasus of Metapontum; see West 1992, p. 234, also Burkert, *Lore and Science*, p. 377.

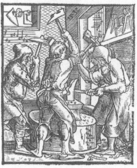

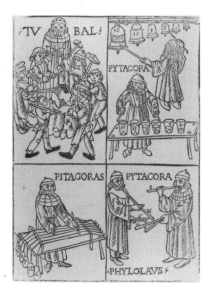

Figure 13. Frontispiece of Marcin Kromer's *Musicae elementa*, Cracow 1542, showing four blacksmiths plying their hammers
Figure 14. Woodcut showing experiments by Pythagoras and Jubal, from Franchino Gaffurio, *Theorica musice*, Milan (F. Mantegazza) 1492, fig. 1.8.1

incomprehensible unless one knew the ancient story, since in this case, Pythagoras is nowhere to be found. In another famous illustration, this time from Martin Agricola's *Musica instrumentalis deudsch* (1529), the philosopher himself can be seen actually weighing the hammers.

By contrast, in Gaffurio's *Theorica musice*, one of the accompanying woodcuts shows not only Pythagoras but also Jubal, his biblical counterpart, engaged in experiments with bells and water glasses of various sizes whose 'harmonic' ratios (16, 12, 9, 8, 6, 4) are clearly indicated (fig. 14).[59] In this instance, however, two strands of legend are woven together. Here, it is with Jubal, 'the father of them that play upon the harp and the organ', that the experiment with the hammers is associated, perhaps reflecting a medieval tradition going back to Aegidius of Zamora that attributed to him, rather than to Pythagoras, the 'discovery' concerning their relative weights.[60]

59 On the competing claims of these semi-legendary figures from Classical antiquity (the pagan tradition) and from the Bible (Christian tradition) to have 'invented' music see James W. McKinnon, 'Jubal vel Pythagoras, quis sit inventor musicae?' *Musical Quarterly*, vol. 64, no. 1 (January 1978), pp. 1–28. For an account of the harmonic ratios and how they are derived see below, ch. 4, pp. 153ff.
60 In the first chapter of the *Theorica musice* Gaffurio writes that 'Josephus and the Holy Scriptures relate that Jubal, from the tribe of Cain, was the first to have instituted [music] by the *kithara* and the organ, after he had searched out [this music] diligently from the various sounds of the hammers'. (Gaffurio, *Theory of Music*, p. 7.)

We, too, may be inclined to question whether Pythagoras was really the first to realize that the primary musical consonances could be expressed mathematically by the ratios between the smallest whole numbers: those same numbers that played such an important part in Pythagorean thinking generally. Surely that discovery must have been made independently in various places and at different times by practising musicians rather than musical theorists. Moreover, it is likely to have been experiments with stretched strings (of gut or woven silk) rather than with bells or hammers or water glasses that immediately revealed these simple numerical relationships. It is apparent from references to the ratios of both string and pipe lengths that, by the time of the Warring States (403–221 BC), the ancient Chinese were well aware of the method by which all twelve semitones could be generated according to mathematical principles.[61] Because of this, several writers have suggested that both the Pythagoreans and the Chinese must have been dependent upon older, Babylonian science for their discovery of these 'musical ratios', despite the fact that no such links between the West and China at this time have been historically proven.[62] But in reality, it would not have been necessary to possess any very elaborate body of mathematical theory in order to make such a straightforward discovery – to realize, for example, that the octave, which appears to us as the first and most easily perceived of all musical consonances, can be created by the sound of two strings or pipes with lengths in a ratio to one another of 2:1.

Why these particular intervals should strike the ear as consonant was more difficult to account for. Several Greek authors were clearly tempted to decide that the primary consonances were pleasing to the ear *because* their constituent tones stood in a simple mathematical relationship to one another. That this was not really an adequate explanation was apparent to more acute minds: for example, to Plato, who sharply criticized the musical theorists of his day for their incapacity to explain why some intervals were consonant while others were dissonant, other than in purely mathematical terms.[63] However, by comparison with their formidable achievements in mathematics and harmonics, the Greeks made little

---

61 Ernest G. McClain, 'The Bronze Chime Bells of the Marquis of Zeng'; see also ch. 1, pp. 34–5.
62 Needham hypothesizes that a common understanding of the mathematical basis to the relationship between the various pitches, found both in China and in Greece at around the same period (sixth–fifth centuries BC), may be traced back to elements of earlier Babylonian science and that Pythagoras' 'discovery' may have been the result of some inspired guesswork: 'Just as Thales used his partial knowledge of Babylonian astronomy to make some lucky predictions, so Pythagoras also may have introduced a limited amount of Babylonian acoustic information which at first was not properly understood.' (Needham 1962, pp. 176–7, 180ff.) See also Ernest G. McClain, *The Myth of Invariance. The Origin of the Gods, Mathematics and Music from the Ṛg Veda to Plato*, Boulder CO/London (Shambhala) 1978.
63 *Republic*, 531c.

headway with the science of acoustics. Despite noticing that a resonating string vibrated at a given speed, they seem not to have grasped the relationship between frequency and wavelength, a discovery that might have helped to explain why certain intervals struck the ear as 'smooth' or 'harmonious' while others did not.[64] Instead, the fact that musical consonances could be shown to correspond to certain ratios merely reinforced the belief (or, according to some writers, may have been the origin of the belief) held by the Pythagoreans that all the constituent elements of the cosmos and of human experience stood in an exact mathematical relationship to one another.[65] In music, to borrow Crocker's striking image, the Pythagoreans thought they saw 'a patch of the basic fabric of the universe'.[66] Music was 'captured in a net of number'. Like geometry, astronomy and arithmetic, it served to demonstrate that 'number holds sway throughout the universe'.[67] Hence the intervals produced in this way were considered 'harmonious' precisely because musical harmony was part of that universal, cosmic harmony manifested in all things.

Pythagoras and Plato

Whereas the elementary data of musical experience might be interpreted as providing support for the Pythagorean world-view, Pythagorean theory seemingly had little impact on such matters as the tuning of instruments or on musical practice generally. That a tone an octave higher really could be produced by stopping a resonating string at the half-way point was, for the Pythagoreans, not a matter of great consequence, any more than the fact that other consonant intervals such as the fifth and the fourth were likewise produced by dividing the same string into two-thirds or three-quarters. The important truths about music were 'to be found in its harmonious reflection of number. As a mere temporal manifestation, the employment of this harmonious structure in actual pieces of music was of decidedly secondary interest.'[68] Nor were Pythagorean principles necessarily applicable to the division of musical space.[69]

---

64 Burkert notes that none of the early Greek writers on acoustics attempted to measure the frequencies of vibration experimentally and that, in the writings of both Plato and Aristotle, rapidity of propagation is often confused with frequency, so that the higher tones are said to reach the hearer more quickly than lower ones (*Lore and Science*, p. 379).

65 Athenaeus in the 'Sophists at Dinner' describes Pythagoras as 'one of many conspicuous for having taken up music as no mere hobby; on the contrary, he explains the very being of the universe as bound together by musical principles'; quoted after Strunk I, p. 92.

66 Richard L. Crocker, 'Pythagorean Mathematics and Music (Part I)', *Journal of Aesthetics and Art Criticism*, vol. 22, no. 2 (winter 1963), pp. 192.

67 *Lore and Science*, p. 378.

68 Mathiesen, *Apollo's Lyre*, p. 352.

69 On the concept of musical space see below, ch. 3, pp. 113ff.

For example, while two tones an octave apart stood in a simple mathematical relationship to one another, 2:1, dividing the span of the octave into two equal parts did not produce a further consonance. On the contrary, what results is one of the most grinding of all dissonances, the tritone (try playing C and F# simultaneously on the piano, the latter being exactly half-way between middle c', for example, and the c" above); while mathematically speaking, the result produced is an 'irrational' number.[70] This, as McClain points out, was the *diabolus in musica* – the 'devil in music' of the medieval theorists, an interval to be shunned whenever possible in a melodic progression.[71] Although mathematical principles of this kind were probably never applied to the actual practice of music, we may nevertheless detect an echo of such numerological-musical calculations in Plato's seemingly fanciful account of the 'true pleasure proper to man's nature', which he describes – bafflingly, unless one has some knowledge of how musical consonances and dissonances were calculated – as being 729 times greater than that of the despot.[72] The number 729 – that is, 3 to the power of 6 – again produces the tritone (six 'fifths' above the fundamental), 'the worst possible dissonance in the musical systems known to Plato and, for that matter, in all Western tonal systems for two thousand years after him'. In describing the relation between 'the good man and the tyrant', what Plato intended to express by the 'discordant' number 729 was thus 'the greatest possible tension within a civilised system'.[73]

Music in Plato's 'Timaeus'

In several of his other dialogues, Plato draws elaborate and sometimes complex analogies between the principles of music and various manifestations of cosmic order. Perhaps the most famous of these is a passage from the *Timaeus* where, in describing how the universe came into being, he explains the systematic dividing up of what he calls the 'world soul', although the language he chooses and the recurrent metaphor of the creator or 'demiurge' busily chopping up a length of fabric tend to make his meaning as obscure as possible:

And he began the division in this way. First he took one portion (1) from the whole, and next a portion (2) double of

---

70 On irrational numbers and the 'harmonic' division of the octave see Richard L. Crocker, 'Pythagorean Mathematics and Music (Part II)', *Journal of Aesthetics and Art Criticism*, vol. 22, no. 3 (spring 1964), pp. 326ff.
71 *Myth of Invariance*, p. 117.
72 *Republic*, 587e.
73 This and the preceding quotation are from Siegmund Levarie, 'Introduction', in McClain, *Myth of Invariance*, pp. xi–xii.

this; the third (3) half as much again as the second, and three times the first; the fourth (4) double of the second; the fifth (9) three times the third; the sixth (8) eight times the first; and the seventh (27) twenty-seven times the first.[74]

Our puzzlement recedes somewhat when we realize that this is a familiar series – or rather, two parallel series – of odd and even numbers together with their squares and cubes: 1, 2, 4, 8 on the one hand, 1, 3, 9, 27 on the other. Plato then proceeds to fill in the intervals between these numbers by dividing them according to either their harmonic or their arithmetic mean.[75] As Cornford and others have shown, a careful reading of these divisions reveals that what is thereby created is, in fact, a musical scale spread over four octaves plus a major sixth, with not only the intervals of the fourth and fifth but also the whole tone and even the semitone all accounted for in purely mathematical terms.[76] Slightly adjusted for easier reading, the result of this process of division and insertion might look like this:

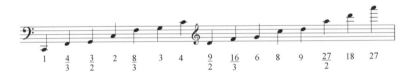

Figure 15. Showing how the fractions produced by Plato's division of the 'world soul' can be translated into musical intervals, after Cornford, *Plato's Cosmology* (1937)

Significantly, no explicit reference is made in this context to any audible music, nor to the harmony of the spheres, even though Plato may well have had that concept in mind. The 'harmony' about which he writes in the *Timaeus* is rather that conjunction between the well-attuned individual soul and the orderly nature of the cosmos: a strange blend of rational mathematics and elaborate number mysticism that characterizes much of his thinking.

---

74 *Timaeus*, ed. Cornford, 35b–c; see *Plato's Cosmology. The Timaeus of Plato translated with a running commentary by Francis Macdonald Cornford*, London (Kegan Paul, Trench, Trubner)/New York (Harcourt, Brace) 1937, p. 66.
75 On these see below, ch. 4, pp. 152–3.
76 Cornford, op. cit., pp. 67, 70ff.; see also D. P. Walker, *Studies in Musical Science*, pp. 7–8 and n. 34.

The Myth of Er

Elsewhere in Plato's writings, the mystical predominates over the rational, as in the famous passage to be found in the last book of the *Republic* where the very workings of the cosmos and the source of its constant motion are revealed not in mathematical but in musical terms. Here, Plato couches his description in the form of a legend, that of Er the Armenian who, springing back to life from his own funeral pyre, told of what he had seen in the shadowy realm that lies beyond death:

On the fourth day, they reached a place whence they could look down from above on a straight beam of light, stretched through the whole of heaven and earth like a pillar ... From there, in the middle of the light, they saw stretched from heaven the end of heaven's chains. For this light is what binds heaven together, holding its whole circumference in, like the undergirding of a trireme. And from the end is hung the spindle of Necessity, by which all the circumferences are turned. The shaft of the spindle and the hook were of adamant, and the whorl partly of adamant and partly of other substances ... There were in all eight whorls, set one within another, with their rims showing above as circles and making up the continuous surface of a single whorl around the shaft, which pierces right through the centre of the eighth ... The spindle is spun upon the knees of Necessity. Up on top of each of the circles rides a Siren, carried around with its revolution, each giving out a single sound, a single tonos; *and from these sounds, eight in all, is made a single* harmonia. *Round about at equal distances are seated three others, each on a throne: the Fates, daughters of Necessity, clothed in white and with garlands on their heads. They are Lachesis, Clotho, and Atropos; and they sing to the* harmonia *of the Sirens, Lachesis of what has been, Clotho of what is, and Atropos of what will be. With her right hand Clotho touches the outer circumference of the spindle from time to time and helps to turn it, while Atropos does the same to the inner circumferences with her left; Lachesis touches inner and outer in turn, using first one hand, then the other.*[77]

---

77 *Republic* 615b–617d. For a detailed account of the musical inferences to be drawn from Plato's exposition of this myth see McClain (as following note), pp. 41ff.

Echoes of Pythagorean thought occur at various points throughout Plato's writings, but nowhere more vividly than in this memorable description of the sounding cosmos.[78] It was the Pythagoreans who, having concluded that the universe and all its parts must be organized according to the same kinds of numerical relations that gave order to the musical scale, first pictured the astronomical firmament in the 'music of the spheres': a concept that bore little or no relation to any music actually played or heard but that profoundly affected later thinking about the supposedly orderly arrangement of the natural and scientific realms.[79] However, it seems to have been Plato who first explicitly associated the movement of the heavenly bodies, as here, with the particular scales and *tonoi* of Greek musical theory. Whether he really meant this elaborate model of the universe to be understood literally or thought that the rotation of the heavenly circles created an audible music is another matter. While the teachings of the Pythagoreans had ensured that the notion of 'cosmic harmony' was well understood, by no means all writers accepted that this was necessarily the same thing as music perceived by the human ear. Aristotle, for example, took issue with those who believed that:

the motion of bodies of that size must produce a noise, since on our earth the motion of bodies far inferior in size and speed of movement has that effect. Also, when the sun and the moon, they say, and all the stars, so great in number and in magnitude, are moving with so swift a motion, how should they not produce a sound that is immensely great? Starting from this argument, and the observation that their speeds, as measured by their distances, are in the same ratios as musical consonances, they assert that the sound given forth by the circular movement of the stars is a harmony.

He also derided the idea that we are unaware of this celestial music, simply because it is always there: 'for, they say, sound and silence are distinguished in relation to one another, so that just as

---

78 On this subject see further Ernest G. McClain, *The Pythagorean Plato: Prelude to the Song Itself*, Stony Brook, NY (N. Hays) 1978. McClain argues that an important group of Plato's writings, which includes the *Republic*, *Timaeus*, *Critias* and *Laws*, revolves around a succession of complex and mutually illuminating musical allegories: see his Introduction, esp. pp. 2ff.

79 Burkert notes that, strictly speaking, the expression 'harmony of the spheres' is misleading applied to any period before that of Eudoxus (a contemporary of Plato who described the orbits of the planets in mathematical terms) 'for then one spoke of bodies, wheels, rings, circles in the sky, but not yet of spheres'. (*Lore and Science*, p. 351, n. 1.)

to blacksmiths the noise makes no difference because they are accustomed to it, so the same thing happens to mankind'.[80]

For our part, we might object that, if Plato really did mean that the music of the spheres was capable of being heard by human ears and if all the tones of the musical scale were sounded simultaneously (as he seems to imply), what would be produced would not be 'harmony' but a kind of celestial cacophony, as if I were to bring my whole forearm down at once on some hapless keyboard. However, what little we know about the music of Plato's time suggests that it was predominantly monodic, consisting of only a single line of melody. For this reason, our own notions of 'harmony' – that is, a combination of notes sounded simultaneously or a succession of chords – would almost certainly have been foreign to the Greek mind. *Harmonia* meant, first and foremost, a fitting-together; applied to music, it denoted the relationships between various notes sounded successively rather than at once. Richard Norton has even suggested that what Plato is describing may not be the heavenly music itself but the scalar *harmonia* that constitutes 'the permanent framework, the reservoir of elements and relations, on which that music is based'.[81] Regarding the Pythagorean tradition generally, he also observes that:

> *not even the most severe of the ancient critics ever commented on the cacophony of a complete scale sounded simultaneously. Perhaps they did not think about it or were grateful that, according to tradition, only Pythagoras could hear it.*[82]

Celestial harmonies from Cicero to Mozart

Commentators may squabble over the details of Plato's account of the 'musical' structure of the universe. However, such disagreements are of little significance compared with the power of the imagery he employs to conjure up in the mind's eye what one writer has called the 'naked glory of the diatonic octave'.[83] So graphic is the language Plato uses, so vividly does he evoke the myriad details of the celestial spheres and the music they supposedly create

---

80 *De Caelo*, 290b12ff. Aristotle concludes his discussion of these matters with the trenchant observation that 'the claim that through the motions of celestial bodies harmony comes into being, in which the tones form *symphoniai*, is, though noble and original, by no means true'.

81 This seems likely; note that in the passage quoted earlier, while each of the Sirens produces a single tone, the three Fates *'sing to* the *harmonia* of the Sirens' (my italics).

82 Richard Norton, *Tonality in Western Culture. A Critical and Historical Perspective*, University Park and London (Pennsylvania State U. P.) 1984, p. 92. For further discussion of these issues, see also Barker 1989, p. 58 and n. 11.

83 West 1992, p. 234.

that, even many centuries later, his description still resonated
with sufficient force to cause artists, poets and musicians from
other periods and cultures to fall helplessly under his spell. Think,
for example, of Milton's poem *Arcades*, where the Genius of the
Wood recounts how:

...in deep of night, when drowsiness
Hath lock'd up mortal sense, then listen I
To the celestial Sirens' harmony,
That sit upon the nine infolded spheres
And sing to those that hold the vital shears
And turn the adamantine spindle round,
On which the fate of gods and men is wound.[84]

That the Myth of Er was indeed the source for a succession of later
treatments of the theme of heavenly harmony can perhaps best be
seen from a comparison of Plato's original with the so-called
Dream of Scipio, a parable based on a vision of the celestial realm
and life after death to be found at the end of Cicero's essay on
politics, *De re publica* (just as the Myth of Er is placed at the end
of Plato's *Republic*). In both their language and content there are
obvious similarities between the two texts. Consider, for example,
the passage in which the younger Scipio enquires as to the source
of that 'great and pleasing sound' that accompanies his dream of
the cosmic afterlife. His grandfather, the celebrated Roman general
Scipio Africanus, replies:

That is produced by the onward rush and motion of the
spheres themselves; the intervals between them, though
unequal, being exactly arranged in a fixed proportion, by an
agreeable blending of high and low tones various
harmonies are produced; for such mighty motions cannot
be carried on so swiftly in silence; and Nature has provided
that one extreme shall produce low tones while the other
gives forth high ... The earthly sphere, the ninth, remains
ever motionless and stationary in its position in the centre
of the universe. But the other eight spheres, two of which
move with the same velocity, produce seven different
sounds – a number which is the key of almost everything
... But this mighty music, produced by the revolution of the
whole universe at the highest speed, cannot be perceived by

---

84 Quoted after F. T. Prince (ed.), *Milton: 'Comus' and other Poems*, Oxford (Oxford U. P.) 1968, pp. 32–3.

*human ears, any more than you can look straight at the
Sun, your sense of sight being overpowered by its radiance.*[85]

Scipio's Dream was repeatedly paraphrased or alluded to by
medieval writers, its popularity being due in part to the famous
commentary by Macrobius.[86] Or it may have been known at
second hand through the gloss on Cicero's text to be found in
Boethius' treatise on music, where the original disposition of the
heavens is varied by assigning the highest tone to the sphere
of the fixed stars, whose rotation is fastest, the lowest to that of
the moon (fig. 16).[87]

Cicero and Boethius are also the most likely sources for a
remarkable medieval hymn, 'Naturalis concordia vocum cum
planetis', the text and music of which were found inserted
between the flyleaves of a manuscript copy of Boethius' *De
institutione musica*, now in the Bibliothèque Nationale in
Paris.[88] The musical notation marks a transitional stage between
the 'heighted neumes' of earlier medieval music and the lined
staff introduced by Guido of Arezzo.[89] It shows incised lines
representing the pitches C and F, in accordance with Guido's
system, suggesting a date sometime during the latter part of the
eleventh century. The music itself is distinguished by its very
wide compass, from low A to a' two octaves above. All of the
notes in between are identified by their ancient Greek
nomenclature, from *proslambanomenos* at the bottom to *nete
hyperboleion* at the top. Each note in the lower octave is linked
with one of the heavenly spheres, that important note *mese*,
described earlier, being here equated with the vault of heaven:
that is, the sphere of the fixed stars. The hymn is accompanied by
a diagram showing the ascending scale of notes with its
corresponding sequence of planetary spheres and (still higher)
angels: one of the earliest surviving visual representations of the
by now hallowed notion of the music of the spheres.

---

85 Cicero, *De re publica*, VI, xviii; see the translation by Clinton Walker Keyes (Loeb Classical Library), London
(William Heinemann)/Cambridge, MA (Harvard U. P.) 1961, pp. 271ff., also Jamie James, *The Music of the
Spheres. Music, Science and the Natural Order of the Universe*, London (Little, Brown & Co.) 1994, pp. 63ff.
James' account of the transmission of what he calls 'the great theme' via Cicero, Macrobius and Martianus
Capella to Ficino, Kepler and ultimately Mozart is fascinating and eminently readable; I have drawn on it
several times in the concluding part of this chapter.

86 *Commentarii in Somnium Scipionis*; the rhetorician Favonius Eulogius, a pupil of St Augustine, also wrote
a commentary on the Dream of Scipio (*Disputatio de Somnio Scipionis*). Cicero's *De re publica* itself
remained lost until 1820, when a manuscript was discovered in the Vatican Library (*Vaticanus 5757 V*); see
the introduction to the translation by Keyes (as preceding note), pp. 9ff.

87 *De institutione musica*, I, 27; see also Jacques Handschin, 'Ein mittelalterlicher Beitrag zur Lehre von der
Sphärenharmonie', *Zeitschrift für Musikwissenschaft*, 9. Jg., 4. Heft (January 1927), p. 196.

88 BN lat. 7203; Handschin, pp. 199ff; see also Meyer-Baer, *Music of the Spheres*, pp. 80ff.

89 On neumes, Guido of Arezzo and medieval musical notation see below, ch. 3, pp. 109ff.

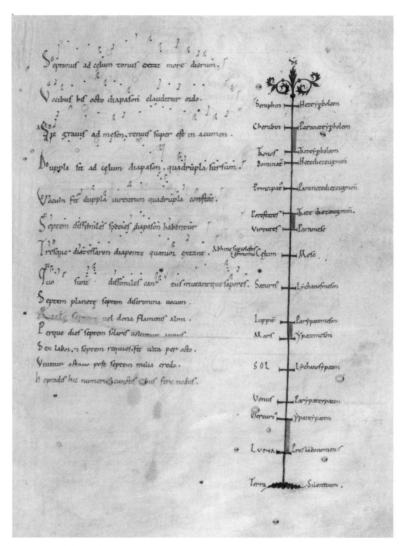

Figure 16. Flyleaf of *c.*11th century manuscript of Boethius, *De institutione musica*, showing the tones of ancient Greek music juxtaposed with the planetary spheres (Bibliothèque Nationale, Paris, MS lat. 7203)

The influence exerted by visions of celestial harmony in general and by the *Dream of Scipio* in particular was surprisingly long-lived.[90] As late as the eighteenth century, none other than the fifteen-year-old Mozart dressed up in musical garb a much-altered version

90 On these notions as reflected in poetry see the classic study by John Hollander, *The Untuning of the Sky. Ideas of Music in English Poetry 1500–1700*, Princeton, NJ (Princeton U. P.) 1961.

of Cicero's fable. His 'dramatic serenade' *Il Sogno di Scipione* was written in anticipation of the celebrations intended to mark the fiftieth anniversary of the ordination of the Archbishop of Salzburg, Sigismund Count Schrattenbach, in January 1772.[91] Unfortunately, the projected performance was cancelled when Schrattenbach died suddenly in mid-December, the day after Mozart and his father returned to Salzburg from a successful tour of Italy. The work, completed but now without a patron to celebrate, lay unperformed for 208 years.[92] Probably the real cause of its neglect was not Mozart's immaturity, since many of his juvenilia have had no difficulty in charming audiences around the world: for example, the delightful string divertimenti KV 136-138 or the early operas *Mitridate, re di Ponto* and *Lucio Silla*, which are roughly contemporary with *Il Sogno di Scipione*. Rather, the problem has to do with Metastasio's text, the poet having transformed Cicero's original into a garbled mish-mash of antique allusions in which the dominant theme has become a choice between unconvincing personifications of pleasure and virtue – both of whom appear, to modern eyes at least, little more than silly geese. Not even Mozart, it seems, could bring to this flat-footed version of the tale very much by way of dramatic coherence. Nevertheless, his music at times touches on the sublime, as in the breathtaking aria 'Ah! perchè cercar degg'io' or, for that matter, the concluding chorus: probably the only parts of the work the composer himself ever heard performed.[93]

The power of music: Giovanni de' Bardi and the Florentine 'Intermedi' of 1589
The oblivion to which *Il Sogno di Scipione* was swiftly consigned is in marked contrast to the success enjoyed by what was arguably the most sumptuous and certainly the most costly of all musical-dramatic visualizations of the harmony of the spheres. This was the staged extravaganza, often known simply as the 'Florentine

---

91 W. A. Mozart, *Il Sogno di Scipione. Azione teatrale*, KV 126 (1771); see *Grove*, vol. 12, pp. 689ff. for a comparison with Mozart's other early dramatic works. An even more belated treatment of this theme can be found in Chateaubriand's novel of Indian life *Les Natchez*, written in the 1790s, in which the saints Geneviève and Catherine ascend through the spheres to the 'world which extends above the region of the stars [whereupon] they heard that harmony of the spheres which the ear cannot grasp'; for discussion and partial translation of this interminable and now justly neglected text, see Joscelyn Godwin, *Music, Mysticism and Magic. A Sourcebook*, London/New York (Routledge & Kegan Paul) 1986, pp. 184ff.

92 Incredibly, the work received its first-ever complete performance during the *Mozart-Woche* held in Salzburg in January 1979. At the time of writing, the only commercial recording was the one based on that 1979 production, available as vol. 31 of the Complete Mozart Edition issued by Philips, 2CD 422 531–2. The accompanying booklet contains much useful information concerning the history of the work, some of which I have incorporated here (as in the following note); see also *Grove*, vol. 12, pp. 689–90.

93 It is thought that these two numbers may have been performed as part of an evening concert Mozart organized in Salzburg some time later in 1772; there is no indication that he ever attempted to have *Il Sogno di Scipione* performed elsewhere.

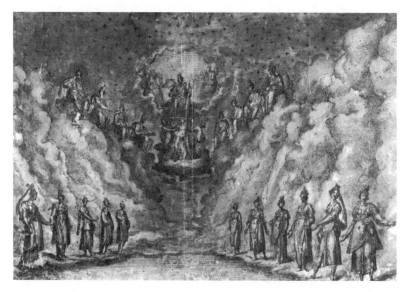

Figure 17. Bernardo Buontalenti, drawing for the *Music of the Spheres*, Florentine *intermedi* of 1589 (Victoria & Albert Museum, London)

intermedi' or *La Pellegrina*, that was performed as part of the celebrations marking the marriage of Ferdinand de' Medici, Grand Duke of Tuscany, to Princess Christine of Lorraine in May 1589.[94] The overall theme of this spectacle, in which poetry, music and scenic design are ingeniously woven together, was the power of music (fig. 17). It consisted in all of six tableaux, inserted between the scenes of a comedy by Girolamo Bargagli to which it bore absolutely no relation. (This to our eyes curious practice of punctuating the scenes of a play with unrelated musical interludes was popular in this period and is the origin of the name *intermedi* given to this particular genre.)[95] Master-minded by Giovanni de' Bardi, patron of the Florentine *camerata*, with verses largely by the poet Ottavio Rinuccini, the music for the *intermedi* was provided by some of the leading composers of the day, among them Jacopo Peri, Cristofano Malvezzi and Luca

---

94 In much of the literature the terms *intermedi* and *intermezzi* are used more or less interchangeably (see e.g. Shearman 1967, pp. 104ff.) but, strictly speaking, the former is the correct name for this genre. On the Florentine *intermedi* of 1589 see *Grove*, vol. 9, pp. 265–7; also the informative notes and texts that accompany the recording by Andrew Parrott and the Taverner Consort, *Una 'Stravaganza' dei Medici: Intermedi (1589) per 'La Pellegrina'*, EMI/Reflexe CDC 7 47998 2.

95 Palisca traces the origins of such productions back to the fifteenth century, noting that they first featured in revivals of classical comedies by Plautus and Terence in Ferrara 'to entertain the audience between acts, or perhaps to make up for a lack of entertainment in the play itself. Later they became common between the acts of modern comedies and other plays ...'; see Claude V. Palisca, *The Florentine Camerata*, New Haven/London (Yale U. P.) 1989, pp. 208–9, also Nino Pirrotta, *Music and Culture in Italy from the Middle Ages to the Baroque*, Cambridge, MA/London (Harvard U. P.) 1984, pp. 210–34.

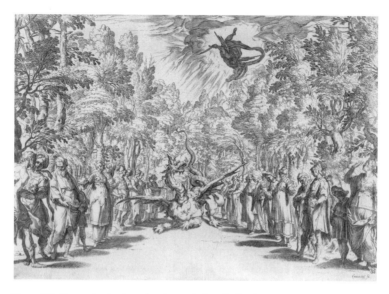

Figure 18. Engraving by Agostino Caracci after design by Bernardo Buontalenti for Apollo's contest with the Delphic python, Florentine *intermedi* of 1589

Marenzio.[96] The costumes and scenic effects were by the Mannerist artist Bernardo Buontalenti, who had spent most of his life in the service of the Medici as architect and artistic master-of-ceremonies.[97] Buontalenti was renowned for his ingenious theatrical devices, which in this case included a fire-breathing dragon, around which the otherwise largely gratuitous third tableau representing Apollo's contest with the Delphic python was constructed (fig. 18). Other scenes, by contrast, were characterized by a more scholarly or antiquarian approach. In particular, the staging of the first of the *intermedi*, whose subject was the Harmony of the Spheres, seems to have followed with astonishing fidelity the details of Plato's description of the music-making heavenly Sirens to be found in the

---

96 The *camerata* was a circle of 'intellectuals, musicians and musical amateurs' who frequented the Florentine home of Giovanni de' Bardi, Conte di Vernio, during the 1570s and 1580s. The term itself appears to have been used for the first time only in 1600, in the dedication to Bardi of Giulio Caccini's opera *L'Euridice*. Caccini, Piero Strozzi and Vincenzo Galilei were the composers directly linked with the *camerata*; the latter, in particular, was preoccupied with reconstructing the compositional methods and performing practice of ancient Greek music. See Palisca, *Florentine Camerata* (as preceding note), esp. pp. 7ff., where the eulogy of Bardi quoted at the beginning of this chapter can be found; also *Grove*, vol. 3, pp. 645ff.

97 For discussion of the costume drawings and of the principal documents on which our knowledge of the staging of the *intermedi* is based see Aby Warburg, 'I costumi teatrali per gli intermezzi del 1589', in Gertrud Bing and Fritz Rougemont (eds), *A. Warburg, Gesammelte Schriften, Band I: Die Erneuerung der heidnischen Antike. Kulturwissenschaftliche Beiträge zur Geschichte der europäischen Renaissance*, rev. ed. Nendeln/Liechtenstein (Kraus Reprint) 1969, pp. 261ff. Warburg's article had originally appeared in *Atti dell' Accademia del R. Istituto Musicale di Firenze (Anno 1895): Commemorazione della Riforma Melodrammatica*, pp. 133–46.

Myth of Er. Necessity, enthroned upon a huge cloud, sat holding the spindle of the cosmos clasped between her knees, with the three Fates below her, while the Planets were located on smaller clouds to the left and right. The celestial group was divided into three choirs, each led by a Fate.

In the run-up to the first performance a few concessions were found necessary, mainly in order to accommodate an ever-increasing cast of performers. By the time the show opened, the total number of Sirens had grown to fifteen, while another dozen or so actors representing gods and heroes were strategically placed in the highest heaven, which in this way must have come to resemble Dante's Empyrean.[98] Despite this, a contemporary description of the *intermedi* by one of the participants (and a confidant of Giovanni de' Bardi), Bastiano de' Rossi, is at pains to stress the authority of Plato for what he and his companions had gone to such lengths to create visually on stage, even quoting chapter and verse from the *Republic*. Over and above the imagery drawn directly from Plato's Myth of Er, one supplementary detail is interesting. Both Rossi and Bardi himself tell us that, since Plato and Aristotle had praised the Dorian mode above all others, it had been personified in the figure of Harmony, who appears during the music that precedes the dialogue of the Fates and the Sirens in the opening scene.[99] Lest this allusion be lost on the *intermedi*-going public, it was reinforced by having a small, rusticated Doric temple prominently positioned down-stage: an explicit linking of the Dorian mode in music with the Doric order in architecture and thus, one assumes, of the symbolic qualities of both.[100] In this way, the staging might be thought to conform to the 'Prescriptions for Intermedi' formulated by Giovanni Battista Strozzi the Younger, author of the texts of the madrigals in the fourth *intermedio*, who insisted that 'everything represented ought to be intelligible to the spectator, and that without effort. Idiots ought to understand it with only the slightest explanation and ought to be able to draw [from it] some interpretation.'[101] Yet the precise significance of such details still eluded many in the audience, as betrayed by more than one contemporary account of

---

98 A selection of virtues was symbolized by the inclusion of real or mythical figures from antique history and legend. For example, justice was personified by Numa Pompilius and filial piety by Aeneas; see Warburg, 'I costumi', p. 274 and n. 1, also Nagler (as n. [103] below), pp. 74–5.

99 Warburg, p. 270; compare pp. 271ff. for the *Descrizione* published by Rossi.

100 Onians notes that the manly, courageous qualities ascribed to this mode by Plato have their equivalent in Vitruvius' association of the Doric order with Latin *virtus*. He also suggests that Bramante may have employed the Doric order, especially in some of the most important of his Roman buildings of the period of Julius II, because of the traditional association of the Dorian mode with *gravitas* and other such suitably manly qualities; see John Onians, *Bearers of Meaning. The Classical Orders in Antiquity, the Middle Ages and the Renaissance*, Cambridge (Cambridge U. P.) 1988, p. 38.

101 Original and translation printed in Palisca, *Florentine Camerata*, pp. 220ff.

the events of May 1589. At least one educated observer, while expressing enthusiasm for the spectacle as a whole, seemingly failed to recognize the character of 'L'Armonia' altogether, describing her merely as 'a woman who, dressed as an angel, sang so beautifully and with such sweet harmony that all were transfixed with admiration'.[102] Another, reporting on the scenic effects, thought she was a Hydra.[103]

Bardi's own thinking about contemporary music and drama in many ways reflected the lively interest in ancient Greek music shared by his associates Vincenzo Galilei and Girolamo Mei as well as their disdain for the complex contrapuntal style that characterized the modern madrigal. Mei, in a letter written to Galilei nearly twenty years earlier, had expressed his firm belief that the music of the ancients had been 'in every song a single air, such as we hear today in church in the recitation of the psalmody of the Divine Office.'[104] In other words, he was convinced that Greek music had been monodic, resembling the single melodic line of ecclesiastical chant. His opinion was based partly on the fact that he had been able to find no mention of polyphony or part writing in any of the ancient theoretical sources he had consulted. Thus, if modern music were to produce the remarkable effects claimed for the ancient modes, composers must return to a simpler, monodic style of writing.

Bardi, too, disapproved of complex polyphony, although he did not go as far as Galilei or Mei. Instead, he advocated singing, whether performed by a solo voice or an ensemble, to the accompaniment of instruments in such a way as to underline the meaning of the text or poem and thus move more effectively the passions of the audience. 'When composing', he wrote in a lengthy epistle to Giulio Caccini, 'you will strive above all to arrange the verse well, and to make the words comprehensible.'[105] In this, his opinions closely resemble those of Strozzi who, in his 'Prescriptions for Intermedi', likewise stressed that an aria or madrigal is most gratifying 'when the words are beautiful and affective, and can be heard'.[106]

Bardi's own sole musical contribution to *La Pellegrina*, his largely homophonic setting of Strozzi's *Miseri abitator' del cieco Averno*, is noticeably more restrained and less complex than its

---

102 Simone Cavallino, *Raccolta di tutte le solennissime Feste nel Sposalitio della Serenissima Gran Duchessa di Toscana ...* (Rome, 1589) cited, together with the likewise contemporary *Diario* of Giuseppe Pavoni, in Warburg, 'I costumi', pp. 280ff.
103 A. M. Nagler, *Theatre Festivals of the Medici 1539–1637*, New Haven/London (Yale U. P.) 1964, p. 76.
104 Letter of May 1572; translated in Palisca, *Florentine Camerata*, pp. 56ff. On the role of monody in the performance of plainchant see below, ch. 3, pp. 107ff.
105 'Discourse ... on Ancient Music and Good Singing', in Palisca, op. cit., pp. 78ff.
106 As n. [101] above.

companion pieces, closer to the affective and monodic *stile rappresentativo* of the following century.[107] His long-standing ambition to reform contemporary music in line with what he believed to have been ancient Greek practice was, however, realized only to a limited degree. Despite his exhortations, many of the virtuoso set pieces that are a feature of the 1589 *intermedi* were, in the end, written in a distinctly 'modern' madrigalesque style. Whether this was because of compromises forced upon him by the expectations of both patron and audience, or because this was the manner already popular at the Florentine court, or because of the collaborative nature of this whole enterprise that claimed the work of so many different hands is difficult to say.

Monteverdi and the beginnings of opera

The première of *La Pellegrina*, on 2 May 1589, so delighted Duke Ferdinand that he had the whole spectacle repeated – twice.[108] He also gave instructions that the verses and music should be printed, thus ensuring their survival.[109] We should be grateful to him for this, since the music itself must count among the most enchanting vocal compositions of the entire sixteenth century. In the form given to the *intermedi*, moreover, we may detect in embryo that division of the musical material into solo arias, choruses and fragments of recitative that would soon become part of opera's accepted conventions. Indeed, *La Pellegrina* has frequently been seen as one of the immediate forerunners of modern opera, that new dramatic genre 'invented' little more than a decade later. This view is in some respects quite accurate, at least as far as the intimate relation between music, poetry and scenic action is concerned, even though there was not a great deal of the latter. What actually took place on stage seems to have been mostly of a rather static nature, closer to the *tableau vivant* than to the operatic comings and goings we are now accustomed to.[110]

But in other respects the comparison with opera is quite misleading. Faced with a work such as Monteverdi's *L'Orfeo* (1607), we

---

107 The simplicity of *Miseri abitator'* is in marked contrast to the preceding number, a polyphonic setting in six parts by Cristofano Malvezzi of the madrigal *Or che le due grand'alme*, again to a text by G. B. Strozzi.

108 The *intermedi* were repeated on 6 May, this time as accompaniment to a quite different comedy entitled *La Zingana*. They were performed once more on 13 May for the benefit of the Venetian ambassadors, together with yet another comedy, Isabella Andreini's *La Pazzia*; for details of these early performances see Warburg, 'I costumi', pp. 261–2, also Nagler, *Theatre Festivals*, p. 90.

109 The original version, edited by Malvezzi, was published in Venice in 1591 under the title *Intermedii et Concerti fatti per la Commedia rappresentata in Firenze ...*; for a modern critical edition of text and music see D. P. Walker (ed.), *Les Fêtes de Florence (1589). Musique des Intermèdes de 'la Pellegrina'*, Paris (Éditions du Centre National de la Recherche Scientifique) 1963.

110 Some of the same poets and composers, including Rinuccini and Peri, who were involved in the staging of *La Pellegrina* were among the creators of the earliest operas, written around 1600: Peri's *Dafne*, based on a text by Rinuccini, Caccini's *Eurydice*, also after a libretto by Rinuccini. We know that Peri's *Dafne* was performed but the music is now lost; Caccini's *L'Euridice* was published in 1600 but was not performed until 1602.

---

are prepared to follow with delightful apprehension the fortunes and disasters that befall the characters on stage. The *intermedi*, by contrast, do not invite us to become emotionally involved in following either what little plot there is or the lives of the personages depicted. We may admire, even be thrilled by, the ingenuity of the spectacle. But confronted with pasteboard figures and a noticeable lack of dramatic coherence, we find ourselves reluctant to engage in that willing suspension of disbelief that is the prerequisite for the appreciation of all dramatic art. We are amused rather than frightened by the murderous sailors who throw the hapless Arion overboard in the scene based on the legend of his rescue by a music-loving dolphin and who are about as convincing as the ugly sisters of pantomime. Nevertheless, it seems that Monteverdi himself may have been inspired by this particular scene. As Ghisi has pointed out, the echo-effects that characterize Orpheus' lament in the last act of *L'Orfeo* are surely composed in imitation of the double echoes that Jacopo Peri wove into Arion's aria 'Dunque fra torbide onde' in the fifth of the 1589 *intermedi*.[111]

The music of the *intermedi* has also been described as 'in-expressive'.[112] However, it strikes me as no more inexpressive than the music Mozart wrote for *Il Sogno di Scipione*, a work that likewise marked not a new departure but the culmination of an existing and highly stylized tradition. What *is* true is that seventeenth-century composers turned increasingly to the medium of opera in preference to that of the *intermedi* (which none the less continued to enjoy a certain popularity) as a means of giving musical form to feelings such as joy and anger, jealousy and grief: in other words, real, believable emotions. Monteverdi, above all, subtly exploited opera's potential for characterizing the tortuous workings of the human psyche, the interweaving of impulse and desire and the tug-of-war between duty and self-interest. Even more remarkably, in his *L'Incoronazione di Poppea*, written in 1642 when the composer was nearly eighty, he represented on stage and before our very eyes, word for word and deed for deed, not the actions of virtuous men (as Plato had demanded) nor even the mythical exploits of gods and heroes but betrayal, intrigue and the ultimate triumph of evil, all clothed in music of unprecedented dramatic power. We shall return to Monteverdi, to seventeenth-century notions of the expressive potential of music and how the Baroque era viewed Greek ideas about the link between music, emotion and morality in Chapter 5.

---

111 Federico Ghisi, 'La tradition musicale des fêtes florentines et les origines de l'opéra', in Walker, *Les Fêtes de Florence* ..., pp. xxi–xxii.
112 For example by Walker (as n. [109]), p. xxvi.

As music became articulated through an exact and systematic division of time (it was the Paris school of the thirteenth century that introduced the mensural notation still in use and still referred to, in England at least, by the original terms of 'breve', 'semibreve', 'minim', etc.), so did the visual arts become articulated through an exact and systematic division of space.

Panofsky, *Gothic Architecture and Scholasticism* (1951)

Many writers on the Middle Ages have been intrigued by the notion that Gothic cathedrals somehow embodied 'musical' principles.[1] This idea – as prevalent in musicological studies as it was, for a time, in writings about architecture – can usually be traced back to a single source: Otto von Simson's *The Gothic Cathedral. Origins of Gothic Architecture and the Medieval Concept of Order*, first published in 1956.[2] Given the extent of the influence exerted by that classic text, it is worth examining Simson's hypothesis as to the relationship between music and architecture in some detail, if only in an attempt to refute it.[3]

Simson's monograph was one of a succession of books and articles about the origins of the Gothic style that appeared during the 1940s and 1950s, mostly written by German (or at least German-speaking) art historians. Others included Hans Sedlmayr's book *The Rise of the Cathedrals* (1950), Erwin Panofsky's essay *Gothic Architecture and Scholasticism* (1951) and Panofsky's edition and translation of the writings of Abbot Suger (1946).[4] One shared characteristic was that all three authors – Simson, Sedlmayr and Panofsky – were clearly determined to associate the tangible realities of Gothic buildings with an intangible and very broadly defined climate of thought.[5] Not only did they discuss and analyse at length the early development of medieval architecture; they also

---

1 In his book *Buildings for Music* – to cite but a single instance – author Michael Forsyth alludes to the medieval belief that the cosmos was ordered by the harmony of Pythagorean numbers, 'musical consonances being one clear example. The Gothic cathedrals were designed according to the ratios of musical consonances, in order to stand as a microcosm of the universe.' (Michael Forsyth, *Buildings for Music. The Architect, the Musician and the Listener from the Seventeenth Century to the Present Day*, Cambridge, 1985, p. 6 and caption to fig. 1.3.)

2 Otto von Simson, *The Gothic Cathedral. Origins of Gothic Architecture and the Medieval Concept of Order*, New York (Pantheon Books/Bollingen Series XLVIII) 1956, 2nd rev. edn 1962.

3 For further discussion of Simson's influence, especially on subsequent writings about medieval music, see the chapter 'Cathedralism' in Christopher Page, *Discarding Images. Reflections on Music and Culture in Medieval France*, Oxford (Clarendon Press) 1993, esp. pp. 18ff.

4 Hans Sedlmayr, *Die Entstehung der Kathedrale*, Zurich (Atlantis) 1950, subsequently translated into English as *The Rise of the Cathedrals*; Erwin Panofsky, *Gothic Architecture and Scholasticism* (London/New York, 1951 and subsequent eds); *Abbot Suger on the Abbey Church of St.-Denis and its Art Treasures*. Edited, translated and annotated by Erwin Panofsky, Princeton, NJ (Princeton U. P.) 1946. Sedlmayr (b. 1896 at Hornstein in the Burgenland) was Austrian, not German.

5 For an example of an even more broadly conceived account of Gothic, see Simson's monumental study *Das Mittelalter II: Das Hohe Mittelalter* (Propyläen Kunstgeschichte Bd. 6), Berlin, 1972.

devoted a good deal of attention to the intellectual background against which that development occurred. *The Gothic Cathedral*, in particular, is as much an exercise in intellectual history as it is a study of individual building types or a description of the physical features of specific works of architecture. In seeking to account for the 'miracle' of Gothic, Simson writes in great detail about Neo-Platonism, which he sees as the dominant intellectual tendency of the cathedral school at Chartres.[6] He discusses the convergence of 'Augustinian and Neo-Platonic trends' that resulted at Chartres in a focus on 'mathematical and musical studies',[7] comparing the teachings of this school with those of 'the Platonizing William of Auvergne' and especially of Alan of Lille (Alanus de Insula, twelfth century AD), who dramatized the image of God as 'master builder ... composing and harmonizing the variety of created things through subtle chains of musical consonances'.[8]

Simson also embraces with barely contained enthusiasm Panofsky's hypothesis that Abbot Suger's 'programme' for the rebuilding of the abbey church of Saint-Denis was influenced by the metaphysics of light propounded by the mystical writer known as Pseudo-Dionysius the Areopagite, whom the monks of Saint-Denis confused with their patron and first Bishop of Paris, the Saint Denis persecuted and beheaded by the Romans.[9] But whereas Panofsky employs a certain caution in associating the metaphysical teachings of 'Dionysius' with notions of cosmic harmony, Simson goes out of his way to link Suger's hypothetical 'programme' with musical imagery. He quotes, not altogether appropriately, from the prefatory paragraphs of Suger's 'little booklet' on the consecration of the church, which describe the reconciliation of contrariety and diversity in nature in terms of 'the single, delightful concordance of one superior, well-tempered harmony'. He comments: 'It is a sublime and ancient thought, voiced by Saint Ambrose and in the eleventh century by Fulbert of Chartres, that all creation is a symphonic praise of the Creator ... According to Suger, this cosmic music conjoins not only the universe with the liturgy; the design of

---

6 For a sceptical view of the alleged importance of the 'school' of Chartres, see the essay 'Humanism and the School of Chartres', in R. W. Southern, *Medieval Humanism and other Studies*, Oxford (Blackwell) 1970, pp. 61–85.

7 Simson, *Gothic Cathedral*, 2nd rev. edn 1962, pp. 125, 188ff. All further references are to this second edition.

8 Simson, pp. 31–2. In his article 'Deus Geometra. Skizzen zur Geschichte einer Vorstellung von Gott', Friedrich Ohly provides an extensive list of other writers who likened the work of God to that of the artist or architect, among them St Augustine, Pseudo-Dionysius the Areopagite, John Scot Eriugena, St Anselm, Hugh of St Victor, Bernard of Clairvaux, Peter Lombard, Thomas Aquinas, Albertus Magnus and St Bonaventure; see Norbert Kamp and Joachim Wollasch (eds), *Tradition als Historische Kraft. Interdisziplinäre Forschungen zur Geschichte des früheren Mittelalters*, Berlin/New York (Walter de Gruyter) 1982, pp. 2–3 and n. 2.

9 See Lindy Grant, *Abbot Suger of St-Denis. Church and State in Early Twelfth-Century France*, London/New York (Longman) 1998, pp. 3–4.

his sanctuary is the visual equivalent of this music.'[10] And, on a still larger scale, Simson obviously believed not just that the notion of musical harmony, conceived in essentially Platonic terms, was one of the forces shaping early Gothic architecture but that many of the great cathedrals and churches of this period can be shown to reflect specifically 'musical' intentions.

Medieval learning and the theory of music

In order to demonstrate what he saw as the profound kinship between medieval architecture and classical notions of harmony and order – that same 'order' emphasized in the title of his book – Simson deployed a number of related arguments. One such argument revolved around what we might call the 'erudition' of the Middle Ages. The extent of that erudition has not always been acknowledged; indeed, some authors in the past denied its very existence. In his treatise *Dodekachordon* (1547), the Swiss theorist Heinrich Glareanus went so far as to describe the preceding era as a 'time when all honourable knowledge together with good scholarship ... were lying asleep', a remark that betrays all the arrogance of the Renaissance polymath.[11] But if anyone ever seriously believed that medieval times were a period of 'ignorance, stagnation and gloom' and that the wisdom of the ancients lay dormant until rediscovered by the early Renaissance, such ideas are now no longer tenable.[12] We know, for example, just how extensive were the holdings of some of the great monastic and cathedral libraries of the Middle Ages, which in many cases possessed complete or partial transcriptions or versions of texts by a wide range of classical authors,[13] among them Vitruvius and (at a somewhat later date) Aristotle.[14] Where Greek and Roman sources were incomplete or entirely lacking, the works of 'transitional'

---

10 Ibid., p. 132; compare Suger's *Libellus alter de consecratione Ecclesiae Sancti Dionysii*, ch. I, in Panofsky, *Abbot Suger*, p. 83.

11 Glareanus, *Dodekachordon* (Basel, 1547), I, xvi, 43; for an English version see Heinrich Glarean, *Dodecachordon*. Translation, transcription and commentary by Clement A. Miller, Rome (American Institute of Musicology) 1965, vol. 1, p. 82. In addition to his interest in music, Glareanus (1488–1563) was also a philosopher, theologian, philologist and historian.

12 See Charles Homer Haskins, *The Renaissance of the Twelfth Century*, New York (Meridian) new edn 1955, p. v. Haskins' monograph, although now outdated, remains unsurpassed as a study of medieval scholarship; for a tribute by other medievalists incorporating a good deal of more recent research, see Robert L. Benson and Giles Constable (eds), *Renaissance and Renewal in the Twelfth Century*, Oxford (Clarendon Press) 1982.

13 Haskins singles out the libraries of Monte Cassino, Tegernsee in Bavaria and Cluny as among those containing extensive collections of writings by classical authors. He also notes a substantial gift to the cathedral library at Rouen that included, in addition to Augustine and Vitruvius, Pliny's *Natural History* and the *Etymologies* of Isidore of Seville (*Renaissance of the Twelfth Century*, pp. 37ff., 72).

14 On medieval knowledge of Vitruvius see Carol Herselle Krinsky, 'Seventy-Eight Vitruvius Manuscripts', *Journal of the Warburg and Courtauld Institutes*, vol. 30 (1967), pp. 36–70; also Stefan Schuler, *Vitruv im Mittelalter. Die Rezeption*, Cologne-Weimar (Böhlau) 1999 for an account of the numerous copies and partial copies of Vitruvius' treatise that, by the end of the twelfth century, were to be found in monastic libraries as far apart as Reichenau in Germany, Gorze in the South Tyrol, and Cluny in Burgundy. Schuler also discusses the influence of Vitruvian notions on a wide variety of medieval thinkers, among them Hugh of St Victor and Vincent of Beauvais.

writers such as Boethius, Cassiodorus and Isidore of Seville supplied the link between classical antiquity and the medieval world. Cassiodorus, who was Boethius' pupil, established a monastery at Vivarium in southern Italy – an important precedent for the monastic centres of learning of the Middle Ages – partially with a view to preserving the knowledge of the ancients within the context of Christianity. He also encouraged the setting up of scriptoria and the copying of Latin texts, although we do not know what happened to his books after his death or whether they found their way into other libraries.[15]

Boethius, for his part, contemplated translating the complete works of both Plato and Aristotle and, in his own writings, paraphrased passages from Plato's *Timaeus* as well as other Greek authors. By means of his widely influential treatise *De institutione musica*, he also ensured the transmission – in detail and *in extenso* – of a good deal of ancient Greek musical theory: not just the now hoary anecdotes about Pythagoras and the hammers or the inflammatory tendency of Phrygian pipe music but more serious and abstruse harmonic science.[16] While giving due weight to the theories of the Pythagoreans, he made some allowance for the more pragmatic standpoint of Aristoxenus, for whom the evidence of the ears – especially in the matter of consonances – was more important than the symmetrical beauty of purely arithmetic relationships.[17] From Boethius' account, medieval musical theorists would have gained at least a partial understanding of the principles on which Greek harmonics had been based: the Pythagorean consonances, the octave as the fundamental unit of musical organization, the different *genera* (diatonic, chromatic and enharmonic) that resulted from different ways of dividing the tetrachord, and the various octave species that produced the different modes or *harmoniai* such as Dorian or Phrygian.[18] Boethius also treats of the idea found in Plato, Aristotle and other writers that these *harmoniai* were

---

15 On Cassiodorus and his library, and what happened to it, see L. D. Reynolds and N. G. Wilson, *Scribes and Scholars. A Guide to the Transmission of Greek and Latin Literature*, Oxford (Clarendon Press) 2nd rev. edn 1974, pp. 72ff.

16 Again, both Gorze and Reichenau owned copies of Boethius' treatise on music. Reginbert's catalogue of new acquisitions for the library at Reichenau between the years 835 and 842 lists 'libri quinque de musica' ('five books on music') of Boethius, while the library catalogue of Gorze, also from the ninth century, contains 'Boetii duo de arte musica' ('two [books] by Boethius on the art of music'); see Michael Bernhard, 'Glosses on Boethius' *De institutione musica*', in André Barbera (ed.), *Music Theory and Its Sources: Antiquity and the Middle Ages*, Notre Dame, IN (University of Notre Dame Press) 1990, pp. 142–3. For an account of Boethius' principal sources, which included the writings of Nicomachus and Ptolemy, see also Chadwick 1981, esp. pp. 84ff.

17 See above, ch. 2, pp. 68ff.

18 For an account of the central place occupied by Boethius' *De institutione musica* in the teaching of music at the University of Paris during the period after 1200, see Christopher Page, *The Owl and the Nightingale. Musical Life and Ideas in France 1100–1300*, London (J. M. Dent & Sons) 1989, esp. pp. 137ff. Page points out, however, that students were likely to have achieved at best only a partial reading of the prescribed text – something not unfamiliar to university teachers today.

associated with different kinds of moral value or emotional effects, underlining the difference in this respect between music and the other 'mathematical arts' (geometry, arithmetic and astronomy):

Of the four mathematical disciplines, the others are concerned with the pursuit of truth, but music is related not only to speculation but to morality as well. Nothing is more characteristic of human nature than to be soothed by sweet modes and disturbed by their opposites.[19]

Boethius has been credited with impressing upon the Middle Ages, largely through his *Arithmetica* and *De institutione musica*, the antique notion that beauty resided in number and ratio, upon which the universe was founded, and that the ordered tones of music were the expression of the same organizing principles. But similar ideas could also be found in the writings of some of the eminent fathers and doctors of the Church, among them St Augustine, for whom (following the Book of Wisdom) the universe had been created in 'measure, number and weight'.[20] In one of the key passages from his treatise *De musica*, Augustine speaks of advancing from the 'traces' (*vestigiis*) left in the mind by the sensory apprehension of music to its 'very sanctuary' where it is 'divested of everything corporeal' (*ubi ab omni corpore aliena est*).[21] His meaning is clear. Music, despite its overt appeal to the senses, was none the less a vehicle by which the mind might be led to an apprehension of the 'intelligible beauty' of pure number and hence to the realization of the divine.

Builders and scholars

As Haskins has remarked, no author had a more persistent influence than Augustine on the higher ranges of medieval thought. 'Every well appointed library of this period' could boast, if not all, then 'a goodly proportion' from among the long list of his works, which were as readily available to the scribe or scholar as Boethius' writings or Pliny's *Natural History*.[22] Only when we pose the question how – or indeed whether – all this classically derived learning was actually applied to medieval building practice do we start to run into difficulties. Simson and others have argued that

---

19 *De institutione musica*, I, i, quoted after Strunk II, p. 138.

20 'We must not despise the science of numbers, which, in many passages of Holy Scripture, is found to be of eminent service to the careful interpreter. Neither has it been without reason numbered among God's praises, "Thou hast ordered all things in number and measure and weight".' (*City of God*, xi, 30; the quotation is from the Book of Wisdom, 11:20.)

21 *De musica*, V, 28; see further Robert J. O'Connell, *Art and the Christian Intelligence in St. Augustine*, Oxford (Basil Blackwell) 1978, pp. 67–8, also ibid., p. 204 and n. 21.

22 *Renaissance of the Twelfth Century*, pp. 78ff.

medieval 'architects' were men of education and some standing, emphasizing how, at times, courts or cathedral chapters would even compete with one another to secure the services of particularly experienced individuals.[23] This, however, was probably the exception rather than the rule. Usually, the person in charge of a project – for a new cathedral, say – would have been the *magister operis*: a master mason who employed a team of assistants and apprentices working under his direction. The extent of the education to which such masters could lay claim has been debated, but they were certainly not 'educated' in the sense that their clerical patrons were educated. They were unlikely to know Latin and may even have been unable to read. That said, many of them clearly possessed a considerable fund of useful knowledge, which included an understanding of the elements of practical if not theoretical geometry – knowledge that was transmitted largely by word of mouth.

It has also been suggested that close and frequent contact between the 'master' and his patron, who may have had no practical knowledge but who perhaps had in mind a symbolic or even philosophical programme for the building under discussion, could amount to a kind of 'informal tutoring' and that a good deal of clerical learning was imported into the craft traditions of the Middle Ages by just such 'informal means'.[24] Even so, as Paul Crossley pointed out, there is no firm evidence for the percolation of theology – nor, one might add, of any form of abstract speculation – into the mason's yard.[25] Other authors warn in equally cogent terms against viewing Gothic architecture as a kind of 'petrified philosophy'. In his study of the Gothic cathedral, 'unquestionably the most intellectually refined architecture yet seen in the medieval West', Christopher Wilson observes that:

short of invoking the theory developed by the Annales *school of cultural historians,[26] that the unity discernible in the attitudes and artifacts of a single era is to be explained by reference to deep and hardly recoverable patterns or*

---

23 Simson 1962, pp. 43ff.; compare also Warnke, 'Die Entstehung eines neuen Architektentypus', in Martin Warnke, *Bau und Überbau: Soziologie der mittelalterlichen Architektur nach den Schriftquellen*, Frankfurt/M. (Syndikat) 1984, pp. 128ff.
24 Lon R. Shelby, 'The Geometrical Knowledge of Mediaeval Master Masons', in Lynn T. Courtenay (ed.), *The Engineering of Medieval Cathedrals*, Aldershot (Ashgate) 1997, pp. 30, 45.
25 Paul Crossley, 'Medieval Architecture and Meaning: the Limits of Iconography', *Burlington Magazine*, vol. 130, no. 109 (February 1988), p. 120.
26 The French journal *Annales d'histoire économique et sociale*, founded in 1929, was identified with a globalizing school of cultural history, of which the most important representatives were Lucien Febvre, Marc Bloch and Fernand Braudel. It later changed its name to *Annales: économies, sociétés, civilisations*.

'habits' of thought, it is difficult to see how the supposed correspondences [between Gothic architecture and Scholasticism] can be accounted for historically. There is absolutely no evidence from this period that any cleric ever became deeply involved in the designing of a major church, though this is not to say that such a thing could not have happened ... [27]

This lack of evidence has proved a stumbling block for many present-day historians, who have shown themselves reluctant to go beyond the details of Gothic buildings in order to explore more far-reaching ideas.[28] Their reluctance might well appear justified, given how little we know about the thought processes of the men who built the great cathedrals of the Gothic era or their opinion of the projects on which they were engaged. Part of the problem is that, by contrast with the numerous texts about the theory of music that have survived from medieval times, we possess no writings of that period that treat seriously of architecture conceived in anything other than practical terms.[29] If, in the absence of written sources of information, a convincing argument were to be made for Gothic buildings having been designed in accordance with some all-embracing, even allegedly 'musical' programme, such an argument would have to be based primarily on the evidence of the structures themselves.

Perhaps the most obvious place to look for this kind of evidence is in the proportions of the buildings. And indeed, if we think of the Gothic cathedral or 'great church' as the defining edifice of the later Middle Ages, it is striking how many seem to employ coherent proportional systems of some kind – systems that mostly (although not exclusively) depend on the same primary ratios from which musical harmony, in the Greek sense, derives. There is, for example, an evident predilection for the octave ratio 2:1, the simplest and most easily apprehended of all musical consonances.

---

27 Christopher Wilson, *The Gothic Cathedral. The Architecture of the Great Church 1130–1530*, London (Thames & Hudson) 1990, pp. 45–6. That there may have existed precisely such affinities (by which I do not mean that one can demonstrate any kind of causal relationship but that there are significant parallels to be drawn between the distinctive patterns of thought manifested in the work of Gothic architects, writers and musicians) is argued below at pp. 127ff.

28 The extent to which scholars have now turned their back on this kind of exploration is made clear, for example, by a recent essay dealing with methodological approaches to the study of Chartres cathedral, in which authors Peter Kurmann and Brigitte Kurmann-Schwarz dismiss the type of synthetic overview for which the 'art historian will often strive' as 'laudable but difficult. It is methodologically far more acceptable in current studies for historians to confine themselves to far narrower questions'; see 'Chartres Cathedral as a Work of Artistic Integration: Methodological Reflections', in Virginia Chieffo Raguin, Kathryn Brush and Peter Draper (eds), *Artistic Integration in Gothic Buildings*, Toronto (Toronto U. P.) 1995, p. 140.

29 It should, moreover, be pointed out that historians of medieval music now consider the earliest musical treatises of this period to date from the years around 1250–60 – that is, a whole century after the first major examples of Gothic building.

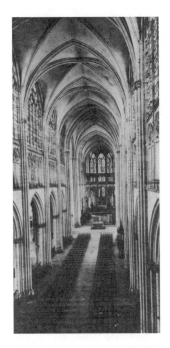
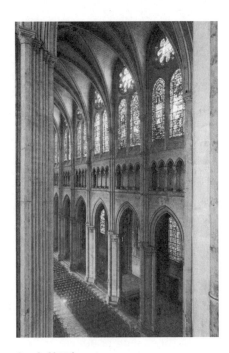

Figure 19. Troyes cathedral looking east, first half 13th century
Figure 20. Chartres cathedral (begun 1194) showing succession of nave bays

Other 'harmonic' ratios – 2:3 for the fifth, 3:4 for the fourth – occur almost as frequently. In his detailed analysis of Troyes cathedral, Stephen Murray, who voices what we might consider a well-founded scepticism about the 'interpretation of the medieval cathedral as the embodiment of sublime neo-Platonic Ideas', finds nevertheless that the central vessel is approximately twice as high as it is wide – a proportion that, in his opinion, 'conveys a general sense of moderation and stability' (fig. 19).[30] In fact, the 'approximation' to which he refers turns out to be a relatively close one, the measurements being given in a footnote: the height of the keystone of the easternmost nave vault 28.85 m (94 ft 10¼ in) as against the 13.94 m (45 ft 8¾ in) span of the central vault. Another equally detailed study, this time of Chartres, likewise appears to show a deliberate – or at least consistent – use of 'musical' ratios, the width of the nave (approximately 44 m; 144 ft) being in a proportion of 4:3 to the gaps separating the glazed areas of the great lateral windows (fig. 20).[31]

30 Stephen Murray, *Building Troyes Cathedral. The Late Gothic Campaigns*, Bloomington and Indianapolis (Indiana U. P.) 1987, pp. 3 and 8, also p. 228 and n. 10.
31 John James, *Chartres. The Masons who Built a Legend*, London (Routledge and Kegan Paul) 1982, p. 149.

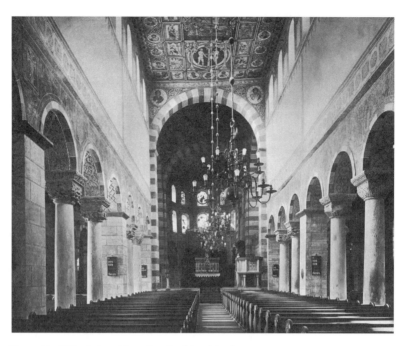

Figure 21. Hildesheim, abbey church of St Michael, *c*.1100

Simson's theory of musical ratios criticized

Not surprisingly, Simson, in keeping with the main thrust of his argument, provides an array of further instances of Gothic buildings in which the application of 'musical' ratios might be construed as deliberate: Sens, for example, where 'the square bays of the nave are twice as wide as those of the side aisles. Owing to the tripartite elevation, it was possible to give the same proportion to the relative heights of nave and aisles ... The octave ratio of 1:2 permeates the entire edifice.'[32] Among other cathedrals where such ratios seem to have been purposefully employed he cites Lausanne (southern transept) and Peterborough as well as the façades of 'Paris, Strassburg [sic] and York', in which 'the consonance of the fifth is sounded'.[33] He also contrasts Chartres with the Romanesque abbey of St Michael at Hildesheim (fig. 21) on account of what he sees as the former's more consistent (and more visibly effective) use of 'musical' ratios.[34]

This comparison that Simson draws between Gothic and Romanesque raises an interesting but thorny point. Like many other

---

32 Simson, *Gothic Cathedral*, p. 144.
33 Ibid., pp. 199–200.
34 Ibid., pp. 212ff.

writers, he stresses the preoccupation of Gothic builders with geometry, as revealed 'even by a glance at Gothic architectural drawings'.[35] He also remarks that the painted representations of heaven that often adorned the Romanesque apse were, in the Gothic era, ousted by the 'pattern produced by the structural members, the vault ribs and supporting shafts ... Whereas the Romanesque painter could deceive the senses with the illusion of ultimate reality, the Gothic builder applied the very laws that order heaven and earth.'[36] In other words, the ambition to represent the merely illusory beauties of nature had been supplanted by a seemingly Platonic concern with the intelligible beauty of number, a beauty that lies at the heart of both geometry and music. If such a concern existed, it would serve to underline the vigour with which Platonic and Pythagorean notions of beauty and number were transmitted to medieval times by St Augustine and other writers.

Simson presses home the advantages of this argument at various points in his book. He claims that churches of the Cistercian order express 'Augustinian' ratios, as in the case of Fontenay abbey, where the width of the crossing in relation to its length produces a ratio of 2:3 – the interval of a fifth.[37] He also notes that the 'musical mysticism of the Platonic tradition' played an important part in the spirituality of the Cistercian movement and of its leader, Bernard of Clairvaux:

To a man steeped, as Bernard was, in the Augustinian tradition, the presence of the 'perfect' ratios must have been as evident in visible proportions as in audible consonances. And the metaphysical dignity of the ratios that he admired in musical composition he cannot have failed to respect in well-proportioned architecture.[38]

But Simson's account, seductive though it may be, brings with it a number of obvious difficulties. For one thing, studies in psychology have shown that our visual perception is quite different from, even if in certain respects related to, our mathematical or musical faculties. Thus, the notion that certain proportions in architecture, if noticed by the eye, would inevitably have called to mind musical

---

35 Ibid., p. 13; compare James, who, in discussing the proportions of Chartres cathedral, observes that in Gothic architecture 'there is not one decision that was not made through geometry'. (*Chartres*, p. 148.)

36 Simson, pp. 38–9, also pp. 5ff. Such an argument appears to be undermined by the largely representational and, in many cases, specifically narrative character of Gothic stained glass, which is unlikely to have struck the medieval viewer as jarringly at odds with the intricate and predominantly abstract tracery by which it is contained.

37 Ibid., pp. 48–50, where other ratios of nave, aisles, etc., are also discussed.

38 Ibid., pp. 39, 42–3.

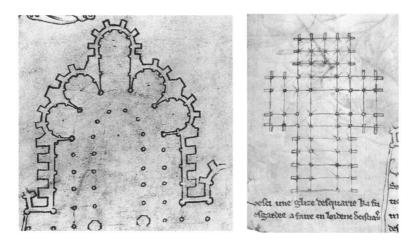

Figures 22 (a) and (b). Details of page from the sketchbook of Villard de Honnecourt showing ground plan of cathedral at Cambrai and *une glize dequarie, c.*1220–40 (Bibliothèque Nationale, Paris, MS fr.19093)

consonances is questionable, to say the least.[39]   For another, architectural and spatial devices such as the double cube or the relationship of half to whole may well have been used primarily – or exclusively – not because they were thought to be 'musical' but because they were found to be visually pleasing, evoking qualities such as moderation and stability in precisely the way that Murray suggests.[40] Such devices do not necessarily indicate any special knowledge of or interest in music. Probably, architects in every period would have tended to favour the same proportions, regardless of any musical association.

Villard de Honnecourt

Apart from buildings, some medieval drawings also seem to show a marked preference for specifically 'harmonic' ratios – 2:1, 3:2 and so on. An example of such a drawing is the ground plan of an 'ideal' church by the thirteenth-century artist Villard de Honnecourt (figs 22 a and b), designed, according to its inscription, for *l'ordene d(e) Cistiaus* ('the order of Citeaux', that is, the Cistercians).[41] Of all the architectural plans and drawings to be found in Villard's famous 'sketchbook', this is by far the most abstracted. Entirely missing are not just practical details such as towers or portals or staircases but

---

39 See below, ch. 4, pp. 156–7.
40 See n. [30] above.
41 See H. R. Hahnloser, *Villard de Honnecourt. Kritische Gesamtausgabe des Bauhüttenbuches ms. fr 19093 der Pariser Nationalbibliothek,* Vienna (Anton Schroll) 1935, plate 28b and text, pp. 65–7; also Simson, p. 199.

even any indication of the mass or thickness of the walls. (The contrast with the adjacent drawing on the same sheet, a ground plan of the choir of the cathedral at Cambrai, on which the variations in the thickness of the walls and the exact disposition of the buttresses are clearly shown, could scarcely be more marked.) In this case, what obviously appealed to Villard was not so much the visual effect of the building as the purely abstract beauty of the mathematical ratios on which his design was based. Here indeed is *une glize desquarie*, just as it says on the drawing: a rectangular church, designed *ad quadratum*, the basic module being represented by the square vaults of the side aisles. This module is multiplied by two, by three, by four, inevitably producing most of the simple ratios on which the primary musical consonances are based. The ratio of the width of the aisles to the width of the nave is 1:2 (*ie* the octave), the width of the transepts to that of the crossing 2:4 (the same octave ratio of 1:2, only doubled). The ratio between the width of the transepts and the length of the apse is 2:3 (fifth), that between the width of the crossing and the length of the apse 4:3 (fourth). Nevertheless, other than the drawing itself, there is no evidence to show that Villard was consciously using 'musical' proportions or that he was aware that such ratios were 'musical' in the first place.[42]

The difficulties in interpreting any medieval building or architectural drawing in terms of a specifically 'musical' programme – despite what might appear at first sight to be a wealth of supporting evidence – may therefore be summarized as follows. On the one hand, the use of proportional systems of various kinds, including the division of the constituent parts of a building according to the simple ratios described above, is quite widespread; but we have no means of demonstrating that such ratios were employed *because* they were considered to be musical.[43] On the other hand, numerous writings of the period testify to an abundance of medieval learning, much of it based directly or indirectly on classical sources, in which images of divine harmony and of God as supreme architect, ordering all creation according to number and proportion, are frequently encountered. But these

---

42 Nowhere in the commentary to his critical edition of Villard's sketchbook does Hahnloser remark specifically on the use of 'musical' ratios; he does, however, compare the geometric *schemata* that seemingly underlie Villard's drawings of several sculptural groups and the division of the figures into unequal parts with Euclid's *Elements*; see Hahnloser, op. cit., pp. 275ff. and esp. p. 278.

43 Elizabeth Read Sunderland has demonstrated the widespread – and perhaps significant – recurrence of particular numbers such as threes, fours, sevens and tens in the ground plans of large abbey and priory churches of the Romanesque period, including Paray-le-Monial, Baume-les-Moines and St Gall; see her article 'Symbolic Numbers and Romanesque Church Plans', *Journal of the Society of Architectural Historians*, vol. 18, no. 3 (October 1959), pp. 94–103.

formulations are so vague and so general and can be interpreted in so many different ways that, in the words of one writer, 'any cap can be made to fit any head'.[44] There is no evidence to suggest that such ideas directly affected architectural practice, even if, in the minds of certain educated patrons, they may have provided the background to the campaigns that led to the erection of some of the most prominent medieval buildings.

Development of polyphony

There is, however, a more illuminating parallel that can be drawn between medieval architecture and music. This has to do not with abstract notions of order and proportion but with actual methods of building and composing, in which the systematic articulation of space, both architectural and musical, played a crucial role. The concept of 'architectural space' is, of course, readily understood and scarcely requires definition. By contrast, what is meant by 'space' in music is not immediately obvious. Moreover, in order to explain how, in medieval music, space might be 'articulated', it is first necessary to give some account of developments in contemporary musical practice. Of these, by far the most important was the invention of polyphony.

For the first thousand years of its history, the music of the Western Church (which is the only European music of this period we know anything about) had two distinctive features. First, it was largely monophonic – that is, it consisted of a single melodic line.[45] Gregorian chant or 'plainchant', as it is sometimes called, was in most cases devoid of the kinds of additional interest that derive from the juxtaposition and interweaving of two or more melodic lines or 'parts'.[46] If there were two parts, this was usually because of the natural differences characteristic of the human voice, which may find it more comfortable to pitch a given note at a lower or higher octave. In the case of an all-male choir (of monks, for example) the naturally lower voices – what we would call the 'basses' – would sing in the bottom register, the 'tenors' an octave

---

44 Eric Fernie, 'The Ground Plan of Norwich Cathedral and the Square Root of Two', in Courtenay, *Engineering of Medieval Cathedrals*, p. 116.

45 The threefold definition given by Yudkin of the characteristics of plainchant is useful here: that it was monophonic; that it was unmeasured (meaning that its note values and rhythms were not explicitly defined); and that it was performed without accompaniment (although at various times, instruments as well as voices seem to have been permitted within the context of the liturgy); see Yudkin 1989, p. 42.

46 Various meanings have been attributed to the term 'plainchant', whose origin, like that of 'organum', is uncertain. In the writings of some thirteenth-century musical theorists, *cantus planus* – that is, the unmeasured music of traditional Christian chant (see preceding note) – is contrasted with the *musica mensurata* that was progressively introduced from about 1200 onwards; see Alec Harman, 'Medieval and Early Renaissance Music', in Alec Harman and Wilfred Mellers, *Man and his Music. The Story of Musical Experience in the West*, London (Barrie and Rockliff) 1962, pp. 2–3.

above: a practice that is known as 'doubling'. Or, sometimes, the range and disposition of notes in a particular chant or melody made it more comfortable to 'double' at the interval of a fifth or fourth, rather than at the octave, resulting in a richer and more sonorous effect.[47] This doubling – the voices moving in parallel from start to finish while singing the same tune – is called 'parallel organum'. The term 'organum' would subsequently acquire other, more complex meanings, but these details of musical terminology need not concern us here. The point is that the only difference between one voice and another was the *pitch* at which the melody was sung, since in strict parallel organum the *interval* (octave, fifth or fourth) separating the two identical melodic lines remained always the same.

In practice, it is unlikely that the singing of medieval chant would have been quite as monotonous as the foregoing description suggests. We know that there were different ways of approaching the 'finals' or ends of verses, where voices that had otherwise been singing a fifth or a fourth apart might move by oblique or contrary motion to arrive at the same concluding note: the unison. Moreover, given mankind's seemingly spontaneous delight in decoration, it was perhaps inevitable that, in the singing of organum, performers should have experimented with musical ornaments of one kind or another. Written sources point to just such simple forms of decoration, the use of contrary motion and even crossing of parts as well as the occurrence of 'impure' intervals – that is, those other than the octave, fifth and fourth. Early compilations such as the ninth-century *Musica Enchiriadis* or, somewhat later, the anthology of alleluias and sequences known as the *Winchester Troper* also reveal an interest in trying to fit together two independent tunes. But in these early forms of polyphonic writing, the additional part often consisted of little more than a succession of reiterated notes, like a drone accompanying the main melody. True polyphony – that is, two or more voices moving independently 'against' rather than 'with' one another, each maintaining its own distinctive melodic shape – in this era did not yet exist.

The second characteristic of early Western Church music turns out to be practically related to the first. By about 800 AD, the liturgical repertoire comprised many hundreds of melodies – the numerous chants, including psalms and hymns, that were an

---

47 In his analysis of the beginnings of part music, Harman also notes how 'in order to bring the melody within the comfortable range of male and female voices, consecutive octaves later became consecutive fourths and fifths, for the normal range of the bass, tenor, alto and soprano are roughly a fourth or fifth apart'. (*Man and His Music*, p. 41.)

integral part of the celebration of the mass or marked the various hours of the monastic day – which all had to be learnt by heart. This was because there existed no agreed system of musical notation, of the kind that would enable a singer to 'sight read' an unknown piece of music in the way we take for granted today. According to St Basil, the 'delight of melody' had been sanctioned by the Church Fathers so that 'through the pleasantness and softness of the sound we might unawares receive what was useful in words'.[48] But whereas the words were transcribed in multiple copies and could be read by anyone who had mastered the skills of literacy, the music to which the words were sung was, in that pre-notational age, simply consigned to memory.[49]

It is therefore hardly surprising that, by the ninth century, at the latest (but probably earlier), there existed considerable variations in the musical observance of the liturgy from one part of Europe to another – a problem addressed at different times by various expedients, including the establishment of a papal choir that would sing only the 'authorized' versions of the chants.[50] Monks were also sent from Rome to their brothers across the Alps in order to instruct them anew in the 'correct' manner of performance.[51] Attempts to impose on the rest of Europe a single, nominally Roman chant repertory were aided by the use of what is termed 'neumatic' notation.[52] However, 'neumes' – a system of what look to us like little more than squiggles or hieroglyphs written above the words of the chant – could serve at best as reminders of music already known (fig. 23). They could not be accurately 'read' in the way that the Latin texts were read, since

---

48 St Basil the Great (*c*.330–79 AD), 'Homily on the First Psalm', in Strunk II, p. 121; compare also St John Chrysostom: 'from the spiritual Psalms ... proceeds much of value, much utility, much sanctity, and every inducement to philosophy, for the words purify the soul and the Holy Spirit descends swiftly upon the soul of the singer.' ('Exposition of Psalm 41', in ibid., p. 124.)

49 For a detailed account of the transition from verbatim memory to the early notational systems used for the transmission of medieval ecclesiastical chant, see Kenneth Levy, *Gregorian Chant and the Carolingians*, Princeton, NJ (Princeton U. P.) 1998.

50 McKinnon ascribes the establishment of the papal choir, the *Schola Cantorum*, and of a standard repertoire of what is loosely called Gregorian (more properly, Roman) chant to the reign of Pope Gregory II (r.715–31 AD) rather than, as often proposed, that of Gregory I (d.604 AD) who, numerous legends notwithstanding, appears to have shown little interest in music. See James W. McKinnon, *Man and Music: Antiquity and the Middle Ages. From Ancient Greece to the 15th Century*, London (Macmillan) 1990, esp. ch. 4, 'The Emergence of Gregorian Chant', pp. 88ff.; also his introduction to Strunk II, pp. 116–17.

51 John 'the Deacon' Hymonides in his *Life of Gregory the Great* reported how 'cantors of the Roman school were dispersed throughout the West and instructed the barbarians with distinction', but that, after they died, 'the Western churches so corrupted the received body of chant that a certain John ... was sent by bishop Vitalian to Britain by way of Gaul; and John recalled the children of the churches in every place to the pristine sweetness of the chant, and preserved for many years ... the rule of Roman doctrine'; quoted after Strunk II, p. 180.

52 Levy considers the standardization of the liturgical repertoire to have been a priority for Carolingian ecclesiastical reformers, ascribing the initiative that lay behind such attempts at standardization to Charlemagne's father Pepin; see Levy 1998, pp. 6–7. He also advances the hypothesis, plausible but as yet unproven, that neumes were already in use by about 800 AD: that is, at least a century earlier than any surviving document containing evidence of neumatic notation.

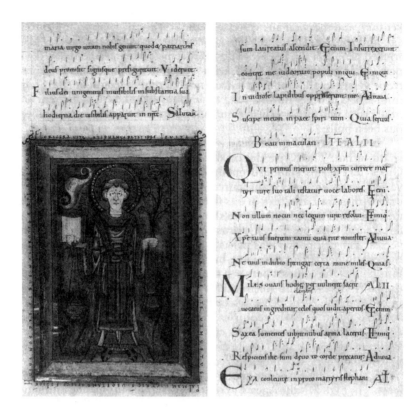

Figure 23. Tropes for the introit of Saint Stephen showing an example of neumatic notation and a miniature of the saint, mid-eleventh century.

they gave no exact indication of either the pitch of any given note or its duration.[53] Despite the later introduction of what were called 'heighted neumes', which provided a few more clues as to the relative positions of different patterns of notes, the problem of holding such a vast musical repertory in memory persisted until the beginning of the eleventh century, when an entirely new system of notation came into use – a system that revolutionized not only the learning and performance of music but also, to some extent, its subsequent course of development.

---

53 'Memory still has the essential role, much as it did during the improvisational, notationless stages that went before ... Neumes are secondary, supplying silhouettes of melodic substances that are fixed and quite accurately remembered, yet useless unless someone has the full melodic substance in memory.' (Levy 1998, p. 3.)

Guido of Arezzo

The invention of the musical staff, or stave, is often credited to Guido of Arezzo (sometimes known as Guido il Monaco – Guido the monk), although it seems that the use of drawn lines and spaces to indicate musical pitches – at first just two lines, later four or five – came about gradually over quite a long period and was probably not the brainchild of any one person. But it was certainly Guido who provided the most systematic and comprehensive explanation of this new method, which became in all important respects the basis of the five-lined stave still in use today, nearly a thousand years later. Guido's 'system' consisted, as does our modern stave, of a sequence of horizontal lines and spaces, arranged one above the other on the page. Any line or space could be made to 'stand for' a particular pitch – F, for example. This was achieved by the simple expedient of choosing whichever line you wanted to signify F or C or any other pitch, and writing the corresponding letter on to it: the origin of our modern 'clef'.[54] (Even today, we sometimes talk about a 'C clef' or an 'F clef' instead of 'alto' or 'bass'.) Notes were then placed on or between the lines, thereby acquiring an unambiguous pitch value, since the musical significance of each line or space remained the same, unless changed by the substitution of a different clef. (For example, if the second line of the stave were defined as 'C', a note placed in the space above it would always be 'D' and so on.) Henceforth, no one who had carefully studied the Guidonian method could be in any doubt about the intended pitch of a given note, about the size of the interval that separated one note from another or the directional flow, the 'shape' of a particular melody.

This remarkable invention had two immediate advantages. The first was that it greatly simplified the task of standardizing the liturgical repertoire, so that, as Guido himself remarked, 'every chant [might] return uniformly to a common rule of art'.[55] The second was that it reduced dramatically the amount of time it took to teach that repertoire: from ten years to two, according to his own estimate.[56] Now, a boy entering a monastery, who perhaps knew by heart only a handful of the many hundreds of chants currently in use, could master the rest quickly and easily by 'reading' the notes, just as we do today. Nor was it merely a question of 'small boys ... who until now have been beaten for their gross ignorance of the

---

54 Guido used the colours red and yellow to indicate the notes F and C: see the 'Prologue to his Antiphoner', translated in Strunk II, pp. 211ff.; also *Grove*, vol. 7, pp. 803ff.
55 Strunk II, p. 212.
56 'For if at present those who have succeeded in gaining only an imperfect knowledge of singing in ten years of study intercede most devoutly before God for their teachers, what do you think will be done for us and our helpers, who can produce a perfect singer in the space of one year, or at the most in two?' (*Epistola de ignoto cantu*, translated by Oliver Strunk, revised by James McKinnon, in Strunk II, p. 215.)

Psalms and vulgar letters' and who 'do not know how to pronounce the words and syllables of the very antiphon which they sing correctly by themselves without a master, something which ... any intelligent and studious person will be able to do if he tries to understand with what care we have arranged the neumes'.[57] Even the Pope was able to verify for himself the efficacy of Guido's method by learning, apparently in next to no time, 'a verse ... without having heard it beforehand, thus quickly finding true in his own case what he could hardly believe of others'.[58]

More problematic is the relationship – if any – between the advent of notation and the subsequent development of polyphony. By the year 1200, there clearly existed a tradition of polyphonic improvisation not only within but also, it appears, outside the liturgy – a tradition largely independent of any kind of writing, musical or otherwise. From a record of his travels compiled by the churchman and historian Gerald of Wales (also called Giraldus Cambrensis or Gerald de Barri, *c*.1146–*c*.1223) we learn of the custom of improvised singing in several parts that was common during the second half of the twelfth century in Wales and also (seemingly, in two parts only) in the north of England, although we cannot be certain how long this practice endured.[59] We also know that, well after written notation came into widespread ecclesiastical use, choristers would still gather around a large book containing transcriptions of the traditional chants, as depicted in fig. 24. While some would intone the familiar melody of the chant itself, others would weave a variety of musical embellishments around it: again, an improvised form of polyphony, known as *discantus supra librum* or 'discant from the book'. Partly on the basis of such evidence, some scholars have argued that notation did not, in itself, facilitate the invention of polyphony. Instead, it offered, so they claim, simply a means of capturing the stage of musical evolution reached at any particular moment – a 'snapshot' view, if you like, of what was already established performing practice.

Perhaps, in an age that hungered as avidly after intellectual or spiritual goods as after material ones, notation also served as a way of advertising the musical wares of a great cultural centre such as

---

57 As n. [54].

58 *Epistola de ignoto cantu*, in Strunk II, pp. 215–16. The pope in question was John XIX, who ruled as Supreme Pontiff from 1024 to 1033.

59 'In their musical concerts they do not sing in unison like the inhabitants of other countries, but in many different parts ... Beyond the Humber, and on the borders of Yorkshire, the inhabitants make use of the same kind of symphonious harmony, but with less variety; singing in only two parts, one murmuring in the bass, the other warbling in the acute or treble'; quoted after Gustave Reese, *Music in the Middle Ages*, London (J. M. Dent & Sons) 1941, p. 387. Gerald of Wales served as archdeacon of Brecknock from 1175 to 1204. His writings provide a vivid account of late twelfth-century ecclesiastical life, especially in Wales.

COLOUR PLATES

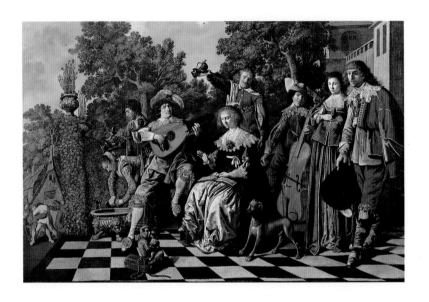

Plate 1. Jan Miense Molenaer, *A Music Party* (*Allegory of Fidelity in Marriage*), 1633, oil on canvas, 99.7 x 141 cm, 39$\frac{1}{4}$ x 55$\frac{1}{2}$ in (Richmond, Virginia Museum of Fine Arts, Adolphe D. and Wilkins C. Williams Collection)

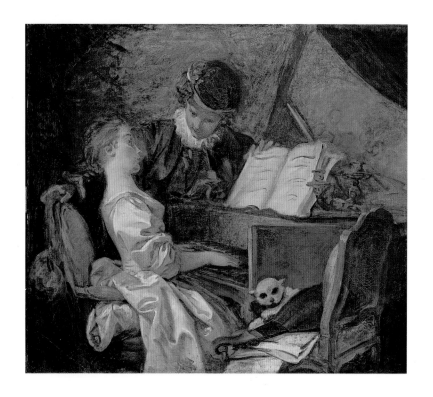

Plate 2. Jean-Honoré Fragonard, *The Music Lesson*, *c.*1765–72, oil on canvas, 110 x 120 cm, 43³₈ x 47¹₄ in (Musée du Louvre, Paris)

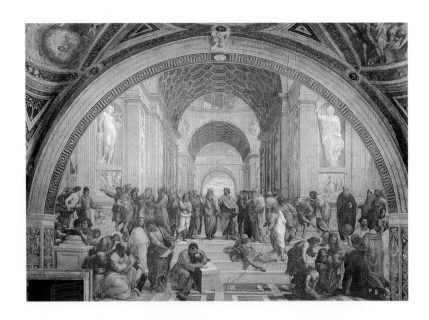

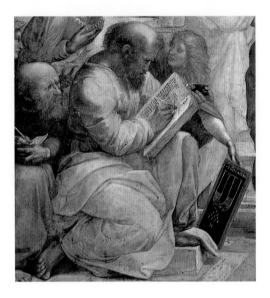

Plate 3. Raphael, *School of Athens*, 1510–11, fresco (Stanza della Segnatura, Vatican Museums)
Plate 4. Raphael, *School of Athens* (detail showing Pythagoras)

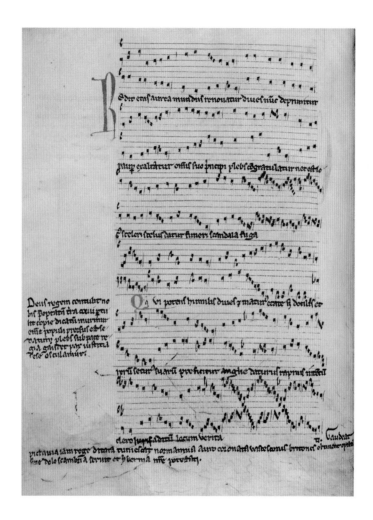

Plate 5. Two-part conductus *Redit aetas aurea*, composed for the coronation of Richard the Lion-Heart (September 1189), 13th-century MS showing the *incipit* with the setting of the words *Dives nunc deprimitur* (Herzog-August Bibliothek, Wolfenbüttel, Inv. no. 628, fol. 101)

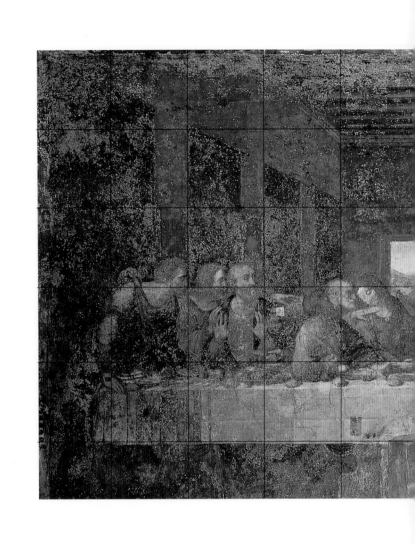

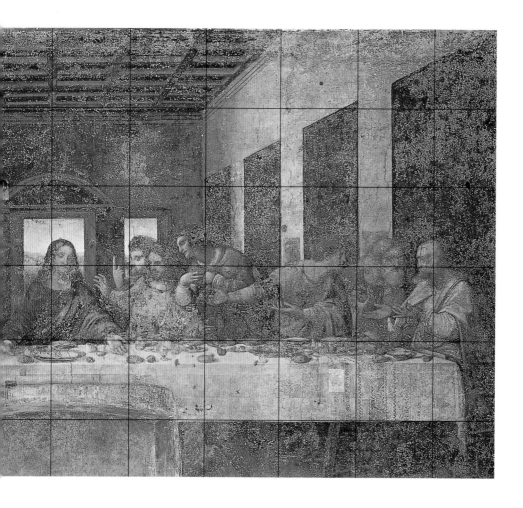

Plate 6. Leonardo da Vinci, *Last Supper*, 1494–7, fresco (tempera and oil on plaster), 460 x 880 cm, $181^1{}_8$ x $346^1{}_2$ in (S. Maria delle Grazie, Milan) showing superimposed grid, after Brachert, 'A Musical Canon of Proportion' (see p. 145)

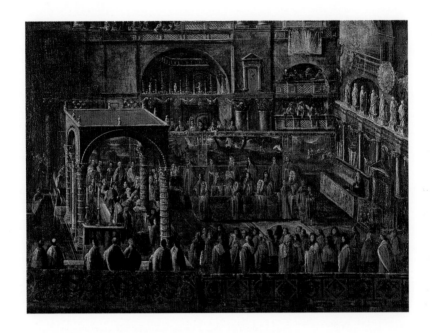

Plate 7. *Consignment of the Sword Given to Doge Francesco Morosini by Pope Alexander VIII in S. Marco*, 1689, painting, showing the placing of musicians in St Mark's basilica during a papal visit to Venice (Civico Museo Correr, Venice)

Paris. Even if it did not directly affect the miraculous flowering of complex polyphony that occurred during the latter part of the twelfth and early thirteenth centuries, it doubtless played a significant role in the seemingly inexorable spread of the Parisian style to other churches and courts throughout Europe. Moreover, the very existence of notation testifies to the vigour with which, during the years after 1200, musicians started to experiment with new and increasingly intricate musical forms. Now, composers (it can scarcely be coincidence that the independent *métier* of composer first makes its appearance at about this time) started devising far longer pieces, whose sheer extent would, in pre-notational times, have severely taxed the memory. Not only that; they also began ingeniously fitting together not just two but three or even four melodies, which, depending on the range of the voices or instruments employed, were invariably arranged 'above' or 'below' one another. As a consequence of this superimposition of simultaneously sounding but independent parts, music acquired – quite literally – a new dimension, for the first time taking full possession of something it had never previously had the means to conquer: vertical space.

Musical space

In writing about the origins of polyphony, I have been freely using terms like 'above' and 'below', 'vertical' and 'horizontal', even though these belong, strictly speaking, to descriptions of visual or tactile, not aural perceptions. Exactly how such expressions came to be appropriated for musical purposes is unclear. We tend simply to take them for granted, as when we speak of a coloratura soprano soaring 'above' the orchestra or a *Heldentenor* 'scaling impossible heights'. Similar uses of 'up' and 'down', 'high' and 'low' to describe various kinds of aural experience are none the less common to many different periods and cultures, perhaps suggesting something deeply ingrained in human thinking about the way we conceive of sound as well as, possibly, some intuitive relationship between musical and spatial perception. Aristotle uses the term 'high-pitched' to describe the voices of women and children, contrasting these with the 'lower' voices of men and remarking that the young of various species of animal are likewise 'high-voiced'.[60]

Instruments, too, are characterized as 'higher' or 'lower'. We speak of the 'upper' parts when, in analysing a modern musical

---

60 'All creatures when they are younger utter a higher sound, except for calves ... In all other kinds of creatures, the female utters a higher sound than the male.' (*De generatione animalium*, 786b7–788b2; quoted after Barker 1989, pp. 80ff.)

score, we turn our attention to the flutes and piccolos, whose music is always to be found higher up the page than that played by 'lower' woodwind instruments such as bassoons. The same is true of each section of the orchestra: the strings, for example, where the parts played by the 'higher' instruments such as violins and violas are printed above those of the cellos and basses. Notes, too, are arranged vertically to form a 'scale' – literally, a ladder;[61] and when we write music using the standard Western system of notation, the 'upper' notes are positioned 'higher' – again literally, in the spatial meaning of the term – on the musical stave than the lower ones. The one exception to this general rule is what are called 'tablatures', graphic symbols that represent not the rise and fall of the melody but successive positions of the hand in playing a stringed instrument such as the lute or, in ancient times, the *kithara*. In such cases, the symbols written on the 'lowest' line may indicate the string furthest from the player, which, depending on how the instrument is held, may be the 'highest' in pitch.[62] It is, however, extremely unlikely that the characteristics of 'highness' to us were those of 'lowness' to the Greeks and vice versa, as has sometimes been suggested.[63] Remarks like Aristotle's, quoted above, concerning the quality of women's and children's voices would surely vitiate any such hypothesis.[64]

The foregoing examples refer, of course, mainly to modern musical convention. But there is plenty of evidence to show that the concepts 'upper' and 'lower' as applied to voices and instruments or 'higher' and 'lower' in respect of pitch were also the stuff of medieval musical discourse. As well as the common use of precisely such terminology to be found in numerous written sources, illustrations that accompanied the various explanations of Guido's system clearly showed 'ascending' and 'descending' parts and 'higher' and 'lower' pitches, arranged above or below one another on his notational staff. Neumes – which, as we saw earlier, were the hieroglyphic predecessors of modern notation – likewise went 'up' or 'down' on the page according to the 'rise' and 'fall' of the melody.

---

61 Ital. *scala*; compare Fr. *échelle*; Ger. *Tonleiter* (literally 'note ladder'), etc.
62 In discussing Boethius' account of the modes and *tonoi*, Chadwick notes that, according to ancient usage, a fourth *below* the *mese* is the *hypate* ('highest'), a fourth *above* it is the *nete* ('lowest'): 'These derive their names from their position on the instrument: the "lowest" string was tuned to the highest pitch, the "highest" to the lowest.' (*Boethius*, p. 93.)
63 For example, by Harman (as n. [46]), pp. 16–17; compare also Meyer-Baer, *Music of the Spheres*, pp. 341ff., who relates the musical tones supposedly produced by the different planets to the positions of the 'lower' and 'higher' (*ie* nearer or more distant) spheres.
64 If further evidence were needed, by the time Ptolemy (Claudius Ptolemaeus) came to write his *Harmonics* the concepts 'high' and 'low' were evidently well established. For example, in Book X of his treatise, in distinguishing between isotonic and anisotonic pitches he compares those at the lower end to the lowing of cows, at the upper to the howling of wolves; see Jon Solomon, 'A Preliminary Analysis of the Organization of Ptolemy's *Harmonics*', in Barbera 1990, p. 78.

'Depictions' of spatial relationships can even be found in actual pieces of music: for example, the two-part *conductus* 'Redit aetas aurea', composed to mark the coronation of Richard the Lion-Heart at Westminster Abbey in September 1189. Here, the words 'Dives nunc deprimitur' ('Now the rich man is trodden down') are set – it can only be deliberately – to a *descending* scale (pl. 5).[65] That this vivid piece of word-painting is wholly intentional is underlined by the fact that (excluding repeats) this is the only moment in the entire piece when the two voices move together, note for note, in stepwise progression.

Of all the forms of music then in liturgical use, the *conductus* offered perhaps the greatest scope for this kind of innovation, since it was the only musical genre to consist, from start to finish, of newly composed melodies. All other types of sacred music were firmly based on the established repertoire of plainsong chants, which, given their hallowed role in the observance of the mass or monastic office, could be neither discarded nor significantly altered.[66] Even so, there was an obvious temptation to 'improve' the liturgical chants by combining them with other melodies which, in the earliest forms of polyphony, were at first added below rather than above the chant-bearing or tenor voice – 'tenor' meaning, in this context, simply 'the holding part'.[67] The *Winchester Troper*, cited earlier, which probably dates from the first quarter of the eleventh century, contains several instances of this kind of two-part writing, where the tenor is still the upper of the two voices.[68]

However, in the period that saw the building of the first Gothic cathedrals – that is, from about the middle of the twelfth century – it gradually became accepted that newly composed music, often referred to by the term 'discant', would be given to the *higher* voices. By contrast with the slowly moving tenor (now the *lowest* voice), these upper parts proceeded more quickly in notes of shorter

---

65 As pointed out by Harman, 'Medieval and Early Renaissance Music', pp. 99-100. In the performing edition by Christopher Page, the *incipit* of the poem is amended to read *Etas auri reditur* in order to preserve the otherwise consistent rhyming scheme; in all the manuscript sources the opening line is nevertheless given as it appears here. See also Page's accompanying notes to his recording *Music for the Lion-Hearted King*, Hyperion CD A66336.

In a letter to the author (June 2003), Christopher Page emphasized just how remarkable this setting of the words must have seemed at that moment in musical history, given that the descending voices are here separated by an interval of a third, then still classified as a dissonance. It is therefore hard to escape the conclusion that the 'composer' attached special importance to this particular phrase and wished it to stand out. I am grateful to Dr Page both for his comments and for supplying a good deal of further useful information in connection with this piece.

66 'Observe also that ... in all except the conductus there is first heard some *cantus prius factus* (called tenor, since it supports the discant and has its place on its own). In the conductus, however, this is not the case, for cantus and discant are written by the same person.' (Franco of Cologne, *Ars cantus mensurabilis*, c.1280; quoted after Strunk II, p. 240.) Note, however, that in earlier sources the term 'discant' is sometimes used to refer to something more like a 'note against note' manner of writing in two or more parts.

67 Lat. *tenere*, to hold.

68 Yudkin, *Music in Medieval Europe*, pp. 342ff.

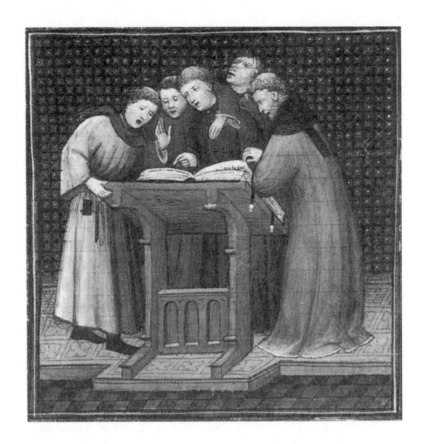

Figure 24. 'Discant from the book', miniature from a late fourteenth-century French Bible

duration, providing a form of ever more complex – some said too complex – decoration.[69] The tenor, on the other hand, was still the principal bearer of the liturgical message, enshrined in the traditional words and melodies of the plainsong. One historian has claimed that, at Notre Dame in Paris, the 'belief that the principal duty of the tenors was to project the plainsong' persisted until at least the sixteenth century – even if, in later and more elaborate forms of polyphony, the words of the psalms or hymns in question were often barely intelligible.[70]

Just as important was the structural role played by the tenor part, whose measured rhythms and simple melodies provided the basis for the more complex rhythmic or melodic patterns given to the upper voices. Thus, it was the tenor that bestowed order, measure and proportion on the entire composition. But while the traditional melodic patterns of the plainsong chants could not be changed, the tenor part itself was now increasingly subject to different kinds of rhythmic variation. Often it would alternate within the same piece between sections based on very long, held notes and more rapidly moving passages in what was known as modal rhythm: fixed metrical patterns, which medieval musical theorists believed were derived from antique poetic metre.[71] The tenor chant could also be repeated in its entirety or divided into shorter sections that were multiplied as many times as was necessary to ensure balance and symmetry. Comparing the two great early masters of the Notre Dame school, Léonin and Pérotin, Gustave Reese points to the latter's fondness for repeating the tenor part in altered rhythmic guise, contrasting the 'rhythmically amorphous character of the tenor' in a typical Léonin discant *clausula* with the rhythmically more organized writing typical of Pérotin's music.[72] 'With Pérotin, both voices of a two-part piece may move in sharply defined independent rhythms. The new two-part *clausulae* add an

---

69 For an example of such criticisms, see the famous diatribe by the English scholar John of Salisbury (mid-twelfth century), who castigated 'long ascents and descents, the dividing and redoubling of notes, the repetition of phrases, the clashing of the voices, while in all this, the high or even the highest notes of the scale are so mingled with the lower and lowest, that the ears are almost deprived of their power to distinguish'; quoted after Harman (as n. [46] above), p. 69.

70 Craig Wright, *Music and Ceremony at Notre Dame of Paris 500–1550*, Cambridge (Cambridge U. P.) 1989, pp. 322ff.

71 The earliest description of modal rhythm is to be found in the anonymous thirteenth-century *Discantus positio vulgaris*, tentatively dated to about 1230; see Strunk II, pp. 218ff.

72 Pérotin has also been identified as the composer of the two great *quadrupla* that have come down to us from this period, *Viderunt omnes* and *Sederunt principes*. These, as far as anyone can tell, are the first examples of four-part writing in the history of European music; on the question of their dating, see Wright, *Music and Ceremony*, pp. 239ff. On the problems of identifying Pérotin, see ibid., pp. 288–94; compare *Grove*, vol. 14, pp. 540ff. On Pérotin's significance, see Stanley Sadie (ed.), *The New Grove Dictionary of Music and Musicians*, London (Macmillan) 2nd edn 2001, vol. 19, pp. 446–51; also Edward H. Roesner, 'Who "made" the *Magnus Liber*?' *Early Music History*, vol. 20 (2001), pp. 227–66.

important element – rhythmic independence of parts – to the technique of polyphony.'[73]

The rise of the motet

A further step in the direction of more rigorous rhythmic and melodic organization is marked by what many historians consider the defining musical form of the later Middle Ages, the polyphonic motet in three or even four parts. This, by the end of the thirteenth century, had evolved into a genre so complicated that it probably taxed the mental capacities of all but the most sophisticated listeners.[74] At least, so thought the theorist Johannes de Grocheio. 'This kind of music', he wrote, 'should not be set before a lay public, because they are not alert to its refinement nor are they delighted by hearing it, but before the clergy [*litterati*] and those who look for the refinements of skills.'[75] In his opinion, only a small, discerning and highly educated audience was capable of appreciating the characteristic subtleties of the motet's interwoven yet independent melodic lines and the different words given to each voice part, which, since they were sung simultaneously, would have been scarcely distinguishable on first hearing.[76] It was also frequent practice for the same motet to combine a Latin chant with one or more completely different texts in vernacular French: a veritable Babel of languages. Some to our ears scandalous motets even superimposed profane words – for example, those of a secular love song – above a liturgical *cantus firmus* (a psalm, say, in praise of the Virgin), thus blurring any clear-cut distinction between secular and sacred music.[77]

Some idea of the impact produced by such experiments is conjured up by a decree issued in 1324 or 1325 by the Avignon Pope John XXII (r.1316–34), who attempted – somewhat belatedly – to ban precisely these kinds of innovation from the domain of liturgical music and who advocated in uncompromising terms a return to the simpler methods of the past:

---

73 Reese, *Music in the Middle Ages*, pp. 299ff. *Clausulae* were semi-independent compositions intended as an alternative to some of the polyphonic settings of the solo or responsorial sections of the liturgical chant. The words sung by the upper voices often served as an elaboration of or commentary upon the liturgical texts sung by the tenor, while the melodies themselves were derived from the original endings of the verses given to the tenor part.

74 I am here referring principally to the sacred rather than the secular motet which, at least in its earliest manifestations, probably consisted of only two parts – a kind of music that was relatively unaffected and easy to comprehend; for an account of the differences between these two genres, see Page, *Owl and the Nightingale*, esp. pp. 148ff.

75 Grocheio, *De musica* (c.1300); see Christopher Page, 'Johannes de Grocheio on Secular Music: a Corrected Text and a New Translation', in C. Page, *Music and Instruments of the Middle Ages: Studies on Texts and Performance*, Aldershot (Ashgate/Variorum Collected Studies Series) 1997, ch. XX, pp. 17ff., 36.

76 For discussion of Grocheio's views see the chapter 'Johannes de Grocheio, the *Litterati*, and Verbal *Subtilitas* in the Ars Antiqua Motet', in Page 1993, pp. 65ff.

77 For an analysis of the mid-thirteenth-century French motet *Quant voi/Au douz Tans*, whose tenor (based on the Latin words *hodie perlustravit*) derives from an Alleluia setting from the Mass for Pentecost, see Yudkin, op. cit., pp. 369, 391ff.

Certain disciples of the new school, much occupying themselves with the measured dividing of time, display their method in notes which are new to us, preferring to devise ways of their own rather than continue singing in the old manner; the music, therefore, of the divine offices is now performed with semibreves and minims, and with these notes of small value every composition is pestered. They truncate the melodies with hockets, they deprave them with discantus, sometimes they stuff them even with upper parts made out of secular song ... We straitly command that no one hence-forward shall think himself at liberty to attempt these methods, or methods like them, in the aforesaid offices, and especially in the canonical Hours or in the celebration of the Mass ... Yet for all this, it is not our intention to forbid ... the use of some consonances, for example, the octave, fifth and fourth, which heighten the beauty of the melody; such intervals, therefore, may be sung above the plain cantus ecclesiasticus, *yet so that the integrity of the* cantus *itself may remain intact and that nothing in the authoritative music be changed.*[78]

While this pointed rebuke did little to retard the pace of musical innovation, it tells us a good deal about other subjects. For example, the scornful allusion to the 'measured dividing of time' points up the greater degree of rhythmic complexity that characterized the 'new musical art' of the fourteenth century.[79] By contrast with the ill-defined note values of monophonic chant, writing in several parts now meant that an agreed system of indicating not only pitch but also time – what was known as *musica mensurata* or 'measured music' – had become increasingly necessary, not least as a means of keeping singers together.[80] On the other hand, the mention of hockets – literally 'hiccoughs', meaning a rapidly alternating rhythmic pattern where one part fits into the gaps left by another – shows that a delight in ornament had extended from the domain of melody to embrace that of rhythm as well. But, above all, this papal edict makes clear how far music had travelled in a comparatively short time. Even in the context of the liturgy, a musically reactionary pope is forced to concede that the days of unadorned

---

78 Adapted from H. E. Woodridge, *Oxford History of Music*, vol. 1, 2nd edn, Oxford, 1929, pp. 294ff.; see also Yudkin, p. 562.

79 See n. [103] below.

80 The *Ars cantus mensurabilis* (see n. [66] above) stresses the importance of the rhythmic patterns that govern the relationship between two or more parts or voices, defining *discant* as 'a consonant combination of different melodies proportionately accommodated to one another by long, short or still shorter sounds'; quoted after Strunk II, p. 228.

plainsong are over. The superimposition of newly composed melodies in the upper voices as a means of decorating the simple forms of the ancient chants had become one of the inescapable realities of early fourteenth-century musical life. Music's conquest of vertical space, which had taken somewhat less than two hundred years to accomplish, was all but complete.

Space in Gothic architecture

If there is one defining characteristic of Gothic architecture, historians usually consider this to be its pronounced verticality – that is, the overwhelming effect of height. One standard account, that by Branner, identifies this upward-soaring aspect of Gothic as its 'most vivid expression', and similar remarks can be found both in general histories of the Middle Ages and in more specialized writings.[81] In his fundamental study of French Gothic, Jean Bony writes of that 'ideal of loftiness … [that] tendency to stretch the naves in height, and at the same time to emphasize the vertical lines of the bay pattern' evident in the great churches of the 'pilgrimage road' such as Conques, Saint-Sernin at Toulouse or Santiago de Compostela.[82] Elsewhere, he calls attention to that 'deliberate insistence on height [that] affects all the proportions of the building' typical of the early thirteenth-century cathedral at Soissons, which, because of its date, is 'still close enough to the beginnings of the [Gothic] movement to preserve much of its original spirit'.[83]

These, however, are not just our own distinctively modern perceptions of Gothic. Observers at the time also commented repeatedly and sometimes critically on the fashion for height. For example, Bernard of Clairvaux, in his celebrated letter to Abbot William of St-Thierry attacking what he saw as the excesses of the Cluniac order, castigated 'the vast height of your churches' as well as their 'immoderate length [and] their superfluous breadth'.[84] Similar sentiments were voiced by Peter the Chanter (d.1197), a dignitary of the chapter of Notre Dame and the person responsible

---

81 Robert Branner, *Gothic Architecture*, New York (George Braziller) 1961, p. 25. An exception to this general rule is Sedlmayr, who described the vault shafts of Gothic cathedrals as not 'rising upwards' but 'growing downwards' (*von oben nach unten*) into the interior (Sedlmayr, *Entstehung der Kathedrale*, pp. 61, 139–40, quoted after Crossley 1988, p. 119). For a critical discussion of Sedlmayr's theories, see Wilhelm Schlink, 'The Gothic Cathedral as Heavenly Jerusalem: A Fiction in German Art History', in Bianca Kühnel (ed.), *The Real and Ideal Jerusalem in Jewish, Christian and Islamic Art. Studies in Honor of Bezalel Narkiss on the Occasion of his Seventieth Birthday*, Jerusalem (Hebrew University/Journal of the Center for Jewish Art) 1988, pp. 275–85.

82 Jean Bony, *French Gothic Architecture of the 12th and 13th Centuries*, Berkeley (California U. P.) 1983, p. 21.

83 Ibid., pp. 5–6.

84 Bernard of Clairvaux's *Apologia ad Guillelmum* is reprinted in V. Mortet, *Recueil de textes relatifs à l'histoire de l'architecture* (Paris, 1911), vol. 1, pp. 366–9. Concerning Bernard's attacks on luxury and ostentation see Christine Smith, *Architecture in the Culture of Early Humanism. Ethics, Aesthetics and Eloquence 1400–1470*, New York/Oxford (Oxford U. P.) 1992, p. 40; also Grant, *Abbot Suger*, pp. 24ff.

for its choir, probably at about the same time that Pérotin was active in the service of the cathedral. One might have thought that Peter's position as *praecentor* at Notre Dame would lead him to express some opinion about the musical innovations of his time, but he makes little mention of music, although he wrote voluminously on other subjects.[85] What roused him to utterance were the symbolic qualities of contemporary architecture. In his forthright view 'to build churches as is done at present is to sin. The *chevets* of our churches should be more humble than their bodies, because of the mystery they symbolize ... Yet today, chancels are built higher and higher.'[86] Elsewhere, evidently with an eye on Maurice de Sully's ambitious building programme for Notre Dame, of which he profoundly disapproved, he enquired scathingly: 'Why do you want your houses so tall? What is the use of your towers and ramparts? Do you believe that the devil cannot scale them? Nay, I say that thereby you will become the neighbour and companion of demons.'[87]

Whether these perceptions were accurate is another matter. Christopher Wilson, comparing Gothic with Romanesque, points out that the first Gothic cathedrals are 'in general no higher than the largest Norman and Anglo-Norman churches', citing as examples of lofty Romanesque Cluny in France at 29 m (96 ft) and Speyer in Germany at 31 m (101 ft).[88] The impression of height conveyed by early Gothic buildings is more a consequence of their manner of construction – in particular, the use of the pointed arch and, especially, the vault rib, which could be 'sprung' from the tops of the columns. These devices not only contributed to an effect of soaring verticality capable of persuading medieval commentators (and ourselves) that edifices in the 'new style' were taller than their predecessors. They also placed in the hands of Gothic architects the means of organizing and unifying the various parts of the building, both ornamental and structural, in a manner never previously attempted.

Numerous writers have been struck by the seemingly greater degree of complexity and yet, at the same time, clarity that characterizes the disposition of parts of the Gothic great church, by contrast with what have been described as the 'oddly assorted pillars' and 'almost haphazard ornamentation' of its Romanesque

---

85 It has been suggested that, despite his nominal responsibility for instructing the choirboys and for the specifically liturgical activities of the choir, Peter may in fact have delegated such matters to the sub-chanter (*succentor*); see John Baldwin, *Masters, Princes and Merchants: The Social Views of Peter the Chanter and his Circle*, Princeton, NJ (Princeton U.P.) 1970, vol. 1, p. 6.
86 Quoted after Allan Temko, *Notre Dame de Paris*, London (Secker & Warburg) 1956, p. 137; see also Baldwin (as preceding note), p. 66.
87 Pierre le Chantre, *Verbum abbreviatum*, quoted after Baldwin, op. cit., p. 68. The particular object of Peter's attack was identified by V. Mortet, 'Maurice de Sully', *Mémoires de Paris*, XVI (1899), pp. 232–4.
88 Wilson, *Gothic Cathedral*, p. 48.

antecedents.[89] The point of the comparison, cited earlier, that Simson makes between the Romanesque abbey of St Michael at Hildesheim and what he sees as the more coherent and organized use of 'musical' proportions at Chartres is precisely to emphasize the supposedly more unified character of Gothic. In a similar manner, describing the period that saw the building of Notre Dame and the other great cathedrals of the Île de France, musicologist Alec Harman alludes – albeit in somewhat general terms – to the 'throbbing waves of sound of a Pérotin *clausula*' and the 'regularly spaced and uniform columns made up of clustered supports for the rib vaulting' as the expression of the same 'desire to unify'.[90] Craig Wright, likewise writing about Pérotin, analyses the composer's tendency to create 'blocks or modules of sound, [which] in turn are balanced, shaped and interposed to produce a brilliantly original form of musical architecture ... What results is a carefully crafted wall of vertical polyphony ... Not only was Perotinus the first to write for four voices, he was the first to realize a wholly new sound ideal for sacred vocal polyphony, one perhaps not out of harmony with the vast, but carefully regulated spaces [of Notre Dame].'[91] And F. J. Smith, in his commentary on one of the most important (and certainly the longest) of all medieval musical treatises, the *Speculum musicae* of Jacques de Liège, describes the thirteenth-century motet as creating 'consonantal archways of sound that interlace each other in polyphonic complexity ... In early polyphony we witness just as careful a building process as went into a cathedral.'[92]

But it is not only musicologists who write in such terms. Art historians, too, have succumbed to the same pervasive but ill-defined feeling that there is some kind of structural parallel to be drawn between medieval music and architecture. In describing the relationship between the width of the window openings and that of the piers at Chartres (see fig. 20), John James writes of a 'contrapuntal positive–negative rhythm' running down the nave between piers and windows;[93] while Jean Bony, analysing the device of the sexpartite vault at Sens (*c.*1145–64), calls attention to the 'superimposed rhythms' that 'gave a sort of contrapuntal movement of large divisions overlying the faster pace of the suite of single bays'. Bony also describes what he sees as 'the systematic application of a simple numerical formula' at Sens, represented by

---

89 Harman,'Medieval and Early Renaissance Music', p. 70.
90 Ibid.
91 Wright, *Music and Ceremony*, pp. 289ff.
92 F. J. Smith, *Jacobi Leodiensis Speculum Musicae, A Commentary*, III, Henryville – Ottawa – Binningen (Institute of Medieval Music) 1983, pp. 20–1.
93 *Chartres*, p. 148.

the frequent recurrence of the number two. The basic unit of spatial division, he writes, is:

two bays coupled beneath a single vaulting unit ... In the upper stories, the perforations of the wall seem to multiply themselves irresistibly in series of twos and fours, the clerestory having been composed in its original state of a pair of windows in each of its panels, while the triforium – which carries the formula to a climax – becomes a sequence of two groups of two openings per bay and repeats that arrangement twice in the length of each double bay unit.[94]

Part of the interest of Bony's account of Sens is that it defines in some detail the complex organizational strategies that gave order and coherence to the interior spaces of the cathedral (fig. 25). But what are we to make of the fact that these and other, very similar strategies can be found – albeit with certain variations – not just at Sens but in other major churches of the period? At Laon, for example, begun around 1165, a vertical reading of the nave elevation shows the duple 'rhythm' of the tribune set against the faster 'threes' of the triforium arches above, while the basic 'tempo' of the whole structure is given by the single arches of the nave arcades, supported on massive columns (fig. 26). At Saint-Rémi in Reims, a building that 'speculates on rhythms and numbers', the external elevation confronts us with something resembling a musical theme and variations, 'three variants of the triplet, three ways of making groups of three openings. It is ... the number three which regulates the form of the screen of narrow arches separating ambulatory from chapels, and which in the tribunes determines the system of vaulting.'[95] Or think of Bourges (*c.*1195–1214; fig. 27), that most breathtakingly spacious of all the great Gothic cathedrals. Looking at the nave in longitudinal section, we are confronted with what appears to be a five-storey elevation; but this is an illusion. There is an 'inner' church and an 'outer' church: a church within a church, so to speak. It is the exaggerated height of the nave arches that allows us to see through them, past the line of the nave itself, as far as the inner walls of the side aisles. Because the articulation of the aisles imitates that of the nave itself, we interpret their three storeys as part of the same, multi-layered elevation. This illusion is reinforced by the way the motif of the triforium arches is repeated in the

---

94 Bony, *French Gothic Architecture*, p. 100.
95 Ibid., p. 147.

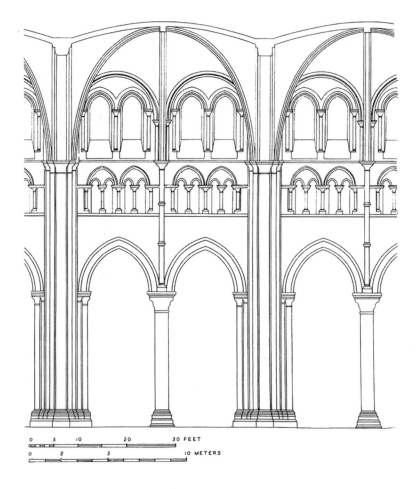

0 5 10   20   30 FEET

0   2   5   10 METERS

Figure 25. Reconstruction of Sens cathedral showing original state of nave elevation

elevations of the side aisles: what Bony calls an 'interplay between two similar sets of forms ... combined in a single overall pattern, like two voices ... following one another at a measured distance and repeating the same theme in two different registers. The unity of that contrapuntal structure overrules the sense of duality.'[96]

Affinities between architecture and music

The fact that modern writers on architecture so frequently draw analogies with music, even using musical terms as specific as 'rhythm', 'counterpoint' and 'fugue', should perhaps give us pause.

---

96 Ibid., pp. 212ff.

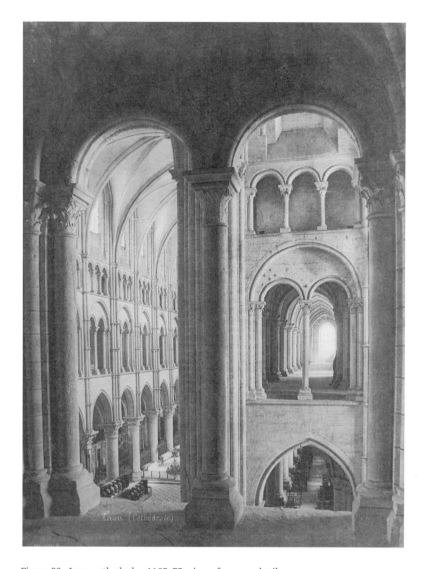

Figure 26. Laon cathedral, *c.*1165–75, view of nave and tribune

Are these just literary flourishes? Or is there, perhaps, some real point to such comparisons? By this I do not mean to imply that, in medieval times, the practice of music influenced the practice of architecture or vice versa. At least, there is no evidence to show that such influences occurred. But despite the obvious differences between their respective media, I think it is possible to recognize a certain affinity or kinship between the systems of spatial and structural organization employed by architects of the twelfth and

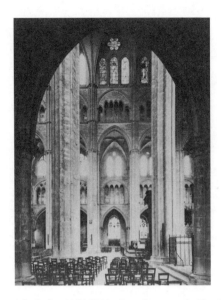

Figure 27. Bourges cathedral, *c*.1195–1214, view of nave and side aisles

thirteenth centuries and the methods of composition practised by
their musical counterparts. Consider, for example, the measures and
proportions of the buildings in question, to which repeated
reference has already been made.[97] I do not for one moment believe
that these proportional relationships were conceived or intended as
'consonances for the eye', as Simson suggests in writing about the
supposedly 'Augustinian' ratios found at Fontenay and elsewhere.[98]
What they *do* appear to show (and a good deal of supporting
evidence exists in the form of drawings and building records) is that
most of the great churches and cathedrals of the Gothic era were not
merely erected but also initially conceived 'from the ground up' –
that is, according to the exigencies imposed by the ground plan. It
was the ground plan that determined the articulation and division
of horizontal space – the relationship between the width of the nave
and its length, between the area of the crossing and the width of the
transepts, and so on – just as the strictly controlled but varying
rhythms of the tenor voice governed music's horizontal dimension:
its extension in time. The ground plan was not in itself ornate (no

97 I am conscious that Robert Suckale, in a valuable article, has argued cogently against drawing 'retrospective
conclusions' concerning any affinity or relationship between architecture and music simply from the
evidence provided by the use of modular or proportional systems of building; see 'La Théorie de
l'architecture au temps des cathédrales', in Roland Recht (ed.), *Les Bâtisseurs des cathédrales gothiques*,
Strasbourg (Éditions les Musées de la Ville de Strasbourg) 1989, p. 50. Compare, however, pp. 128–30 below
for texts by medieval writers on music, which appear to show that theorists at that time themselves thought
in such terms.

98 See above, pp. 104ff and n. [37].

one would think seriously about decorating the *plan* of a Gothic building, except perhaps in terms of the disposition of the side chapels, especially those around the apse), any more than the traditional chant borne by the tenor voice could be musically decorated, other than by forming it into more complex rhythmic patterns. Decoration, if it was to occur, was added *vertically*, in architecture as in music: in the springing of vaults, the use of tracery and the division of the upper storeys into smaller and more complex elements, each being given its particular kind of ornament whose relative complexity contrasted with the simple division of nave and aisles into larger and smaller bays.

However, just as in music the more complex rhythmic patterns given to the higher voices were often derived from those of the tenor, in architecture, too, the spatial articulation of the upper reaches of the building was in many cases dictated by the disposition of the lower columns or piers, which not only provided structural support but also gave the basic unit of measurement to the edifice as a whole. This can be seen in the anything but random proportions of the upper storeys – the clerestory, triforium and so on – and the use of subsidiary structural elements that are repeated according to what appears to be a standard module, like the twos and fours so clearly stated at Sens. Moreover, even the smallest decorative details (for example, parts of the tracery) are often found on closer examination to have been derived from larger structural forms. It is also intriguing to find that, after various experiments with four-storey elevations (as at Laon), from the second quarter of the thirteenth century onwards the most frequent model for the Gothic cathedral was based on three storeys. Perhaps it is merely coincidence that, in the same period, although musical writing in four parts certainly occurred (as in the case of Pérotin's two great *quadrupla*, mentioned earlier),[99] the most frequently encountered form of the polyphonic motet is likewise in three parts, with two more ornate and intricate voices – the *triplum* and the *motetus* – superimposed above the simpler and, in every case, slower melody of the tenor chant.

The role of architecture in medieval musical theory

In modern art-historical writing, analogies between medieval architecture and music have usually been, as suggested earlier, of a rather general kind. Among the few authors to have noticed that there was a more specific comparison to be drawn was Panofsky

---

99 See above, p. 117 and n. [72].

who, in his much-criticized essay *Gothic Architecture and Scholasticism*, commented on the multiplication and replication of standard measures and types of decoration in Gothic buildings.[100] In the same essay, he drew attention to the manner in which, in the case of the spoken or written word, the 'intellectual articulation of the subject matter implies the acoustic articulation of speech by recurrent phrases, and the visual articulation of the written page by rubrics, numbers and paragraphs'.[101] From this he concluded that a tendency towards more coherent systems of organization was one of the defining characteristics of Gothic generally and that the same tendency directly affected all the arts, music being no exception. He also likened music's exact and systematic division of time, reflected in the precisely measured note values indicated by the names breve, semibreve and so on, to the no less exact and systematic division of architectural space, although in the case of architecture he apparently had in mind the clear separation of what he called 'functional contexts' rather than any system of proportional relationships or 'musical ratios' of the kind Simson describes.

But while modern writers have tended to overlook this more precise form of analogy between Gothic architecture and the *musica mensurata* of the thirteenth and fourteenth centuries, it is clear from medieval writings on music that such analogies occurred naturally to at least some observers of the contemporary musical scene. For example, in the seventh and last book of his enormous treatise *Speculum musicae*, probably written in about 1330, the theorist Jacques de Liège turns his attention to topics such as discant and the introduction of mensural music. He also discusses how the composer should set about organizing the musical material at his disposal. Reaching for an architectural comparison in a way that suggests it would have been readily understood by his readers, Jacques remarks how the foundation of a building supports its other parts and how the elevation must be determined by the proportions of the ground plan, likening this to the pattern of the discant voice, which 'cannot be arbitrary' but must be in relation to the tenor:

For who can devise a discant without the tenor, who can construct a building without a foundation? And just as a building owes its proportions to [those of] the foundation, so that it should be constructed not at the whim of the craftsman but according to the exigencies of its

---

100 *Gothic Architecture and Scholasticism*, Cleveland/New York (Meridian Books) 2nd edn 1957, reprint 1966, pp. 48ff.
101 Ibid., pp. 38–9.

foundation, so too the discant should not be composed according to fancy, but must be determined by the exigencies and ratios of the notes of that same tenor part and should harmonize with these. Thus the discant depends upon the tenor, derives its proportions from it, and has to be in harmony not disharmony with it. The tenor is not derived from the discant, but the other way round.[102]

Musically, Jacques de Liège was a conservative. Part of his treatise is devoted to attacking the *ars nova* of his contemporary Jehan des Murs (to whom, ironically, the *Speculum musicae* was once attributed) and to praising the simpler, less affected musical styles of the past.[103] But similar analogies can also be found in the writings of others more in tune with the here-and-now of contemporary musical practice: theorists like Johannes de Grocheio, whom we met earlier in connection with the fearsome complexities of the polyphonic motet.[104] The content of his treatise *De musica* (late thirteenth century) is of particular interest because, rather than music conceived in an abstract sense or ancient harmonic theory, what Grocheio discusses is the music actually written and performed in the Paris of his own day.[105] In the case of motets, he observes that the tenor is composed first and then the upper voices: a point of obvious relevance to the foregoing discussion. (Franco of Cologne, in his *Ars cantus mensurabilis*, also remarks that, in the composition of a *conductus*, the tenor comes first – which is interesting since, as already noted, the *conductus* was the one form of music based solely on newly composed melodies, in which, therefore, the tenor was not derived from the established plainchant repertory.)[106] And, pointing to the derivation of the upper voices from the melody and rhythm of the tenor part, Grocheio, too, turns with apparent ease to architecture in search of a suitably vivid comparison. 'The tenor', he declares, 'is the part

---

102 'Quis enim sine tenore discantat, quis sine fundamento aedificat? Et sicut aedificium debet proportionari fundamento ut fiat aedificium non ad libitum operatoris sed secundum exigentiam fundamenti, sic nec discantans ad libitum suum notas proferre debet sed secundum exigentiam et proportionem notarum ipsius tenoris ut concordent cum illis. Discantus igitur a tenore dependet, ab eo regulari debet, cum ipso concordare habet, non discordare. Non tenor de discantu sumitur, sed e converso'; quoted after Roger Bragard (ed.), *Jacobus of Liège. Speculum Musicae* (*Corpus scriptorum de musica* no. 3), Rome (American Institute of Musicology) 1973, vol. 7, ch. 3 ('Unde dicitur discantus'), p. 9. A fragment of the same passage is quoted in a footnote by Simson, p. 191, n. 23 but without discussion or any clear indication of its context or source.

103 *Ars nova*, literally the 'new art'. Originally the title of a treatise of the early 1300s by Philippe de Vitry that describes a more flexible system of mensural notation, the term is often used to refer to fourteenth-century music as a whole. However, rhythmically more intricate music had already been provided for in late thirteenth-century treatises and reached new heights during the same period in the works of composers such as Petrus de Cruce.

104 See above, pp. 118ff.

105 For an account of Grocheio, who remains little studied, see *Grove*, vol. 9, pp. 664ff.; also Page 1997 (as n. [75] above); Schueller, *Idea of Music*, pp. 413ff.

106 See n. [66] above.

upon which all the others are founded, as the rooms of a house or edifice [rest] upon a foundation, and it regulates them and gives the stance, as bones do, to the other parts.'[107]

Music and architecture in paradise

Comparisons like these are found only occasionally in medieval writings on music, although the confidence with which they are employed suggests that, by the late Middle Ages, they formed part of an established tradition of discourse. The surviving evidence is now so scanty that we can no longer reconstruct with certainty the breadth of that tradition. However, it clearly extended to other areas of intellectual life such as literature and poetry. Consider, for example, the allusions to both music and architecture that occur repeatedly in Dante's *Divine Comedy*, especially in the *Paradiso*, where references to music are legion. In the sphere of Venus, Dante encounters two separate rounds of dancers, one slower and one faster. He compares their motion to a part song, in which one voice holds sustained notes while the other moves against it:

as two voices may be told apart
if one stays firm and one goes lower and higher;
so I saw lights circling within that light
at various speeds ...[108]

In her book *Music of the Spheres*, Kathi Meyer-Baer comments that what Dante describes in the *Paradiso* are evidently the forms of music of his own time.[109] She remarks on how, in the sphere of Mars, the poet hears a song without being able to understand its beautiful unity, like someone who, unaccustomed to hearing polyphony, cannot follow the texture of its parts.[110] This she interprets as an allusion to the polyphonic motet with its texts in different

---

107 'Tenor autem est illa pars, supra quam omnes aliae fundantur quemadmodum partes domus vel aedificii super suum fundamentum et eas regulat et eis dat quantitatem quemadmodum ossa partibus aliis', quoted after Page, 'Johannes de Grocheio' (as n. [75]), pp. 37–8; compare Ernst Rohloff, *Die Quellenhandschriften zum Musiktraktat des Johannes de Grocheio*, Leipzig (VEB Deutscher Verlag für Musik) 1972, p. 146. A complete English version of Grocheio's text, without commentary, can be found in Albert Seay (trans.), *Johannes de Grocheo. Concerning Music (De Musica)*, Colorado Springs (Colorado College Music Press, Translations no. 1) 1967.
108 *Paradiso*, VIII, 17–20. In quoting from Dante I have followed the John Ciardi translation: Dante Alighieri, *The Divine Comedy*, New York/London (W. W. Norton) 1970. The same passage (in a different translation) is quoted by Pirrotta who, like myself, believes there is parallel to be drawn between Dante's musical imagery and late thirteenth-century polyphony of the Parisian school; see 'Dante *Musicus*: Gothicism, Scholasticism, and Music', in Nino Pirrotta, *Music and Culture in Italy from the Middle Ages to the Baroque*, Cambridge, MA/London (Harvard U. P.) 1984, pp. 23ff.
109 Meyer-Baer 1970, pp. 125ff., 127.
110 'So from that choir of glories I heard swell/So sweet a melody that I stood tranced/Though what hymn they were singing, I could not tell' (*Paradiso* XIV, 121–3).

languages, which remained one of the dominant musical genres of the fourteenth century and survived even into the fifteenth. She also stresses that, for Dante, the two highest heavens are filled with nothing but motion, sweet singing and, above all, light, as if he were being 'guided through a grandiose building full of light and splendor'. Since the utilization of light, made possible by often vast expanses of stained glass, was – just as much as height – one of the defining characteristics of French Gothic architecture, she argues that those vivid passages in which the poet's experience of light is conjoined with that of music may have been inspired by Dante's memories of France. Other details in the *Paradiso*, she thinks, may owe their origin to French cathedrals. 'If', she writes, 'it is true that Dante had studied in Paris ... could not the sculpture of the orders of angels and the music-making Elders on the portals of Chartres and the stained-glass paintings of the rose windows have given him the inspiration for his description of paradise with circles of angels and the court of the saints in the heavenly rose?'[111]

Whether Dante actually visited Paris now seems impossible to ascertain. William Anderson's biography of the poet notes merely that the 'weight of modern opinion' is against the probability of his having done so and similar remarks can be found in other, more recent publications.[112] Nevertheless, an old tradition that Dante studied in Paris can be traced as far back as Boccaccio and Villani, and what the *Enciclopedia Dantesca* calls 'a good knowledge on Dante's part of the Parisian university world' seems to be reflected by various details in the *Paradiso* – for example, the placing of Thomas Aquinas and Albertus Magnus, both associated with the University of Paris, amongst the first garland of souls.[113] Other allusions suggest, if not an actual stay in France, then at least a certain familiarity with Parisian life and customs, as when, in *Purgatorio* XI, Dante encounters the illuminator Oderisi and tells him that, in Paris, the verb used to describe his art is *alluminar*.[114] But perhaps the most persuasive touch of all is to be found in the *Inferno*, where the poet likens a stone wall that crosses the burning sand to the 'great dikes', which:

---

111 Meyer-Baer 1970, p. 128.
112 William Anderson, *Dante the Maker*, London (Routledge & Kegan Paul) 1980, p. 160. For a more extreme view, compare Zygmunt G. Baranski, *Dante e i segni. Saggi per una storia intellettuale di Dante Alighieri*, Naples (Liguori) 2000, p. 19, who dismisses Dante's visit to Paris as 'invented'.
113 'una buona conoscenza da parte di D[ante] del mondo universitario parigiano ...'; see the entry 'Parigi' in U. Bosco (ed.), *Enciclopedia Dantesca*, Rome (Istituto dell'Enciclopedia Italiana fondata da Giovanni Treccani) 1973, vol. 4, p. 306.
114 'Aren't you Od'risi?' I said. 'He who was known as the honor of Agobbio, and of that art Parisians call *illumination*?' (*Purgatorio* XI, 79–81).

*the Flemings in the lowland between Bruges
and Wissant, under constant threat of the sea,
erect ... to hold back the deluge.*[115]

Could Dante really have conjured up so striking an image, had he not been to the Low Countries himself to see these things? But if he did undertake such a journey, he would surely have stopped in Paris *en route*, given all the other circumstantial details that seem to point to such a visit. While the imposing space and light of the great Parisian Gothic churches like Notre Dame could scarcely have failed to impress the awe-struck visitor, Dante may also have noticed a certain similarity between this architectural setting and the music performed there. That music would certainly have included not only traditional plainchant but also examples of the new polyphony, which now played an increasingly important role in the context of the liturgy. As we have seen, one distinctive feature of motets and other forms of polyphonic writing was that they usually incorporated more florid upper parts whose structure was partly determined by the simpler melody and rhythm of the tenor chant. To a mind as acute as Dante's, would it not have been obvious that Gothic architecture was likewise conceived in terms of a succession of carefully contrived modular relationships, expressed not just horizontally but also vertically, the more intricate of these being encountered not at the lower levels of the building but in the upper reaches of the façade or nave elevation?

That Dante was indeed struck by just such similarities, even to the extent of drawing deliberate parallels between these two forms of art, is suggested by several passages that appear in the final cantos of the *Paradiso*. To take a single example: in his upward progress from one heavenly sphere to the next (the fact that it is an ascent – in other words, the vertical aspect of the poet's journey – is repeatedly stressed) he is met with music of various kinds. In the lower regions, this consists merely of a single, slowly moving voice line. As he moves higher, several voices are heard, singing simultaneously, while the rapidity of their motion increases. Here, for the first time, choral as well as solo singing is heard; but, in the still higher sphere of the Sun, it is evident that the music sung by the revolving dancers is now polyphonic, comprising several simultaneous melodies:

---

115 *Inferno*, XV, 4–6. I am grateful to my colleague Jonathan White of the Literature Department at Essex University for drawing my attention to these details.

I saw that wheel of glories start
and chime from voice to voice in harmonies
so sweetly joined, so true from part to part ...[116]

Dante's memorable description of the celestial edifice and its ascending spheres, complete with ever more intricate forms of musical accompaniment, may owe more than hitherto acknowledged to his encounter with the new art of Paris – that is, assuming that such an encounter really occurred. But, as Pirrotta points out, it would not have been essential for Dante to visit Paris in order to be aware of new musical styles. Even if his Parisian sojourn is an invention, as modern writers have claimed, there existed a native school of polyphony that arose in Italy during the late Middle Ages, seemingly independent of ultramontane musical influences.[117] Significantly, what we know of such polyphony derives largely from descriptions of music and musical forms to be found in contemporary treatises on poetry, among them Dante's own *De vulgari eloquentia* of *c*.1306.[118] In either case, Paris or no, those 'deep and hardly recoverable patterns of thought' manifested by various forms of medieval art begin to seem slightly more recoverable when we realize that, in sketching before the mind's eye the architecture of paradise, Dante was perhaps forging an analogy with the new music that flourished in Europe during the half century before the *Divine Comedy* was written. The fact that similar analogies can be found in the writings of musical theorists at that time suggests they may have played a significant part in thinking about medieval art and architecture more generally – even if the men who actually created the great Gothic cathedrals left behind them, other than the buildings themselves, so little trace of their deliberations.

---

116 *Paradiso*, X, 145–7.
117 In the same context, Pirrotta draws attention to examples of French motets that are included in a Florentine *laudario* of this period; see 'Dante *Musicus* ...', p. 24.
118 See Michael Long, 'Trecento Italy', in McKinnon 1990, pp. 246ff.

IV DIVINE HARMONIES

The very same numbers that cause sounds to have that concinnitas, *pleasing to the ears, can also fill the eyes and mind with wondrous delight. From musicians therefore who have already examined such numbers thoroughly, or from those objects in which Nature has displayed some evident and noble quality, the whole method of outlining* [finitio] *is derived ...*

Alberti, *On the Art of Building* (1452)

The principles of Gothic building had been based upon a considerable fund of first-hand experience, most of it transmitted from one generation to another by word of mouth. But, as we saw in the previous chapter, if that knowledge had its counterpart in abstract speculation, we know little or nothing about it.[1] Most records of artistic activity that survive from the Middle Ages are of a stubbornly practical kind. Documents detailing the deliberations of cathedral chapters or the doings of some of the larger medieval workshops usually reflect mundane preoccupations such as the supply of materials, contracts of employment and attempts to raise money. By contrast with the formidable quantity of medieval writing about music, it seems that medieval architects made little attempt to propagate or preserve in written form theories about their art. As James Ackermann has observed, the desire to formulate and spread a doctrine of architecture is 'to a degree, a sign of the Renaissance'.[2] In essence, the same is true of painting and all forms of visual art.[3]

In the Renaissance – by which, in this context, I mean that flowering of the arts and sciences that occurred in Italy during the fifteenth and sixteenth centuries – the situation is quite different: there is almost too much writing about art. This sudden proliferation of literary activity is partly accounted for by the rapid growth of printing, which had swept aside many of the

---

1 Modern historians frequently remark on the absence of theory in Gothic architecture. See, for example, the study by Dieter Kimpel and Robert Suckale, *Die gotische Architektur in Frankreich 1130–1270*, Munich (Hirmer) 1985, p. 144. Here, the authors observe that, while a few medieval clerics may have known their Vitruvius, there is no evidence that his precepts were utilized in practice: 'There were methods and principles, but these existed independently of any theoretical superstructure and were applied unsystematically and inconsistently throughout the period under discussion.'

2 James S. Ackermann, '"Ars Sine Scientia Nihil Est": Gothic Theory of Architecture at the Cathedral of Milan', *Art Bulletin*, vol. 31 (1949), pp. 84–111, reprinted and updated in idem, *Distance Points. Essays in Theory and Renaissance Art and Architecture*, Cambridge, MA/London (MIT Press) 1991, p. 212.

3 In his *Art and Beauty in the Middle Ages* (New Haven/London, 1986), Umberto Eco devotes a brief section (pp. 100–2) to what he calls medieval treatises on art, of which the most significant is the eleventh-century *Schedula diversarum artium* by Theophilus; see Theophilus, *De diversis artibus*, ed. and trans. by C. R. Dodwell (London, 1961). These, however, are for the most part either collections of technical precepts or theological reflections on the place in God's universe assigned to the beauties of nature on the one hand, to man-made (allegorical or symbolic) images on the other.

obstacles to disseminating more widely a particular body of ideas. Now, architects like Alberti and Palladio addressed themselves to not only their patrons but to the world at large by means of the formal treatise: in Palladio's case, the *Four Books on Architecture* (1570), Alberti, still more of a polymath, wrote an important text on each of the major arts: painting, sculpture and architecture. Leonardo evidently intended to publish a treatise on painting but in the end bequeathed to posterity only a mass of disconnected notes on a bewildering variety of subjects.[4] Raphael and Michelangelo, by contrast, turned to the medium of writing in order to express themselves not in theoretical propositions but in poetic form.

Some artists, of course, remained silent about their opinions or intentions; but when they did, there was no shortage of other writers to fill the gap. There were theorists such as the mathematician and friend of Leonardo, Luca Pacioli, who published a treatise on 'divine' proportion. There were chroniclers of artistic events like Vasari, who transmitted much essential information about the most celebrated artists of his time. There were scholars and humanists, too: men like Daniele Barbaro, patriarch-elect of Aquilea and a staunch friend and patron of Palladio, to whom the sixteenth century owed a new, comprehensively annotated edition of Vitruvius' *Ten Books*. And there were other, more shadowy figures such as the Dominican friar Francesco Colonna, whose misdemeanours (which included making an unsubstantiated allegation of sodomy against four other members of his order) caused him to be banished from his monastery of SS. Giovanni e Paolo in Venice and denied the right to say mass or hear confession. But if his failings were larger than life, he also seems to have possessed other, more positive qualities. In particular, most historians now ascribe to Colonna one of the most remarkable pieces of writing of the entire Renaissance: the *Hypnerotomachia Poliphili* (*The Strife of Love in a Dream* or *Dream of Poliphilus*), an architectural fantasy *all'antica* in which erotic visions, the symbolic meanings of the classical orders and references to the affective powers of music are interwoven like threads in some bizarre but colourful tapestry.[5]

---

4. On the status of Leonardo's surviving manuscripts and the fate of his projected *Treatise on Painting*, of which only a fragment of the original survives, see *The Literary Works of Leonardo da Vinci. Compiled and Edited from the Original Manuscripts by Jean Paul Richter*, London (Phaidon), 3rd edn 1970 (cited hereafter as Richter 1970), vol. 1, pp. xi ff.; also the introduction to Martin Kemp (ed.), *Leonardo on Painting*, New Haven/London (Yale U. P.) 1989.

5. On the attribution of the text to Colonna as well as the sometimes lurid details of his life see Francesco Colonna, *Hypnerotomachia Poliphili. The Strife of Love in a Dream. The Entire Text translated for the First Time into English with an Introduction by Joscelyn Godwin*, London (Thames & Hudson) 1999, esp. pp. xiv–xv. For a divergent opinion as to the author of the text see Liane Lefaivre, *Leon Battista Alberti's Hypnerotomachia Poliphili. Recognizing the Architectural Body in the Early Italian Renaissance*, Cambridge, MA/London (MIT Press) 1997.

The liberal and the mechanical arts

From this wealth of writing emerge several recurrent themes that bear directly on the relationship – real or imagined – between music and the visual arts. First, there is the question of the relative status of different forms of art. If this had been a matter for discussion in medieval times – if, on occasion, visual artists had sought to rise above their relatively lowly position by professing more sophisticated intellectual or theoretical concerns – we have scant evidence of it.[6] Nevertheless, the problem of status had, in a sense, been inherited from the Middle Ages, along with the schema of what were called the 'seven liberal arts': astronomy, geometry, arithmetic, music, grammar, logic or dialectic and rhetoric. As is clear from this list, most of these were not 'art' – at least, not as we would understand the term today. Moreover, in order to grasp what was meant by 'liberal' we must go back to classical authors like Seneca who, in identifying what he called the *studia liberalia*, had sought to define those mental pursuits worthy of free men, 'liberated' from any preoccupation with practical use or earning a living.[7] Not all sources agree on the exact nature of these pursuits, nor even how many of them there were. The Roman writer Varro (116–27 BC) arrived at the figure of nine liberal arts by including in his definition both architecture and medicine, while as late as the twelfth century Honorius of Autun (Honorius Augustodunensis), in his *De animae exsilio et patria*, names physics (here meaning medicine), mechanics and economics as the eighth, ninth and tenth liberal arts.[8] But by medieval times it had become largely even if not universally accepted that the liberal arts indeed numbered only seven. These were further divided into the *trivium*, which embraced the verbal arts of grammar, logic or dialectic and rhetoric, and the *quadrivium*, comprising the four mathematical arts: astronomy, geometry, arithmetic and music.[9]

Perhaps the clearest exposition of their nature and properties can be found in a famous allegorical text of the early fifth century AD,

---

6 Concerning the aspirations of medieval architects to be seen as geometers, geometry being regarded as a superior form of mental attainment, see Robert Suckale, 'La Théorie de l'architecture au temps des cathédrales', in Roland Recht (ed.), *Les Bâtisseurs des cathédrales gothiques*, Strasbourg (Éditions les Musées de la Ville de Strasbourg) 1989, p. 48 and n. 50 for further refs.

7 *Ad Lucilium epistulae morales*, trans. R. M. Gummere, London (Heinemann: Loeb Classical Library), 3 vols, 1917–25: 90.13. In this, Seneca was doing little more than echoing Aristotle, who denied the epithet 'liberal' to any activity undertaken for the sake of material reward, dismissing as vulgar 'all such arts as deteriorate the condition of the body and also the industries that earn wages; for they make the mind preoccupied and degraded' (*Politics* 1337b); see also Elspeth Whitney, 'Paradise Restored. The Mechanical Arts from Antiquity through the Thirteenth Century', *Transactions of the American Philosophical Society*, vol. 80, pt 1 (1990), p. 26.

8 Ibid., p. 61. Whitney also notes that 'medicine, gymnastics, agriculture, mechanics, navigation and, sometimes, painting' could also be regarded as in some sense liberal because, like the fully fledged liberal arts, they had 'virtue or intellectual wisdom as their end'. ('Paradise Restored', p. 43.)

9 The first writer to allude specifically to the mathematical arts as the *quadrivium* appears to have been Boethius; see Boethius, *De arithmetica*, I, 2. Compare Richard Johnson, 'The Allegory and the Trivium', in *The Quadrivium of Martianus Capella* (as following note), pp. 92ff.

De nuptiis Philologiae et Mercurii et de septem artibus liberalibus libri novem (The Marriage of Philology and Mercury and the Seven Liberal Arts) by the Carthaginian writer Martianus Capella.[10] This tale, in some ways resembling Cicero's *Dream of Scipio*, exerted a powerful grip on the medieval mind. Nearly five hundred years after it was written, post-Carolingian writers still alluded to *De nuptiis* in such a way as to make clear that every educated person was expected to know it.[11] It tells the story of Mercury's courtship of and marriage to Philologia. Having, like Scipio, traversed the celestial spheres, the happy couple celebrate their nuptials, in the course of which the seven liberal arts in the guise of bridesmaids put in an appearance, each being described and personified in turn and at considerable length.[12] Last to appear, in the place of honour, is Harmony, 'the one bridesmaid who is the particular darling of the heavens'. Architecture and medicine, by contrast, who had been 'standing by, among those ... prepared to perform', are told that, in order to hasten the proceedings, their services are no longer required. Apollo is heard to remark disparagingly that 'since these ladies are concerned with mortal subjects and their skill lies in mundane matters, it will not be inappropriate to disdain and reject them'.[13]

It is worth noting that, in this account of the celestial realm, it is now the nine Muses who turn the spheres and make them emit different sounds – a variant upon Plato's myth of Er, in which this task was performed by Sirens.[14] (By adding the sphere of the earth, which does not rotate and which emits no sound, Martianus also increases the number of spheres – traditionally eight – to nine, in order to match that of the Muses.) Urania, their leader, turns the outermost sphere of the fixed stars, which revolves fastest and has the highest pitch. The text does not say whether the perfect harmonies of the spheres and of the Muses' song are the same and circumvents the problem of identifying the nine Muses, the eight spheres and the seven liberal arts with exact musical intervals. That it manages to avoid getting bogged down in such *minutiae* may, it has been suggested, have had something to do with its subsequent popularity.[15]

---

10 See *Martianus Capella and the Seven Liberal Arts*, I: *The Quadrivium of Martianus Capella*, by William Harris Stahl, Richard Johnson and E. L. Burge, New York/London (Columbia U. P.) 1971 (commentary) and II: *The Marriage of Philology and Mercury*, New York (Columbia U. P.) 1977 (translation). On the significance of the *Marriage of Philology and Mercury* see further Meyer-Baer, *Music of the Spheres*, pp. 33–5; also Schueller, *Idea of Music*, pp. 258ff.

11 For example, by Regino of Prüm (d.915 AD) in his *Epistola de harmonica institutione* addressed to Archbishop Rathbod of Treves; for partial translation see Meyer-Baer, *Music of the Spheres*, pp. 349ff.

12 The seven liberal arts, as they appear in Martianus's allegory, are usually referred to as bridesmaids, but as Stahl points out they are really handmaidens presented by Mercury to his bride, in other words a form of dowry. (*The Quadrivium of Martianus Capella*, p. 24.)

13 *Marriage of Philology and Mercury*, p. 346.

14 For discussion of both Plato's myth of Er and Cicero's *Dream of Scipio* see above, ch. 2, pp. 81ff.

15 Meyer-Baer, op. cit., p. 35.

Equally striking is the fact that architecture, which Varro had been prepared to add to the number of the liberal arts, is here dismissed with the epithets 'mortal' and 'mundane'. Nor was there any place for painting and sculpture, which were not usually ranked among the liberal arts at all. (Although a number of antique authors had written approvingly about painting, Seneca specifically *excluded* painters from the company of liberal artists, along with parfumiers, cooks and all who create 'aids to luxury'.) In failing even to mention them, Martianus was thus merely following classical precedent.[16]

The worth of painting

Attitudes like these, which had been passed down from Classical antiquity via the Middle Ages, profoundly influenced Renaissance thinking about the nature and purpose of the visual arts. There was no denying that painting and sculpture were usually practised for money: something that constituted, at least in the eyes of some writers, a considerable disadvantage. Moreover, both these arts were often regarded as merely the products of eye and hand rather than of the faculties of judgement or intellect. Despite claims made by theorists like Alberti, who argued strenuously for the intellectual worth of painting, it was difficult for visual artists to escape the opprobrium that attached to merely manual labour – the 'mechanical' aspect of their profession.[17] In his *Tractato di pictura*, published in Rome in 1509, Francesco Lancilotti tells of a vision of a lady, Painting, who complains about not being included among the seven liberal arts. In her lament, couched in poetic metre, *la profondissima Pittura* castigates the ignorance of those who

... know not who I am, wretched mortals!
I who can enable him who loves and follows me
With unbounded power to soar without wings
Even unto heaven. He who calls my art mechanical
Let him read on, and he will see ...[18]

---

16 *Ad Lucilium* 88.18; Whitney, p. 26.

17 In his *Book of the Courtier* (*Il Cortigiano*), Baldassare Castiglione refers to the arts of drawing and painting as things which 'nowadays ... may appear mechanical and hardly suited to a gentleman'; quoted after Francis Ames-Lewis, *The Intellectual Life of the Early Renaissance Artist*, New Haven/London (Yale U. P.) 2000, p. 1. Castiglione's remarks may have had more to do with the social standing of the artist than with his claims to intellectual worth; elsewhere, he describes painting as a 'most worthy and noble art', remarking that 'anyone who does not esteem the art of painting seems to me quite wrong-headed'.

18 Richter 1970, p. 21 (author's translation). By the same token, it was (according to Vasari) precisely Lorenzo de' Medici's intention in taking Michelangelo under his protection to produce artists of superior *ingegno*, more remote from what is termed *ogni cosa meccanica*; see John Onians, 'On How to Listen to High Renaissance Art', *Art History*, vol. 7, no. 4 (December 1984), p. 427. The term *ingegno*, which in some contexts might be translated as either 'intellect' or 'ingenuity', is here perhaps best rendered as 'power of invention'.

Pomponius Gauricus raised a similar objection on behalf of sculpture, claiming for it, rather than painting, a place as 'eighth sister' alongside the seven liberal arts.[19] Leonardo, on the other hand, decried sculpture, which he described as an 'extremely mechanical operation, generally accompanied by great sweat which mingles with dust'. In his so-called *Paragone*, where Leonardo embarks on a detailed comparison between the arts, he contrasts the sculptor 'plastered and powdered all over with marble dust, which makes him look like a baker' (what more hideous insult could be imagined?) with the painter – clearly an allusion to himself – who

sits before his work at the greatest of ease, well dressed and applying delicate colour with his light brush ... He often enjoys the accompaniment of music or the company of authors of various fine works that can be heard with great pleasure without the crashing of hammers or other confused noises.[20]

This, in the context of what was sometimes a bitter rivalry between advocates of different forms of art, was one possible strategy. One could distance oneself from the 'mechanical' aspect of one's calling, in this instance simply by suggesting that painting (by contrast with sculpture or architecture) was scarcely a manual occupation at all. But if the idea was to claim a more exalted status not just for painting but for the visual arts generally, then another way of helping them – as Vasari put it – to 'rise suddenly and free themselves of knavery and beastliness'[21] was to point to their supposed affinities with music, which had long since enjoyed an unquestioned place among the liberal arts, as a respected member of the *quadrivium*.

Music as a model worthy of emulation

In this context, we should also remind ourselves that the term 'music' had a rather special meaning, at least for those writers who insisted on comparing the supposed merits and defects of the different arts.

---

19 *De sculptura* (Venice, 1499), cited after Onians (as preceding note), p. 413.
20 Quoted after Kemp, *Leonardo on Painting*, pp. 38–9. Leonardo's description of the sculptor 'looking like a baker' is probably a jibe at Michelangelo; for another example of the animosity between them, compare Michelangelo's letter to the historian Benedetto Varchi dated 1549 in which he writes disparagingly of Leonardo: 'He who wrote that painting was nobler than sculpture, if he understood as much about the other subjects on which he wrote, my servant could have done better'; the original quoted in Paola Barocchi (ed.), *Trattati d'arte del cinquecento fra Manierismo e Controriforma* (3 vols), vol. 1, Bari (Laterza) 1960, p. 82.
21 ' ... uscir un tratto fuori della furfanteria e delle bestiacce'; letter dated 9 May 1566 to Don Vincenzio Borghini, in *Le opere di Giorgio Vasari, tomo viii, scritti minori*, Florence (G. C. Sansoni) 1882, p. 405. There must surely be a better rendering of *bestiacce* than 'beastliness', which is Richter's suggestion, but 'bestiality', which springs to mind as another possibility, likewise seems somewhat wide of the mark (and perhaps also conjures up the wrong associations).

In most cases, it had precious little to do with the 'sensual impact of lived music experience' or with that abundant flowering of musical life that graced the churches and courts of Renaissance Italy. Instead, 'music' – quadrivial music, that is – meant in essence that same abstract, harmonic science to which antique theorists had devoted so much attention and which medieval authors assigned to the same category as astronomy, arithmetic and geometry because all these 'arts' (we would call them sciences) led the mind to an understanding of quantity. The teachings of Pythagoras, the dialogues of Plato (especially the *Timaeus*, now increasingly studied in the translation by Marsilio Ficino) and, above all, the *De musica* of Boethius were still the principal sources on which Renaissance thinking about this more abstract kind of music depended. The influence of some of these writings is apparent, for example, in the treatises of Franchino Gaffurio, choirmaster at Milan cathedral and a distinguished theorist and composer, whom we met in Chapter 2 in connection with Raphael's *School of Athens* (see pls. 3, 4).[22] Gaffurio's *Theorica musice* (The Theory of Music) of 1492 is indebted to Boethius in a variety of ways. Not only is it divided into five books, like Boethius' account of musical theory, but also – again like Boethius – Gaffurio views music not primarily as an art but as a science: the science of harmonics.[23] Tellingly, the first illustration in his later treatise *De harmonia musicorum instrumentorum opus*, published in 1518, shows Gaffurio himself seated in a *cathedra* lecturing to his students. On his right are three organ pipes of differing lengths, on his left three strings (fig. 28). The dimensions of both strings and pipes are clearly indicated, 3:4:6: the interval of the octave, divided by the harmonic mean, thereby producing the two other primary consonances, the fifth and the fourth.[24] Next to the strings is placed a pair of dividers. The intended meaning of this image is unambiguous: music is to be regarded as synonymous with number and ratio.

Leonardo and music

Gaffurio, Pacioli and Leonardo were all in Milan during the last years of the fifteenth century. Leonardo was active in the service of the Milanese court, Pacioli was giving lectures on mathematics and Gaffurio's duties as *maestro di cappella* at the cathedral would also

---

22 See above, ch. 2, pp. 72–5.
23 See Franchino Gaffurio, *The Theory of Music*. Translated, with Introduction and Notes, by Walter Kurt Kreyszig. Edited by Claude V. Palisca, New Haven/London (Yale U.P) 1993; also Claude V. Palisca, *Humanism in Italian Renaissance Musical Thought*, New Haven/London (Yale U.P) 1985, esp. pp. 161, 166ff. for a detailed analysis of Gaffurio's sources.
24 On the arithmetic, geometric and harmonic means see below, pp. 152ff.

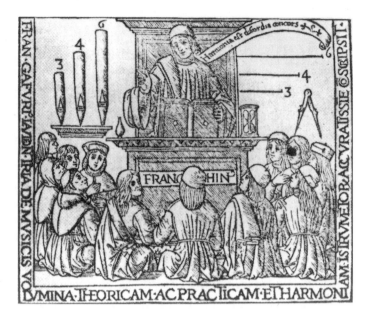

Figure 28. Franchino Gaffurio, *De harmonia musicorum instrumentorum opus*, Milan (da Ponte) 1518, first illustration showing Gaffurio lecturing

have included a fair amount of teaching.[25] Both he and Pacioli probably influenced Leonardo's ideas about music and number expressed in the following well-known extract from the *Paragone*, where the artist not only demands equal treatment for both music and painting but also refers specifically to what he terms the 'proportionality' of the latter:

Music can only be called the sister of painting, being dependent upon hearing, a sense second only to sight. Harmony is created by the conjunction of its proportional parts, which are sounded simultaneously, being conjured up or dying away at one or more harmonic intervals. These intervals delimit the proportions out of which such harmony is composed, in the same way that human beauty is derived from the contours of the limbs. But painting excels and surpasses music, because it does not perish as soon as it has been created, which is music's misfortune ...

---

25 For a document of 1493 alluding specifically to Gaffurio's lectures see Palisca, *Humanism*, p. 8; also P. O. Kristeller, 'Music and Learning in the Early Italian Renaissance', *Journal of Renaissance and Baroque Music*, vol. 1 (1947), pp. 255ff. It is thought that Gaffurio may have occupied a chair at the University of Pavia, but this was probably only a grace and favour appointment.

[moreover,] the painter's work endures for many years, and is of such excellence that it keeps alive the harmony of its constituent parts, which nature, despite her powers, is not able to preserve ... Therefore, since you have placed music among the liberal arts, either you must put painting there or else remove music.[26]

Threatening to eject music from the *quadrivium* unless painting were admitted might seem somewhat brutal. A subtler way of proceeding would be to claim equal status for the visual arts on the grounds that they were, in one way or another, actually *like* music. For such a claim to be convincing it was necessary to show that their resources were in essence the same – or at least, since music's exalted position derived principally from its identification with number and proportion, that the other arts had a similarly mathematical basis. This seems to be precisely what Leonardo is seeking to do in respect of painting. His various notes are, as already remarked, incomplete or disorganized and his ideas are sometimes repeated in different guises or in different contexts. But it is noticeable how much attention he pays to the question of the mathematical basis of pictorial composition, including the recently devised method of perspectival construction. This was a topic that had already been discussed by other writers, Alberti and Piero della Francesca among them. Their concerns were, however, different in certain respects from Leonardo's and from each other's. Alberti was preoccupied with a form of pictorial realism and the demand that objects in a picture should appear 'like real objects'.[27] The rules and proportions he enumerates in his treatise on painting were all intended to serve the same purpose: namely, the elucidation of his system for representing objects as they exist in three-dimensional space. Piero, like Leonardo, was interested in the mathematical basis of perspective and in the canon of proportion that governs the relationship between figures seen from different viewpoints and at various distances. Both he and Leonardo evidently concluded that figures placed at equal

---

26 *Leonardo on Painting*, pp. 34ff., 37.

27 It has been argued not only that the structure of Alberti's *De pictura* reveals a knowledge of classical precepts concerning the art of rhetoric, but also that Alberti believed painting capable of moving and persuading the viewer in accordance with the same precepts. If this were the case, it would be entirely consonant with the aim of raising the status of painting since rhetoric, like music, enjoyed an unquestioned place among the liberal arts. See John R. Spencer, 'Ut Rhetorica Pictura. A Study in Quattrocento Theory of Painting', *Journal of the Warburg and Courtauld Institutes*, vol. 20 (1957), pp. 26–44, also Thomas Puttfarken, *The Discovery of Pictorial Composition. Theories of Visual Order in Painting, 1400–1800*, New Haven/London (Yale U. P.) 2000, pp. 55ff.

distances upon a perspective grid diminish in size in a way that could be expressed as a succession of simple fractions: three-quarters, two-thirds, one half. But, while they arrived at very similar conclusions, it was Leonardo who stressed the coincidence between these mathematical ratios and the harmonic proportions that underlay the primary musical consonances. In a manuscript of around 1492, he wrote:

I grade the things before the eye as the musician grades the sounds that meet his ear ... I shall make my rule for distances ... as the musician has done for sounds; because, although all these are in fact linked and touch upon one another, he has fixed intervals from tone to tone, has called them first, second, third, fourth, fifth and has thus named, from step to step, the variety of higher and lower tones.[28]

This passage, somewhat obscure in its language but which is cited in almost every book on Leonardo, has caused scholars some difficulty. Martin Kemp, who in his monograph *The Science of Art* scrutinizes the artist's ideas on perspective in some detail, remarks in this connection only that such systems of proportional diminution convinced Leonardo that he was 'dealing with a form of visual harmonics in which the perspectivist forms his "intervals" in the way the musician does with his notes'.[29] Emanuel Winternitz, who devoted several detailed studies to Leonardo's relationship with music, specifically associates the artist's description of 'objects as they confront the eye in a continuous receding row or chain' with the 'musical tones that, by their numerical ratios ... form a scale'.[30] While conceding that the 'mathematical rationalization of pitch values' was 'commonplace in Leonardo's day', Winternitz describes this comparison between the ratios that determine the intervals of the musical scale and Leonardo's account of perspective as 'farfetched'. Instead, he argues that references to the 'proportionality' of both music and painting may point not to those arithmetical proportions on which musical harmony is based but to the potential dividing up of *time* (that is, the durational aspect of music) according to certain precise ratios.[31]

---

28 MS 2038, quoted after Thomas Brachert, 'A Musical Canon of Proportion in Leonardo da Vinci's *Last Supper*', *Art Bulletin*, vol. 53 (1971), p. 461; the same passage is cited in Rudolf Wittkower, 'Brunelleschi and "Proportion in Perspective"', *Journal of the Warburg and Courtauld Institutes*, vol. 16 (1953), p. 286 and n. 4. Wittkower also draws attention to the fact that the fractions $\frac{1}{2}$, $\frac{1}{4}$, $\frac{1}{3}$ represent a 'harmonic' progression.

29 Martin Kemp, *The Science of Art. Optical Themes in Western Art from Brunelleschi to Seurat*, New Haven/London (Yale U. P.) 1990, p. 46.

30 Emanuel Winternitz, 'The Role of Music in Leonardo's Paragone', in Maurice Natanson (ed.), *Phenomenology and Social Reality. Essays in Memory of Alfred Schutz*, The Hague (Martinus Nijhoff) 1970, p. 285.

I do not find this argument convincing. Indeed, Winternitz himself, in a subsequent reworking of his earlier writings on Leonardo and music, entered his own caveat, remarking that whereas contemporary musical treatises were full of references to numerical ratios between tones of different pitch, 'no treatise on Music of Leonardo's day developed the notion of musical form as a balance between the parts of a composition'.[32] (This is not strictly true: the *Practica musice* by Gaffurio contains perhaps the most thorough discussion of musical proportion to be found in any Renaissance treatise, including mensural proportion, featuring among its musical examples the use of isometre, a principle probably derived from the isorhythms employed by medieval composers.)[33] But, rather than posing insuperable difficulties, the above-quoted passage from the *Paragone* surely points to something quite straightforward. As already remarked, figures of equal size placed at successive intersections of Alberti's monocular perspectival grid, if seen from a central viewpoint, appear to diminish in size in a way that can be expressed as a series of simple fractions. Leonardo, with his scientific and mathematical turn of mind, had merely noticed that these fractions – one half, two-thirds, three-quarters – were the same as those from which the primary consonances (the octave, the fifth and the fourth) were derived.[34] Arguably, it is in this sense that his otherwise puzzling reference to the 'harmony of those proportional parts' that distinguished both music and painting is to be understood.

Determining how – or whether – these kinds of 'musical' principles might have affected the actual practice of painting is less straightforward. For example, it has often been said that Leonardo himself employed a 'musical canon of proportion' in the design of his *Last Supper* (pl. 6), perhaps the most famous of all Renaissance murals which, now heavily restored, can still be seen on the wall of the refectory of the convent of S. Maria delle Grazie in Milan.[35] The complex analysis of the fresco proposed by Thomas Brachert appears to show the artist consistently exploiting an elaborate

31 Winternitz bases his argument not upon the *Paragone* but upon a passage from a Leonardo manuscript (BM Arundel 263, 1736: 'if the line is infinitely divisible, so is the section of time resulting from such division ...'); see 'The Role of Music...', p. 294. Note that Pacioli, whose remarks often appear to echo those of Leonardo, in his *De divina proportione* also compares perspective, which uses 'natural number according to any definition and measure as represented by the line of sight', with music, which 'employs heard number and measure *as expressed in the time of its continuances* ...' (my italics; cited after Onians, 'On How to Listen to High Renaissance Art', p. 413).
32 Emanuel Winternitz, *Leonardo da Vinci as a Musician*, New Haven/London (Yale U. P.) 1982, pp. 211–12.
33 *Grove*, vol. 7, pp. 77ff. See also below, p. 168 and n. [104] for a definition of isorhythm.
34 On the distinction Leonardo draws between 'artificial' and 'natural' perspective see Kemp, *The Science of Art*, p. 49; it is the latter form of perspective that is concerned with the perception of the relative sizes of actual objects in nature.
35 For an up-to-date account of the latest restoration of the fresco, see Pinin Brambilla Barcilon and Pietro C. Marani, *Leonardo, The Last Supper*, Chicago (University of Chicago Press) 2001.

rectangular grid whose lateral division into twelve equal parts permits the generation of a variety of 'musical' ratios, a suggestion that seems all the more plausible, given the manifestly artificial, stagy, non-naturalistic disposition of the figures.[36] It is also relatively easy to divide the shallow, boxy space represented in the fresco by imposing on it various species of grid pattern whose intersections relate not only to the placing of the principal *dramatis personae* but also to the pattern of the coffered ceiling and the arrangement of the flanking tapestries.[37] However, there is no compelling evidence to show that Leonardo employed precisely these ratios *because* they were musical. An artist indifferent or even hostile to music might unthinkingly have chosen the same ratios in laying out any kind of regular or symmetrical composition. If, moreover, Leonardo did apply 'musical' principles to the composition of the *Last Supper*, this appears to have been the only painting in which he did so.

In fact, we know that, far from being indifferent to music, Leonardo was profoundly interested in its practical as well as its theoretical aspect.[38] This is attested to both by his own writings and by several early accounts of his life, according to which he was considered an accomplished musician, accustomed to entertaining courtly gatherings by singing and accompanying himself on the *lira da braccia*.[39] He also invented musical rebuses – puzzle pictures that sometimes include fragments of notation – and made a large number of highly original and sometimes improbable designs for musical instruments.[40] Some of these designs, which seem to betray an obsessive preoccupation with devices for mechanizing the playing of things like trumpets or drums, are more akin to his drawings for siege engines and other weapons of war; they do not, in themselves, provide evidence of any particular musical propensity. Rather, it is the artist's theoretical writings that show more clearly the importance he ascribed to music. In particular, his at first sight merely passing remark about its capacity for 'delineating things unseen' ('figuratione ... delle cose invisibili') appears to us, from our vantage point of half a millennium later, to

---

36 Brachert's article 'A Musical Canon of Proportion' (see n. [28] above) appears to show the consistent employment throughout the fresco of a modular system based on the ratios 12:6:4:3; on musical ratios and the generation of the 'harmonic' mean, see below, pp. 152ff.

37 For more detailed discussion of the compositional basis of Leonardo's fresco, including the unresolved ambiguities over the size and shape of the ceiling coffers and whether we are, in fact, meant to 'read' the ceiling as consisting of twelve or thirteen coffers see Kemp, *The Science of Art*, pp. 47ff.

38 In an appendix to *De divina proportione*, Pacioli describes Leonardo as 'the most excellent painter of perspective, architect, musician, and man learned in all virtues'; quoted after Winternitz, *Leonardo da Vinci as a Musician*, p. 13.

39 Concerning Leonardo's musical accomplishments, see Emanuel Winternitz, 'Leonardo and Music', in Ladislao Reti (ed.), *The Unknown Leonardo*, London (Hutchinson) 1974, esp. pp. 111–12.

40 Ibid., pp. 114, 116ff.

stand quite outside its own time, prefiguring in a remarkable fashion the Romantic era's intense interest in music's supposedly abstract qualities. If, as Winternitz pointed out, Leonardo had never said anything else on this subject, this definition alone would be enough to convince us of his 'profound understanding of the nature of Music as a discipline that is not bound to copy nature but with an unparalleled degree of freedom creates forms ... out of a material neither tangible nor visible.'[41]

Proportion in Renaissance music and architecture

If architects and architectural theorists, too, wanted to claim a more exalted status for their art, they could avail themselves of much the same strategies we have already encountered in the context of painting. They could seek to demonstrate that the methods of architecture were, by their very nature, akin to those of music. Or they could strive consciously to apply musical principles to the practice of actually designing and erecting buildings. The argument that the methods of music and architecture were alike is not difficult to make, since architecture by definition deals in relations between quantities and in proportions of various kinds. (How wide? How thick? How tall?) By far the greater number of comparisons between architecture and music found in theoretical writings of this period turn on what were, by now, well-established notions of 'harmonic' proportion: that is, harmony conceived in the antique sense as synonymous with number or ratio.

But while there is (*pace* Winternitz) little evidence to show that theorists compared *painting* with music conceived as movement *in time*, at least some writers on *architecture* do point specifically to the temporal aspect of music: the exact division of musical space in terms not only of pitch but also of rhythm. We cannot know for certain whether there had been earlier speculation about a possible analogy between architecture and the rhythmic aspect of the new music that came into fashion during the last quarter of the thirteenth century. As mentioned in Chapter 3, one of the most significant musical achievements of the later Middle Ages had been the introduction of mensural notation: a system that, as well as indicating the exact pitch of notes, also gave unambiguous directions as to their duration.[42] It would seem an obvious step to compare, if only in tentative fashion, the greater rhythmic possibilities afforded by this new system with the various ways of articulating architectural

41 Winternitz, 'Role of Music...', p. 296, also idem, *Leonardo da Vinci as a Musician*, pp. xxii and 222–3. The phrase 'figuratione ... delle cose invisibili' comes from the section of the *Paragone* entitled 'Conclusion of the Discussion between the Poet, the Painter and the Musician'; see Richter 1970, pp. 79–80.
42 For an account of this and discussion of the concept 'musical space', see above, ch. 3, pp. 113ff.

form, which, in the case of Gothic buildings, included the purposive repetition of decorative or structural elements at precisely determined intervals so as to create or imply certain kinds of visual rhythm.[43] However, it is clear from surviving documents that, in the Renaissance, just this kind of speculation actually occurred. For example, in the first version of Francesco di Giorgio's treatise on architecture, dating from the 1470s, we read:

Music, too, appears necessary for the relationships and proportions of each building. And as music has its long and very long intervals, its breves and semibreves which correspond in their proportions, so too the same is necessary in a building. And when there is a dissonant note in music the whole tune is discordant, and the same happens in a building: it will be badly composed and discordant if all the elements do not correspond.[44]

And in the *Hypnerotomachia Poliphili*, that strange 'dream work' to which reference has already been made, Colonna describes the architect's method of dividing the square, here taken as the basic unit of measurement, in terms of an analogy *both* with the manner in which the musician will divide up the scale (that is, pitch) *and* with the establishment of rhythmic measures and proportions – the element of time:

I have spoken in several places about the proper goal of architecture, which is its supreme invention: the harmo-nious establishment of the solid body of a building. After the architect has done this, he reduces it by minute divisions, just as the musician sets the scale and largest unit of rhythm before subdividing them proportionately into subdivisions and small notes. By analogy with this, the first rule that the architect must observe after the conception of the building is the square, which is subdivided to the smallest degree to give the building its harmony and consistency and to make the part correlate with the whole.[45]

---

43 Ibid., pp. 124ff.
44 Quoted after Onians 1988, p. 181.
45 Colonna, op. cit. (see n. [5] above), p. 47.

Vitruvius, Alberti and the principle of 'harmonic' ratios

Architecture, apart from its more obvious affinities with the proportional systems on which music was based, enjoyed a further unique and enviable advantage compared with painting or sculpture. Writers on the visual arts possessed no antique written sources to which they could turn in search of support for their ideas, other than the works of classical authors who had discussed other 'related' topics such as poetry, drama and rhetoric. Architectural writers, on the other hand, could (and did) invoke the textual authority of the ancients by referring to the only treatise on the art of building to have survived from classical times: the *Ten Books on Architecture* by the first-century Roman architect Vitruvius.[46] The profound effect this ancient text exerted on the subsequent development of Renaissance theory can scarcely be exaggerated.[47] As Krautheimer has pointed out, the most important architectural treatise of the fifteenth century, Alberti's *De re aedificatoria*, is in many ways indebted to Vitruvius, not least in its manner of arrangement and the triad of terms *firmitas*, *utilitas* and *venustas* that Alberti borrows as part of his definition of the tasks of architecture.[48] A century later, Palladio insisted that, in preparing his own *Four Books on Architecture*, he had 'perused with great care the writings of those who, endowed by generous fortune with great intellects, have enriched this most lofty science', his choice of words clearly indicating that, to his mind also, the status of architecture and of the architect was a question of some importance.[49] Among his predecessors he particularly praised Alberti, while the contemporary sources on which he drew included Pietro Cataneo, Vignola's *Regola delli cinque ordini dell'architettura* and the treatise on architecture by Sebastiano Serlio. But above all the moderns he placed Vitruvius, 'the only ancient writer on this art', whom he had chosen as 'master and guide' (*per maestro, e guida*).[50]

---

46 For a sceptical view of the identity of the author of this famous text see Lionel March, *Architectonics of Humanism. Essays on Number in Architecture*, Chichester (Academy Editions) 1998, pp. 137ff. March suggests that 'Vitruvius' may have been a fiction invented by the Roman 'polymathic encyclopaedist' Marcus Terentius Varro (see also above, pp. 137ff) and that Vitruvius and Varro were perhaps the same person.

47 For a detailed account of the various fifteenth- and sixteenth-century editions and translations of Vitruvius see Alina A. Payne, *The Architectural Treatise in the Italian Renaissance* (as n. [60] below).

48 See Richard Krautheimer, 'Alberti and Vitruvius', *Studies in Early Christian, Medieval and Renaissance Art*, New York/London (New York U. P./University of London Press) 1969, pp. 323–32. For discussion of the so-called 'Vitruvian triad', see the glossary appended to Alberti, *On the Art of Building* (as n. [63] below), pp. 426–7. The terms *firmitas*, *utilitas* and *venustas* are not easy to translate; what Alberti (and Vitruvius) had in mind were evidently qualities such as the stability or permanence of the building, how far it was suited to the purpose for which it had been designed, and its grace, beauty or elegance.

49 Foreword to Book I of the *Quattro libri*; quoted after *Andrea Palladio, The Four Books on Architecture*. Translated by Robert Tavernor and Richard Schofield, Cambridge, MA/London (MIT Press) 1997, p. 5.

50 Palladio, loc. cit. In the early chapters of Book I, Palladio makes repeated mention of Vitruvius, sometimes more than once on a page. Further references occur at intervals throughout the *Quattro libri*, especially in Book IV, where he specifically discusses ancient Roman architecture.

The fact that Vitruvius had highlighted the importance of musical training for architects and also had a good deal to say about topics such as harmony, number and proportion rendered his ideas still more beguiling. Just how beguiling is shown by the prominence given to music in the various commentaries on Vitruvius' text, especially that printed in Barbaro's edition of 1556, for which Palladio provided the illustrations.[51] Even theorists of music seem to have viewed the *Ten Books on Architecture* with respect. For example, in his influential treatise *Le istitutioni harmoniche* of 1558 the distinguished composer Gioseffo Zarlino turned to Vitruvius for support in arguing the thorny question of whether or not the interval of a fourth should be viewed as a consonance.[52]

The account of music Vitruvius gives is, however, in certain respects curious and sometimes bizarre. Passing references to affinities between music and other forms of intellectual endeavour occur quite frequently, but are couched in somewhat general terms, as in the first chapter of Book I, where he remarks that 'astronomers and musicians discuss certain things in common: the harmony of the stars, the proportions of squares and triangles, that is, the intervals of the fourth and fifth, and with geometers they speak about vision'.[53] For more specific observations on music the reader must turn to the fourth chapter of Book V, which is devoted entirely to harmonics. This Vitruvius describes as 'an obscure and difficult subject, especially ... for those who cannot read Greek', perhaps because he is anxious to divert attention from his own less than perfect grasp of the musical terminology of the ancients.[54] He then proceeds to give an extended account of Greek harmonic theory, including a definition of the three *genera* (enharmonic, chromatic and diatonic), based almost entirely on Aristoxenus. In this chapter, Vitruvius appears content to paraphrase; he adds no observations of his own, nor does he comment on the nomenclature Aristoxenus employs, on the division of the tetrachord into 'tones and semitones' and so forth. He also makes no attempt to relate these 'harmonic principles' to the actual practice of architecture; but in the following chapter, which treats of the 'sounding vessels' (*echea*) utilized in the building of theatres, he makes clear that these are to

51 Wittkower, *Architectural Principles*, p. 65, also p. 132, citing the commentary to Book I of the 1556 edition of Vitruvius, where Barbaro writes in seemingly Augustinian terms: 'The rules of arithmetic are those which unite Music and Astrology; for proportion is general and universal in all things given to measure, weight and number.' (I, i, 16.) For a more detailed account of Barbaro's interpolations see Elizabeth Cropper, *The Ideal of Painting. Pietro Testa's Düsseldorf Notebook*, Princeton, NJ (Princeton U. P.) 1984, pp. 137ff.
52 'Vitruvio anco nel Cap. 4 del Quinto libro della Architettura è di parere, ch'ella [la Quarta] sia Consonanza'; *Ist. harm.*, III, 5 (*Opere*, vol. 1, p. 186).
53 *Ten Books*, I, i, 16.
54 Ibid., V, iv, 1.

be 'tuned' according to their proportions in such a way that 'when touched, they may produce with one another the notes of the fourth, the fifth and so on up to the double octave'.[55] Here, he is clearly preoccupied with the acoustics of the building, the purpose of the 'sounding vessels' being to allow the actors' voices to resonate with maximum clarity. At the same time, his description of the *echea* in terms of '*diatesseron*, *diapente* and so on' indicates that he expected architects to be familiar with this kind of specifically musical (and specifically Greek) terminology.

Other passages from the *Ten Books on Architecture* confirm our initial impression: namely, that in drawing comparisons with music, what Vitruvius had in mind were primarily practical rather than abstract-symbolic considerations.[56] In the opening chapter he appears to be making a strong case for an architect acquiring some musical knowledge ('the architect should know music in order to have a grasp of canonical and mathematical relations'),[57] but he goes on to observe merely that such knowledge is useful when it comes to the correct tensioning of catapults. The chapter that deals with the dimensions of temples stresses the importance of symmetry and proportion, 'whose principles architects should take the greatest care to master'.[58] Here, 'musical' ratios such as the fifth, the octave and the double octave (2:3, 1:2, etc.) do indeed occur, but, in determining the width of the distance between the columns of a portico in relation to their height, Vitruvius is again swayed by practical considerations, noting that both:

pycnostyle and systle [intercolumniations of one-and-a-half and two column widths respectively] have practical disadvantages. When the matrons mount the steps for public prayer or thanksgiving, they cannot pass through the intercolumniations with their arms about one another, but must form single file.[59]

These, along with a few other passing references, might appear somewhat flimsy foundations on which to construct elaborate theories about the use of 'musical' ratios in architecture. Nevertheless, it seems to have been precisely the notion of harmonic

---

55 Ibid., V, v, 1.
56 Scholfield also notes that Vitruvius' interest in music 'arose, not from the possibility of applying the theory of harmony to the problem of architectural proportion, but simply from the importance of acoustics in the design of theatres. The myth which identifies Vitruvius with the "musical" theory of architectural proportion seems to have originated in the sixteenth century, and has continued up to the present day'; see P. H. Scholfield, *The Theory of Proportion in Architecture*, Cambridge (Cambridge U. P.) 1958, p. 36.
57 *Ten Books*, I, i, 8
58 Ibid., III, i, 1.
59 Ibid., iii, 1–3.

proportion – something Renaissance writers to a large extent read into, rather than actually found in, Vitruvius' treatise – that was accorded particular attention.[60] In *De re aedificatoria*, for example, Alberti gives far more space to questions of ratio and proportion than does Vitruvius himself, although his definitions at times resemble more closely those of the Pythagorean Archytas – in particular, Alberti's account of how the various proportional 'means' are to be determined.[61] Archytas had distinguished between three ways of dividing a string or monochord, corresponding to three different species of ratio. The first of these he calls the arithmetic mean, where the second of three terms (for example 6, in the series 4, 6, 8) exceeds the first by the same amount as that by which the third exceeds the second.[62] Alberti describes it as follows:

Once two extreme numbers have been set, the longest being eight, for example, and the shortest, say, four, add them together, to produce twelve; divide this into two parts and take one of them: its value will be six. This number is called the arithmetical mean, being equidistant between both extremes, four and eight.[63]

A second kind of ratio or proportion is termed geometric, as expressed by the series 2, 4 and 8. Here the second term stands in relation to the first as does the third to the second (four is twice two, just as eight is twice four). The third kind, called 'harmonic', Alberti describes as 'a little more laborious'. Here, the largest number exceeds the middle term by a certain fraction of itself (for example, 6 exceeds 4 by one third of 6, *ie* 2), while the middle term exceeds the smallest number by the same fraction of the latter (4 exceeds 3 by one-third of three, that is to say 1: hence, 6:4:3).[64] Taken in

---

60 In her study of the reception of Vitruvius' text, Payne likewise remarks that its 'reticence' did not prevent Renaissance architects from reading their own questions into it, so that *De architectura* became 'an accretive and adhesive object'. Thus, a significant degree of 'unreading' is required in order to 'peel off the accumulated layers of interpretation and allow us to gauge or even notice *what was really there*'; see Alina A. Payne, *The Architectural Treatise in the Italian Renaissance. Architectural Invention, Ornament and Literary Culture*, Cambridge (Cambridge U. P.) 1999, pp. 35ff.

61 Renaissance writers were a little distrustful of Vitruvius' account of harmonics because of his almost total reliance on Aristoxenus; they would have preferred a source more consonant with the Pythagorean-Platonic tradition.

62 'There are three means in music. One is arithmetic, the second geometric, the third subcontrary, which they call harmonic ...' (Archytas frag. 2, from Porphyry, *Commentary on Ptolemy's 'Harmonics'*, in Barker 1989, p. 42); see also Schueller, *Idea of Music*, p. 22.

63 Leon Battista Alberti, *On the Art of Building in Ten Books*, translated by Joseph Rykwert, Neil Leach and Robert Tavernor, Cambridge, MA/London (MIT Press) 1988, p. 308.

64 Alberti describes it somewhat differently: 6, the largest number, is the double of 3, the smallest. If the 'harmonic' mean is 4, then the interval (*ie* 2) separating it from the largest number is in the same proportional relationship to that separating it from the smallest number (*ie* 1), since 2 (the interval between 6 and 4) is the double of 1 (the interval between 4 and 3). (Alberti, loc. cit.; see also Barker 1989, p. 42 for an explanation of how the basics of Greek harmonic theory are derived from the application of the three means.)

combination, these various species of proportion can be used to generate precisely those musical intervals recognized as consonant by Greek musical theory: the octave, the fourth and the fifth.

Let us take an example. As we saw in Chapter 2, the octave ratio 2:1 cannot be harmoniously divided into two equal parts; but if, in order to avoid using fractions, we choose larger numbers in the same ratio – say 12 and 6 – we can insert both the harmonic mean (8) and the arithmetic mean (9) between them. The ratio 9:12 equals 3:4, which represents the interval of a fourth, while 8:12 equals 2:3, which is a fifth. Thus the series 6, 8, 12 divides the octave into a fourth followed by a fifth (for example, C–F–C), while the series 6, 9, 12 produces a fifth followed by a fourth (C–G–C). All that remains to be accounted for is the stepwise interval between the fifth and the fourth, which is the *tonus* or whole tone, expressed as the ratio 9:8. Upon these simple relations all the more complex structures of Greek harmonics are ultimately built, since combining the two series described above (thus: 6, 8, 9, 12) produces the fixed notes bounding a pair of disjoined tetrachords (two fourths separated by the interval of a tone) – in other words, precisely the division of the octave described by Aristoxenus and other musical theorists.[65]

Obviously, 'musical' proportions of this kind, once expressed as arithmetical ratios, could be applied without difficulty to the design of buildings. For example, a rectangular church or assembly hall whose length might be 60 ft, its height 40 and its width 30 would manifest the 'harmonic' proportion 6:4:3. It is clear that Alberti had just these kinds of relations in mind when, in the fifth chapter of Book IX of *De re aedificatoria*, he writes:

We define harmony as that consonance of sounds which is pleasant to the ears ... From the different contrasts between these sounds arise the varying harmonies which the ancients have classified into set numbers corresponding to the relationships between the consonant strings ... In the consonance called diapason *one number is double the other, such as two to one, or one to a half; in the triple, three to one, or one to a third; in the quadruple, likewise four to one, or one to a quarter. To sum up, then, the musical numbers are one, two, three and four; there is also* tonus, *as I mentioned, where the longer string is one eighth more than the lesser. Architects employ all these numbers in the most convenient manner possible: they use them in pairs, as in*

---

65 For a more detailed account see above, ch. 2, pp. 68ff. The same numbers 6, 8, 9, 12 are shown in Gaffurio's illustration of harmonic experiments undertaken by Jubal and Pythagoras (see fig. 14).

laying out a forum, place, or open space, where only two dimensions are considered, width and length; and they use them also in threes, as in a public sitting room, senate house, hall, and so on, when width relates to length, and they want the height to relate harmoniously to both.[66]

In Chapter 6 he continues in a similar vein, consistently employing the same specifically musical terminology. The intervals he singles out are, once again, the Pythagorean consonances, corresponding to the ratios of the smallest whole numbers. In this chapter he refers not only to the *diapason* (octave) and *tonus* (second, or whole tone) but also to *diapente* (fifth, also called *sesquialtera*) and *diatesseron* (fourth or *sesquitertia*),[67] using these terms in order to describe the proportional relationships between the dimensions of different kinds of *area* or ground plan:

To begin with the area, *since it is determined by two dimensions: an* area *may be either short, long or intermediate. The shortest of all is the quadrangle with all four sides of equal length ... After this come the* sesquialtera, *and another short area is the* sesquitertia. *So these three relationships, which we call 'simple', apply to the short area. There are three appropriate to the intermediate area as well, the best of which is the double, followed by that composed of the double* sesquialtera. *This latter is constructed as follows: having established the lesser dimension of the area – for example, four – construct the first* sesquialtera, *making six; to this add another, making the length nine. Thus the length is twice the width plus a further double* tonus ...

When working in three dimensions, we should combine the universal dimensions, as it were, of the body with numbers naturally harmonic in themselves ... Numbers naturally harmonic include those whose ratios form proportions such as the double, triple, quadruple and so on. For a double may be constructed from the single by adding a sesquialtera *and then a* sesquitertia.[68]

---

66 Alberti (as n. [63] above), p. 305; see also the notes and glossary to that edition for explanation of the terminology employed.

67 The *diatesseron* (interval of a fourth) does not have a ratio of 1:4, as claimed in the notes to Bk. 9, ch. 5 of Alberti, *On the Art of Building*; if it did, it could not be the same as *sesquitertia*, whose ratio is correctly given as 3:4. See Alberti, op. cit., p. 409 and nn. 83, 84; also Scholfield 1958, p. 56 for a comparative table of ratios, their Latin and Greek names and their musical equivalents.

68 *On the Art of Building*, p. 306. In his article 'La bellezza numerabile: l'estetica architettonica di Leon Battista Alberti' (in Rykwert and Engel 1994, pp. 292ff.), Paul von Naredi-Rainer suggests that a more detailed scrutiny of Alberti's building practice would reveal the use of proportions other than those of the Pythagorean *tetraktys*, corresponding to more 'modern' consonances such as the major or minor third; see also the same author's *Architektur und Harmonie. Zahl, Maß und Proportion in der abendländischen Baukunst*, Cologne (DuMont) 6th rev. edn 1999.

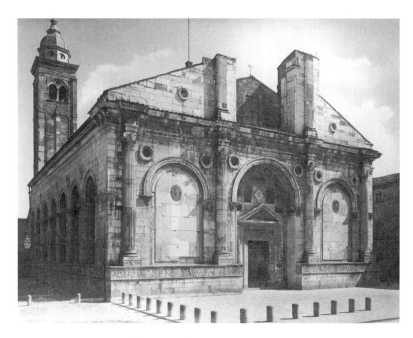

Figure 29. Leon Battista Alberti, church of S. Francesco (Tempio Malatestiano), Rimini

Alberti's choice of an abstruse and archaic vocabulary drawn from Greek harmonic science may have been partly a matter of showing his respect for the authority of the ancients. Demonstrating his familiarity with classical precepts was a way of underlining his credentials as well as making his *Ten Books* seem, perhaps, more like those of Vitruvius. But while the musical terminology Alberti uses may appear somewhat old-fashioned to modern readers, some of what he says about the relationship between architecture and music is strikingly new. As Christine Smith remarks, the Neo-Platonists believed that music could induce a certain tranquillity of mind in those capable of intellectually apprehending its harmonious proportions. Alberti, by contrast, attributes this function to 'music as aurally perceived ... Beauty, while it may inhere in number, is recognized only by the pleasure it affords the senses and emotions.'[69]

That Alberti really meant the 'harmonies' of architecture to be satisfying to the eye, just as the harmonies of music were satisfying to the ear, is made explicit in his famous letter concerning the

---

69 *Architecture in the Culture of Early Humanism*, pp. 92, 94. The affective properties of music are also discussed at length in Alberti's *Profugiorum ab Ærumna*; see Alberti, *Opere volgari, a cura di Cecil Grayson*, vol. 2: *Rime e trattati morali*, Bari (Laterza) 1960, vol. 2, pp. 107ff.

execution of his proposed façade for the church of S. Francesco in Rimini (fig. 29).[70] Here, the problem was how to reconcile an existing building with his new design, which, he insists, cannot be integrated with the dimensions of the nave, because 'the widths and heights of the chapels disturb me'. (By this, he surely means that he finds their proportions aesthetically displeasing. Therefore, according to his instructions, the façade was to 'stand by itself'.) But he is adamant that the 'measures and proportions' of the pilasters must be respected, since 'we want to help that which has been made and not spoil that which has to be made ...' Otherwise, anything that you change will bring *all this music* into discord.'[71] Here, it is clear that 'music' is meant not as a vague and generalized metaphor standing merely for order or regularity. Rather, the passage points to what Alberti saw as the viewer's capacity to perceive harmony visually, since 'when the mind is reached by way of sight or sound, or any other means, *concinnitas* [harmony] is instantly recognized'.[72] But despite his injunctions, it seems that changes still took place. His account of what he intended for S. Francesco does not accord exactly with the image of the façade as it appears on the bronze foundation medal, while the church as it exists today is different again, making it difficult to judge whether the 'musical' effect he envisaged would, in practice, have been evident to the viewer.

Zorzi and Palladio

Alberti was not the only architectural theorist to believe that the beholder could visually apprehend the abstract 'harmonies' of proportion, regarded as a potential source of aesthetic pleasure. More than a century later, an identical supposition underlies a report by Palladio evaluating his colleague Lodovico Beretta's proposed design for the new cathedral at Brescia. Here, Palladio writes that 'the proportions of voices are harmonies for the ears; those of measurements are harmonies for the eyes', adding in somewhat lapidary fashion that 'such harmonies usually please very much, without anyone knowing why, except for those who study

---

70 See Howard Saalman, 'Alberti's Letter to Matteo de' Pasti Revisited', in Cecil L. Striker (ed.), *Architectural Studies in Memory of Richard Krautheimer*, Mainz (Philipp von Zabern) 1996, pp. 147ff.; also Joseph Rykwert, 'I committenti e il loro edifici. Sigismondo Malatesta di Rimini e il Tempio Malatestiano', in Rykwert and Engel 1994, pp. 378ff.

71 ' ... si discorda tutta quella musica ...' quoted after Saalman, op. cit., pp. 148–9; the italics are mine.

72 Alberti, *On the Art of Building*, op. cit., p. 302. While it is tempting to translate *concinnitas* as 'beauty', Alberti defines it as 'a form of sympathy and consonance of the parts within a body' (see the glossary to *On the Art of Building*, p. 422). Thus, it is closer to the antique meaning of *harmonia*, discussed earlier: that is, a proper (and appropriate) fitting together of parts.

the causes of things.'[73] And in the foreword to the last of his *Four Books on Architecture*, Palladio discusses in similar fashion the design of churches generally:

If we consider ... how the heavens change the seasons of the world by their continuous revolutions ... and how they maintain themselves by the sweetest harmony of their measured movements, we cannot doubt that, since these small temples which we build must be similar to this vast one which He, with boundless generosity, perfected with but a word of command, we are bound to ... build them in such a way and with such proportions that together all the parts convey to the eyes of onlookers a sweet harmony ...[74]

For our part, we may object that modern perceptual studies – for example, Helmholtz's investigations into the physiology of hearing – have largely discredited the notion that the eye responds to 'harmonious' proportions in ways similar to the manner in which the ear takes in musical consonances.[75] But that is not the point at issue; Renaissance architects and architectural theorists clearly believed that it did. Such ideas were also consonant with their own religious convictions, which were often a mixture of Christian doctrine and antique cosmology in more or less equal proportion. If, as defined by Scripture, the cosmos was the embodiment of that divine order of which 'God, the supreme architect, is master and author', the primary task of architecture must be to emulate that order, especially in those buildings dedicated to divine worship.[76] The fact that musical consonances were considered simply another manifestation of that same order made the application of 'musical ratios' to the design of such buildings all the more commendable, given their supposed effects upon the eyes and minds of the faithful.

---

73 '... secondo che le proportioni delle voci sono armonia delle orecchie così quelle delle misure sono harmonia degli occhi nostri, la quale secondo il suo costume sommamente diletta, senza sapersi il perchè, fuori che da quelli che studiano di sapere le ragione delle cose'; for a transcription of Palladio's report dated 7 May 1567 see Zorzi, *Le chiese e i ponti* (as n. [77] below, pp. 88–9).

74 Palladio, op. cit., p. 213. In his study of the Villa Foscari at Malcontenta, Forssman writes that Palladio 'believed in the absolute truth and divine origin' of such proportions; their use, therefore, 'guaranteed the participation of his buildings in the harmony of creation'; see *Visible Harmony: Palladio's Villa Foscari at Malcontenta*, Stockholm (Sveriges arkitekturmuseum) 1973, p. 35. March, discussing the underlying aesthetic of Humanism, stresses the 'idea of the artist working as second Nature, so that an artefact is designed as a microcosm of the universe. If the universe has mathematical origins – Pythagorean, or even more precisely, Timaean, after Plato – then so should the highest creations of humankind.' (March 1998, prologue, p. ix.)

75 Forssman, *Visible Harmony*, p. 35. As early as 1683, the French architect Perrault pointed out that the 'knowledge we have, by means of the ear, of what results from the proportions of two strings, wherein the harmony consists, is quite different from the knowledge we have, by the eye, of what arises from the proportion of the parts of which a column is composed'; see Claude Perrault, *Ordonnance des cinq espèces de colonnes*, quoted after Scholfield 1958, p. 72.

76 *God, the supreme architect*: see Zorzi 1967 (as following note).

Certainly, it is striking how often topics such as musical harmony and proportion occur in the context of discussions that have specifically to do with the qualities of sacred architecture. A vivid example of this can be found in a celebrated memorandum of 1535, written by the Franciscan friar Francesco Zorzi, concerning the completion of Sansovino's church of S. Francesco della Vigna in Venice. This document, published by Wittkower and cited by nearly every subsequent writer on Renaissance architectural theory, proposed a specifically 'musical' programme which, its author insisted, should determine the relationship between the various dimensions of the building. Zorzi's own credentials were, it must be said, irreproachable. In 1525 he had published a treatise entitled *On the Harmony of the Entire Universe* (*De harmonia mundi totius*), in which his debt to Plato's cosmology and to antique numerology is unmistakable. In advocating a musical system of proportions for S. Francesco, he cites both Plato and Aristotle in support of his ideas as well as the Temple of Solomon and the Ark of the Covenant by way of biblical precedent. Like Alberti, Zorzi uses the same ancient musical terminology to identify the underlying consonances on which his scheme will depend. Again like Alberti, he was clearly thinking not in terms of imperceptible abstractions but of the kind of visual harmony capable of being appreciated in purely sensuous terms:

The width of the chapels will be three paces in triple proportion to the nave of the church, which is a diapason *[octave] and* diapente *[fifth] and with the width of the* cappella grande *it will be double, which results in a* diapason ... *Thus all the measurements of the plan, lengths as well as widths, will be in perfect consonance and will necessarily delight those who contemplate them, unless their sight be dense and disproportionate.*[77]

But while Renaissance architects acknowledged that the properly composed work of architecture should embody the same laws of harmony and proportion that were manifested by music, it is now difficult to establish whether these 'musical' principles, so often alluded to, were ever consistently applied to the design of actual buildings.[78]

---

[77] The original document is transcribed in Giangiorgio Zorzi, *Le chiese e i ponti di Andrea Palladio*, Neri Pozza Editore [Venice] 1967, p. 35; for an English translation see Wittkower, *Architectural Principles*, p. 156. Zorzi's memorandum is also discussed in Deborah Howard, *Jacopo Sansovino. Architecture and Patronage in Renaissance Venice*, New Haven/London (Yale U. P.) 1975, pp. 66ff.

[78] In his monograph *Pythagorean Palaces: Magic and Architecture in the Italian Renaissance*, G. L. Hersey points to the discrepancy between the mathematical beauty of linear diagrams and the physical intractability of real buildings. 'What', he asks, 'is to be done with actual palaces and their thick walls? Are these thicknesses included, excluded or split by the *linee occulte*? ... Then too, the original buildings have settled and have been remodeled; whatever ideal geometry they ever had is compromised. Finally, the original builders seldom worked to fine tolerances.' (Hersey 1976, pp. 166–7.)

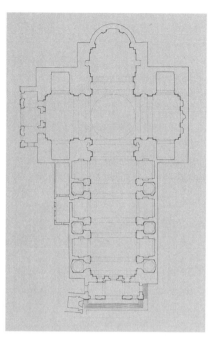

Figure 30. Ground plan of church of S. Andrea, Mantua, drawing by Prue Chiles, from Robert Tavernor, *On Alberti and the Art of Building*

This is due partly to changes that occurred during construction work, partly to the inevitable vicissitudes suffered by structures over the course of time. We know, for example, that the nave of Alberti's church of S. Andrea in Mantua was extended later in the sixteenth century. If, as Tavernor proposes, its original length was 120 *braccie*, then the proportions of the main part of the church would have exhibited the exact 'harmonic' ratio 6:3:2, since different surveys agree that the height and width of the nave amount to 60 and 40 *braccie* respectively (fig. 30).[79] These, however, were also the proportions of the Temple of Solomon – sixty by thirty by twenty cubits, as we read in the Book of Kings – a precedent repeatedly cited throughout medieval times and well into the Renaissance.[80] Alberti may have used these ratios at S. Andrea for precisely that reason; Tavernor points to a number of other parallels between details of the church and descriptions of the Solomonic temple.[81]

79 Tavernor, *On Alberti and the Art of Building*, pp. 172–3. For detailed measurements and diagrams of the plan and elevation of the church showing the use of a repeating module of 20 *braccie* see Livio Volpi Ghirardini, 'Sulle tracce dell'Alberti nel Sant Andrea a Mantova. L'avvio di un analisi archeologica e iconometrica', in Rykwert and Engel 1994, pp. 224, 227ff.
80 Regarding the ambiguities attaching to this precedent see also John Onians, 'The Last Judgement of Renaissance Architecture', *Journal of the Royal Society of Arts*, no. 128 (October 1980), esp. pp. 719ff.
81 Tavernor, loc. cit. (as n. [79]).

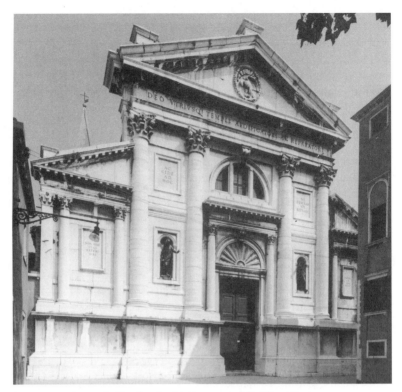

Figure 31. Andrea Palladio, church of S. Francesco della Vigna, Venice

Zorzi, in his memorandum concerning S. Francesco della Vigna, likewise alludes to Solomon's Temple, although he confuses its proportions with those dictated by God to Moses for constructing the Ark of the Covenant, while the measurements he himself proposes for the ground plan – 9:12:27 (paces) – in fact correspond to neither.[82] Nevertheless, most of his recommendations concerning the dimensions of the church were followed in practice, the principal exception being the height of the ceiling which, as Wittkower notes, should have related to the width of the nave in the ratio 4:3 (musically, the interval of a fourth or *diatesseron*) and which Zorzi had wanted to be flat and coffered. Moreover, when Palladio completed the façade of S. Francesco, some thirty years after the original memorandum was submitted, he too adhered to Zorzi's scheme of harmonic proportions (fig. 31). Whether he did so for musical reasons is impossible to say. He may have merely been

---

82 'Pondering on this mystery, Solomon the Most Wise gave the same proportions as those of the Mosaic tabernacle to the temple which he duly erected' (Zorzi 1967, p. 35). As specified in Exodus 25, the dimensions of the Ark of the Covenant were one and a half cubits in height, the same in breadth and two and a half cubits in length; those of Solomon's Temple, as already noted, were sixty by thirty by twenty cubits.

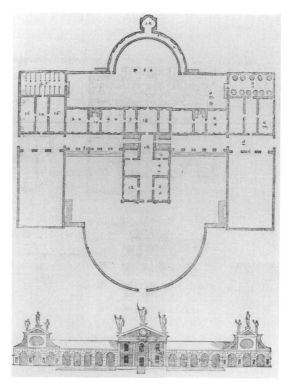

Figure 32. Andrea Palladio, ground plan and elevation of the Villa Barbaro, from *Quattro Libri* (London, RIBA)

fulfilling his predecessor's wish that the front 'should correspond to the inside of the building ... From it one should be able to grasp the form of the building and all its proportions; so that, inside and outside, all should be proportionate.'[83]

Palladio's musical villas

It has also been suggested that Palladio may have had 'musical' proportions in mind when designing a number of secular buildings dating from the later part of his career – that is, after his collaboration with Daniele Barbaro dating from the later part of his career – that is, after his collaboration with Daniele Barbaro on the latter's Vitruvius edition of 1556. Nearly all these buildings are villas and houses commissioned either by musical patrons – that is, families and individuals (including Barbaro himself) for whom the performance and discussion of music were of some importance – or

---

83 Ibid., p. 157. Wittkower also notes that, while most of the actual proportions of S. Francesco do not correspond exactly to Zorzi's carefully chosen ratios, 'the divergences are small and due to the kind of irregularities that occur in practice ...' (p. 105).

by patrons with a known interest in architectural theory (fig. 32).[84] The only notable exception is the Villa Emo near Treviso, which does appear to be based on a sequence of musical proportions and where allegories of Architecture and Music appear in the frescoes, but where the intellectual interests of the patron are not known. In such cases, we might think it appropriate for the architect to display his skill at manipulating 'harmonic' ratios, although here, the same difficulty arises that we have already encountered in examining the carefully ordered composition of Leonardo's *Last Supper*. Even if we limit ourselves solely to the 'Pythagorean' consonances, expressed by the ratios of the smallest whole numbers, it is quite likely that various combinations of these numbers or their multiples will occur in the ground plan of any largely symmetrical building.[85] Since many of Palladio's buildings are more or less symmetrical in plan and elevation, as emphasized by the drawings reproduced in his *Four Books on Architecture*, we may be tempted to call these buildings 'musical' or ascribe musical intentions to their author, ignoring the fact that an architect who had not the slightest interest in notions of visual harmony nor any intention of applying 'musical' principles might still end up choosing these same numbers, simply because they lie so readily to hand.

An alternative (and more generous) method of determining which are the 'harmonic' ratios, proposed by Howard and Longair in their analysis of Palladio's villas, makes it even more likely that we shall find music wherever we go. This involves taking the successive notes of the diatonic scale (C, D, E, etc.) and assigning a numerical value to each of the intervals produced when two notes are sounded together: thus C + C: unison = 1:1; C + D: second (the interval Alberti calls *tonus*) = 9:8; C + E: major third and so on.[86] Defined in this way, of the whole numbers between 1 and 100 no fewer than thirty-four are 'harmonic', including all those from one to six.[87] Therefore, juxtaposing any of these thirty-four numbers will automatically produce a 'harmonic' ratio. Using this system it is relatively easy to show that many of Palladio's later buildings exhibit musical proportions of one kind or another – and not just one but often

84 For an account of the villas in question and of Palladio's use of musical ratios, see Deborah Howard and Malcolm Longair, 'Harmonic Proportion and Palladio's *Quattro Libri*', *Journal of the Society of Architectural Historians*, vol. 41, no. 2 (May 1982), pp. 116–43.
85 March (*Architectonics of Humanism*) notes whereas the 'occurrence of ubiquitous ratios like 1:1 and 2:1' is often held to 'reflect the prime musical consonances of the unison and the octave', in reality 'almost anything will give rise to such a simple idea of something and its double – including music'. Likewise, the 'occurrence of ratios like 3:2, 4:3, 5:4 and even 5:3' is thought to 'confirm the usage of the secondary musical consonances of the perfect fifth, the perfect fourth, the major third and the major sixth', whereas 'they might simply arise from the employment of the 3, 4, 5 triangle to set out an architectural design'; see March 1998, p. 101.
86 Howard and Longair, pp. 120–1 and Table 1.
87 Ibid., p. 121.

several series or sequences of just such simple numerical relationships. However, there is no documentary evidence to show that this method of calculation was ever consciously employed in the creation of actual works of architecture. In this respect, Howard and Longair's article is commendable for the caution with which the authors proceed to their conclusions: a caution that may serve as a warning to writers who believe they have detected similarly musical ambitions in other works of Renaissance painting, sculpture and architecture.

But while we cannot prove that these particular numbers or ratios were chosen for reasons that have anything to do with music, it is sobering to find that, at least in certain of Palladio's villas, not only the particular dimensions of individual rooms but also the ratios of *every* dimension (in plan) of *every* room can be related musically to every other dimension of every other room.[88] This result is so difficult to achieve that it can scarcely have come about accidentally, just as a consequence of calculating in basic whole numbers.[89] An architect might well design individual rooms or perimeter walls according to simple dimensions that could – in theory, at least – be united in musical ratios, but such a system is most unlikely to pervade a whole building without conscious manipulation. This display of virtuosity would have been consistent with the belief, expressed in Palladio's report on the design of the cathedral at Brescia, that musical ratios in architecture should be perceptible to the eye. It also corresponds to the ideals expressed in the foreword to the second book of his *Quattro libri*, where he writes about making smaller rooms correspond to the larger ones, and these to the whole fabric of the villa, in such a way as to produce 'a certain harmony'.[90]

Brunelleschi, Dufay and S. Maria del Fiore

For much of the Renaissance, the relationship between music and other forms of art was a noticeably one-sided affair. Music, regarded in the abstract, enjoyed universal approbation; to succeed in imitating it, many theorists believed, was among the highest aims to which the plastic arts should aspire. However, at least one counter-example of music supposedly imitating a well-known work of architecture has been so frequently cited that it merits at least a brief discussion here. It is Guillaume Dufay's isorhythmic motet

---

88 By way of a deliberate counterweight to this kind of argument, March points to a series of projects by Palladio that do *not* exhibit musical proportions (*Architectonics of Humanism*, pp. 216ff.).

89 A fact pointed out by Deborah Howard, letter to the author, May 2001. I am grateful to her and to Malcolm Longair for their advice concerning Palladio's use of musical proportion and Palladio problems generally.

90 Wittkower, 1962, p. 130.

Nuper rosarum flores, written for the dedication of Florence cathedral in March 1436. This motet exhibits several striking features that appear in need of explanation, among them the use of two tenor voices and a carefully contrived system of proportional relationships that governs the way the music is structured, with the numbers four, seven and twenty-eight predominating.[91] There are four voices and four main sections, each consisting of twenty-eight measures, although their actual lengths vary from one to another in the ratio 6:4:2:3. This is because, at the start of each section, Dufay introduces a new mensuration sign that changes the value (that is, the relative duration) of the notes and rests allocated to the lower voices. Although the two tenor parts are written in the same notes and have approximately the same repeating rhythm throughout (hence the term 'isorhythmic'), the duration of each section differs from that of the next in a proportion precisely determined by these special signs.

One explanation, suggested by Charles Warren in a famous article of 1973 entitled 'Brunelleschi's Dome and Dufay's Motet', is that the structure of the music was meant to 'echo' that of the recently completed dome of the cathedral – an act of musical homage, if you like.[92] Warren proposes that the overall design is 'not purely musical after all, but the result of a deliberate attempt on the part of Dufay to create a sounding model of Brunelleschi's architecture'. Even the two tenor parts, he thinks, may have been fashioned in emulation of the famous double shell of Brunelleschi's dome, the outer cupola of which had been placed over the internal vault to protect it from the weather and also to give it, as one contemporary description records, 'a more magnificent and swelling form'.[93]

Elsewhere in his article, Warren extends this musical 'metaphor' to the building as a whole. He points, for example, to the proportions of the nave (fig. 33), which consists of four huge bays whose dimensions can be related to those of the central crossing area by a series of complex ratios, and compares these with the proportional schema on which Dufay's motet is based, with its four sections and its repeated use of fours and sevens. The aim of this exercise is to demonstrate a virtually perfect correspondence between the structure of the music and that of the building for which it was written.

Numerous art historians have since followed – or at least alluded to – Warren's theory. However, his ideas about a possible

---

91 On the structural function of the tenor part in polyphonic motets of the thirteenth and fourteenth centuries see above, ch. 3, pp. 117ff.
92 Charles W. Warren, 'Brunelleschi's Dome and Dufay's Motet', *Musical Quarterly*, vol. 59, no. 1 (January 1973), pp. 92–105.
93 Ibid., pp. 92ff., 98; the passage quoted by Warren, in which this description of the dome occurs, is taken from a notarial record of the Florentine Wool Guild (Arte della Lana) dated 1420.

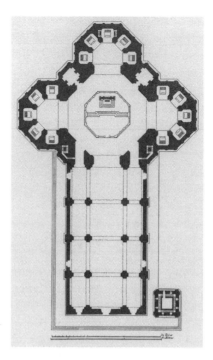

Figure 33. Ground plan of Florence cathedral

relationship between the music and the architecture bring in their train a number of difficulties.[94] To start with, the notion that the 'doubled' tenor in *Nuper rosarum flores* was meant as a specific allusion to the structure of Brunelleschi's dome seems suddenly less plausible once we realize that other musical compositions exhibit precisely the same feature. Dufay's own earlier motet *Ecclesie militantis* also uses two tenors, this time singing two different texts. (The tenor parts in *Nuper rosarum flores* are both based on the same chant, 'Terribilis est locus iste', taken from the Introit of the Mass for the Dedication of a Church.) But *Ecclesie militantis* was written for the coronation of Pope Eugenius IV in 1431; it has nothing to do with Florence cathedral. Moreover, the use of two (or even more) tenors is specifically provided for in earlier theoretical treatises such as the *Speculum musicae* of Jacques de Liège, already cited in Chapter 3 as one of the most important – and

---

94 Most writers on art and architecture, if they refer to the matter at all, have cited Warren's conclusions without objection. See for example Tavernor 1998, pp. 73ff ('it has been argued that the motet composed ... by the Burgundian Guillaume Dufay has a structure that complements and harmonizes with the enclosure in which it was performed'); compare Dale Kent, *Cosimo de' Medici and the Florentine Renaissance. The Patron's Oeuvre*, New Haven/London (Yale U. P.) 2000, p. 126, who refers in passing to Dufay 'whose motet echoed the harmony and proportion of the cupola itself'.

certainly one of the longest – medieval textbooks on music. Dufay, a deeply scholarly man, may well have had just this kind of theoretical precedent in mind when composing his isorhythmic motet, a musical form that itself harks back to the complex metrical schemes favoured by composers of the Middle Ages.[95]

Other writers, too, have objected to Warren's account of the relationship between Dufay's motet and the architectural space in which it was performed. For example, in her study *Architecture in the Culture of Early Humanism*, Christine Smith points out that his derivation of the measurements of Florence cathedral by a system of *quadratura*, 'although it might reflect the process by which the building was designed, has no relation to how its measurements were perceived in the Quattrocento'.[96] There is, she emphasizes, nothing in the numerous records relating to the duomo to suggest that its measures and proportions would actually have been 'read' or understood in the way that Warren implies. Moreover, contemporary sources are noticeably silent about specific details of the music that accompanied the inauguration of the cathedral, how it struck the listeners, even how it was performed. One notable eye-witness of the 1436 dedication ceremony, Giannozzo Manetti, while enthusing at length about the splendour of the occasion, fails to mention Dufay altogether. He merely describes how, following the elevation of the host, 'every part of the basilica resounded to the harmonious concord of so many different instruments ... that murmured in our ears with I know not what ineffable sweetness, such that it rightly seemed as if the songs of angels, even the melodies of heaven itself were reaching us here on earth below'.[97] As David Fallows remarks, this 'glorious example of humanistic rhetoric' provides 'little useful information other than that the occasion was a magnificent one with a lot of music from both singers and instrumentalists'.[98]

But perhaps the most comprehensive rebuttal of Warren's theories is that offered by American musicologist Craig Wright in his essay 'Dufay's *Nuper rosarum flores*, King Solomon's Temple, and the Veneration of the Virgin'.[99] There are two principal strands to Wright's argument. The first is that, to put it bluntly, the figures do

---

95 For an excellent and vivid account of Dufay generally see David Fallows, *Dufay* (*The Master Musicians*), London (J. M. Dent), 2nd rev. edn 1987, esp. pp. 45–6 for discussion of *Nuper rosarum flores* and the 1436 dedication ceremony.

96 Smith, *Architecture in the Culture of Early Humanism*, p. 94.

97 'Oratio ... de secularibus et pontificalibus pompis in consecratione basilicae florentinae' (1436); for the complete Latin text see Eugenio Battisti, 'Il mondo visuale delle fiabe', *Archivio di filosofia* 1960/ii-iii: *Umanesimo e esoterismo*, appendix, pp. 310ff. Manetti's references to the splendour of the music, quoted here, are scattered between pp. 317 and 319.

98 Fallows, loc. cit. (as n. [95] above).

not add up. In order to demonstrate the supposed resemblances between the measurements of the cathedral, based on a repeating module of twenty-eight *braccie*, and the strikingly symmetrical structure of the motet, consisting of four sections each twenty-eight measures long, Warren is forced into all kinds of arithmetical jiggery-pokery: massaging certain figures by increasing them to fit his theory, rounding them up to whole numbers and 'adjusting' the dimensions of the nave by measuring it from well inside the crossing. The second is that, if Dufay's proportional system of 6:4:2:3 corresponds to anything, its most likely source is, once again, the biblical account of the Temple of Solomon, the dimensions of which are spelt out with admirable precision in at least three different passages from the Old Testament.[100] To demonstrate just how apposite an allusion this would have been, Wright adduces a dazzling array of earlier sources, among them various instances of biblical exegesis from the Venerable Bede to Honorius of Autun, in which the Solomonic temple is cited as antecedent of the Christian church. To these we may add the famous depiction of S. Maria del Fiore by the fourteenth-century master Andrea di Bonaiuto (Andrea da Firenze) in the Spanish chapel of S. Maria Novella in Florence, in which the building – in reality, still unfinished, but shown in Andrea's fresco complete with its projected dome – is associated with Christ's church on earth: the 'church militant', personified in the right-hand portion of the painting by the Dominican order.[101] Admittedly, Wright, too, finds himself obliged to massage the figures somewhat in order to achieve a perfect correspondence, since the length of the Solomonic temple must be taken twice – once in its entirety and a second time divided into two sections, the hall and the sanctuary – if the ratio 6:4:2:3 is to be produced. He might also have added, although he does not, that the dimensions actually specified in the Book of Kings and elsewhere, three-score cubits (length) by thirty cubits (height) by twenty cubits (width) represent a 'harmonic' ratio, 6:3:2.

There is, however, another kind of argument we could make concerning the relationship between *Nuper rosarum flores* and the architecture of Florence cathedral. That the motet did indeed celebrate the building for whose dedication it was composed is beyond doubt. This is clear from the text alone, perhaps written by Dufay himself, which alludes specifically to 'this vast temple' and to the 'celestial virgin' who was its patron.[102] But the church itself was

---

99 In *Journal of the American Musicological Society*, vol. 47 (1994), no. 3, pp. 395–441.
100 I Kings 6; also II Chronicles 3; Ezekiel 41–2.
101 For a detailed discussion of the iconography of this painting see Joseph Polzer, 'Andrea di Bonaiuto's *Via Veritas* and Dominican Thought in Late Medieval Italy', *Art Bulletin*, vol. 77, no. 2 (June 1995), pp. 266ff. As Polzer remarks (p. 268), Andrea's depiction of the completed building must have been based on a model.

begun in 1296 and is a predominantly medieval structure. Even Brunelleschi's dome, often seen as one of the first great monuments of Renaissance architecture, conforms in its essentials to a design originally proposed in 1367, albeit with minor changes.[103] Is it merely coincidence that the music written for the dedication ceremony is also cast in a compositional form – that of the isorhythmic motet – associated primarily with the music of the later Middle Ages? As Fallows remarks, Dufay's ingenuity in exploiting the various possibilities offered by an intricate sequence of isorhythmic and isomelic relationships[104] seems to betoken a somewhat old-fashioned preoccupation with 'numerical system and entelechy', while the simultaneous singing of different texts ('*Nuper rosarum flores*' ... '*terribilis est locus iste*') also resulted in a 'richness ... born partly of aural confusion' perhaps more pleasing to 'the Gothic mind ... than to the contemporaries of Donatello and Brunelleschi'.[105] Evidently thinking along similar lines, Wright stresses that whereas Dufay composed his motet during his stay in Florence, 'the cradle of Renaissance humanism', the piece with its four homologous sections is 'devoid of any humanistic influence ... a distinctly medieval creation'. This 'medieval' flavour is further accentuated by the sharp contrast between *Nuper rosarum flores*, with its distinctive number symbolism and hierarchical structure, and the kind of musical rhetoric 'intensifying the meaning of the text through purposeful changes in register, texture, metre, harmony' that would soon be employed by the outstanding composer of the next generation, Josquin des Près.[106]

But while Florence cathedral is still a recognizably medieval building, in certain respects it is also strikingly modern. Quite apart from Brunelleschi's awe-inspiring dome, the elegantly proportioned nave (fig. 34), with its four giant bays, breathes a spirit of clarity and rationality noticeably at odds with the intricate medieval decoration and sometimes fussy detailing of the exterior.[107] This lucid and logical articulation of the internal structure has no real parallel in any other major work of architecture completed in Italy during this

---

102 As in all traditional forms of the motet, the words given to the tenor voices are those of the ancient plainchant service; in *Nuper rosarum flores*, however, the two upper voices sing a newly composed Latin poem. On the likelihood that Dufay was the author of this poem see Wright 1994, p. 398 and n. 7.

103 The proposed design was ratified the following year; thereafter, successive *capomaestri* in charge of work on the cathedral had to swear not to deviate from the agreed design. See Franklin K. B. Toker, 'Florence Cathedral: The Design Stage', *Art Bulletin*, vol. 60, no. 2 (June 1978), pp. 214ff., 227.

104 'Isorhythmic': consisting of a succession of identical or nearly identical rhythmic patterns, often repeated in one or more voices but with different pitches; 'isomelic': repeating the same melodic pattern, usually in altered rhythm; see further *Grove*, vol. 9, p. 351.

105 Fallows, op. cit., pp. 103ff. (also for an account of Dufay's isorhythmic motets generally).

106 Wright 1994, p. 439.

107 As Ross King points out in his study of Brunelleschi's career and achievements, the dome of S. Maria del Fiore remains to this day the highest and widest masonry dome ever raised; see *Brunelleschi's Dome. The Story of the Great Cathedral in Florence*, London (Pimlico) 2001, esp. pp. 160ff.

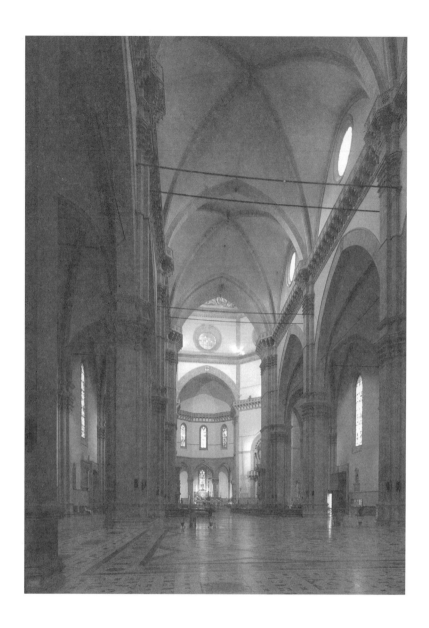

Figure 34. Florence cathedral, after 1357, view of nave

period. In similar fashion, Dufay chose to exploit a musical form that is essentially medieval in origin, but he consciously imposed upon this archaic genre a structure that is radically new. There is no obvious precedent for the use of a concluding section that is longer than its predecessor – the consequence of its altered note values, already referred to. And while the *fact* of two tenor voices is not unique to this motet, the way in which the tenor parts in *Nuper rosarum flores* are structurally functional, repeatedly following and overlapping one another in quasi-canonical sequence, is likewise without precedent. For example, the two tenor parts in *Ecclesie militantis*, already mentioned, are relatively brief by contrast with those employed in *Nuper rosarum* and the real structure of that earlier piece is based not upon the *cantus firmus* but upon the other and longer repeating melody.

The fact that none of the educated and highly cultured listeners who witnessed the dedication ceremony actually commented upon these particular features of Dufay's motet or its appropriateness to the setting in which it was performed need not discomfort us unduly. The musically more adept among them must surely have been conscious of the novelty of his composition – especially its structure, which is readily apparent at first hearing. This was, after all, precisely the kind of audience Johannes de Grocheio had described in writing about those capable of appreciating the subtleties of the polyphonic motet: a genre by now outdated, but which in its final flowering Dufay raised to new heights of sophistication.[108]

Music and architecture at St Mark's, Venice

Churches often served as a focus for civic pride, as was the case with Florence cathedral – something made abundantly clear by contemporary accounts of the dedication ceremony. Their most important function, however, was to provide the physical setting for the observance of the liturgy, in which music usually played a significant part. Therefore, another way of thinking about the relationship between sacred music and church architecture is in terms of the liturgical function both were intended to fulfil. In this respect, it is instructive to compare the spatial articulation of St Mark's Basilica in Venice, and the ways in which the building was used, with the distinctive and, in some respects, peculiar form given to Venetian church music of the late Renaissance and early Baroque. A particular tradition that developed in Venice during the sixteenth

---

108 On Grocheio and the polyphonic motet see above, ch. 3, pp. 118ff.

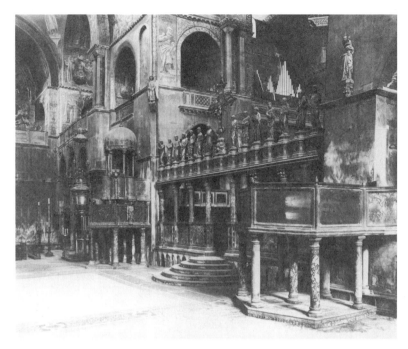

Figure 35. St Mark's, Venice, showing crossing with transept and organ lofts above

century was that of polychoral singing – that is, the use of two or more choirs, sometimes referred to as *cori spezzati*. This tradition can be traced back at least as far as the 1550s, when the famous Netherlandish composer Adrian Willaert (appointed *maestro di cappella* in 1527) published his so-called *salmi spezzati*: settings of the psalms that had been written specifically for the double choir of St Mark's.[109] A notable feature of the basilica itself was that it had not one but two main organs and therefore two organ lofts of roughly equal size, located on opposite sides of the building (fig. 35). Because of this, some writers have toyed with the idea that in performing *salmi spezzati* the singers, usually consisting of a larger *ripieno* chorus and a smaller group of soloists, must have been divided between these two organ lofts. If this were the case, we might reasonably have concluded that this particular musical form, which came to be associated specifically with Venice and with St Mark's, in a sense 'corresponded' to the architecture of the church.

However, documents of that time – for example, the *ceremoniali* that describe various details of liturgical procedure – paint a rather

---

109 *Di Adriano et di Jachet: I salmi appertinenti alli vesperi … da cantare a uno et a duoi Chori* (Venice, 1550).

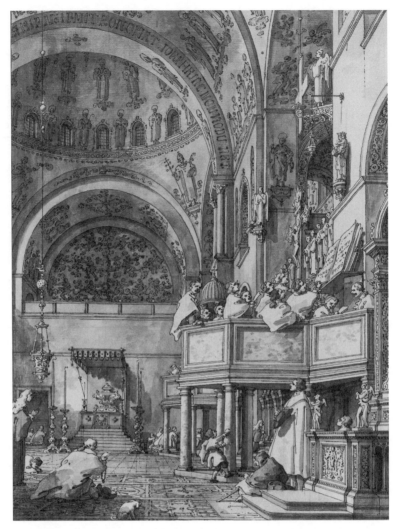

Figure 36. Canaletto, drawing showing crossing and transept of St Mark's with musicians singing, 1766, pen and wash, 47 x 36 cm, 18$\frac{1}{2}$ x 14 in (Hamburg, Kunsthalle)

different and in some ways more complicated picture.[110] It seems that, in the sixteenth century, the choristers of St Mark's could be stationed in a variety of places. These included – oddly, perhaps, to our eyes – the large hexagonal pulpit that occupied the central

110 These documents, many of them discovered and published in the last thirty years, are described and summarized in an article by David Bryant, 'The "Cori Spezzati" of St Mark's: Myth and Reality', *Early Music History*, I (1981), pp. 165–86, which also contains a revealing account of the musical traditions of the basilica during this period and their relation to its architecture; also J. H. Moore, 'The *Vespro delle Cinque Laudate* and the Role of *Salmi Spezzati* at St Mark's', *Journal of the American Musicological Society*, vol. 34 (1981), pp. 249–78.

crossing area to the right of the iconostasis, known as the *pulpitum magnum cantorum* (or, more vulgarly, as the *bigonzo*: the 'tub').[111] A drawing by Canaletto of 1766 (fig. 36), recording what was undoubtedly long-established practice, depicts the singers crammed into this pulpit and looking rather uncomfortable, although their discomfort was still greater on those occasions when the doge occupied the *pulpitum magnum* and the singers were obliged to move over to the smaller pulpit on the other side of the crossing: the *pulpitum novum lectionum*.[112] And there were other possible locations, too: for example, in front of the steps leading to the high altar or in the two *pergoli* (tribunes or choir boxes) overlooking the new and larger choir stalls, which were installed in the first half of the sixteenth century as part of Jacopo Sansovino's remodelling of the choir of the building.[113]

What the same documents seem to show is that the very places that were *not* used in this period – at least, not for the performance of *salmi spezzati* – were the two main organ lofts. There would have been several possible reasons for this. Musicologists now think it likely that these settings of the psalms were performed not antiphonally but responsorially, which means that they did not depend for their effect on fragments of melody being passed back and forth between two contrasting choirs.[114] Instead, the smaller group of singers, consisting perhaps of no more than four soloists, would intone the first verse (sometimes half a verse) of the psalm in question and the rest of the choir would then 'respond' by joining in. If *salmi spezzati* were performed in this way, physically separating the singers would, from a purely musical standpoint, have made little sense. Nor did the acoustics of the building really lend themselves to such a manner of performance. Given the long reverberation times and confusing echoes that are among the more awkward features of the basilica, the organ lofts were simply too far apart for singers divided between them to be able to reproduce any such close-knit music accurately. Despite being split into two groups, it is more likely that the singers would still have stood together, either crammed into the *pulpitum novum lectionum* or, more frequently, in the *bigonzo*, as shown in Canaletto's drawing.

---

111 References to the singers occupying one or other of the two pulpits adjacent to the iconostasis can be found as early as 1564; for the documentary evidence see Bryant, op. cit., pp. 170ff.

112 A painting by Canaletto of about 1760, now in the Museum of Fine Arts in Montreal, also clearly shows singers occupying the *pulpitum magnum* – that is, the right-hand pulpit.

113 For an account of this remodelling see Bruce Boucher, 'Jacopo Sansovino and the Choir of St Mark's', *Burlington Magazine*, vol. 118, no. 881 (August 1976), pp. 552–66, also idem, *The Sculpture of Jacopo Sansovino*, New Haven/London (Yale U. P.) 1991, pp. 55ff.

114 Bryant., pp. 169ff. and n. 13 for references to earlier hypotheses about how Willaert's *salmi spezzati* would have been performed.

Therefore, in the case of *salmi spezzati*, it seems that the architecture of St Mark's exerted little direct influence on traditions of musical performance. However, other factors (including purely economic ones) may well have encouraged composers to think about ways of exploiting the possibilities for spatial contrast afforded by the physical layout of the basilica. Under the direction of the eminent theorist Gioseffo Zarlino, *maestro di cappella* from 1565 to 1590, the musical establishment of St Mark's increased considerably. 'Such an adornment', reads a citation of 1588 appointing a third organist, 'are the concerts performed in our church of San Marco with so much public dignity on solemn feast days in which most of the city participates that we must seek in every way to expand and augment them.'[115] In other words, the Procurators of St Mark's, whose responsibility it was to manage the basilica's resources, were now prepared to spend more lavishly on what were, for that period, relatively large numbers of performers. With these more copious forces at their disposal, composers like Andrea and Giovanni Gabrieli and Giovanni Bassano began to experiment with new kinds of polychoral writing.[116] The Gabrielis, in particular, wrote their *concerti* and *sacrae symphoniae* for three or even four 'choirs' made up of different groups of instruments as well as voices, whose contrasting tonal values were emphasized by their physical separation within the church. The effect of these *concerti* – occasional pieces having no fixed place within the liturgy – must have been markedly different from that produced by the purely vocal settings of the psalms and vespers. On those occasions when choral and instrumental forces were combined, it seems that the choristers continued to take up their position as before: that is, somewhere on the floor of the church. The reasons for this may have been practical as well as musical. Members of the choir had other duties such as lining up for processions and it would have been inconvenient to keep climbing up and down the narrow stairs leading to the galleries. The instrumentalists, on the other hand, had no such duties to perform, which meant that they could be placed in a variety of locations: for example, high up in the organ lofts, where they were sometimes joined by small numbers of solo singers. That this is what actually happened is demonstrated both by contemporary documents and by various fragments of visual

---

115 Quoted by John Eliot Gardiner in the booklet accompanying his recording of the *Vespers* of 1610, Archiv 429 565–2 (1990), p. 12.

116 Andrea Gabrieli and his nephew Giovanni both held the position of organist at St Mark's during the later sixteenth century; see Eleanor Selfridge-Field, *Venetian Instrumental Music from Gabrieli to Vivaldi*, Oxford (Blackwell) 1975, esp. pp. 6ff.; compare also the same author's 'Gabrieli and the Organ', *Organ Yearbook*, 8 (1977), pp. 2ff.

evidence. For example, a frequently cited *ceremoniale* of 1564, alluding to a 'beautiful Mass of the Trinity with the Collect of St Mark', describes how the players 'sound *piffari* ... behind the High Altar, and at the Elevation they sound cornetts or other instruments, and in this as in all important solemnities they sing and play from the organ lofts'.[117] A late seventeenth-century painting by an unknown artist, now in the Museo Correr, Venice, shows just the kind of disposition of musical forces described in the *ceremoniale* (pl. 7). Alternatively, singers and instrumentalists alike could be stationed in the *nicchie* (niches) on either side of the icono-stasis: smaller galleries into which portative organs were moved on special occasions.

Ad hoc solutions were sometimes needed in order to address the purely practical problems that arose as a consequence of these experiments. Singers or players stationed in close proximity to the organists often had difficulty in seeing the main *ripieno* choir, standing some distance away, usually at floor level: a difficulty that was solved by employing an assistant conductor to relay the beat.[118] On the other hand, the long reverberation times, referred to earlier, posed less of a problem, since the whole point of this kind of music – unlike the responsorial settings of the Vesper psalms – was that it was conceived antiphonally: that is, it was built out of distinct blocks of sound that alternated and contrasted with one another. In such cases, the resonant acoustic of St Mark's was a positive advantage, since it lent greater sonority to the tonal contrasts between different groups of singers and players, while dramatic spatial effects could be heightened or made to seem more surprising by concealing some of the musicians, the sound produced by these unseen performers echoing 'from side to side and from dome to dome' of the ancient basilica.[119] It is not difficult to imagine the powerful impression created by the interaction between music performed in this way – that of the Gabrielis, for example – and the architectural setting for which these compositions were conceived, especially on great feast days of the church such as Christmas and Easter when, according to tradition, even larger numbers of players and singers were employed.[120]

---

117 Venice, Archivio di Stato, Procuratia de supra reg. 98 (1564). *Piffari* is a word of German derivation, used in Italy from the fourteenth century onwards to refer to double-reed wind instruments of the shawm family and, by extension, to wind players in general; see Michael Long, 'Trecento Italy', in McKinnon 1990, p. 257.

118 For an account of the documentary evidence for this and the other musical practices described here, see Bryant, op. cit., esp. pp. 175ff.

119 Ellen Rosand, 'Venice, 1580–1680', in Curtis Price (ed.), *Man and Music: The Early Baroque Era. From the late 16th century to the 1660s*, Basingstoke (Macmillan) 1993, p. 80.

120 Several writers have suggested that composers consciously took account of the acoustics of particular buildings in which their music was performed. See, for example, Thurston Dart, *The Interpretation of Music*, London (Hutchinson's University Library) 1954, pp. 56ff.; also Forsyth 1985, pp. 3ff. The way in which the *canzone* and *concerti* written by the Gabrielis, uncle and nephew, were composed seems to be a particularly striking example of this deliberate tendency.

Still more remarkable, precisely because of its imaginative use of space, must have been the effect produced by Monteverdi's famous *Marian Vespers* (*Vespro della Beata Vergine*) of 1610. Monteverdi had been invited to apply for the post of director of music at St Mark's after the previous holder, Giulio Cesare Martinengo, died in July 1613. When he was subjected to a lengthy (and successful) audition or *prova* in the basilica on 15 and 19 August that same year, he probably used the *Vespers* as his party piece. Apart from any other considerations, the texts he had set to music, which included psalms and motets in praise of the Virgin as well as the Marian hymn *Ave maris stella*, would have been particularly appropriate to the Feast of the Assumption, celebrated on the 15th of that month. But the way the music is written also suggests that Monteverdi, still employed at the Gonzaga court in Mantua when his *Vespers* were first published, may have had the physical layout as well as the human resources of St Mark's in mind – as if he already had his eye, so to speak, on this particular job.

Monteverdi's *Vespers* is a huge work, made up of numerous contrasting sections. One of its distinctive features is that many sections are markedly antiphonal in character. Although we do not know exactly what the composer intended, we have only to glance at the score to imagine different groups of singers and instrumentalists answering one another in turn across the vast and reverberant spaces of the basilica. Various details such as the use of solo *cornetti* – the curved, valveless wooden trumpets that in 'authentic' performances of early music (and in capable hands) can still conjure up a haunting, magical sound quite unlike anything else – or the deliberate 'echo' effects that characterize the concerto *Audi coelum* would have made little sense if the singers or players had simply been standing next to one another. Rather, individual soloists must surely have been placed at some distance from the main body of singers: perhaps high up in one or other of the *nicchie* on opposite sides of the church, or in the organ lofts themselves, or in any of the various locations where, as the *ceremoniali* make clear, musicians could be stationed or concealed.

As *maestro di cappella* at St Mark's for much of the early seventeenth century, Monteverdi could rely on musical forces even more numerous than had been available to Willaert or even Zarlino. A full performance of the *Vespers* might well involve twenty or more instrumentalists, with a choir of perhaps thirty.[121] These

---

121 On the larger numbers of both salaried and occasional musicians employed at St Mark's during the early years of the seventeenth century see Rosand, op. cit., p. 78; also *Grove*, vol. 19, pp. 614ff.

greatly augmented resources made possible a richness of sound and a complexity of spatial effects that, in earlier times, would scarcely have been imaginable. In the light of such evidence, it might be argued that changes in style, which became apparent towards the end of the sixteenth century and which Monteverdi himself ultimately carried to perfection, owed as much to economic as to musical or architectural considerations. But it was not these economic factors in themselves that determined the form of the music. Rather, the more generous resources at his disposal allowed Monteverdi to exploit still more thoroughly than his predecessors the opportunities for contrast offered by the physical setting for which that music was created.

As it happens, Monteverdi's choral works represented not only the culmination but also the end of this particular stylistic tradition. Although he brought in talented younger composers like Cavalli in an attempt to ensure the continuity of high musical standards, Monteverdi himself had no significant followers. By the mid-seventeenth century, the music composed at St Mark's had assumed a somewhat simpler form, was easier to perform and was for the most part devoid of the complex polyphonic writing and use of *cori spezzati* that had been the hallmarks of the preceding century. In the disastrous plague of 1630, moreover, a number of musicians died and, for a period, music making ceased altogether. Thereafter, despite attempts to renew the strength of its choir, St Mark's never fully regained its position as the most important centre of musical life in the city – a position increasingly challenged by newly founded opera companies and by the emphasis placed on the teaching and performance of music by the major Venetian hospital churches such as the Pietà.[122]

---

122 See Rosand, loc. cit., for an account of the increasingly important part that opera companies played in Venetian musical life during the latter part of the seventeenth century. On the role of music at the Incurabili – one of the four major hospital churches that were, in effect, also music conservatories – see Howard, *Sansovino*, esp. pp. 92ff. For a description of music at the Pietà – another of the four churches – compare the same author's 'Giambattista Tiepolo's Frescoes for the Church of the Pietà in Venice', *Oxford Art Journal*, vol. 9 (1986), no. 1, pp. 11–28. The two other churches were the Mendicanti (by Scamozzi) and the Ospedaletto (S. Maria dei Derelitti, after designs by Massari).

V MODE AND MOOD

The basis of music is sound. Its aim is to please and to arouse various emotions in us. Melodies can be at the same time sad and enjoyable.

Descartes, *Compendium Musicae* (1618)

Many writers have described the years around 1600 as a watershed – most notably, perhaps, Arthur Koestler in his great tale of scientific discovery *The Sleepwalkers*.[1] Still more apt might be the metaphor of some vantage point or summit, from which scientists and men of letters could gaze in opposite directions. They could look back on what had gone before them, on what had been primarily an age of metaphysical belief. Or they could peer inquisitively forward to an era in which 'reality' would become more closely identified with the physical world, now seen as the proper object of scientific enquiry.[2] Widespread interest in topics such as the nature of gravity, how forces acted at a distance and the laws governing the behaviour of moving bodies reflected a growing conviction that there remained 'few things that cannot be weighed, numbered and measured' – a conviction as evident in Galileo Galilei's studies of dynamics as it is in his father Vincenzo's experiments that sought empirically to determine the mathematical laws governing musical consonances.[3]

Investigating quantifiable phenomena of this kind meant asking some searching questions about the way things actually worked: questions that usually began with the word 'how?' How did the heavenly bodies revolve? How, indeed, did they produce music; and, if they really did, why was no one able to hear it? In fact, several ancient Greek philosophers had already asked the same question, among them Aristotle, who was characteristically sceptical about the frequently proposed explanation for our inability to hear celestial music, namely that, like those who live by a waterfall or who work amid the continuous din of a smithy, we have become inured to its constant sound.[4] Other writers thought the problem had more to do with our own stubbornly corporeal nature. Milton, for example, remarked that the 'heavenly tune', while keeping 'unsteady

---

1 Arthur Koestler, *The Sleepwalkers. A History of Man's Changing Vision of the Universe*, London (Penguin/Arkana) 1989 (original edition 1959). Part Four of Koestler's book, which deals mainly with Kepler, is entitled 'The Watershed'. Joscelyn Godwin, writing about Athanasius Kircher (1602–80), likewise refers to what he calls the 'watershed period in Western Culture'; see *Music, Mysticism and Magic. A Sourcebook*, London/New York (Routledge & Kegan Paul) 1986, p. 153.

2 Koestler attributes the seventeenth-century concern with 'hard fact and exact measurement' in part to the needs of 'ocean navigation, the increasing precision of magnetic compasses and clocks, and the general progress in technology'. (*Sleepwalkers*, p. 290.)

3 The quotation is taken from Galilei's 'Special Discourse Concerning the Diversity of the Ratios of the Diapason'; see 'Three Scientific Essays by Vincenzo Galilei', in Palisca, *Florentine Camerata*, p. 181.

4 *De Coelo*, 290bff.: see above, ch. 2, pp. 82–3, also pp. 84ff. for the account given by Scipio Africanus (in Cicero, *Somn. Scip.*).

Nature' to her law, remained inaudible to those 'of human mould, with gross unpurgèd ear'.[5] In this, he does little more than echo Shakespeare's Lorenzo who, in the *Merchant of Venice* (*c*.1596–7) regales Jessica with an account of that 'harmony' that is 'in immortal souls' and that imitates the music of the spheres, only to assure her that 'whilst this muddy vesture of decay doth grossly close it in, we cannot hear it'.[6]

Myth, legend and modern science

An insistence on the need for physical explanations and the importance of empirical data might well be counted among the hallmarks of modern science.[7] But in the late sixteenth and early seventeenth centuries, those same concerns went hand in hand with a profound respect for antiquity, whose legends and beliefs still, to a large extent, affected scientific thinking.[8] This tension between conflicting world views is clearly apparent in the life and work of the famous mathematician Johannes Kepler (1571–1630). Kepler is now revered as one of the intellectual giants of the Baroque era, and his *Astronomia Nova* (1609) and *Five Books of the Harmony of the Universe* (1619) still stand as milestones in the history of astronomy. It is therefore somewhat surprising to find that their author genuinely believed in a real (albeit soundless) music of the spheres and thought that the planets as they turned in their orbits together produced a kind of polyphony. In 1617, two years before the *Five Books* were finally published, he wrote to his friend Wackher von Wackenfels about the celestial harmonies in language that has a distinctly Pythagorean ring:

We and the entire choir of planets revolve around the sun,
subservient to him, as it were … as for the heavenly tones,
they are to be reproduced in the usual manner of notation …
Indeed, the tones of the individual [bodies] are thus distinct,
of course, with respect to the pitches, varying in height, of the
musical scale.[9]

---

5 Milton, 'Arcades', quoted after F. T. Prince (ed.), Milton: *'Comus' and other Poems*, Oxford (Oxford U. P.) 1968, p. 33.
6 *Merchant of Venice*, V, 1.
7 Much the same point is made by Gouk, who writes that, in the years around 1600, the term 'science' 'chiefly denoted a body of theoretical knowledge or doctrine about a specific subject'. This kind of knowledge is in contrast to what she calls 'natural philosophy', defined as a form of investigation requiring the 'accumulation of data by means of observation and experiment'; see Penelope Gouk, *Music, Science and Natural Magic in Seventeenth-Century England*, New Haven/London (Yale U. P.) 1999, pp. 9–10.
8 The intellectual and ideological tensions and contradictions characteristic of this period have been frequently described by other authors; see, for example, Gary Tomlinson, *Monteverdi and the End of the Renaissance*, Oxford (Clarendon Press) 1987, esp. ch. 1, 'Oppositions in Late-Renaissance Thought', which includes a discussion of both Galileo and Monteverdi.
9 Johannes Kepler, *Gesammelte Werke, VI: Briefe*, pp. 244–55, quoted after Eric Werner, 'The Last Pythagorean Musician: Johannes Kepler', in LaRue 1967, p. 869. On the ways in which specifically musical theories influenced Kepler's thinking see Bruce Stephenson, *The Music of the Heavens. Kepler's Harmonic Astronomy*, Princeton, NJ (Princeton U. P.) 1994, esp. ch. 5, pp. 75ff.

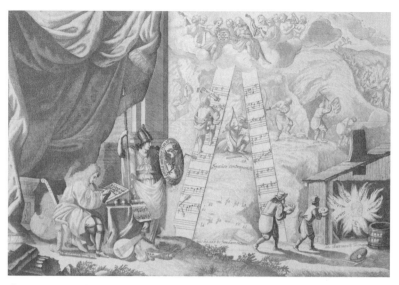

Figure 37. Frontispiece from the lute book by W. L. von Radolt, *Allertreueste Freundin*, 1701, engraving by Hoffman and Hermundt after Waginger

Much of Kepler's scientific thinking is riven by just such contradictions. His calculations of planetary distances and motions, based largely on the meticulous observations of the great Danish astronomer Tycho Brahe, occupied his attention for nearly a quarter of a century, finally yielding a more complete understanding of the movements of the heavenly bodies than any earlier scientist had attained. Kepler's theories – in particular his third or 'harmonic' law of planetary motion – provided the foundation upon which, little more than fifty years later, the Newtonian model of the universe would be constructed. But they scarcely left room any longer for antique notions of celestial harmony: notions to which, paradoxically, he himself clung with all the fervour of religious belief. Eric Werner neatly summed up the ambivalence that characterized not just Kepler but many of his contemporaries when he wrote:

while the Third Law was far ahead of its time – Galileo pronounced it false still in 1632, and only Newton proved it – in his way of thought Kepler harked back more than two millennia, to the Pythagoreans. Yet he demanded strictly empirical proofs, not speculative arguments. This Janus-faced attitude is characteristic of most pioneers of science during the late Renaissance.[10]

---

10 Werner, op. cit., p. 868.

A similar ambivalence pervaded not only scientific enquiry but also other areas of intellectual life. Treatises that deal with the arts of poetry, music and painting look constantly to classical philosophy and literature for support of what often turn out to be surprisingly new ideas. At times, however, it is clear that at least some antique beliefs and legends were beginning to lose their hold on the modern imagination. This waning influence is betrayed, for example, by the numerous dutiful but uninspiring illustrations to be found on the title pages of seventeenth-century collections and anthologies of music (fig. 37). Many of these, as well as depicting various ancient or modern instruments, reproduce long-established and clearly now outworn symbols or attributes of the past: music-making angels or the figures of Harmony and Measure as we encounter them still in the designs for Bardi's Florentine *intermedi*.[11] The same tales are represented visually again and again, as in the engraving by F. Baronius after Paul Schor, printed as the frontispiece to Athanasius Kircher's *Musurgia universalis* (1650), which depicts at lower right a figure symbolizing Music, at lower left that of Pythagoras, while between them the incident of the hammers is shown taking place in a forge (fig. 38). Interestingly, the female figure to the right has a bird perched somewhat precariously on her head. This may be an allusion to the legend of the daughters of Pierus, who were turned into cawing magpies as punishment for their presumption in challenging the Muses to a singing competition, which, needless to say, they lost.[12] If this *is* the intended allusion, it also recalls the libretto of the 1589 *intermedi*, since the story of the Pierides provided the subject-matter for the second *intermedio*, with texts by Rinuccini and music by Luca Marenzio. To judge by the way it is represented here, it seems that this, too, was a legend that had, by the 1650s, lost much of the significance it originally possessed.

Even the hallowed story of Pythagoras and the hammers could no longer evade the new spirit of scientific enquiry. It had been obvious for some time that there was something fundamentally wrong with the traditional account of his discovery of the proportional relationships that underlay the primary musical consonances. If the various antique versions of the tale were to be believed, it had been the sound of the hammers actually hitting the anvil that first alerted him to the 'harmonious' relationship between their respective weights. This, as noted in an earlier chapter, cannot possibly be true, although it appears that not until the first half of the seventeenth

11 On these see above, ch. 2, pp. 87ff.
12 As also pointed out by Joscelyn Godwin, *Athanasius Kircher* (London, 1979), p. 68. The tale of the Pierides is told in Book V of Ovid's *Metamorphoses*.

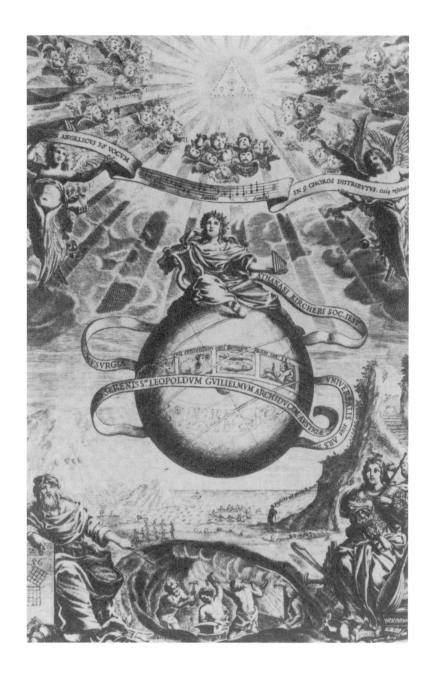

Figure 38. Frontispiece from Athanasius Kircher's *Musurgia universalis*, 1650, engraving by F. Baronius after Paul Schor, with the figures of *Musica* and Pythagoras

century did anyone actually bother to experiment with hammers and anvil in order to disprove the story. The person in question was the French philosopher Marin Mersenne who, in his *Harmonie universelle* of 1636, acidly describes the Pythagorean legend as 'patently false, as can be seen if one experiments with an anvil',[13] implying that he himself had actually tried it out. Several early biographies of Pythagoras also relate how he proceeded to take the hammers home with him (how did the blacksmiths occupy themselves then, one wonders?) and carefully suspended them from strings of equal length and thickness.[14] What he discovered – so the story goes – was that, since the weights of the hammers were in the 'correct' arithmetic ratios, the strings whose tension had been correspondingly increased sounded the intervals of the octave, the fifth and the fourth; and this part of the story, at least, seems to have gone unquestioned until the time of Vincenzo Galilei.[15] It was Galilei who showed that this experiment will almost work – but not quite. The correct intervals cannot be produced if the weights of the hammers are in a straightforward arithmetical relationship to one another, as shown in the woodcut from Gaffurio's treatise reproduced in Chapter 2 (see fig. 14).[16] Rather, it is the square of their respective weights that will bring about the desired result.[17] This discovery apparently delighted Newton, since it coincided with his own inverse square law of gravitational attraction which, he concluded, must have been known to the ancients, implying that this was what Pythagoras had

---

13 Marin Mersenne, *Harmonie Universelle, contenant la théorie et la pratique de la musique* (Paris, 1636). Édition facsimile ... ed. F. Lesure, Paris (Éditions du Centre National de la Recherche Scientifique) 1975 (3 vols), *Livre quatrième de la composition*, Pr. iv (vol. 2), p. 216.
14 Macrobius, *Comm. in Somn. Scip.*, II, i; Boethius, *De institutione musica*, I, x–xi.
15 In Book I, ch. 8 of his *Harmonics*, Ptolemy expressed scepticism as to whether the correct intervals will be produced in this way, but only because he doubted whether it was possible to conduct the experiment under what we would call 'controlled' conditions (having regard to the quality, thickness, etc., of the different strings), not because he questioned the mathematical basis according to which the ratios were to be calculated; see Barker 1989, p. 291, also ibid., pp. 256ff. for Nicomachus's account of Pythagoras' experiment with the hammers.
16 See above, p. 76.
17 Palisca notes that Galilei's discovery is adumbrated in his *Discorso intorno all'opere di Gioseffo Zarlino da Chioggia* (Venice, 1589); see *The Florentine Camerata*, p. 155, also pp. 162-3. The exact details are spelt out in the unpublished *Discorso particolare intorno alla diversità delle forme del diapason*, translated in ibid., pp. 180ff. This may have formed the basis for the imaginary exchange between Sagredo and Salviati concerning ratios, weights and consonances in Galileo Galilei's *Discorsi e dimostrazioni matematiche intorno a due nuove scienzie*, Leyden (Elseverius) 1638. See further D. P. Walker, 'Vincenzo Galilei and Zarlino', in Walker 1978, pp. 25–6; also Frieder Rempp (ed.), *Die Kontrapunkttraktate Vincenzo Galileis*, Cologne (Arno Volk) 1980.
18 In his article 'Newton and the wisdom of the ancients', Piyo Rattansi notes that, according to Newton's interpretation of events, Pythagoras must have 'recognized that the harmony of the spheres required the force of the Sun to act upon the planets in that harmonic ratio of distance by which the force of tension acts upon strings of different length – that is, inversely as the square of the distance'. Newton himself added drily that 'Pythagoras and the sages who invented the mystical philosophy of the ancients were men by far the most acute, as Macrobius relates' (in John Fauvel, Raymond Flood, Michael Shortland and Robin Wilson (eds), *Let Newton be! A New Perspective on his Life and Works*, Oxford (Oxford U. P.) 1988, pp. 189–90); see also Gouk 1999, pp. 253–4.

really meant all along by the 'music of the spheres'.[18] We may think this ironic, since it was Newton's discoveries, even more than those of Kepler, that finally put paid to anyone seriously believing any longer in the idea of celestial music.[19]

Music ancient and modern

Writings by sixteenth- and seventeenth-century musical theorists likewise betray an ambivalence similar to that which gripped their counterparts in the sciences and the other arts. On the one hand, their minds were, at times, clearly focused on questions that begin once again with the word 'how?' How was it that some intervals were perceived as consonant while others were dissonant? How could one determine what emotional or expressive value attached to one interval by comparison with another? On the other hand, it seems as if discussion of these questions could scarcely be carried on for more than a few sentences without some reference being made to the antique, and to ancient Greek music in particular, about which every writer was evidently expected to hold some opinion. This applies not only to those whose interests were primarily antiquarian and who were anxious to rediscover or re-create the lost music of antiquity; it is also true of writers whose main concern was with contemporary musical practice. Throughout the Renaissance and early Baroque, the latest developments in contemporary music tended to be either explained or criticized in terms of a comparison with Greek musical theory or with what the music of antiquity was believed to have been like.[20] This preoccupation is reflected in the titles of a succession of treatises, from Nicola Vicentino's *Antique Music Adapted to Modern Practice* of 1555 to G. B. Doni's *On the Superiority of the Old Music ... whereby the Old and New Music in all their Aspects are Precisely Compared*, which appeared almost a century later, in 1647.[21] The sometimes acrimonious debates and disagreements

---

19 Note that the same discovery concerning the squares of the ratios had also been announced by Mersenne ('j'ai montré ... que les poids doivent pour le moins être en raison doublée des termes qui contiennent les Consonances') in his *Harmonie Universelle*, p. 216. In his correspondence and elsewhere, Mersenne acknowledged Galilei's priority in discovering the laws governing strings, pipes and bells; see Palisca, *Florentine Camerata*, p. 162 and further refs.

20 On occasion, antique writers on music such as Aristoxenus are specifically cited and their theories used as ammunition, as in the case of Ercole Bottrigari's criticisms of Francesco Patrizi, in *Il Patricio, overo De' tetracordi armonici di Aristosseno* (Bologna, 1593); see Claude V. Palisca, 'The Artusi-Monteverdi Controversy', in Denis Arnold and Nigel Fortune (eds), *The New Monteverdi Companion*, London (Faber) 1985, pp. 128–9.

21 Nicola Vicentino, *L'antica musica ridotta alla moderna pratica* (Rome, 1555); Giovanni Battista Doni, *De praestantia musicae veteris libri tres ... in quibus vetus ac recens musica, cum singulis earum partibus, accurate inter se conferuntur* (Florence, 1647). The phrase 'adapted to modern practice' is found in a number of writings of this period; see, for example, the third edition of Adriano Banchieri's *Cartella musicale nel canto figurato ... in questa terza impressione ridotta dall' antica alla moderna pratica* (Venice, 1614).

provoked by these publications – a true 'quarrel of the ancients and moderns' – often turned on the alleged superiority of antique music. Gioseffo Zarlino, whom we have already encountered as Monteverdi's predecessor as *maestro di cappella* at St Mark's in Venice, remarked scathingly on the complexities of contemporary polyphonic writing, typified by the compositions of sixteenth-century madrigalists like Cipriano de Rore (a composer greatly admired at that time including, as it happens, by Zarlino himself), which he compared unfavourably with the simpler declamatory style of the ancient Greek composer-poets:

That the music of our own day can induce in us various passions, just as it did in antiquity, can occasionally be seen when some beautiful, erudite and elegant poem is recited to the accompaniment of some instrument. Then, the listeners are greatly moved, and incited to various emotions, such as laughing, or crying, and other such things ... If such effects were wrought by music in antiquity, it was recited as described above, and not in the way that is used at present, with a multitude of parts, and so many singers and players that at times nothing is heard but a jumbled din of voices and instruments ... But when music is recited with taste, approaching more closely the manner of the ancients, that is, in a simple style, singing to the sound of the lira, *lute or other similar instruments ... then one can see its effects. For indeed, those songs in which brief subjects are treated in but few words, as is customary today in certain canzonets known as madrigals, are capable of moving the soul but little.*[22]

One intriguing thing about this extract from Zarlino's treatise on harmony is the apparent confidence with which he describes the musical practice of the ancients, a subject about which, in reality, next to nothing was then known. Of the few surviving fragments of Greek music, not until the start of the seventeenth century were the hymns attributed to Mesomedes published by Vincenzo Galilei in the second edition of his *Dialogo della musica antica e della moderna*, and even these were merely transcribed in their original notation, which Galilei had been unable to decipher.[23] In fact,

---

22 Gioseffo Zarlino, *Le istitutioni harmoniche*, II, 9, in *De tutte l'opere del R. M. Gioseffo Zarlino ... Il primo volume, contenente l'Istitutioni harmoniche divise in quattro parti ... in Venetia, MDLXXXIX, Apresso Francesco de' Franceschi Senese*, p. 92; all further references are to this 1589 edition. For a slightly different translation of the same passage, see Palisca, *Humanism*, pp. 371ff.

23 See D. P. Walker, 'Musical Humanism in the Sixteenth and Early Seventeenth Centuries' [part 1], *Music Review*, vol. 2 (1941), p. 2 and n. 7; also Michaelides, *Encyclopaedia*, p. 288.

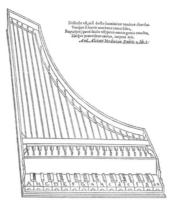

perciocche in loro senza alcuna necessità farebbono multiplicate le chorde: le quali(oltra le mostrate) nò sarebbono atte ad esprimere altri concenti più dilesteuoli, di quelli che son no vdire quelle,che sono collocate nel mostrato istrumento; i quali veramēte sono Diatoni ci, ouer Chromatici,o pure Enharmonici. Et se alcuni credessero, che potessino esprimere altri concenti,che li tre sopradetti; di gran lunga s'ingannano: perche niuna altra spe cie di Diatonico, ne di Chromatico, ne di Enharmonico si può ridurre alla sua perfes sione : come vederemo altroue : & come facendone ogni proua, ciascuno dassè lo potrà vedere. Ma perche io credo,che homai la Diuisione di cotali generi & la loro natura sia nota a ciascuno ingegnoso: però non mi estenderò più oltra, in voler dare di loro al cuna ragione : conciosia che gran parte delle difficultà , che potranno occorrere & saranno di qualche importanza in questa Scienza ,si potranno vedere dimostrate & con ogni diligenza esplicate nelle nostre DEMOSTRATIONI harmoniche: le altre cose più si lasciaro al giudicio del discreto Lettore , che si hauerà nel maneggio de i Numeri & delle Misure ottimamente essercitato. Dirò adunque per concludere, che questo è vn Istrumento ,sopra il quale si potrà essercitare ogni ottimo Sonatore,non so lamente

Figure 39. Plate from Zarlino's *Le istitutioni harmoniche*, showing panharmonic harpsichord with divided keyboard, accompanied by a quotation from Andrea Alciato's *Emblematum liber*

Zarlino was well aware of the fact that, as he put it, 'modern music is practised differently from ancient music' and that there was 'no example or vestige of it which can lead us to a true and perfect knowledge'.[24] Despite his admiration for the ancient Greek composers and the 'marvellous effects' he believed they had been capable of creating, he cautions against wasting time, 'a thing more precious than anything else', in an attempt actually to re-create the music of the past. Those who occupy themselves in this way, he writes, 'do not realize that we do not yet have a full knowledge [even] of the diatonic *genus*, and truly they do not know in what manner the modes were used, according to the custom of the ancients'.[25] He also ridicules the ideas of Vicentino and others, who advocated reviving the antique *genera*, by including in Book I of his *Istitutioni harmoniche* a woodcut showing a keyboard with nineteen notes to the octave, the black keys being further divided so as to provide additional pitches: for example, between the notes e and f (fig. 39). As if to pour scorn on Vicentino's lack

---

24 *Ist. harm.*, IV, 1; *Opere*, vol. 1, p. 377.
25 Ibid., IV, 3; *Opere*, vol. 1, p. 386.

of learning, this illustration is accompanied by a quotation from Andrea Alciato's *Emblematum liber* (1531), one of the most famous emblem books of the sixteenth century, which reads *Difficile est nisi docto homini tot tendere chordas*: 'It is difficult, unless he is skilled, for one man to span so many strings.'[26]

Words and music: Monteverdi's 'second practice'

Fifty years after the first publication of Zarlino's *Istitutioni harmoniche*, the same preoccupation with ancient Greek ideas and the relationship between music and text was evidently in the forefront of Monteverdi's mind when he sought to defend the new style that he called *la seconda pratica*: 'the second practice'. This was a freer, more expressive and more dissonant manner of writing, where harmony and counterpoint were no longer governed by the laws of consonance and dissonance laid down by Zarlino.[27] Apparently, Monteverdi intended to write a pamphlet, or perhaps even an entire treatise on this topic, under the title *Seconda pratica overo Perfettione della moderna musica* ('The Second Practice, or Perfection of Modern Music'). In the end, all that appeared was a brief letter printed by way of a preface to his fifth book of madrigals (1605).[28] Addressed to the 'studious reader', this famous letter makes, as it happens, no mention whatever of antiquity. However, Monteverdi's brother Giulio Cesare, evidently anxious that the composer's intentions should be properly understood, published a lengthy commentary, in which he quotes repeatedly from Plato: both from the *Gorgias* and the *Republic* (in the translation by Marsilio Ficino) as well as from Ficino's *Compendium in Timaeum*. We can only assume that this commentary was written with his brother's approval and that it reflects Monteverdi's own thinking. Part of Giulio Cesare's 'explanation' reads as follows:

He [the composer] will take his stand upon the consonances and dissonances approved by mathematics ... likewise [he] will take his stand upon the command of the words, the chief mistress of the art considered from the point of view of the perfection of the melody, as Plato affirms in the third book of his Republic *... Here is what Plato says:* Sola enim melodia ab omnibus quotcunque distrahunt animum retrahens contrahit in se ipsum *[For only*

---

26 See Paul P. Raasveld, 'Echoes of Andrea Alciato's "Foedera" in the Musical Theory of his Contemporary Gioseffo Zarlino', *Emblematica*, vol. 7, no. 12 (winter 1993), pp. 387–95.

27 Palisca, 'The Artusi-Monteverdi Controversy', pp. 127–58; also *Grove*, vol. 15, pp. 228–9.

28 C. Monteverdi, *Il quinto libro de' madrigali* (Venice, 1605); see Margaret Murata, *The Baroque Era*, in Oliver Strunk (ed.), *Source Readings in Music History*, rev. edn by Leo Treitler, New York (W. W. Norton) 1998 (cited hereafter as Strunk IV), p. 536.

melody, turning the mind away from all things whatsoever that distract, reduces the mind to itself]. And not harmony alone, be it ever so perfect, as the Reverend Zarlino concedes in these words: 'If we take harmony absolutely, without adding to it anything else ... in a certain way it intrinsically prepares for and disposes [us] to joy or sadness, but it does not on this account lead to the expression of any extrinsic effect.'[29]

To us, it may appear strange that debate about Monteverdi's distinctive use of dissonant intervals (his madrigals had been attacked by the Bolognese theorist Giovanni Maria Artusi, mainly because of their frequent use of undisguised dissonances) should turn on observations about music and words made some two thousand years earlier by Plato and other ancient Greek philosophers. But in most seventeenth-century discussions of questions to do with harmony and counterpoint, consonance and dissonance, the arguments put forward by the various opposing parties tended likewise to revolve around the issue of music's relationship to the text. In the case of those who advocated a return to archaic musical practice, this may have been because ancient Greek music was thought to have been primarily vocal, consisting of declamation reinforced by instrumental accompaniment. Or it may have been because Plato had disdained the notion of music without words (which suggests that it may have been none the less commonly practised), describing it as merely 'confusing'.[30] But, regardless of their standpoint, almost everyone agreed that music, viewed as a serious form of art rather than mere mindless entertainment, was indissolubly linked to what were essentially narrative purposes. Artusi himself, quoting the opinion of a somewhat shadowy figure identified only as 'L'Ottuso academico' ('obtuse academic'), writes that 'the singer is the soul of music ... it is he who, in sum, represents the true meaning of the composer to us'.[31] Only gradually did the growth and increasing popularity of purely instrumental music lead writers and composers to wonder whether, or in what way, particular combinations of musical tones and intervals might be expressive in themselves or consider how music might be used in order to convey purely 'abstract' meanings.[32]

---

29 Quoted after Strunk IV, pp. 541–2.
30 See above, ch. 2, pp. 67–8.
31 Palisca, 'The Artusi-Monteverdi Controversy', pp. 150–1. On the probable identity of Artusi's 'obtuse academic' see ibid., pp. 136ff.; for further discussion of the controversy itself compare Tomlinson 1987, pp. 21ff.
32 Various seventeenth-century compilations of instrumental music were apparently conceived in terms of their 'affects' upon the listener: for example, the *Affeti Musicali* by the composer Biagio Marini (Venice, 1617). Despite the fact that its subtitle specifies *canzone* and *arie*, and that two of the four parts are given as *canto primo* and *canto secondo*, the music itself is exclusively instrumental; for a modern edition see *Biagio Marini. String Sonatas from Opus 1 and Opus 8*, transcribed and edited by Thomas D. Dunn (*Collegium Musicum*: Yale University Second Series, vol. X), Madison, WI (A-R Editions, Inc.) 1981.

Theories of music applied to painting

For Renaissance scholars who wrote about the music of the past, the shortage of surviving examples from Greek antiquity came as something of a disappointment. But, in the absence of the music, they could at least turn to a substantial body of theory: not only treatises handed down in the form of medieval copies but also, in many cases, versions of those same treatises now translated from the original Greek into Latin or even the vernacular. By comparison, those who wrote about the visual arts had no such ancient treatises on painting or sculpture they could rely on. Heroic efforts were made, for example by the Dutch theorist Franciscus Junius, to assemble all the scattered references that could be found in Pliny or Cicero or other classical sources and cobble them together into something resembling an antique theory of painting. Other writers on art like Giovanni Pietro Bellori adopted a similar strategy. Bellori's theories, as first proposed in his lecture entitled 'The Idea of the Painter, Sculptor and Architect' delivered before the Accademia di S. Luca in Rome in 1672, greatly influenced French academic theory.[33] But the fact remained that no comprehensive account of any of the visual arts had passed down from antiquity to modern times, with the sole exception of Vitruvius' *Ten Books on Architecture*. Partly for this reason, seventeenth-century writers on painting turned readily to aspects of musical theory, wondering whether ideas concerning music's expressive potential might provide a model after which some account of the affective character of painting could be formulated. The fact that these musical writings invariably cited the authority of the ancients can only have made such ideas more appealing.

Several topics that provoked animated debate among musical theorists in the years around 1600 were also of interest to writers concerned to develop a more cogent theory of the visual arts. One such topic had to do with what has been called the 'expressive value' of intervals. The increased complexity of polyphonic writing, as it had developed over the preceding century and a half, now led musical theorists to define intervals in two different ways. The first of these is the simpler of the two, where 'interval' denotes merely two notes sounded together. On any keyboard instrument, strike the notes C and G simultaneously. What you will hear is the 'interval' of a fifth. This, like the octave or the fourth, appears more

---

[33] Franciscus Junius, *De pictura veterum* (1637); Giovanni Pietro Bellori, *Le vite de' pittore, scultori e architetti moderni* (1672); for extracts from both as well as a useful introduction to theoretical writings of this period generally see Charles Harrison, Paul Wood and Jason Geiger (eds), *Art in Theory 1648–1815. An Anthology of Changing Ideas*, Oxford (Blackwell) 2000, pp. 1–28, 96ff. (cited hereafter as *Art in Theory* I).

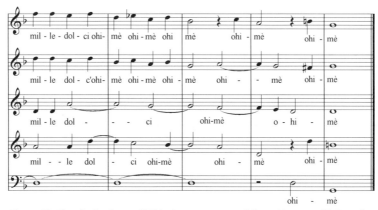

Figure 40. The closing bars of 'Ohimè se tanto amate', from Monteverdi's *Fourth Book of Madrigals* (1603). Here, the effect of the repeated word 'ohimè' ('alas') is heightened by the use of undisguised dissonances – precisely the feature of Monteverdi's music to which the composer Artusi so pointedly objected (see above, p. 189).

pleasing to the ear – that is, 'smoother' or more 'natural' – than other intervals. Octaves, fifths and fourths were therefore held to be consonant and had been defined as such by various antique theorists, albeit for reasons that were primarily mathematical rather than aesthetic.[34] Other intervals, by contrast, were considered dissonant because they appeared 'harsh' or 'grating': for example, the major seventh (c–b) or the minor second (c–d flat). Most Renaissance textbooks on harmony forbade the use of these dissonant intervals, even in fast-moving polyphony, unless they were 'prepared' in the form of a suspension or by some other means. These precepts did not, however, prevent composers like Monteverdi from making repeated use of just such dissonances, whether 'prepared' or not, which were exploited for the sake of greater expressiveness (fig. 40).

But 'interval' can also mean the distance between two notes when sounded sequentially, instead of together. (For example, the rising leap formed by the first two notes of *Auld lang syne*: 'Should auld acquaintance be forgot ...' is the 'interval' of a fourth.) Renaissance and Baroque theorists spent a good deal of time reflecting on the specific character of various intervals, understood in this sense. They sought to define how and in what context they should be used and the emotional meanings that clung to them. In his *Dialogo* of 1581, Vincenzo Galilei observed that 'joy and sadness, and the other passions, can be caused in the listener not only by high and low sounds, and by rapid or slow movements, but also by the different quality of

---

34 See above, ch. 2, pp. 77ff.

the intervals'.[35] Whether those intervals were larger or smaller, major or minor, rising or falling – all this seemed profoundly to affect their meanings. Mersenne, in his *Harmonie universelle,* describes the major imperfect consonances (that is, thirds and sixths) as 'very suitable for joy, and for expressing virile and courageous actions', the minor for 'flattering and for softening the passions, and for expressing sadness and pain'.[36] Elsewhere in his same compendious treatise, he relates the size and direction of intervals to human actions and movements, writing that 'semitones and accidentals represent tears and groans because of their small intervals, which signify weakness; for little intervals, either ascending or descending, are like children, like old people or those who have recently had a long illness.'[37]

That major intervals were happier or more gay than minor ones, which were perceived as sad or melancholy, was a matter of fairly general agreement. In his *Istitutioni harmoniche*, Zarlino had declared that the 'property and nature' of the imperfect consonances was that 'some of them are lively and cheerful [while] some, although they are sweet and smooth, tend somewhat towards sadness or languor', explaining this in terms of the quality of the 'third above the final'. While the terminology used is that of medieval musical theory, the account he gives is precisely the same as the one we would give today. A triad is defined as major or minor depending on the quality of the third: thus C–E–G for the major triad and C–E flat–G for the minor. The explanation for the different effects thereby produced, Zarlino thought, was mathematical, since the consonances are 'placed according to the nature of the sonorous number ... that is, the fifth ... divided harmonically into a major third and a minor third; which gives much pleasure to the ear.'[38]

Descartes on music

Although musicians and musical theorists were preoccupied with defining the expressive character of intervals and of particular

---

35 Quoted after 'The Expressive Value of Intervals', in Walker 1978, p. 65.
36 Mersenne, *Harmonie Universelle, livre troisième des genres*, Pr. xviii (vol. 2), p. 188.
37 Ibid., *Livre second des chants*, Pr. xxvi (vol. 2), p. 173. In similar vein, in his *L'antica musica ridotta alla moderna pratica* (1555) Nicola Vicentino writes of the minor third that 'its nature is very feeble, and is rather sad, and likes to descend ... [or] when it ascends slowly, it will have the nature of a man when he is tired ... this consonance is very suitable for sad words when it is prolonged'. (Walker, 'Expressive Value ...', as n. [35] above, p. 64.) Vicentino's statement is especially interesting because his mention of the minor third being 'prolonged' suggests that he is thinking of this interval harmonically: that is, in the first of the two senses defined above.
38 *Ist. harm.*, III, x; *Opere*, vol. 1, pp. 191–2. A similar explanation is given in Sethus Calvisius' *Melopoeia sive melodiae condendae ratio* (Erfurt, 1592), which notes that 'the most joyful modes are Ionian, Lydian and Myxolydian, because the fifth is divided harmonically. The sadder and more languid [modes], on the other hand, [are] Dorian, Phrygian and Aeolian because of the arithmetic division of the same interval. For everywhere the harmonic division expresses a smoother sound than the arithmetic'; quoted after Joel Lester, 'Major-Minor Concepts and Modal Theory in Germany, 1592–1890', *Journal of the American Musicological Society*, vol. 30, no. 2 (summer 1977), p. 221.

COLOUR PLATES

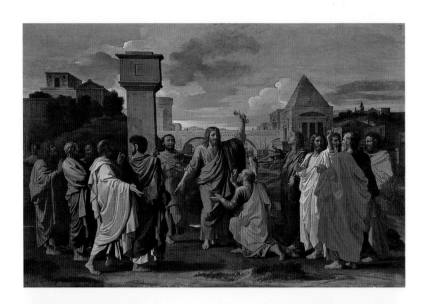

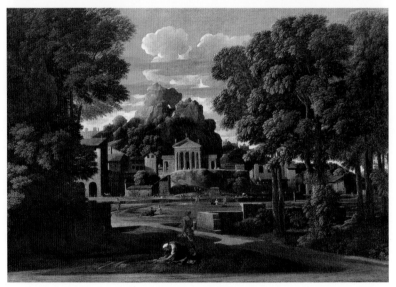

Plate 8. Nicolas Poussin, *Ordination*, from the second series of the *Seven Sacraments*, 1647, oil on canvas, 117 x 178 cm, 46 x 70 in (National Galleries of Scotland, Duke of Sutherland Collection, Edinburgh)

Plate 9. Nicolas Poussin, *Landscape with the Ashes of Phocion*, 1648, oil on canvas, 116 x 176 cm, 45^5_8 x 69^1_8 in (Walker Art Gallery, Liverpool)

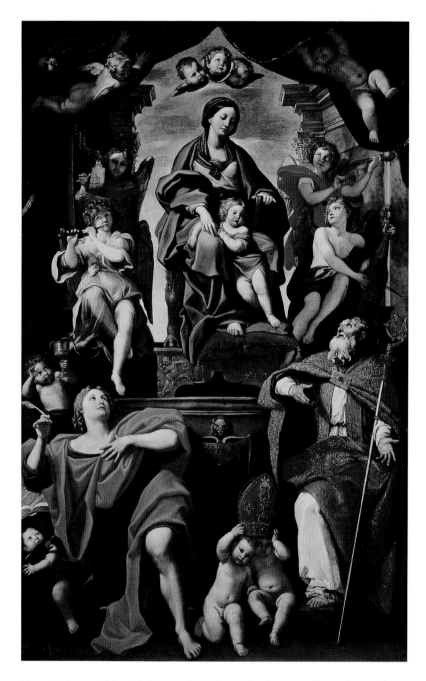

Plate 10. Domenichino, *Madonna with Saints John the Evangelist and Petronius*,
1626–9, oil on canvas, 420 x 267 cm, 165³⁄₈ x 105¹⁄₈ in (Galleria Nazionale,
Palazzo Barberini, Rome)

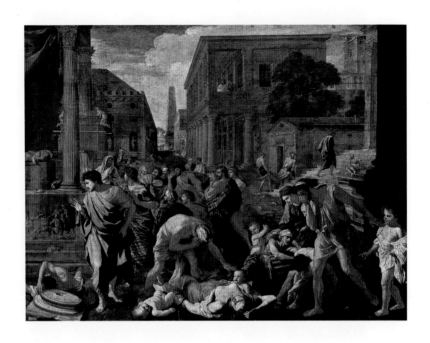

Plate 11. Nicolas Poussin, *The Plague at Ashdod*, c.1630, oil on canvas, 148 x 198 cm, 58^1_4 x 78 in (Musée du Louvre, Paris)

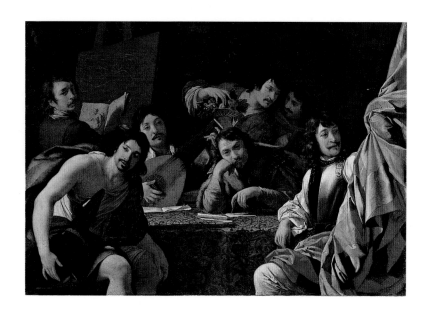

Plate 12. Eustache Le Sueur, *The Music Party* (*Réunion d'Amis*), *c.*1640, oil on canvas, 136 x 195 cm, 53^{1}2 x 77 in (Musée du Louvre, Paris)

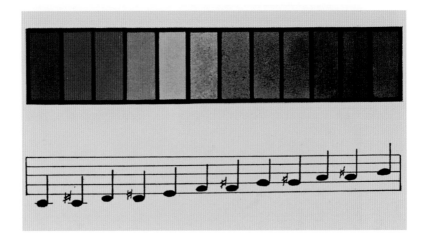

Plate 13. Rimington's table of correspondences between colours and musical pitches ('Chromatic scale in Music and Colour') from A. W. Rimington, *Colour-Music*, London, 1912, after p. 20

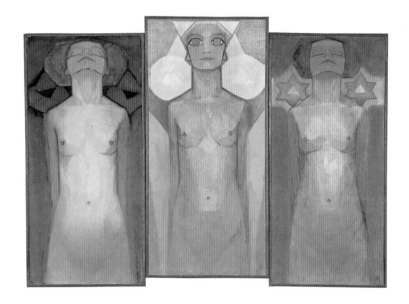

Plate 14. Piet Mondrian, *Evolution*, 1910–11, triptych, oil on canvas, 183 x 87.5 cm,
72 x 34^{1}₂ in (central panel), 178 x 85 cm, 70 x 33^{1}₂ in (each side panel)
(Haags Gemeentemuseum, The Hague)

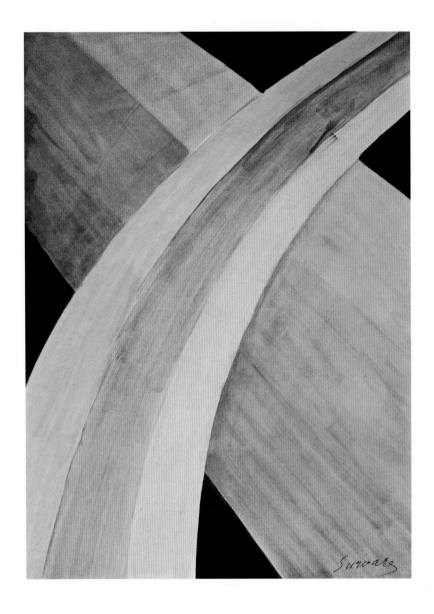

Plate 15. Léopold Survage, study for *Rhythmes colorées*, 1913, watercolour and ink on paper, 33 x 31 cm, 13 x 12^3$_8$ in (Museum of Modern Art, New York)

kinds of harmonic progression, the effects that these were capable of producing upon the listener were rarely, if ever, judged sufficient or satisfying in themselves. Just as debate about Monteverdi's 'expressive' use of dissonances had turned upon their relationship to the words, the affective properties of music in general were discussed almost exclusively with reference to the meaning of the text or libretto and how that meaning might be expressed or reinforced. Not until the early years of the seventeenth century did a philosopher (rather than a musician) devote serious attention to the affective properties of chords and intervals, considered independently of any verbal element. This was Descartes, whose brief *Compendium of Music* was written as early as 1618 during an uneventful period of military service spent by its author in Brabant. It betrays a seemingly innate curiosity regarding the nature of musical sounds: not only their physical characteristics but also their psychological or emotive effects.

It is true that some of what Descartes says appears to differ little from remarks made by other, more traditional theorists of music. He writes, for example, that 'the major third and the major sixth are more pleasing and more gay than the minor third and minor sixth; this is well known to composers ...'[39] There is nothing revolutionary about that: one can find similar observations in many sixteenth- and seventeenth-century musical sources, some of which have already been cited. But it is clear that he was also thinking in terms of the intrinsic meanings and affects of music rather than just the expression of words, as when he declares that 'time in music has such power that it alone can be pleasurable by itself; such is the case with the military drum ...'[40] Hollander suggests that Descartes' primary concern was not with the relationship between text and musical setting in vocal music, which is clearly true. For Descartes 'the essence of music is instrumental sound, or the vocal intonation of sound modelled on the former, the voice being treated merely as another instrument ... In short, the effects of music upon feelings are purely matters of acoustics and physiology.'[41] Nor is he concerned, unlike so many of his contemporaries, with the music of antiquity or traditional classifications of the various branches of music. His 'little book' dismisses the 'historical, metaphysical and cosmological synthesis of *musica speculativa*' in its very announcement of intention – that same announcement quoted at the

---

39 René Descartes, *Compendium of Music (Compendium Musicae)*. Translation by Walter Robert. Introduction and Notes by Charles Kent (*Musicological Studies and Documents*, 8), Rome (American Institute of Musicology) 1961, p. 27.

40 Ibid., p. 15.

41 Hollander, *Untuning of the Sky*, p. 179.

beginning of this chapter: 'The basis of music is sound. Its aim is to please and to arouse various emotions in us.'[42]

For the next century and a half, arguments raged back and forth as to the merits or defects of music when freed from any verbal associations. To us, the vehemence with which this discussion was conducted must appear somewhat surprising. When we think of the early eighteenth century, we think not only of Handel's operas and oratorios or the Passions and church cantatas of J. S. Bach but also of Handel's *concerti grossi* and keyboard sonatas as well as Bach's *Brandenburg Concertos*, his sublime *Goldberg Variations* or his magisterial *Art of Fugue* – all purely instrumental compositions. Yet as late as 1711 Sir Richard Steele, writing in the *Spectator*, still cast doubt on whether music without words could possibly lay claim to any serious value. His remarks were part of a heated exchange over the alleged superiority of English opera or music accompanying texts with English words, which is starkly contrasted with the Italian opera introduced into England by Handel and others. In the course of this argument, Steele prints a letter that, while stressing the need to associate music with words that should be both audible and comprehensible, also makes a more widespread disdain of instrumental music abundantly clear. It is worth quoting *in extenso*:

Believing your Method of Judging is, that you consider Musick only valuable as it is agreeable to and heightens the purpose of Poetry, we consent that That is not only the true Way of relishing that Pleasure, but that without it a Composure of Musick is the same Thing as a Poem, where all the Rules of Poetical Numbers are observed, but the Words of no Sense of Meaning ... Meer musical Sounds are in our Art no other than nonsense Verses are in Poetry. Musick therefore is to aggravate what is intended by Poetry; it must always have some Passion or Sentiment to express, or else Violins, Voices, or any other Organs of Sound, afford an Entertainment very little above the Rattles of Children.[43]

Lomazzo's 'Treatise on Painting'

By the end of the Renaissance, discussions about the affective properties of harmonies and intervals had become commonplace – and not only in musical circles. On the contrary, they would have been just as familiar to artists and theorists of art who took an interest in musical matters. One such theorist was the Milanese

---

42 Ibid., p. 177; *Compendium of Music*, p. 11.
43 *Spectator*, no. 258 (26 December 1711).

Gian Paolo Lomazzo, who wrote what was probably the most influential treatise (in his case, on painting) of the entire sixteenth century: his *Trattato dell'arte della pittura* (1584). Lomazzo's *Treatise* went through three published editions in little more than a year: a remarkable achievement for that period.[44] It was also quickly translated into English. More than a century later, the ideas it contained were still being cited in England, even by an artist as sceptical as the painter and satirist Hogarth.[45]

Lomazzo grew up in Milan, the same flourishing musical environment that nurtured the painter Arcimboldo, whose experiments with colour and musical notation are discussed in the next chapter. His own interest in music is amply documented by his various writings. In his *Idea del tempio della pittura*, Lomazzo stresses, as does Vitruvius, the essential role that an understanding of music, like that of architecture, plays in the education of the artist, 'without which the painter cannot attain perfection'.[46] He was clearly familiar with Vitruvius' *Ten Books on Architecture*: not only the text itself but also the commentaries by Barbaro and Cesariano in which, as previously noted, a good deal of attention is paid to musical questions. He also refers tantalizingly to the ideas of the contemporary architect Giacomo Soldati – who, it seems, had invented a sixth order of architecture: the 'harmonic' order, which was intended to embrace the harmonious proportions inherent in the other five classical orders (Tuscan, Doric, Ionic, Corinthian and Composite). We know little about Soldati, other than the fact that he was employed by Emanuele Filiberto, Duke of Savoy, and that he was active as a military architect and hydraulic engineer.[47] And we know nothing at all about his use (if he ever actually used it) of the 'harmonic order' which, Lomazzo tells us, was 'easily distinguished by the ear' but which the eye found it 'more difficult' to identify.[48] However, architectural treatises of the late sixteenth and early seventeenth centuries from Vignola to Scamozzi via Giovan Battista Villalpando abound in similarly vague references to the 'harmonious' proportions to be employed by architects – references that still draw heavily on Vitruvius' account of the orders and on the Pythagorean notion of 'musical' ratios.[49]

---

44 For an account of the various editions of Lomazzo's treatise on painting see Gian Paolo Lomazzo, *Scritti sulle arti, a cura di Roberto Paolo Ciardi*, Florence (Marchi & Bertolli) 1973, vol. 1, pp. lxxxiii ff.

45 Hogarth refers several times to Lomazzo (whom he calls, perhaps deliberately, Lamozzo) in his *Analysis of Beauty* (1753).

46 *Idea del tempio della pittura*, ch. viii, *Delle scienze necessarie al pittore; Scritti*, vol. 1, p. 273.

47 Wittkower, *Architectural Principles*, pp. 120ff.

48 *Scritti*, p. 274.

49 Wittkower, *Architectural Principles*, gives a succinct account of these and other architectural theorists and of the usually vague or general uses of such musical analogies that occur in their writings.

In another essay, his fantastic-allegorical *Book of Dreams*, Lomazzo not only mentions figures as diverse as Aristoxenus, Beelzebub and Sappho but also lists in passing an astonishing array of names of contemporary composers and musicians. Some are still famous, like the madrigalist Cipriano da Rore; others are now unidentifiable or barely heard of. He also writes – knowledgeably, it seems – about all those who 'divided music into the enharmonic, chromatic and diatonic' and who distinguished the principal modes of ancient music 'according to the names of their regions: Phrygian, Lydian, and Dorian'.[50]

But it is Lomazzo's *Treatise on Painting* that affords perhaps the most instructive comparison with contemporary musical theory, as can be seen from his account of colour. Not only do colours, Lomazzo claims, have a certain 'agreement or disagreement' between themselves, but he also considers them capable of calling forth in the observer precise emotional states.[51] He discusses each colour in turn, starting with black and white and proceeding via red, turquoise and yellow. In Chapter 3 of his *Trattato*, where this more detailed analysis of colours is found, their affective properties are mainly linked with symbolic associations, at least partly derived from antiquity. (For instance, red is associated with revenge or with the red mantle traditionally used to cover the bodies of Christian martyrs.)[52] But in the introductory chapter, where the effects of colour are described in a more general fashion, any reference to such symbolic values is entirely lacking; instead, colours are described solely in terms of their effect upon the viewer's mood or emotions.

It is hard to escape the conclusion that, to a painter well-informed about music like Lomazzo, contemporary theories about the expressive capacities of tones and intervals must have offered an enticing model for his account of the affective properties of colours. He writes, for example, that:

because all colours have different qualities, therefore they cause diverse effects in the beholders ... black, light, earthy, lead-like, and obscure colours, by reason of their heavy qualities, being apprehended by the eye, do breed in the mind of the beholder tardity, musing, melancholy, &c. Black, green, the colour of the sapphire, reddish, or obscure, or the

---

50 *Libro de sogni, Ragionamento quarto; Scritti,* vol. 1, pp. 68ff.
51 *Scritti,* vol. 2, p. 170. The English translation by Richard Haydocke (see n. [53] below) renders this as 'a natural concord and discord' between colours, although Lomazzo himself does not use quite the same image, alluding merely to their 'amicizie et inimicizie naturali' (their natural sympathy or antipathy to each other).
52 *Trattato,* Bk. 3, ch. xiv: *Del color rosso; Scritti,* vol. 2, p. 181.

*colour of gold and silver mixed together as yellow yield a
pleasurable sweetness. Red, fiery, flame colour, violet,
purple, the colour of iron red hot, and sanguine cause
courage, providence, fierceness and boldness by stirring up
the mind like fire. Gold colours, yellows, light purples, and
other bright colours make a man vigilant, adding grace and
sweetness. The rose colour, light greens, and bright yellows,
yield joy, mirth, delight, &c.*[53]

Some writers have found this discussion of the effects of colour
surprisingly modern, by contrast with various archaic aspects of
Lomazzo's theory of painting.[54] But in fact, his treatise manifests
precisely the same tension or ambivalence we have encountered
several times in writings not just about music but also about
scientific and literary questions. On the one hand, a good deal of
time is spent discussing rather prosaic things like narrative,
gesture, the motion of figures and the depiction of natural
phenomena such as wind and waves. Much of what Lomazzo writes
is unashamedly derivative, as when he describes the proportions of
the human figure in terms of musical consonances. The ratio of the
breadth of the foot to the height of the instep, he writes, is a
diatesseron, that of the distance from the shoulder to the elbow and
from the elbow to the wrist a *diapente*.[55] Such remarks are
indistinguishable from those of Vitruvius or Alberti or any of the
authors whose ideas about musical proportion we have examined in
the preceding chapter.

In book three of his *Treatise*, on the other hand, Lomazzo writes in
a more original manner about the qualities of painting generally. As
noted earlier, he goes to considerable lengths to define the affective
properties of colours and explain how certain colours come to be
invested with particular kinds of emotional significance. Nowhere,
however, does he suggest that we should exploit colours solely on
account of their expressive potential, regardless of narrative or
subject. Indeed, he clearly believed the opposite: namely, that colour
should be employed in an appropriate manner, as befits the nature of
the subject and the forms or objects depicted. In this respect, his
views closely resemble more conservative aspects of contemporary

---

53 *Trattato*, Bk. 3, ch. xi: *De gl'effetti che causono i colori.* Because it is of some interest in its own right, I have
   followed the late sixteenth-century English translation: *A Tracte containing the Curious Artes of
   Painting Carving and Building. Written first in Italian by Io: Paul Lomatius painter of Milan and
   Englished by R[ichard] H[aydocke]* (Oxford, 1598), Bk. 3, p. 112, but I have tidied up the irritating
   archaic spelling.
54 For example, see Ciardi, in Lomazzo, *Scritti*, vol. 2, p. 177 and n. 1.
55 *Trattato*, Bk. 1, ch. vi; *Scritti*, vol. 2, pp. 44ff. As noted elsewhere, the *diatesseron* is the interval of a fourth,
   the *diapente* that of a fifth.

musical theory, which sought to comprehend the expressive character of consonances and intervals mainly in order to convey effectively the passions reflected in the text, poem or libretto.

Theories of the modes revisited

Another topic of potential interest to musicians and visual artists alike had to do with the 'modes' of ancient Greek music (although the word 'mode' derives from the Latin *modus*, Greek writers referring instead to *tonoi* or *harmoniai*).[56] As we saw earlier, musical theorists of the sixteenth and seventeenth centuries frequently squabbled over how the means of musical expression at their disposal might best be adapted to the moral content of a given text or poem. This was a problem to which, it seemed, the modes might offer a ready-made solution, even though most Renaissance and Baroque music appeared quite incapable of producing the powerful effects upon the moral disposition of the listener described by philosophers in antiquity.[57] Many people thought this was because modern methods of composition were actually based not on the *tonoi* and *harmoniai* of ancient Greek music but on the 'modes' of plainchant. Confusingly, medieval theorists had called these by the same names as the Greek modes (for example, Dorian or Phrygian), ignoring the fact that their underlying patterns of notes were entirely different – and therefore, one presumes, their effect on our emotions. Nevertheless, the idea that the 'modes' might offer, even in their modern guise, the prospect of unlocking 'the powers of music over human feelings and morals' was too seductive simply to be thrown away.[58] Well into the seventeenth century, writers on both music and art still clung with touching loyalty to the endlessly repeated stories of Timotheus rousing Alexander to warlike fury and then calming him again by playing first in one mode, then in another, or of Pythagoras quietening the jealous lover driven to arson by an excess of Phrygian pipe music.[59]

---

56 See above, ch. 2, pp. 63ff.
57 This defect of modern music gave rise to considerable perplexity among musical theorists and a good deal of bad-tempered debate. Doni, for example, in his *Compendio del trattato de' generi e de' modi della musica* (Rome: Andrea Fei, 1635) quoted the opinion of Galilei, who had written scathingly that 'our own modes all have the same colour, taste and smell; for indeed, the way they are employed today, it is practically impossible to detect the difference between one mode and another.' (*Compendio ...*, ch. 2, p.8.)
58 Palisca, *Humanism*, pp. 12-13.
59 Lomazzo also mentions the tale of Timotheus and Alexander several times in his *Trattato*: for example, at the beginning of Book II, where he compares the painter's mastery of gesture and facial expression to 'those Miracles of the ancient Musicians, who with the variety of their melodious harmony, were wont to stir up men to wrath and indignation, love, wars, honourable attempts, and all other affectations'. As Korrick stresses, Lomazzo here takes for granted the 'distinct rhetorical character' of the musical modes, pointing out that Poussin was therefore not the first to draw an explicit association between their emotive or suggestive power and the expressive devices used by the painter: see Leslie Korrick, 'Lomazzo's *Trattato ... della pittura* and Galilei's *Fronimo*: Picturing Music and Sounding Images in 1584', in Katherine A. McIver (ed.), *Art and Music in the Early Modern Period. Essays in Honor of Franca Trinchieri Camiz*, Aldershot (Ashgate) 2003, pp. 193ff, 195–6. Unfortunately, this valuable article appeared too late for me to address fully the several interesting issues it raises.

Since, moreover, there appeared to be an antique mode to suit any kind of subject-matter or narrative content, it was perhaps inevitable that, sooner or later, someone would try to adapt this remarkably convenient model of affective stimulus and response to contemporary discussion of the visual arts. That someone was the French seventeenth-century painter Nicolas Poussin, and it was almost certainly as a consequence of his influence and prestige that the 'doctrine of the modes' eventually found a place in French academic theory of painting.[60]

Poussin explained his ideas about the modes in a famous letter he wrote in 1647 to one of his most important patrons: Paul Fréart, Sieur de Chantelou. Chantelou, it seems, had complained that a picture done for him, the rather sombrely painted *Ordination* (pl. 8) from the series the *Seven Sacraments*, was less appealing than the *Finding of Moses* (or *Moses Saved from the Waters of the Nile*), which Poussin had sent the same year to another collector, the banker and silk merchant Jean Pointel. Judging by its appearance, Chantelou had concluded that his picture must have been painted with less love. Poussin replied that it was, in the end, not the amount of love you put into a picture but its subject that determined the manner in which it was painted. Thus the 'nature of the subject' was ultimately responsible for his patron's disappointment, since different subjects 'require a different treatment'. On to this seemingly obvious remark he then tacked the extended discussion of the various antique modes (Dorian, Phrygian, Lydian, etc.) already quoted in Chapter 2 above.[61] Oddly, although he specifically mentions poetry and, of course, painting in this letter, Poussin makes no explicit reference to music as such. But it is clear from the context, the way in which the ancient nomenclature is used and an examination of the sources on which he drew that it was the musical modes of antiquity he had in mind.

Poussin and Zarlino

After his death in 1665, Poussin's followers cited the views stated in his various letters as evidence of the artist's formidable erudition.

---

60 The sequence of events that led to the theory of the modes becoming an accepted, albeit largely unexamined part of French academic doctrine has been traced by Jennifer Montagu, 'The Theory of the Musical Modes in the Académie Royale de Peinture et de Sculpture', *Journal of the Warburg and Courtauld Institutes*, vol. 55 (1992), pp. 233–48; see also idem, *The Expression of the Passions. The Origin and Influence of Charles Le Brun's Conférence sur l'expression générale et particulière*, New Haven/London (Yale U.P.) 1994, esp. ch.2.

61 Poussin's letter to Chantelou is translated in Blunt 1967, pp. 368–70, alongside a transcription of the French original. In quoting from this letter, I have usually followed Blunt's translation, but I have made a few small changes for the sake of clarity or style, mainly in those passages that employ specifically musical terminology. For earlier quotation, see ch. 2 above, p. 64.

Whether his letter to Chantelou really establishes him as an especially learned man or demonstrates any real understanding of musical theory is another matter.[62] Research has shown that many of his notes about theoretical aspects of painting, on which the legend of his intellectual attainments was largely based, were copied from other writers. We also know that the principal source of his remarks about the musical modes was a text we have already encountered several times in the course of this chapter: Zarlino's *Istitutioni harmoniche*.[63] A recent study by Frederick Hammond has suggested that Poussin may have had privileged access to a copy of the 1589 edition of Zarlino's writings. In the early seventeenth century, such a copy could be found in the collection of Cardinal Francesco Barberini, who commissioned several pictures from Poussin during the artist's early years in Rome.[64] The patronage of the Barberini family (Francesco's uncle Maffeo had become pope in 1623, taking the name Urban VIII) extended to a wide circle of musicians and intellectuals: men like the antiquarian and collector Cassiano dal Pozzo, for whom Poussin painted his first version of the *Seven Sacraments*, and the musical theorist Giovanni Battista Doni, who served as the Cardinal's secretary.[65] Apart from which, there were other painters Poussin encountered during his stay in Rome, among them artists like Pietro Testa, who appears to have been greatly interested in music, perhaps because of the influence exerted by his teacher Domenichino.[66] It may have been one of the more musically minded of this circle of acquaintances who drew Poussin's attention to Zarlino's treatise, from which he proceeded to copy more or less verbatim a number of scattered passages, mostly from Part IV – that is, the portion that deals specifically with the history and usage of

---

62 Thomas Puttfarken has suggested that, faced with the lack of major commissions for large-scale decorative schemes, it was almost certainly a deliberate strategy on Poussin's part to build himself up in the eyes of his patrons as an accomplished *savant*, capable of finding the appropriate tone even for the most recondite subjects from classical mythology and the Old and New Testament; see 'Poussin's Thoughts on Painting', in Katie Scott and Genevieve Warwick (eds), *Commemorating Poussin. Reception and Interpretation of the Artist*, Cambridge (Cambridge U. P.) 1999. Poussin's strategy was evidently successful, as witnessed by the various laudatory statements cited in Puttfarken's article (see esp. pp. 59ff.), among them that by Fréart de Chambray who, in his *Idée de la perfection de la peinture* (1662), described Poussin as 'universally intelligent in all the fine arts'.

63 It was Anthony Blunt who first identified Poussin's debt to Zarlino, but he did not immediately publish his findings; instead, they were summarized by Paul Alfassa in his article 'L'Origine de la lettre de Poussin sur les modes d'après un travail récent', *Bulletin de la Société de l'Histoire de l'Art Français* (1933), pp. 125–43.

64 Frederick Hammond, 'Poussin et les modes: le point de vue d'un musicien', in Olivier Bonfait et al. (eds), *Poussin et Rome* (Actes du colloque de l'Académie de France à Rome, 16–18 novembre 1994), Paris (Réunion des musées nationaux) 1996, pp. 76ff.

65 Concerning Doni and others who enjoyed the protection of the Barberini, see Frederick Hammond, *Music and Spectacle in Baroque Rome. Barberini Patronage under Urban VIII*, New Haven/London (Yale U. P.) 1994, pp. 26ff., also pp. 99–102.

66 On the circle of artists in Rome that included not only Poussin but also Domenichino, Pietro Testa and others see Cropper 1984, pp. 3ff.; also R. E. Spear, *Domenichino*, New Haven/London (Yale U. P.) 1982, esp. pp. 42ff.

the musical modes. Nowhere in his letter to Chantelou, however, does he acknowledge the source of any of these quotations.

What did Poussin mean by this piece of unabashed plagiarism? One hypothesis is that his aim was to give his patron a 'lesson in criticism' and that he turned to Zarlino for authority in order to amplify his own arguments about the role of theory and practice, reason and sense in formulating artistic judgements.[67] For this purpose he relies quite literally on Chapter 36 of Zarlino's account of the modes, entitled 'The Senses are Fallible, and Judgements should not be Made Solely by their Means, but Should be Accompanied by Reason'. Poussin echoes this statement, which Zarlino had in turn copied from Boethius,[68] in his assertion to Chantelou that 'to judge well is very difficult unless one has great knowledge of both the theory and practice of this art. We must not judge by our senses alone but by reason.' But while Poussin had evidently read Zarlino's text with close attention, he did not always copy it, as in this instance, word for word. In other cases, it is instructive to compare his 'borrowings' with the original, both because of the changes made and also because of what got left out. Some of Poussin's alterations were clearly undertaken for a quite specific purpose. Zarlino writes, for example, that the various modes were 'capable of inducing different passions in the souls of the listeners [*ascoltatori*]'. Poussin keeps precisely the same wording but changes 'listeners' to 'viewers' [*regardans*], for obvious reasons. But in other places, the changes he made alter the sense of the original in more subtle ways, as in the following passage from his letter:

The word Mode means, properly, the ratio *or the measure and the form that we employ to do anything, which compels us not to go beyond it, making us work in all things with a certain middle course or moderation. And so this mediocrity or moderation is simply a certain manner or determined and fixed order in the process by which a thing preserves its being.*

A number of commentators both ancient and modern have been misled by Poussin's reference to '*ratio*' and 'measure'. They have thought that, by using the term 'ratio', he must be pointing to the

---

67 Cropper 1984, p. 140.
68 *Non omne iudicium dandum esse sensibus, sed amplius rationi esse credentum* (Boethius, *De Institutione Musica*, I, 8).

orderly aspect of music and its dependence upon arithmetic and proportion, as so many of his predecessors had done. Among those so misled was the eminent French academician Charles Le Brun, one of Poussin's staunchest admirers, who declared that 'keeping to that harmonic proportion which musicians observe in their compositions, his aim was that in his paintings all things should be in consonance with one another [que toutes choses gardassent des accords réciproques] and hence conspire to one and the same end'.[69] But the musical modes have nothing to do with ratio or proportion. As previously explained, it is the consonances and intervals that can be derived from arithmetical ratios – not the modes, which were merely different sequences of notes, in some ways resembling our modern scales. Rather, the explanation is that Poussin has, in transcribing the original, omitted a vital half-sentence. At this early point (in the original, the quotation occurs at the beginning of the first chapter of Part IV of *Istitutioni harmoniche*) Zarlino had not even got as far as discussing the character of the musical modes. Instead, he writes in far more general and indeed abstract terms:

One should be aware that this word 'mode', apart from all its other meanings, which are many, properly means 'reason', namely, that measure or form which we adopt in everything we do, preventing us from going too far and making us act in all things with a certain restraint or moderation. And in truth, it is well named, for (as Pindar says) 'in everything there is mode, or measure.'[70]

Equally baffling, until one goes back to the original source, is Poussin's description of the characteristics of the Phrygian mode, which he claims the Greeks used:

because its intervals were smaller than those of any other Mode and because its effect was sharper. These two manners and no others were praised and approved by Plato and Aristotle, who deemed the others useless; they held in high esteem this vehement, furious and highly severe Mode that strikes the spectator with awe.

Poussin's references to Plato and Aristotle and his characterization of the Phrygian mode as 'vehement and furious' situate this passage

---

69 Quoted after Montagu, 'The Theory of the Musical Modes', pp. 237–8. Le Brun's remarks were made in the context of a lecture by Jean-Baptiste Champaigne given before the Académie on 1 March 1670.

70 *Istitutioni harmoniche*, IV, 1; *Opere*, vol. 1, p. 377. The italics, indicating the phrase omitted by Poussin, are mine.

firmly within the ambit of classical discussion about the moral significance of different kinds of music. The only trouble is that the Phrygian mode is not sharper nor does it have smaller intervals than any other mode. In fact, no one mode has smaller (or larger) intervals than any other. What determines the size of the intervals is the choice of *genus*: diatonic, chromatic or enharmonic. It is the enharmonic that uses the smallest intervals, dividing the tetrachord (interval of a fourth) into a ditone (two whole tones) plus two quarter tones, these being smaller than any interval now used in conventional Western music. But the enharmonic *genus* could, as far as we know, be applied to any mode; it was not the peculiar preserve of the Phrygian. However, we still do not fully understand how or why ancient Greek musicians chose particular combinations of mode and *genus* or whether one combination was thought more 'permissible' than another. And despite efforts made by Renaissance theorists such as Mei or Doni to recover aspects of Greek music, such questions had certainly not been answered by Zarlino's time. Indeed, Zarlino specifically cautions against those who 'believe that they can put into use the chromatic and enharmonic *genera*, abandoned for so great a span of time, even though they do not know the style of these *genera* nor have any vestige of them', likening such theorists to alchemists frustrated in their attempts to discover 'what they will never be able to find, namely, that which they call "quintessence"'.[71]

So how did this confusion arise? Again, let us compare Poussin's statement about the characteristics of the Dorian and Phrygian modes with Zarlino's original. Poussin writes:

Observing these effects, the wise ancients attributed to each [Mode] a special character and they called the Dorian the Mode that was firm, grave and severe, and they applied it to matters that were grave, severe and full of wisdom. And passing on from this to pleasant and joyous things they used the Phrygian Mode because its intervals were smaller [pour avoir ses modulations plus menues] than those of any other Mode and because its effect was sharper.

Zarlino's text has:

On account of these effects, the ancients attributed the properties I have described to the Dorian mode, and applied it to matters that were severe, grave and full of wisdom.

---

71 *Istitutioni harmoniche*, IV, 3; *Opere*, vol. 1, p. 386.

And when they abandoned these and moved on to things that were pleasant, happy and light-hearted, they used the Phrygian mode, its divisions being more rapid than those of any other mode, and its harmonia *higher than that of the Dorian* [essendo che i suoi Numeri erano più veloci de i numeri di qualunque altro Modo, & la sua Harmonia più acuta di quella del Dorio].[72]

There is an important difference between the original version of this passage and Poussin's transcription of it. In describing the Phrygian mode, Zarlino writes not about its 'sharper character' and 'smaller intervals' but about its overall pitch, which, given the way the Greek *tonoi* and *harmoniai* were arranged, is higher than that of Dorian. He also refers to the more agitated rhythms ('numeri più veloci'), which were thought appropriate to the particular character of this mode. Thus, according to Zarlino's account, the 'smaller intervals' about which Poussin writes were conceived of as rhythmic, not melodic. One might argue at length over precisely what Poussin meant by 'modulations plus menues', but one possibility is that this is a simple case of mistranslation. Another is that he had no idea what Zarlino was talking about.[73]

'Mode' and 'mood' in Poussin's paintings

Poussin's famous explanation to Chantelou has been the subject of a good deal of art-historical debate. Until now, opinion has been more or less evenly divided between scholars who believe that Poussin read carefully and thought deeply and that his use of musical analogy must therefore have served some real, albeit elusive purpose and those who consider his letter too superficial and too confused to be a coherent statement of his aesthetic aims.[74] The fact that he had, on one interpretation at least, seemingly read and copied Zarlino's text without understanding it would appear to support the latter view. Moreover, several writers have pointed out a further obstacle to taking Poussin's remarks about the modes seriously, namely the difficulty of relating all these generalities to

---

72 *Istitutioni harmoniche*, IV, 5; *Opere*, vol. 1, pp. 388–9.

73 In his article 'Poussin et la musique', A. P. de Mirimonde likewise suggests that Poussin may simply have failed to understand Zarlino and also points to the artist's misreading of the passage that concerns the Phrygian mode (*Gazette des Beaux-Arts*, VI, vol. lxxix, March 1972, p. 131).

74 An example of a writer who adheres to the first of these views is Cropper, who enjoins us to 'remember that Poussin read texts critically and intelligently' (*Ideal of Painting*, n. 199 to p. 142). For an opposing view see the article 'Poussiniana. Afterthoughts Arising from the Exhibition' by Denis Mahon, who describes Poussin's letter as 'trivial' and the artist's account of Zarlino's theories as 'utterly chaotic and confused', remarking that 'if Chantelou had not happened to irritate [Poussin] … with some not very tactful or understanding comment, it is unlikely that the so-called "Theory of the Modes" would ever have been heard of.' (*Gazette des Beaux-Arts*, VI, vol. lx, July–August 1962, pp. 125–6.)

the specifics of his pictorial practice. If he were in earnest about his intention to paint 'within a year' a picture in the Phrygian mode, which one is it? And if we thought we knew, what pictorial characteristics would enable us to identify it with reasonable certainty? An examination of his *oeuvre* reveals, it is true, a few pictures that might, with only a small effort of the imagination, be thought candidates for having been deliberately painted in a particular 'mode': *Landscape with the Ashes of Phocion*, for example (pl. 9), which is 'broad, severe and static' and therefore might plausibly be defined as 'Dorian', or the *Rape of the Sabine Women*, with its 'vehemence and its violent, repeated movements', which has been linked with the 'Phrygian' mode.[75] However, paintings of this kind are far outnumbered by others, such as *The Israelites Gathering Manna*, in which internal contrast plays a vital role, making any association with one particular mode dubious in the extreme.[76] Nor do late works like *Landscape with Diana and Orion* or *Apollo and Daphne* immediately lend themselves to interpretation in terms of any precise musical analogy.

This obvious difficulty has led many commentators on Poussin to agree that, serious or not, his remarks cannot be interpreted literally and that their intended import is of a more general or metaphorical kind.[77] This is clearly true. Poussin never gets round to directly comparing colour, line or composition to any of the constituent elements of music such as melody or rhythm. Unlike many of his more intellectually inquisitive contemporaries, he does not try to account for the effects supposedly produced by the different musical modes: grave, frenzied, gay and so on. Nor does he explain how similar effects might be achieved by painting, if indeed that was his aim. The theorist André Félibien, who after Poussin's death did much to popularize his 'theory' of the modes, doubted that it was. Citing the legend of Erik II, King of Denmark, who was so inflamed by martial music that he killed four members of his entourage (evidently a reworking of the story of Timotheus and Alexander), he remarks that it would be 'dangerous ... if painting had the same force to move our passions as music ... It was not the intention of Poussin to put those who looked at his pictures in such great danger.'[78] Poussin also makes no attempt to derive from all these scraps of musical theory anything resembling rules or

---

75 Alain Mérot, *Nicolas Poussin*, London (Thames & Hudson) 1990, p. 202.

76 Puttfarken, in discussing this painting, also observes that it would be 'impossible to subsume both the starving Israelites and those which have been rescued by the manna under one single mode'. (*Roger de Piles' Theory of Art*, p. 36.)

77 Thus, for example, Mérot (as n. [75]) who writes that 'Poussin originally took up the concept of the modes in a metaphorical sense to clarify his explanation to a disgruntled patron' (p. 203).

78 André Félibien, *Entretiens sur les vies et sur les ouvrages des plus excellens peintres anciens et modernes;* quoted after Puttfarken, *Roger de Piles*, p. 33.

precepts for visual art. In the later seventeenth and early eighteenth centuries, his followers tried to extract just such precepts from his letters and his other scattered writings. But despite their efforts, we must reconcile ourselves to the fact that, in the end, he never told anyone how to paint a picture in the Phrygian mode. He merely told Chantelou that he himself intended to do so.

The modes in seventeenth-century musical practice

The fact that Poussin's account of the modes is couched in such general terms, lacking any specific application to painting, leaves us pondering the same questions that have tormented many of his biographers. Why did he reach out for an analogy between painting and music in the first place? What real benefit did he think he might obtain from it, other than the short-term advantage of perhaps silencing an otherwise querulous patron? And why, in particular, did he rely so heavily on Zarlino, whose *Istitutioni harmoniche* was nearly a century old by the time he discovered it? Was the aim of the exercise merely to impress Chantelou with his knowledge of musical matters? If so, there were other, more modern authors to whom he could have turned: Doni, for example, who as recently as 1635 had published his influential *Compendio del trattato de' generi e de' modi della musica* (Treatise on the *genera* and on the modes in music).[79] Poussin may not have been as well versed in musical matters as artists like Domenichino or Testa, but he can scarcely have been deaf to the animated debates going on around him as to the respective merits of the 'old' and the 'new' music. Those debates were not confined to the realms of abstract theory; they also affected contemporary musical practice. Both Doni and Domenichino, in particular, were preoccupied with re-creating the musical usage of the ancients, which meant trying to understand not only the modes themselves and what they signified but also the correct use of the three *genera*. To this end, they designed and constructed new instruments capable of playing these archaic harmonies and scales: Doni's famous amphichordal lyre or 'Lyra Barberina' (fig. 41),[80] Domenichino's di- and tri-harmonic viols and lutes, as well as harps with three courses of strings which, we are told, he built 'with his own hands'.[81] A harp of this kind, based no doubt on

---

79 As pointed out by Cropper 1984, p. 141.
80 See Claude V. Palisca, 'G. B. Doni, Musicological Activist and his "Lyra Barberina"', in E. Olleson (ed.), *Modern Musical Scholarship*, Stocksfield/Boston/Henley/London (Oriel Press) 1980, pp. 180ff.; also *Grove*, vol. 5, pp. 550ff.
81 According to the *Vite* (c.1670) of Giambattista Passeri, cited by Renato Meucci, 'Domenichino "musicologo" e le origini della Sonata a tre', in the catalogue *Domenichino 1581–1641*, Rome (Palazzo Venezia) 1996–7: Milan (Electa) 1996, pp. 311ff. Meucci also provides a detailed account of Domenichino's musical experiments and the unusual instruments he designed and constructed.

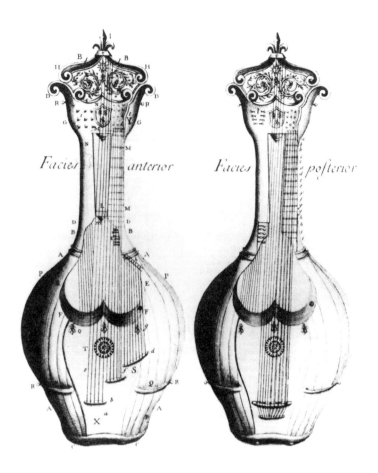

Figure 41. Giovanni Battista Doni, *Lyra Barberina*, 1763, engraving showing two views of his 'amphichordal lyre'

his own experiments, can be seen in Domenichino's painting *Madonna with Saints John the Evangelist and Petronius* (pl. 10). There were even composers like Pietro della Valle who attempted to revive elements of ancient Greek musical practice by writing music for just such instruments. Della Valle's *Dialogo di Ester*, which was composed under Doni's influence and which boasted 'modulati in varij Tuoni', was performed in Rome at the Oratorio del SS. Crocifisso in April 1640 – that is, just prior to Poussin's brief return to France – albeit without much success.

The *Dialogo di Ester* has not survived and we do not know what the 'varij Tuoni' were, but we can gain some idea from the same composer's *Dialogo per la festa della santissima Purificazione*, written in the same year, which actually specified the modes on which it was based: 'Dorio, Frigio, Eolio, Lidio e Hipolidio'.[82] Did Poussin know of works such as these or even hear them performed? If he did, the modes and *genera* must have seemed to him not just some faint echo of classical times or an antiquated piece of musical jargon. On the contrary, they must have appeared immediately relevant to contemporary artistic practice, audibly present in the work of modern composers who were themselves in thrall to the antique, in whose proximity he found himself and whose aims he may have regarded as in some ways comparable to his own.[83]

Painting and poetry

But while ideas about the modes and the expressive qualities of music generally may have been useful to Poussin in other ways, it is clear that Zarlino's theories, in particular, had a special resonance for him. What one commentator calls a 'more charitable' view of the artist's purpose in writing to Chantelou is that he was trying to say something about the specifically visual nature of his work for which, prior to his 'discovery' of the composer's writings, he had been able to find 'no appropriate language or terminology'.[84] This seems highly plausible. Virtually all discussion of painting up to the seventeenth century – that is, discussion of anything other than purely technical matters – had borrowed its vocabulary from earlier theories about the *verbal* arts. The main ingredients of Renaissance and Baroque pictorial theory – notions such as decorum or the unity of time, place and action – derive from classical authors who had, in fact, written about poetry, drama and rhetoric.[85] While such ideas could conveniently be applied to the narrative aspects of painting – gesture, facial expression, even the relationship between the principal figures – they left other, equally significant things like colour, light and shade and overall composition unaccounted for. Did Zarlino's account of the expressive uses of music – even though it, too, turned on the relationship between music and words – provide Poussin with the 'appropriate language' he was groping for when he tried to formulate ideas about the 'specifically visual'

---

82 Hammond, 'Poussin et les modes', p. 83; also Hammond 1994, p. 102.
83 Della Valle's *Dialogue for the Feast of the Purification*, his only surviving composition, written for the Oratorio della Valicella, was not in fact performed. There were, however, other works of this kind, including his *Dialogo della partenza*, also of 1640, and his last composition, the *Dialogo di Luys Camões* 'set to music ... in a mixture of the diatonic, chromatic and enharmonic *genera* and in seven different modes', which della Valle sent to King John IV of Portugal in April 1649; see *Grove*, vol. 5, pp. 347ff.
84 Puttfarken, 'Poussin's Thoughts on Painting', 1999, p. 66.
85 As John R. Spencer has pointed out, the comparison that sprang most readily to the fifteenth-century mind was between painting and rhetoric, for which the most important classical sources were Cicero and Quintilian. Aristotle's theories of poetry and drama were the object of revived interest following the publication of his *Poetics* in Italian translation (1549); see Spencer 1957, pp. 26ff.

aspect of his art? A further passage from the same letter to Chantelou suggests that it did, even though Poussin has now apparently finished discussing the modes and has moved on to a different topic, that of poetry. In this paragraph he singles out Virgil, writing in particular about the Roman poet's use of language:

Good poets have used great diligence and marvellous artifice in adapting their choice of words to their verse ... as Virgil has observed throughout his poetry, because to all three manners of speech he accommodates the actual sound of the verse with such skill that he seems to set before our eyes with the sound of the words the things about which he is writing. Thus in speaking about love, one can see that he has artfully chosen certain words that are sweet, pleasing, and which fall most gracefully upon the ear. Where he sings of a feat of arms or describes a naval battle or mishap at sea, he has chosen words that are hard, sharp, and unpleasing, so that on hearing or pronouncing them they induce fear ...[86]

At first sight, there is nothing very startling about this extract. In the seventeenth century, Virgil's name nearly always cropped up in discussions of poetry as an example of a classical writer skilled in choosing the appropriate manner of poetic diction.[87] Or rather, the only startling thing about it is that, as Blunt first pointed out, Poussin has again copied a lengthy passage straight out of Zarlino, even though it has nothing to do with music. Copied it, moreover, word for word and line for line, even down to the examples chosen such as 'naval battles' and 'mishaps at sea'.[88]

Instead of simply pointing the finger at Poussin's lack of originality or castigating him for his slavish adherence to another man's text, it is worth asking what it was about this passage from the *Istitutioni harmoniche* that captured his attention in the first place. The answer is surely that, despite the seemingly inevitable reference to Virgil and his 'three manners of speech', what Zarlino is saying amounts to something more than just another re-formulation of the age-old notion of poetic decorum. He is pointing, above all, to the *sound* of the words. To avoid any misunderstanding, he even

---

86 Blunt 1967, p. 370.
87 For example, in the commentaries of Aelius Donatus, who identified particular texts of Virgil with the different styles of oratory as defined by Cicero: the *Aenead* with the grand, the *Georgics* with the intermediate, and the *Eclogues* with the lowly; see Jan Bialostocki, 'Das Modusproblem in den bildenden Künsten. Zur Vorgeschichte und zum Nachleben des "Modusbriefes" von Nicolas Poussin', *Zeitschrift für Kunstgeschichte*, vol. 24 (1961), pp. 130ff.
88 For Zarlino's original see his *Istitutioni harmoniche*, I, 2; *Opere*, vol. 1, p. 8. The paragraph from Poussin's letter cited above is a literal translation of the Italian.

repeats the same remarks several times. In Virgil's poetry, Zarlino thinks, it is not merely the choice of words but also their sound that conjures up fear or makes us think of love. By this he does not mean, of course, that their sound can be divorced from their sense, any more than the artist is at liberty to employ colours and forms without regard for the subject shown in the painting. Their purely sonorous aspect can, nevertheless, be considered separately, as one does in preferring one word to another simply for the sake of its sound or one interval or chord to another for the sake of its 'harsher' or 'sweeter' character.

It may have been this passage, coupled with Zarlino's discussion of the modes, that first set Poussin thinking about whether theories of this kind might serve equally well if applied to painting. Could not colours and lines, light and shadow be chosen, not for their own sake, but with fastidious regard for the subject depicted, thereby creating an effect no less precise than that which the tones of music or the sound of the words in poetry were capable of producing?[89] As we saw earlier, the tones and intervals of music had long been an object of detailed scrutiny, in an attempt to determine their emotive or 'affective' properties, which could be exploited in such a way as to reinforce or heighten the meaning of some text or libretto. But, leaving aside Lomazzo's observations on colour, the idea that the forms and colours of painting might affect the viewer's emotions in no less systematic a fashion was quite new. Poussin's remarks on the modes were meant to focus attention on a question that had, until now, been little regarded: how might the resources intrinsic to visual art, by analogy with those of music, be reliably employed so as to produce on the part of the spectator a response that was clearly appropriate to the subject of the picture? Seen in this light, everything Poussin quoted without acknowledgement in his letter to Chantelou served but one purpose: to underline the care and judgement he had expended upon the purely visual aspect of his *Ordination* (see pl. 8), sombre though its effect might be. The fact that his grasp of musical matters was less than perfect, to the extent that he somewhat garbles the passages borrowed from Zarlino, only makes his enthusiasm for these – to him – unfamiliar ideas all the more touching.

Moreover, Le Brun, in commenting on Poussin's *Plague at Ashdod* (pl. 11), showed more perceptiveness than he has sometimes been

---

89 There are other instances where allusions to painting, to music and to the verbal arts of drama and poetry were all neatly wrapped up together to form a single package. Mersenne, for example, wrote that 'music is an imitation or a representation just as poetry, tragedy, or painting is, as I have said elsewhere. For it does with sounds or the articulated voice what the poet does with verse, the actor with gestures, and painting with light, shadow and colours'; *Harm. Univ.*, *Livre Second des Chants*, Pr. ii (vol. 2), p. 93.

given credit for. Having defined its principal subject as the 'maladie contagieuse et la désolation des Philistins', he specifically draws attention to how the artist has established 'le caractère lugubre par une lumière faible [et] par des teintes sombres' (its mournful character by means of feeble lighting and sombre colours) – that is, precisely those elements of painting that eluded the definitions provided by theories of poetry or rhetoric, but for which Zarlino's modes might seem to offer a suitable metaphor.[90] On the other hand, no matter what Le Brun might have thought, Poussin's 'theory' of the modes had, in the end, nothing to do with classical notions of harmony or proportion. Nor, indeed, does it have any bearing on the presence – or absence – of camels in painting.[91]

Poussin's influence

Poussin's ideas about music were cited several times by Le Brun, if only in rather general terms. However, not until the end of the seventeenth century did the text of his now-famous letter to Chantelou become more widely known. By that time, Poussin had, in effect, been canonized by his admirers, who not only tried to extract from the notes published by Bellori something resembling a doctrine of painting but also turned to his remarks on a variety of subjects, including the modes, in search of support for their own ideas. Antoine Coypel, for instance, writes that colour not merely requires to be used correctly (like drawing) but also has the 'power to express emotions ... One must choose, as musicians do, a mode which suits the subject ... whose character may be joyful, or horrifying, or sad.'[92] He also seemed to think that a comparison with music might help to explain how painting was capable of producing an effect that is immediate – 'au coup d'oeil'. By this, he perhaps meant that our response to paintings should be as intuitive and spontaneous as the way in which we respond to music. But that is not what Coypel says: he says that painting, like music, can produce its effect 'at a single glance'. This, of course, is manifestly untrue. One thing that music cannot do is convey anything (or anything of significance) in a single instant, since it requires the unfolding of time not only in order to be performed but also in order to be understood.

---

90 Montagu, 'The Theory of the Musical Modes' (as n. [60] above).

91 For an account of the famous debate before the Académie (7 January 1668), in the course of which Le Brun used the 'theory' of the modes in order to defend Poussin's omission of ten camels which, it had been claimed, were an essential part of the biblical story on which his painting *Rebecca and Eliezar* was based, see Christopher G. Hughes, '*Embarras* and *Disconvenance* in Poussin's *Rebecca and Eliezar at the Well*', *Art History*, vol. 24, no. 4 (September 2001), pp. 493–519; also Puttfarken, 1999, p. 66; Montagu, p. 236; Montagu 1994, pp. 9ff.

92 *Sur l'esthétique du peintre* (1721); quoted after Bialostocki, op. cit., p. 135.

It seems that other writers who turned just as readily to a comparison between painting and other forms of art had no more understanding of music, how it actually worked or what its terminology signified. Thus Henri Testelin, secretary of the French Academy under Colbert, not only claimed (quite wrongly) that Poussin 'usually' painted in the Phrygian mode but also invented a new mode of his own: the Corinthian. (Interestingly, the idea that one could paint in any given mode now seems to be taken for granted.) Félibien thought the Lydian mode appropriate for bacchanales, something no writer in antiquity had ever suggested; and, like Testelin, he too invented a previously unheard-of mode, the Lesbian, which he considered especially suitable for expressing 'choses magnifiques'. The amusing and erudite article by Jennifer Montagu on the Académie Royale and the reception of Poussin's theories, already cited, traces the use of such ill-conceived analogies through to their last, barely audible gasp in French nineteenth-century academic theory – a tale that, as she observes, ends not with a bang but a whimper.[93]

But long before then, the modes themselves had more or less disappeared from musical usage, having finally been supplanted by the major and minor keys that dominated European music until the late nineteenth century. If, in the Romantic era, theorists of painting still alluded to the modes, they tended to do so anachronistically and to little purpose. By that time, there was no longer anything of significance to be gained from an analogy between painting and antique conceptions of music. At worst, such analogies merely contributed to the ill-digested rhetoric that disfigured writing about art. At best, they were just another piece of that increasingly dispensable baggage inherited from our classical past.

'The Rhetoric of the Gods'

The drawings that accompanied Denis Gaultier's *La Rhétorique des Dieux*, a famous anthology of pieces for lute, provide a further example of how visual artists responded to ideas about the antique modes and their 'marvellous effects'.[94] Gaultier was one of the great French lutenists of the seventeenth century and a prominent member of an extended musical family. Given the extent of his reputation in his own lifetime, it is surprising how little we know

---

93 Montagu also provides full references to other seventeenth-century sources such as Testelin or Félibien, here cited in passing; see 'The Theory of the Musical Modes ...', esp. pp. 240ff.

94 Mirimonde (see n. [73] above) also juxtaposes a description of *La Rhétorique des Dieux* with his analysis of Poussin's 'theory of the modes', but he does so mainly in order to illustrate the many discrepancies between the traditional attributes of the modes, the iconography of Bosse's illustrations (see below, pp. 215ff) and the character of Gaultier's music. ('Poussin et la musique', p. 132ff.)

about him.[95] We cannot even be certain whether he was involved in selecting the musical material that constituted *La Rhétorique des Dieux* or to what extent he influenced the form this compilation took, its manner of organization, even its appearance. We do, however, know who was responsible for assembling and preserving this unique collection of musical manuscripts. Anne-Achille de Chambré served as *trésorier de guerre* to Louis II, Prince de Condé during the disturbances of the *Fronde* and in 1664 was appointed *agent général* of the French West India Company.[96] He was also a distinguished patron of the arts. Gaultier probably taught music to his daughter, who confusingly was also called Anne. A painting by Eustache Le Sueur, now in the Louvre, shows a gathering of friends at de Chambré's house; in their midst is a figure playing the lute, commonly identified as Gaultier himself (pl. 12).[97] It was de Chambré who commissioned artists (among them Le Sueur and Robert Nanteuil), goldsmiths, bookbinders and poets to create a sumptuous receptacle for Gaultier's compositions: a leather-bound album, richly decorated and with a dozen or more illustrations, that today is among the treasures of Berlin's Kupferstichkabinett.

The music from *La Rhétorique des Dieux* comprises dance movements of various kinds – mostly traditional forms such as the *galliard*, *allemande* or *courante*. These are grouped under the names of the twelve modes – Dorian, Hypodorian and so on – steadfastly ignoring the fact that the pieces themselves are clearly tonal rather than modal. One has only to listen to a couple of movements from the first sequence of dances to convince oneself that they are in the key of D – not the Dorian mode.[98] There are other discrepancies, too, between the album and its musical contents. Although there is a section allocated to the Lydian mode, complete with heading and an accompanying illustration, the following

---

95 On Gaultier and *La Rhétorique* see David J. Buch, 'The Coordination of Text, Illustration, and Music in a Seventeenth-Century Lute Manuscript: *La Rhétorique des Dieux*', *Imago Musicae*, VI (1989), pp. 39–81; also *Grove*, vol. 7, p. 189; Hammond, 'Poussin et les modes', p. 85; Hollander, *Untuning of the Sky*, pp.217ff.

96 *Fronde*: period of unrest that occurred between 1648 and 1653 during the minority of Louis XIV of France, when many French nobles and parliamentarians sided against the Queen Regent Anne of Austria and her minister Cardinal Mazarin. 'Le grand Condé' was a cousin of the king and, in the first phase of the disturbances, remained loyal to him. Disappointed, however, in his hopes of political power, he subsequently allied himself with the insurgents, risking total defeat in a pitched battle against Royalist forces that took place beneath the walls of Paris in July 1652. The post of *trésorier de guerre* held by de Chambré might best be translated as 'campaign manager'.

97 Until the nineteenth century, the picture was attributed to Vouet. In his catalogue of le Sueur's paintings, Mérot questions the traditional identification of the other figures shown in this group portrait but accepts that the lutenist is Gaultier: see Alain Mérot, *Eustache Le Sueur 1616–1655*, Paris (Arthena) 1987, pp. 173ff and cat. no. 21.

98 For the reader who needs persuading of the beauty and subtlety of Gaultier's music, there is an outstanding recording by lutenist Hopkinson Smith of three of the sequences of dances from *La Rhétorique des Dieux* on Astrée, CD E7778.

manuscript pages are blank, suggesting that the volume itself was created first and that Gaultier's compositions were inserted – not altogether appropriately – at some later date.[99] Apart from the illustrations, the music is accompanied by two sonnets and an elaborate preface that declares the overall 'theme' of the undertaking to be the manner in which the 'rhetoric of the Gods' addresses itself to human understanding, predicting confidently that those 'possessed of music' will find in these compositions:

complete satisfaction, inasmuch as the Author has with such art and such skill ... so perfectly represented the nature of the passions that even the most debased spirits will be elevated unto the most sublime virtue.

But the preface also notes that, since music has the:

capacity to arouse certain passions ... the drawings by Sieur Bosse, done by himself, which represent the twelve modes ... depict in each case those actions to which the modes give rise as well as the instruments, both ancient and modern, most appropriate to them. Even the architecture has been made to conform to these modes. In each illustration there can be found a lute together with an opened book in which the mode in question is notated.[100]

The aim of writing music that would show off the characteristics of the different modes was not new. Apart from experiments by composers like della Valle, mentioned earlier, by the time *La Rhétorique des Dieux* was compiled there existed a number of French seventeenth-century compositions that, to judge by their titles, were conceived with precisely that aim in mind. Among them were works such as Charles Guillet's *Vingt-quatre fantasies ... disposées suivant l'ordre des douze modes* (1610) and Arthus Aux Cousteaux's *Les Quatrains de Mr. Mathieu mis en musique ... selon l'ordre des douze modes* (1643). *La Rhétorique des Dieux* was unusual only inasmuch as the various musical groupings were matched by illustrations that were meant to convey visually the specific character of each mode. These, as the preface indicates, were mostly the work of the artist Abraham Bosse, although Le Sueur

---

99 Buch 1989, pp. 43–4, 70ff; see also ibid., pp. 42–3 for an indication of the content and layout of *La Rhétorique*.

100 From the preface to the *Rhétorique des Dieux*, quoted after the facsimile edition by André Tessier and Jean Cordey, *La Rhétorique des Dieux et autres pieces de luth de Denis Gaultier*, Paris (Société française de musicologie) 1932. In the last of Bosse's illustrations, representing the Hypoionian mode, the lute is shown appropriately put away in its case.

seems to have provided at least two original drawings for the volume, which were subsequently copied by Bosse and Nanteuil. It is possible that Le Sueur was originally meant to take more of a hand in the illustrations and that his participation was cut short by his death in 1655. If so, this would help to establish an approximate date for *La Rhétorique*, which is ascribed by some sources to 1652, by others to between 1655 and 1660.[101]

Unfortunately, when we come to examine Bosse's charming drawings of gods and goddesses surrounded by cherubs and cupids along with various instruments, the disjunction between grandiose ambitions and artistic execution appears well nigh complete. Although the purpose of these drawings, as the preface makes clear, is to represent actions and motifs suited to the character of the mode in question, for much of the time, in their iconography and style they call to mind nothing more vividly than the dutiful frontispiece engravings that so often introduced seventeenth-century anthologies of printed music, to which reference has already been made.[102] In a few cases, admittedly, we can perhaps find rather more to link the style of the drawings – the lighting, setting and so forth – with the music than Montagu suggests.[103] For example, Bosse's illustration for the Lydian mode depicts a tomb-like vault complete with weeping figures and a putto who, with covered head, beats upon a muffled drum: all appropriate enough, since this was a mode frequently associated with lugubrious subjects, while the drawing itself is rendered in a suitably funereal tone (fig. 42). In the case of the Phrygian mode, the corresponding illustration confronts us with warlike motifs including sword and drums as well as a depiction of an *aulos*, an instrument widely considered to be of Phrygian origin. Other drawings show fragments of classical architecture chosen to match the mode in question – for example, the by now unquestioned association of the Doric order with the Dorian mode (fig. 43).

In a valuable article analysing *La Rhétorique de Dieux*, David Buch also draws attention to the fact that the last four drawings in the album depict only modern instruments, not antique ones. He admits to being puzzled by this, but the reason is surely that these drawings were meant to illustrate the four 'modern' modes – Ionian and Aeolian along with their plagal variants (Hypoionian and

---

101 For further information on the dating of the volume and what details are known about Gaultier and Chambré on the basis of contemporary documents see Monique Rollin and François-Pierre Goy (eds), *Oeuvres de Denis Gautier*, Paris (CRNS-Éditions) 1966, pp. xi ff.; also Mérot, 1987, pp. 295–6.
102 See above, p. 182.
103 In fact, Montagu's view is that Bosse makes no attempt to adapt the style of his drawings to the particular modes they accompany; see 'The Theory of the Musical Modes ...', p. 236 and n. 12.

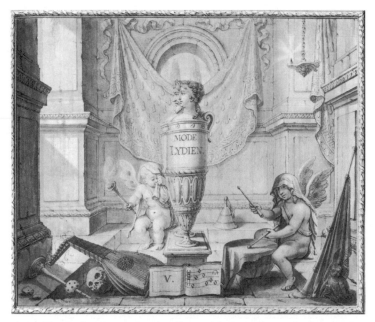

Figure 42. Abraham Bosse, drawing illustrating the Lydian mode, from Denis Gaultier's *La Rhétorique des Dieux* (Kupferstichkabinett, Berlin: MS. 78.C.12)

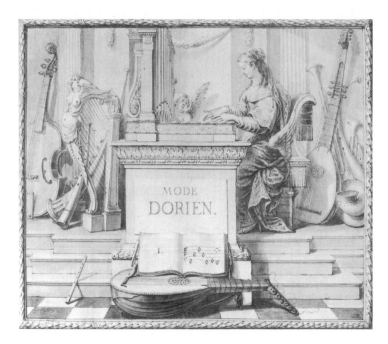

Figure 43. Abraham Bosse, drawing illustrating the Dorian mode, from Denis Gaultier's *La Rhétorique des Dieux* (Kupferstichkabinett, Berlin: MS. 78.C.12)

Hypoaeolian).[104] These, following the precepts of Glareanus, had been added to the eight church modes or 'tones' of medieval music as recently as the sixteenth century. Their introduction completed the octave made up of twelve semitones as well as sanctioning the use of what we would now call the major and minor scales, which Glareanus regarded as the modal species most frequently encountered in the music of his own day.[105] It is interesting to find that Bosse was aware of this distinction between the 'old' and the 'new' modes (or had been made aware of it by some musically minded person, probably de Chambré) and sought a way of expressing it in iconographic terms – evidence, perhaps, of a conscious effort to forge closer links between music and illustration.

But if, by now, legends of the effects produced by the modes – like the unheard music of the spheres – no longer possessed the power of inspiring artists to create anything other than a wholly conventional form of visual imagery, one remarkable feature of *La Rhétorique des Dieux* is that the compositions included in the album were, without exception, purely instrumental. Even fifty years earlier, a composer who set himself the task of representing the human passions would almost certainly have thought first of music serving as the accompaniment to some text, whether in the form of a madrigal, a ballad or an operatic aria. But the 'theme' of *La Rhétorique des Dieux* is the power of music to persuade or move us, regardless of any verbal element. This is underlined by the preface, which declares that 'this manner of expression may rightly claim the title "rhetoric of the Gods", human understanding being capable of conceiving no more eloquent form of language'. The message could scarcely be more explicit. While the rhetoric of mortals is composed of words, that of the gods – 'divine rhetoric' – is music itself, here represented as a higher species of eloquence, superior to oratory or any of the verbal arts.[106]

---

104 Bosse's drawings that accompany the other, traditional modes include numerous depictions of antique instruments including *syrinx*, *kithara* and *aulos*, in contrast to his illustrations for the last four modes (Ionian – Hypoaeolian), where no such ancient instruments are included. Buch, in his article 'The Coordination of Text, Illustration, and Music ...', states merely that, since these four modes were 'considered ancient', he can think of 'no apparent reason why only modern instruments would be depicted' (Buch 1989, p. 61).

105 On Glareanus see (briefly) above, ch. 3, p. 97; also *Grove*, vol. 7, pp. 422–4. His 'system' of twelve modes, explained in his treatise *Dodekachordon* (Basel, 1547) was adopted by many later theorists including Zarlino. During the seventeenth century it was also used in practice by a growing number of composers.

106 The same point is made in one of the two dedicatory sonnets that accompanied *La Rhétorique*, by the now forgotten poet Gauquelin, which praises the volume for not having 'been sired by the liberal arts' (by which is undoubtedly meant the verbal rather than the mathematical arts); see Buch 1989, pp. 49ff.

VI MELODIES FOR THE EYE

The knowledge of colours bears so strong an analogy with the science of Musick that some have been Induc'd to think that the Identical principles, for the composition of musick would equally serve for those of colours.

Hogarth, *Analysis of Beauty* (1753)

One should beware of concluding that there exists any kind of analogy between our perception of colours and that of musical tones; for our perceptions have nothing in common with the objects by which they are caused.

Diderot and d'Alembert, *Encyclopédie* (1751–72)

Music and colour

In modern critical writing, metaphors that have to do with colour are routinely employed in order to describe aspects of our musical – that is, auditory – experience. Precisely because expressions like 'orchestral colour' are now so commonplace, few people would insist on their being pedantically explained. Many listeners would probably agree that Ravel's orchestration of Mussorgsky's *Pictures at an Exhibition* is somehow more 'colourful' than the original piano version, even though it is hard to define exactly *why* particular instruments or combinations of instruments are thought to add 'colour' to a musical composition. Similarly, composers like Berlioz and Debussy are considered great orchestral 'colourists', whose works have repeatedly been described in visual terms. (Adjectives such as 'shimmering' or 'transparent', for example, are often used in order to evoke the unparalleled subtleties of Debussy's orchestration.)[1] And opera lovers will easily recognize the ample figure of the *coloratura* soprano, whose part is embellished with a dazzling array of musical ornaments of one kind or another – ornaments that are likewise said to lend 'colour' to the music.

But it is not just a modern idea that music can be 'coloured' by various means. One of the three *genera* of ancient Greek music was called 'chromatic', showing that comparisons between colours and musical sounds sprang as readily to the Greek mind as they do to ours. And while repetition of the simple rhythmic patterns that provided the basic measures of a polyphonic motet was known in medieval musical parlance as *talea*, the more complex and highly decorated forms of melodic embellishment were called *color*,

---

1 'The blending effect of reverberance [in music] is like the brush strokes in an Impressionist painting, which obscure the subject so that the onlooker is induced to project his senses and emotions into the work in order to perceive the image. The shimmering music of Debussy, its colors sparkling and ethereal, even seems to possess its own "built-in" reverberance.' (Forsyth 1985, p. 17.)

implying that these, too, were considered to be a form of 'colouring'.[2] In this instance, it is unlikely that any very sophisticated analogy with visual experience was intended, since there is no sustained discussion of such analogies in any of the numerous medieval texts on polyphony. Nor did musical theorists of that time have in mind the use of colour by painters or illuminators – a topic to which they scarcely refer. Only in the Renaissance did writers on music start to use more specific comparisons between sounds and colours in order to illustrate their ideas. Vincenzo Galilei, whose interest in ancient Greek musical practice led him to consider the possibility of reviving the antique modes and *genera*,[3] not only thought the composer could 'colour' a piece of music by using the chromatic *genus*; he also believed the musician could find in his own art an equivalent for nearly all significant aspects of painting, among them outline and shading. In his unpublished *Discorso intorno all'uso dell'enharmonio, et di chi fusse autore del cromatico* ('Discourse on the use of the enharmonic [*genus*] and on who invented the chromatic') he wrote:

The diatonic serves the musician not unlike the way drawing the contours and profiles serves the painter, after which the shadows and shadings serve to denote to the sight where the bodies he seeks to represent are in relief or depressed. The composer colours the perfect diatonic design with the chromatic; he then gives it the ultimate perfection (as far as concerns the sounds and chords) with the 'enharmonic'.[4]

Other writers drew parallels with colour in an attempt to explain, for example, why certain consonances seemed to give greater pleasure than others. According to Zarlino, it was those intervals that are most remote from the primary consonances (the octave and the fifth) that afforded the greatest delight. (This view by no means commanded universal assent. The eighteenth-century theorist Dortous de Mairan believed precisely the opposite, namely that our enjoyment of musical chords depended on the ratio between the rates of vibration of their constituent notes and that the simpler that ratio became, the greater was our pleasure.)[5] In his *Istitutioni harmoniche*, Zarlino likens that delight to the enjoyment we derive

---

2 See *Grove*, vol. 4, p. 584.
3 On these see above, ch. 2, pp. 69ff.
4 Quoted after Palisca, *Florentine Camerata*, p. 162.
5 Jean-Jacques Dortous de Mairan, *Discours sur la propagation du son dans les differents tons qui le modifient* (1737); for an account of Mairan's musical theories see Franssen 1991 (as n. [46] below), esp. pp. 42–3.

from our contemplation of 'intermediary' colours such as red or green, by contrast with the extremes of black and white:

In the same way that white and black give less pleasure than other, intermediate or mixed colours, just so, the perfect consonances give less pleasure than others that are not so perfect. Thus green and red and blue and other such colours are more pleasurable, and reveal themselves as more attractive because they are more distant ... Likewise, our hearing rejoices more in those intervals which are more remote from the simple consonances, finding them more attractive than ones which are nearer.[6]

The harmony of colours

Just as musical theorists drew on the language of visual experience, writers on art from the Renaissance onwards freely adapted musical ideas and even musical terminology to their own ends.[7] Consider, for example, the seemingly inevitable references to the 'harmony' of a painting that seem to crop up whenever a topic such as pictorial composition is discussed. 'Harmony' in the antique sense had meant a proper fitting together: a metaphor that might be thought wholly appropriate to the process of selecting and composing from among the various resources at the painter's disposal. But it is clear that, when writing about 'harmony', later authors did not always have any very precise analogy with music in mind – any more than when we ourselves say that the atmosphere in a meeting was 'harmonious' or that the drawing-room furniture has been chosen to 'harmonize' with the colour scheme.[8] In discussions about painting, the term 'harmony' often points to nothing more revolutionary than the idea that a picture should be well-ordered, its composition correctly balanced, the disposition of figures and individual parts logical and clearly thought out. Thus, in his *Cours de peinture par principes* (1708), the French theorist Roger de Piles associates musical harmony with one of his favourite notions, that

6 *Ist. harm.* III, 8. Like many writers in this period, Zarlino describes red, green and so forth as 'intermediate' because he imagines colours to be arranged on a linear scale between black and white, an essentially Aristotelian view that hampered a more comprehensive understanding of the nature of colour; see further John Gage, *Colour and Culture. Practice and Meaning from Antiquity to Abstraction*, London (Thames & Hudson) 1993, ch. 13 'The Sound of Colour', pp. 227ff. and esp. pp. 231–2.

7 Some writers thought the widespread use of such terminology significant in itself. In his *L'Art de peindre* (1761), Claude-Henri Watelet wrote that painting and music 'both have their tones, their chords, their nuances ... these common terms mark their resemblances'; quoted after Maarten Franssen, 'The Ocular Harpsichord of Louis-Bertrand Castel' (as n. 46] below), p. 47.

8 In his book *Colour-Music*, Alexander Wallace Rimington wrote: 'Most people are pleased by the furnishing and decoration of a room if it is harmonious, and displeased by a glaring discord in a picture or a wall-paper, a dress or an advertisement-board' (Rimington 1912, p. 24); on Rimington himself see below pp. 255 ff.

of the 'tout-ensemble' or 'overall effect' of painting. 'It is not enough', he writes, 'that each part has its particular arrangement and propriety; they must all agree together in the picture, and make but one harmonious whole.'[9] While he specifically likens this 'agreement' to a 'concert of music' in which all the parts 'must agree together in a harmony which unites them', he does not pursue any further the implications of what is, in this case, little more than a figure of speech. Harmony is here synonymous with order and equilibrium – above all, with pictorial unity, which De Piles saw as the most important quality of a successful painting.[10]

Other writers, in search of more specific affinities between music and painting, were intrigued by the idea that there might be such a thing as a 'harmony of colours'. Pietro Testa, in his notes for an intended discourse on the theory of painting, wrote how artists like himself were concerned with the 'principles of sight, with shadows and lights and reflections, with the way forms diminish virtually to a point, how colours diminish in intensity through weakness in light or from distancing, how colour harmonies are made according to the rules of music, and other similar things.'[11] Elsewhere in the same notebook, he writes that by the 'principles of the rules of harmony in music are to be understood the rules of colour, the former having high and low notes as limits, the latter light and shade. We must approach these extremes with those temperaments that are in music like steps, and in this we are assisted greatly by the order of the lights that are secondary, tertiary and so on *ad infinitum*, which are called reflections.'[12]

We ourselves might object that 'colour harmony' is, in the end, also a figure of speech, just like the 'harmony' of a picture. But it was a metaphor that proved especially useful to seventeenth-century writers concerned to formulate new ideas about the particular character and function of colour in painting. For example, in the context of French art, Poussin was frequently cited as a painter skilled at using colour in order to create carefully calculated emotional effects, which were thought comparable to the responses elicited by the tones of music.[13] André Félibien, in the preface to his report on the conferences of the French Academy, confidently declared

---

9 *The Principles of Painting*, London (J. Osborn) 1743, quoted after *Art in Theory* I, p. 313.
10 In order to proceed more rapidly with my own argument, I have simplified and abbreviated what was in reality an extended discussion among sixteenth- and seventeenth-century theorists of painting about the precepts that should govern pictorial composition. This topic has been well covered in the art-historical literature; for the best of recent accounts, see Puttfarken 2000, passim, also the same author's *Roger De Piles' Theory of Art* (1985).
11 Quoted after Cropper, *Ideal of Painting*, p. 77. The passage occurs on folio 13v of Testa's notebook; the original is transcribed by Cropper, p. 225.
12 Notebook, 43; Cropper, p. 138.
13 For a more detailed discussion of Poussin and music, see above, ch. 5, esp. pp. 199ff.

that Poussin was 'so much Master' of all the different manners of painting and had 'laid down so certain Rules for them, that he has given his Pictures the Force to express what Sentiments he pleased, and to inspire the Soul of the Beholder, in the same Manner as in Musick these Modes which have been mentioned move the Passions'. He also attributed to Poussin the belief that 'as in Musick the Ear is not delighted but by a just Agreement of different Voices or Sounds: So in Painting the Eye is not charmed but by a fine Harmony of Colours, and a just Agreement of all the Parts with one another'.[14]

While we may doubt whether pious formulations of this kind bore much resemblance to Poussin's own intentions, it is none the less striking how writers in this period often associated the idea of musical harmony with the need for specific rules or principles that might govern artists' use of colour. Félibien, as we saw, ascribed Poussin's mastery of colours to the fact that the great painter had 'laid down so certain Rules for them' – even if, in the end, Poussin had done no such thing. He also remarked trenchantly upon how 'in several other Arts, particularly Musick and Poetry, which are congenial to painting, standard Rules have been found out to bring them to Perfection, though all who know them are not equally capable to put them in Practice'.[15] Similar concerns were voiced by other theorists active elsewhere in Europe. The Spanish painter Jusepe Martinez, in his *Practical Discourse on the Most Noble Art of Painting* (*c.*1675), wrote that:

the colours of a painting are to the eye what the strings of a musical instrument are to the ear. Therefore unison or unity, through which a design becomes harmonious, must be accomplished with moderation as far as colours are concerned lest their vivacity cause them to clash with one another ... Even if [the figures] were in correct proportion, the painting will win small praise if the artist neglects this harmony in the colours.[16]

It is not difficult to see the point of these comparisons between painting and music. Martinez's statement conveys all too vividly the disquiet felt by those writers on art who, in the course of what had become a long-running debate about the respective importance of *disegno* and *colore*, turned their attention to the attributes of colour rather than draughtsmanship. Obviously, the artist's selection and

14 André Félibien, Preface to the *Seven Conferences* ...; *Art in Theory* I, pp. 116–17.
15 Félibien, op. cit., p. 109.
16 Taken from ch. vii, 'Concerning Colour'; *Art in Theory* I, p. 194.

juxtaposition of colours should be convincing when compared with objects in nature, just as drawing aimed to capture the forms and outlines of things as they appeared before the eye. However, some theorists of painting felt that colours should also be satisfying in themselves and in combination with one another. They should not clash, nor should the relationship between them be manifestly arbitrary. But what should govern the choice and disposition of colours, other than merely individual sensibility? The painter might glory in the subtleties that colour, with its seemingly infinite number of tones and gradations, placed at his disposal. He might, on the other hand, shake his head in despair at the accusation that his actual *use* of colour corresponded to no known laws of nature capable of being precisely formulated. As we have seen, painters and architects had, in the past, tried (occasionally) painting pictures and (more frequently) designing buildings based on 'musical' systems of proportion – that is, the same mathematical ratios that produced the primary consonances in music. But Aristotle had hinted that colours, too, might be 'well-ratioed' in the same way that musical consonances had been found to correspond to simple, mathematical relationships. Might it be possible to demonstrate that colour was indeed governed by mathematical laws capable of being applied to the practice of painting in the same way that the rules governing the use of consonance and dissonance were applied to the practice of music? And, in general terms, could it be shown that the organization and division of colours was just as systematic and as orderly as the ways in which the tones of music were organized?

Such an enterprise was, of course, fraught with difficulty. For one thing, there are significant differences between our experience of colour and our perception of musical sounds. Certain colours have strong emotive associations. These are, in part, a matter of convention: think of the symbolic use of colours such as gold and purple in heraldry or regalia. They are also partly to do with physiological or psychological factors. 'Seeing red' or being 'red with anger' are not empty phrases; on the contrary, they are firmly rooted in actual physiological occurrences. Individual pitches, on the other hand, have no such direct associations, even though in the course of time certain keys such as D major came to have particular symbolic connotations. (There were, in part, practical reasons for this: for example, the limited number of keys in which, prior to the late eighteenth century, ceremonial or martial music could be played by instruments like trumpets and drums.)[17] Moreover, a

---

17 Henry Purcell, for example, in his *Orpheus Britannicus* (1698) ascribed particular emotional associations to different keys; for discussion of their characteristics as employed in the works of composers such as Purcell and Blow, see Jensen 1976, esp. pp. 101ff.

particular sequence or juxtaposition of colours does not suggest anything resembling a tonal centre in the way that, for instance, b followed by c′ implies the key of C since, in the absence of any other tonal information, we will tend to perceive b as the leading note (the seventh note of the diatonic scale) resolving on to the keynote or 'tonic'. But, while we attribute certain kinds of 'movement' to colours in themselves, 'warm' colours being described as advancing towards the spectator whereas 'cold' colours seem to recede, the simple juxtaposition of colours such as red and orange does not necessarily convey any sense of movement or direction.

The physical characteristics of colour also differ in several important respects from those of musical sound. Colours are permanent – at least, they are as permanent as anything can be in a world subject to change and decay – whereas musical tones are transitory and can be preserved only by artificial means. Colour is absolute whereas pitches are relative. Red is red and remains the same colour even if we give it another name, since there is only one frequency range that corresponds to the colour we call 'red'. (A different range of frequencies will produce a different colour sensation.) But the note we call a′ has, at different times, been equated with a variety of pitches – *ie* frequencies. It is not its frequency that is significant but its relationship to all the other notes that together form a scale. When, moreover, two or more notes are sounded simultaneously so as to form a chord, each constituent element will still be clearly perceptible – or it will, given a little practice. But you can practise all you like and still not be able to distinguish blue and yellow as separate colours, once they have been physically combined to make green. Mixing colours produces a new colour, whereas mixing musical tones does not produce a new tone or pitch. As for the ratios of colours, it is true that colours can be mixed together in certain proportions (say, two parts red to one part yellow) according to the ratios by which musical consonances are produced – 1:2, 2:3 and so on. But secondary colours produced in this way are not manifestly more 'consonant' than colours created arbitrarily or by 'irrational' mixtures.

Scale and spectrum in Newton's optical theory

Upon this darkness fell the somewhat fitful illumination afforded by Sir Isaac Newton's optical theories. These, in contrast to the dominant Aristotelianism of the seventeenth century, offered new ways of thinking about the physical resemblances between colours and musical tones. Newton's experiments to determine the refrangibility of white light seemed to reveal a striking similarity between the division of the octave by seven tones (*doh–re–mi–fa–soh–la–ti*) and the division of the spectrum into seven colours. In his *Optical Lectures* of 1670–2, he announced his measurements of the width of each colour as it appears in the spectrum and noted that these relative widths corresponded to the differences in the length of a string sounding the successive notes of the diatonic scale.[18] This meant that, in theory at least, it should be possible to determine the proportional relationships between one colour and another in a manner analogous to the way musical consonances can be described in terms of their arithmetical ratios. It was even suggested that these 'proportional relationships' might help to explain why some colours appeared to harmonize with one another whereas others did not.

However, in a letter of 1675 addressed to the Royal Society, in which he sketched the resemblance between the vibratory characteristics of colour and those of sound, Newton wrote with apparent hesitation:

As the harmony and discord of sound proceeded from the proportions of the aereal vibrations, so may the harmony of some colours, as of golden and blue, and the discord of others, as of red and blue, proceed from the proportions of the aethereal. And possibly colour may be distinguished into its principal degrees, red, orange, yellow, green, blue, indigo and deep violet, on the same ground that sound within an eighth [ie octave] is graduated into tones. [fig. 44][19]

675.]   ROYAL SOCIETY OF LONDON.   253

Y the centres of those femicircles, X Z the length of a mufical ftring double to

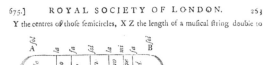

X Y, and divided between X and Y, fo as to found the tones expreffed at the fide (that is X H the half, X G and G I the third part, Y K the fifth part, Y M the eighth part, and G E the ninth part of X Y) and the intervals between thefe divifions exprefs the fpaces which the colours written there took up, every colour being moft brifkly fpecific in the middle of thofe fpaces.

Figure 44. Isaac Newton, diagram showing 'musical' division of the spectrum, from a letter of 1675 addressed to the Royal Academy, published in Thomas Birch, *History of the Royal Society of London*, 1757, III, p. 263

---

18 Newton, *Optica*, Part II, Lecture 11; see Alan E. Shapiro (ed.), *The Optical Papers of Isaac Newton*, vol. 1: *The Optical Lectures 1670–1672*, Cambridge (Cambridge U. P.) 1984, pp. 541ff.
19 Quoted after John Gage, *Colour and Meaning. Art, Science and Symbolism*, London (Thames & Hudson) 1999, p. 140. Newton's letter remained unpublished until the mid-eighteenth century, when it appeared in Thomas Birch's *History of the Royal Society of London* (1757), III, p. 263, complete with accompanying diagram.

It is clear from his use of language ('may proceed ... possibly') that the great scientist was by no means sure of his ground. He was right to be diffident: the parallel he had drawn between the arrangement of colours in the spectrum and the succession of pitches in the musical scale was open to objection on a number of counts. For example, there was no good reason to identify just seven spectral colours; indeed, there was no reason to specify *any* particular number of colours, since colours form a continuum, proceeding by infinitesimal gradations from imperceptibility (beyond violet) at one end of the spectrum to imperceptibility (beyond red) at the other. (In this, colour *does* in fact resemble musical sound, since a similar continuum of pitch extends from one end of the audible scale to the other. Imagine slowly sliding your finger along the fingerboard of a violin at the same time as bowing the string, excruciating though the effect might be.) The only limiting factors are our ability actually to distinguish individual colours from one another – an experiment Newton himself repeated on several occasions, sometimes with the help of an assistant.

This seemingly limitless variety of colour, coupled with the relative imprecision of the method by which individual colours had been isolated, provoked several later writers into criticizing the Newtonian system. One such criticism was aired by the Irish painter James Barry who, in a lecture to the Royal Academy delivered during the 1790s, declared:

Our philosophers have pretended to discover in the rainbow just seven primitive colours ... But if they mean by primitive colours, colours simple and uncompounded of any others, why seven, when there are but three? If they mean only to enumerate the differences, without regarding the actual fact of the procreation of the compounds from the primitives, why more than six, or, why not double that number, or even more, if all the intermediaries are attended to?[20]

In fact, Newton was far from consistent about opting for seven prismatic colours. In his lectures, he described the characteristics of eleven principal steps of colour from 'scarlet, or purple [*purpureus*]' at one end of the scale to indigo and violet at the other by way of three different kinds of green. Elsewhere, in drafts for the *Opticks* and in his optical papers, he seemed to favour a system

---

20 James Barry, *The Works* (2 vols) 1809, vol. 1, pp. 524–6, quoted after Gage 1993, p. 108.

based on five rather than seven colours.[21] It has even been suggested that he may have arrived at the otherwise arbitrary number of seven because he noticed the particularly narrow width of the orange band within the spectrum.[22] Thinking that this might be compared to one of the two semitones that form part of the diatonic scale (for example, in the 'natural' scale of D minor, the distance between e and f and between b and c'),[23] he looked for another equally narrow band of colour. This he 'found' in the conveniently placed but to some eyes illusory tint of indigo, occurring (as it should, if it is to correspond to the scale) between blue and violet. However, only in his *Optica* did he actually spell out his reasons for 'inserting' these two colours into the spectrum alongside what he calls the 'other five pre-eminent colours'.[24]

In the end, Newton's attempts to demonstrate an affinity between colour and musical sound were no more rational or coherent than the ideas put forward by many of his predecessors. Those attempts may even have been driven more by his mystical and alchemical interests and his belief in the possibility of finding a system of correspondences underlying all things than by the processes of experiment and deduction.[25] (In a private letter of May 1698, he affirmed his conviction that 'some general laws of the Creator prevailed with respect to the agreeable or unpleasing affection of all our senses, at least the supposition does not derogate from the wisdom or power of God, and seems highly consonant to the macrocosm in general'.)[26] His discoveries may have led to a greater understanding of the chromatic resources available to painters and encouraged thinking about the ways in which colours and musical tones might be combined. However, they did not in themselves constitute a 'harmonics of colour' any more than the vaguely formulated and subjectively based observations made by earlier writers. In Newton's Cambridge lectures, in which he argued for the 'musical' division of the spectrum of white light, he noted with satisfaction that his system of measurements – that is, of the widths

---

21 In a letter published in the *Philosophical Transactions of the Royal Society of London* for 1671–2, Newton specified as the primary colours '*Red, Yellow, Green, Blew*, and a *Violet-purple*' but adds, as if by way of an afterthought, '*Orange*' and '*Indico*' [sic], at the same time pointing to 'an indefinite variety of Intermediate gradations'; see 'A Letter of Mr Isaac Newton ...', in Cohen 1958 (as n. [47] below), p. 54.

22 For a detailed account of the relationship between musical theory and Newton's optical experiments, see Penelope Gouk, 'The Harmonic Roots of Newtonian Science', in Fauvel et al. 1988, pp. 101–25.

23 See below, pp. 238ff.

24 See Shapiro 1984, pp. 542–3 and n. 19. *Optica* is the name usually given to one of the two principal versions of Newton's optical lectures, the other being known as the *Lectiones opticae*; both are reprinted in Shapiro's edition of Newton's optical papers.

25 On Newton's 'irrational' beliefs of this kind see John Henry, 'Newton, Matter and Magic', in Fauvel et al. 1988, pp. 127–45; also Jan Golinski, 'The Secret Life of an Alchemist', in ibid., pp. 147–67.

26 To John Harrington, 30 May 1698, quoted after Shapiro, p. 547, n. 28. Compare Gouk who, in *Music, Science and Natural Magic*, describes Newton's intellectual goal as having been 'nothing less than to comprehend the whole of creation and the divine plan for mankind within it' (Gouk 1999, p. 229).

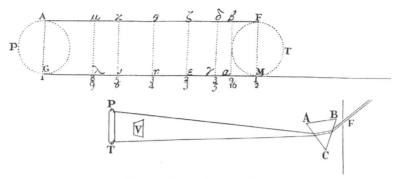

Figure 45. Isaac Newton, diagram showing 'musical' division of the spectrum, from *Opticks*, London, 1704, Book I, pt. ii, fig. 4

of colours and the intervals of the musical scale – 'agrees with the phenomena very well'. But, as far as any possible affinities between music and painting are concerned, he merely remarked that this system 'perhaps involves something about the harmonies of colours (such as painters are not altogether unacquainted with, but which I myself have not yet sufficiently studied) perhaps analogous to the concordances of sounds'.[27] And in his *Opticks*, a book that did much to establish Newton's wider reputation, although he summarized once again his measurements of colours and musical intervals (fig. 45), he drew no specific conclusions from their apparent correspondence, nor did he add any further comment to the passage in which those measurements were reiterated.[28]

Arcimboldo

Newton's *Opticks* was first published in 1704. By then, drawing comparisons between colours and musical tones had been something of a hobby horse among both artists and musicians for more than a century. It seems that one of the first practitioners to attempt to define more precisely the relationship between the tones of music and the colours of the spectrum was the Milanese artist Giuseppe Arcimboldo (1527–93), for a time court painter and artistic factotum to the Habsburg Emperor Rudolf II in Prague. Save for his works, we know next to nothing of Arcimboldo at first hand. Moreover, what

27 Shapiro, in his notes to this passage from the *Optica*, also stresses Newton's 'doubled reluctance here to commit himself to the analogy between musical and color harmony', pointing to the repeated *fortasse* ('perhaps'); see ibid., pp. 545–7 and n. 28.

28 *Opticks*, Book One, Part II, pr. iii. In his preface to the Dover paperback edition of the *Opticks*, Cohen notes that the *Principia*, on which Newton's fame is now largely based, was more or less incomprehensible to all but the most mathematically agile minds of the seventeenth century. Even the philosopher Locke admitted that his grasp of mathematics would never be sufficient to enable him to read Newton's book. The *Opticks*, by comparison, was written in a far more accessible manner and was less dependent on an understanding of mathematics; see *Opticks, or a Treatise on the Reflections, Refractions, Inflections and Colours of Light*, New York (Dover) 1952, pp. ix ff.

we can plausibly reconstruct of his ideas about art must be gleaned from secondary sources. Of these, the most important are Lomazzo's *Treatise on the Art of Painting* and the quasi-Platonic dialogue *Il Figino, overo del fine della Pittura* by the Mantuan-born cleric Gregorio Comanini.[29] Comanini was, like Lomazzo, on friendly terms with Arcimboldo during the latter's final years in Milan. Despite the difficulties it poses, *Il Figino*, printed in Mantua during Arcimboldo's lifetime, has always commanded a certain respect.[30] For one thing, it is improbable that the text would have been sent for publication without the artist's approval. For another, it contains a good deal of information that can, in all likelihood, only have been obtained from Arcimboldo himself.[31] From it, we learn of his interest in the Pythagorean consonances and the mathematical ratios by which these were determined, of his attempts at formulating a scale of values from light to dark according to similar principles, of how:

he identified the tones and semitones, the diatesseron *and the* diapente, *the* diapason, *and all the other musical consonances with colours, in the same manner by which Pythagoras defined the harmonic proportions ... Thus, darkening one white by twice as much as he did another, he formed the same proportion as the* diapason, *ascending by eight degrees of darkness from the purest white, counting this same white as the first degree from which he started. Furthermore, just as the one, by the tensioning of strings in the* sesquitertial *proportion arrived at the* diatesseron *or fourth, so the other, by adding black to white in the* sesquitertial *proportion when compared to another white, likewise formed that same ratio by which the* diatesseron *is produced – that is, four to three ... Pythagoras saw that from the* diatesseron *and the* diapente *was born the* diapason, *and Arcimboldo, observing these same proportions, produced the octave in his colours. From the triple proportion, the one arrived at the* diapason diapente, *which is the twelfth; using the same proportion, the other proceeded to assign twelve degrees from darkness to white ... Having*

---

29 For an account of Lomazzo's *Treatise* see above, ch. 5, pp. 194ff.
30 *Il Figino, overo del fine della Pittura. Dialogo del Rever[endo] Padre D. Gregorio Comanini ... Ove quistionandosi se l'fine della pittura sia l'utile overo il diletto ...*, Mantua (Francesco Osanna) 1591. For extracts from sixteenth-century sources relating to Arcimboldo including Lomazzo and Comanini see 'Antologia di testi del XVI secolo, a cura di Piero Falchetta', in the catalogue of the exhibition held at the Palazzo Grassi, Venice, *Effetto Arcimboldo. Trasformazioni del volto nel sedicesimo e nel ventesimo secolo*, Milan (Bompiani) 1987, pp. 143–98.
31 'The dialogue was printed for the first time in Mantua in 1591, and it is unthinkable that Comanini would have sent it for printing without first seeking the consent of the Master'; see Tonino Tornitore, 'Musica per occhi', in *Effetto Arcimboldo* (as preceding note), p. 345. The same author describes *Il Figino* as 'una fonte per molti versi degna di fede ...'

mastered this system, Mauro Cremonese della Viuola,
musician to the Emperor Rudolf II, was able to locate on the
graviciembalo *all those consonances which Arcimboldo had*
indicated in colour on a chart ... [32]

Here our difficulties begin. Comanini, in his dialogue, does not shirk
the details of Arcimboldo's 'system'. However, it is far from clear
whether what he is talking about is a colour scale or a scale of
values from light to dark: a grey-scale, as Gage and others have
suggested.[33] Perhaps the most persuasive reading of this puzzling
passage from *Il Figino* is that proposed by musicologist Austin
Caswell, who believes that, in the first instance, Arcimboldo applied
a series of calculations based on Pythagoras simply to a scale of
tonal values graduated between white and black.[34] He then had a
musician, the mysterious 'Mauro Cremonese', verify the accuracy of
his calculations by 'playing' the corresponding intervals at the
keyboard.[35] Only then, it seems, did he involve colours in his attempt
to devise a visual equivalent of polyphonic music: a leap into the
unknown. According to this new system, white was assigned to the
lowest part, corresponding to the bass voice in vocal polyphony,
with further colours (green, blue, etc.) being added as required by
the polyphonic structure of the music:

And what I have said about black and white together, I also
say about all the other colours; for just as he gradually
darkened white so as to make it correspond to the higher
pitches [riducendolo ad acutezza], *so he did with yellow and*
all the others, using white for the lowest of the voices, the
bass, green and blue for the middle parts, and charcoal grey
and dark brown for the highest ones; for each of these
colours follows and darkens the other inasmuch as white is
darkened by yellow, yellow by green, green by blue, blue by
grey and grey by brown, just as the bass is followed by the
tenor, the tenor by the alto and the alto by the soprano ...[36]

---

32 Translated from the modern edition of *Il Figino* printed in Paola Barocchi (ed.), *Trattati d'Arte del Cinquencento*, vol. 3, Bari (Laterza) 1962, pp. 368ff.

33 See also Gage 1993, pp. 230ff. for an account of Arcimboldo's ideas on colour and music.

34 Austin B. Caswell, 'The Pythagoreanism of Arcimboldo', *Journal of Aesthetics and Art Criticism*, vol. 39, no. 2 (winter 1980), p. 159.

35 Neither Tornitore nor Levi nor anyone else has been able to discover anything about the mysterious Mauro Cremonese – not even any other mention of his existence. Tornitore notes that he appears in no dictionary of music, nor in any record of the names of eminent citizens of Cremona. Levi describes him merely as a musician who has 'not been precisely identified by those versed in musicology'; see Tornitore, 'Musica per occhi', p. 356, also Levi (as following note), p. 92.

36 *Il Figino* (as n. [32] above), p. 370; see also Lionello Levi, 'L'Arcimboldi musicista', in Benno Geiger, *I dipinti ghiribizzosi di Giuseppe Arcimboldi, pittore illusionista del cinquecento (1527–1593)*, Florence (Vallecchi) 1954, pp. 91–2.

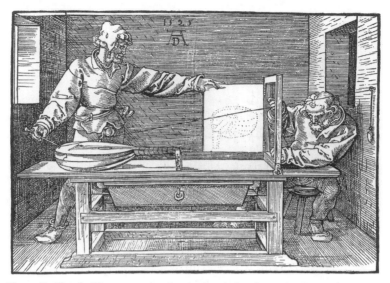

Figure 46. Albrecht Dürer, engraving showing lute in foreshortening, from *Unterweisung der Messung*, Nuremberg, 1525 (Munich, Staatliche Graphische Sammlung)

As for the instrument on which a rendering of Arcimboldo's colour notation was performed, this, too, has been a matter for disagreement. Various commentators have persuaded themselves that it must have been some kind of chromatic keyboard, similar perhaps to the *clavecin oculaire* invented more than a century later by the enterprising French Jesuit Louis-Bertrand Castel.[37] Seductive though this hypothesis might be, it is clear from the context that Comanini's allusion to a *graviciembalo* refers instead to something more like a harpsichord or virginal, both of which were then in common use: in other words, a perfectly ordinary keyboard instrument. The fact that a musician was able to 'play' Arcimboldo's colour chords served merely as confirmation of the accuracy with which they had been calculated, according to the principle of musical ratios; at least, this appears to be the sense of the passage from *Il Figino* in which the experiment is described. Caswell is surely correct when he suggests that the artist was not writing for some new-fangled 'colour harpsichord' but was more interested in undertaking a 'scientific excursion into the twin realms of sight and sound, conducted for the purpose of accurate mathematical measurements of the intervals found in both sensory domains by

---

37 E.g. Levi, op. cit., pp. 90–1, who refers to Arcimboldo's ambitions as an enterprise 'without precedent; its sequel was the *Optique des couleurs*, which appeared in 1740, where its author, Bertrand Louis [sic] Castel, published a description of his *clavecin oculaire*.' For a review of earlier literature relating Arcimboldo to Castel see Tornitore, op. cit., n. 3 on pp. 354–5

means of the Pythagorean ratios derived from music'.[38] Arcimboldo's innovations were not, it seems, intended as an alternative system of musical notation, nor were they meant to engender any form of quasi-synaesthetic experience.

Further confusion has been generated by a misreading of an anonymous inventory of the works of art, artefacts and curiosities preserved in Prague Castle, compiled in 1621.[39] This, it has often been alleged, makes passing reference to a 'perspective lute' (*Perspektivlaute* or *liuto prospettico*) supposedly acquired (or invented?) by Arcimboldo. Again, it is tempting to conclude that this was another ingenious audio-visual device dreamed up by our ever-resourceful artist.[40] However, closer inspection shows that the original entry, dated 6 December 1621, refers not to a musical instrument at all but to a picture, since it is located in that part of the inventory (item 811ff) concerned exclusively with paintings ('Folgen ferner die gemaehl …') alongside other works by Arcimboldo.[41] Somewhat more likely is Tonino Tornitore's suggestion that the entry could refer to an impression of or copy after an engraving by Dürer from the series *Unterweisung der Messung* (Nuremberg, 1525) showing an artist drawing a lute in foreshortening with the help of a perspective frame and stretched string (fig. 46).[42] Rudolf II, Arcimboldo's employer, was a known admirer and avid collector of Dürer's works.[43] That the subject of a lute drawn in perspective was common in this period, no doubt as a way of proving that one had mastered the skill of depicting awkwardly shaped objects seen in foreshortening, is also affirmed by a further inventory of the treasures from Prague Castle, which identifies one painting as 'Ein perspective mit einer lautenschlagerin'.[44] Coincidentally, this unattributed picture is listed between two other works by Arcimboldo, nos. 58 'Ein Vertunno von Arcimboldo' and 60 'Ein Flora vom Arcimboldo'.

38 Caswell (as n. [34] above), p. 156.
39 See Heinrich Zimmermann (ed.), 'Das Inventar der Prager Schatz- u. Kunstkammer vom sechsten Dezember 1621, nach Akten des k. u. k. Reichsfinanzarchivs in Wien', *Jahrbuch der Kunsthistorischen Sammlungen des Allerhöchsten Kaiserhauses*, vol. 25, Vienna/Leipzig (F. Tempsky/G. Freitag) 1905, II. Teil, pp. xiii ff.
40 It was Zimmermann who attempted to link this 'lute' with a 'perspektiflauten', listed in a copy of one of three inventories of the Imperial collections in Prague, previously published in a nineteenth-century edition by Dudik. ('Nun hat Bela Dudik im Sommer 1851 bei einer Durchforschung schwedischer Archive allerdings drei Inventare der Prager Kunstkammer … gefunden, die er in den *Mittheilungen der k. k. Central-Commission zur Erforschung und Erhaltung der Baudenkmale*, XII Jg., Wien 1867, S. xxxiii ff veröffentlichte.') In his own edition of the 1621 inventory, Zimmermann merely inserts as a query against item 1061 ('Eine lauten vom Arciboldo') the brief remark: 'Ob identisch mit Dudik A348 (S.xxxix): Ein perspektiflauten?' see Zimmermann 1905, pp. xiv ('Vorbemerkung') and xliii ('Inv. No. 19421 vom 6 Dezember 1621').
41 Compare item 1062 'Ein kopf von kreüterwerk vom Arsimboldo (Orig.)'; Zimmermann, p. xliii.
42 Tornitore, op. cit., pp. 347ff., where he declares that the so-called perspective lute '… resterà per sempre un oggetto misterioso … certamente non si tratta di uno strumento audiocoloristico (un liuto che emetta colori e troppo anchè per una fantasia arcimboldesca) …'
43 See Dorothy Limouze, 'Engraving at the Court of Prague', in Eliška Fučikova et al. (eds), *Rudolf II and Prague. The Court and the City*, London (Thames & Hudson) 1997, pp. 172ff., 175.
44 Inventory no. 19437 (April 1635), item 59; Zimmermann, p. lix.

Arcimboldo's system of imagined correspondences between colours and musical tones seemingly had little impact on his contemporaries, which perhaps explains why it is now so difficult to reconstruct precisely what his intentions may have been. His choice of colours and their distribution appears to have been largely arbitrary. There is no reason why, for example, blue and green rather than any other colours should be assigned to the tenor and alto parts in polyphony nor why the *darker* tones should be linked to the *higher* pitches. In this respect, he was quite different from Castel who, although professedly anti-Newtonian, nevertheless took as the starting point for his experiments the physically well-grounded comparison that Newton had drawn between the seven prismatic colours and the seven notes of the diatonic scale. Indeed, it is strange that Arcimboldo should ever have been considered a forerunner of Castel, since the Frenchman's purpose was, in the end, quite different from his. Castel's aim was to fabricate an instrument that, when played, produced to the observer's astonished gaze a succession of coloured lights (or coloured ribbons or pieces of paper, depending which of the many descriptions of his *clavecin oculaire* one relies on), each colour corresponding to a different note on the keyboard. Arcimboldo clearly had no such aim in mind. Nor were his experiments with various modulations of tone and colour meant to be 'performed', whether on a keyboard or by any other means.[45] Instead, they were part of that more general enquiry into the systematic nature of colour with which, as we have seen, so many later artists were preoccupied.

Father Castel and his 'ocular harpsichord'

In recent years, the enigmatic figure of Louis-Bertrand Castel (1688–1757) has attracted a good deal of scholarly interest.[46] Although many of his contemporaries dismissed him as a crank, new research has shown how prominent a role he played in French eighteenth-century intellectual life. He enjoyed intimate friendships with Montesquieu and with Bernard le Bovier de Fontenelle, secretary of the Parisian Académie Royale des Sciences.[47] He was

---

45 Gage notes that Arcimboldo had 'no means of gauging the proportions of black and white in the intermediate hues, and that his Aristotelianism was still an obstacle to linking the notion of musical consonances practically to the idea of colour harmonies'. He also discounts the idea that Arcimboldo wrote any colour 'compositions' or that the 'plotting of his colour-consonances on the keyboard gave any pleasure to the eye'; see Gage 1993, p. 230.

46 Among recent studies, the most valuable are the excellent and well-balanced article by Maarten Franssen, 'The Ocular Harpsichord of Louis-Bertrand Castel. The Science and Aesthetics of an Eighteenth-Century *Cause Célèbre*', *Tractrix. Yearbook for the History of Science*, 3 (1991), pp. 15–77, and the proceedings of the colloquium on Castel held at Clermont-Ferrand in 1994, edited by Roland Mortier et Hervé Hasquin and published in the series *Études sur le XVIII Siecle*, vol. 23: *Autour du Père Castel et du clavecin oculaire*, Brussels (Éditions de l'Université de Bruxelles, Groupe d'étude du XVIII Siècle) 1995.

47 Fontenelle was 'perpetual secretary' of the French Academy of Sciences during the early 1700s, a post he held for more than thirty years. In that capacity, he wrote an *éloge* of Newton, who had been *associé étranger* of that institution, following the English scientist's death in 1727. Translated into English, it remained a standard biography of Newton for much of the eighteenth century; see Charles Coulston Gillispie, 'Fontenelle and Newton', in I. Bernard Cohen and Robert E. Schofield (eds), *Isaac Newton's Papers and Letters on Natural Philosophy and Related Documents*, Cambridge (Cambridge U. P.) 1958, pp. 427ff.

scientific editor of the respected Jesuit journal *Mémoires de Trévoux*[48] and a frequent contributor to the *Mercure de France*. His most celebrated invention, the *clavecin oculaire* or 'ocular harpsichord', captured the attention of some of the foremost intellects of his day. Among them were Diderot, who included an entry about it in the *Encyclopédie*, and the composer Telemann, who translated a description of it for a German audience.[49]

But despite the efforts of various scholars, many aspects of Castel's attempts to relate colour to musical sound remain tantalizingly obscure. There seem to have been two main phases to his experiments, so different from one another that they might almost be regarded as two separate projects. Castel announced his first idea for what he called a 'harpsichord for the eyes' in an article published in the *Mercure de France* in November 1725. At this point, his main aim was, as he put it, 'to render sound visible' – not only sound but:

all that music of which sound is capable ...to paint sounds, I say, really *paint them; not merely paint them, but paint them using the* appropriate colours – *in a word, to render sounds perceptible to the eye, just as they are to the ear, in such a way that a deaf person would be capable of* enjoying *and of* judging *the beauty of a piece of music.*[50]

In the course of his article, Castel acknowledged two main sources of inspiration. One was the writings of his Jesuit predecessor Athanasius Kircher (1602–80), whom he later called 'my true, my first, and as it were my only master'.[51] In his *Musurgia universalis* – that monumental compendium of seventeenth-century learning, with its characteristic blend of scientific observation and mystical belief – Kircher had expounded his doctrine of the 'harmonic' organization of the human body and the elements. He illustrated his ideas by means of elaborate tables of correspondences between various natural and celestial phenomena, among them birds and mammals, minerals and gemstones, angels and planets, colours and musical tones. He also described the characteristics of sound, which he christened the 'ape of light', writing that colours, too, 'have their

---

48 Its proper title was *Mémoires pour l'histoire des sciences et des beaux-arts*. As a member of the editorial team, Castel was the sole expert on mathematics and physics from 1720 until his resignation in 1746; see Franssen 1991, p. 16.

49 Georg Philipp Telemann, *Beschreibung der Augen-Orgel oder des Augen-Clavicimbels ... aus einem französischen Briefe übersetzt* (Hamburg, 1739); see Franssen 1991, p. 28, also Wilton Mason, 'Father Castel and his Colour Clavecin', *Journal of Aesthetics and Art Criticism*, vol. 17, no. 1 (September 1958), p. 108.

50 'Clavecin pour les yeux, avec l'art de Peindre les sons, & toutes sortes de Pièces de Musique', *Mercure de France*, IX (November 1725), p. 2553. Castel's article is in the form of a letter dated 20 February 1725.

51 *Mémoires de Trévoux*, October 1735, p. 2033.

harmony, which pleases no less than music and which, being the counterpart of musical harmony, possesses great power to affect one's state of mind'.[52]

An unusual feature of Kircher's theories is that he associated colours not with individual *pitches* but with musical *intervals*, the more consonant intervals being compared to the brighter colours, the more discordant to the darker ones.[53] He does not, however, appear to have envisaged any kind of instrument, musical or otherwise, capable of manifesting these correspondences. Nor did he think primarily in terms of the emotional or psychological effect produced upon the viewer or listener by the simultaneous conjunction of these two forms of sensory experience.

The other important starting point for Castel's deliberations was Newton. This may appear strange, since Castel has often been called anti-Newtonian. But he had studied Newton's *Opticks* carefully, the French translation of which he reviewed in the *Mémoires de Trévoux* in 1723.[54] In the same article in the *Mercure de France* where his ideas were first announced, Castel himself acknowledged that he had, indeed, been influenced by Newton's discoveries:

The fact is certain: colours have their precise tones, which between themselves adhere to the same proportions as do the tones of music. This has been verified by the celebrated Englishman M. Newton ... You have only to consult [Newton's Opticks] *in order to find there all the colors well-*diapasonned *with their octaves, fifths, thirds and sevenths.*[55]

At this early stage, the instrument Castel envisaged was probably soundless. 'The movement of the keys', he wrote, 'will cause colours to appear, with all their [different] combinations and correspondences: in a word, with all their harmony, which corresponds exactly to any kind of music'.[56] There is no mention of the colours being accompanied by any audible music. Instead, Castel's purpose was 'to bestow on colours, over and above their harmonic order, a certain vivacity and lightness which they never have on an immobile and inanimate canvas'.[57] In other words, his instrument should be capable of investing colour with the

---

52 *Musurgia universalis,* vol. 2, p. 223.
53 For a succinct description of Kircher's system of correspondences between musical tones and intervals and other natural and unnatural phenomena, see Albert Wellek, 'Renaissance- und Barocksynästhesie. Die Geschichte des Doppelempfindens im 16. und 17. Jahrhundert', *Deutsche Vierteljahrsschrift für Literaturwissenschaft und Geistesgeschichte,* Halle/S., Bd. IX (1931), esp. pp. 549ff.
54 *Mémoires de Trévoux,* August 1723, pp. 1428–50. Castel's later book on Newton, *Le Vrai système de physique générale de M. Isaac Newton* (1743) was much more critical; see Franssen 1991, p. 18.
55 'Clavecin pour les yeux' (as n. [50] above), p. 2560.
56 Ibid., p. 2568.
57 Ibid., pp. 2574–5.

transient and volatile characteristics of music – even of imitating music's rhythmic aspect, so that, as Hogarth later observed, a 'jig in notes would be litterally [sic] a jig in Colours'.[58]

Castel's article does not disguise the fact that, until now, its author had given little thought to the purely practical question of how a device linking colours with musical tones might be made to work. Towards the end of his life, he wrote ruefully that it had been 'in effect, only an idea, and I had no intention of carrying it out'. Nor had he seriously entertained the notion of constructing any kind of instrument himself. It was, he proclaimed, 'not as an artisan but as a philosopher' that he had undertaken to demonstrate 'this new art'.[59] Elsewhere, he compared himself to an architect, whose task it was to come up with the concept or design; he was not, he insisted, a mason responsible for actually building the edifice in question.[60] The fact that, by 1725, he had done nothing whatever by way of actually realizing his ideas is betrayed by a passing remark, half-buried in his first article about the harpsichord, where he admitted that 'the most difficult part remains to be accomplished, or to put it better, everything remains to be accomplished'.[61]

Somewhat to Castel's surprise, what had hitherto been little more than vague daydreams and dimly perceived analogies were quickly taken up by an enthusiastic but also critical readership. He received a number of queries and suggestions in response to his article, which prodded him into providing further elucidation of his ideas. He also came under increasing pressure to prove that those ideas were capable of being translated into practice. Soon, it dawned on him that only by fabricating a real ocular harpsichord, instead of merely describing it, could he demonstrate that the 'colour music' he envisaged was capable of both arousing and satisfying the emotions, as he had claimed.[62]

Faced with the prospect of actually trying to build a 'harpsichord for the eyes', Castel went rather quiet. But by the summer of 1735, a whole decade after his first article on the subject had been published,

---

58 Rejected draft for chapter 12 'Of Colours with reguard to Beauty', published in William Hogarth, *The Analysis of Beauty. With the Rejected Passages from the Manuscript Drafts and Autobiographical Notes.* Edited with an introduction by Joseph Burke, Oxford (Clarendon Press) 1955, p. 176. In the same passage, Hogarth refers specifically to 'Pare Castle Dr. of the Surbon' and to his harpsichord 'on which he wrote a pretty large Treatise' – evidence that Castel's ideas on colour and music were well known in England. The reference is probably to the lengthy description of the *clavecin* published in the *Mémoires de Trévoux* in 1735; see n. [63] below.

59 'Clavecin pour les yeux', p. 2561.

60 'I am a mathematician, a philosopher, if you like, but I am not of the opinion that I have to be a mason in order to make my mark as an architect'; see [Anon.], *Esprit, saillies et singularités du P. Castel* (Amsterdam/Paris, 1763), quoted after Mason 1958, p. 112.

61 'Clavecin pour les yeux', p. 2561.

62 In the *Encyclopédie*, Diderot remarked that 'the manufacture of this instrument is so remarkable that only an unenlightened public could complain that it is always being built but is never finished'; see *Encyclopédie ou Dictionnaire raisonné des sciences, des arts et des métiers*, vol. 3 (Paris, 1753), p. 512.

it became apparent that he had since been working on an instrument that differed in almost every important respect from his original idea. If the first version of his *clavecin oculaire* – whether really constructed or merely imagined – had been both soundless and essentially Newtonian as regards its underlying conception, the second version was quite the opposite. Like many people, Castel had been struck by the correspondence Newton had pointed out between the seven colours of the spectrum and the seven notes of the diatonic scale; but he had also been troubled by some of the inconsistencies of Newton's account, to which reference has already been made. His disquiet was no doubt aggravated by the fact that he persisted in thinking in terms of a scale of C major, failing to notice that Newton, as we noted earlier, had in mind a 'natural' scale of D minor (d e f g a b c), corresponding to the Dorian 'mode' of medieval church music.

Castel also found it hard to accept that violet, the 'lowest' colour in the spectrum, could stand for the keynote, regarded as the starting point of the diatonic scale. Eventually, he convinced himself that Newton, despite the English scientist's formidable reputation and all the scientific apparatus at his disposal, had not studied the prism closely enough and that the basic components of white light were, in fact, only three: red, yellow and blue. Perhaps influenced by Rameau's notion of a *basse fondamentale* in music, Castel now equated the tonic or 'fundamental', upon which the musical scale was based, with blue. This had two advantages. It solved the problem of what to do with violet, which he had never been able to accept as identical with the tonic, since it was obviously not a primary colour. But it also meant that yellow and red, the other true primaries, could be made to coincide with the third and fifth notes of the scale – that is, the other constituents of the major triad (for example: C–E–G).

Moreover, having carefully considered the distances between the remaining colours, Castel came to the conclusion that there existed precisely twelve in all, which could therefore be arranged so as to correspond to the twelve semitones of the chromatic scale: in his eyes, a far more satisfactory and plausible solution. He provided an exhaustive account of the new version of his harpsichord in a six-part article published in the *Mémoires de Trévoux* during the summer and autumn of 1735.[63] It must have been this later version that was described by Diderot in the third volume of the *Encyclopédie*, under the heading 'clavecin oculaire', since he, too, lists colours equivalent to the twelve semitones of the chromatic scale. (In fact, he lists thirteen, starting with blue–celadon–green

---

[63] 'Nouvelles expériences d'optique et d'acoustique', *Mémoires de Trévoux*, August–December 1735.

and returning once more to blue at the higher octave: presumably a different shade of blue.) He also equates the triad *doh–mi–soh* with the three primary colours: blue, yellow and red.[64] Diderot skates affably over the various manifest difficulties, merely remarking that colours will be arranged in octaves 'according to the same system as notes' and that the eye will take as much pleasure in the 'melodies and harmonies' created by colours as does the ear in the melodies and harmonies of music.[65]

Early performances

Castel's 'system' was complete. Or at least, it was complete in theory. In practice, he was still left with the problem of translating his ideas into reality. From this point on, the story of what became of his invention and the various stages in its development becomes increasingly tangled. We know that visitors to his studio saw a harpsichord of some kind; but was it a model they saw, a prototype, or a fully fledged musical-optical machine? It was probably a model, given the difficulties to which Castel often alluded and the fact that he was constantly short of money, but we cannot be sure. Was it, by contrast with the soundless first version, a functioning musical instrument that generated pitches as well as colours? This seems almost certainly to have been the case. Yet no account of the *clavecin* specifies precisely how sounds and colours were linked. Significantly, some writers sketched a variety of possible mechanisms, as if Castel had still not decided which method he should use. At one point, he experimented with dyeing skeins of silken thread in many different tones of the same colour, from darkest to lightest, perhaps intending to furnish his 'ocular harpsichord' with coloured ribbons or fabrics of some kind. Telemann, on the other hand, mentions painted boxes, fans and pieces of coloured enamel, while an anonymous writer who charted the various stages in the development of the *clavecin* noted that 'in 1730 [Castel] made a trial with colored slips of paper, masked with cartridge ... an easy spring, under the stress of the finger upon the keys of the Harpsichord, raised the colored paper above its cover, so as to make the color appear and vanish like lightening.'[66]

It is difficult to make much sense of all this conflicting evidence. However, that some sort of playable instrument was actually

---

64 *Encyclopédie*, vol. 3, pp. 511–12. Diderot also discussed Castel's ocular harpsichord in some detail in his *Lettre sur les sourds et les muets*.

65 Not all writers were as enthusiastic as Diderot about the effect the ocular harpsichord was likely to produce. Among Castel's critics were the Abbé Prévost, who thought that the rapid movements of the colours would merely 'annoy and trouble the sight', and Voltaire, who speculated that the 'passage of various colours before the eyes may perhaps not fail to shock, dazzle and exhaust'; see Franssen 1991, pp. 40–1.

66 *Explanation of the Ocular Harpsichord upon Shew to the Public*, London (Hooper and Morlay) 1757, pp. 2–3.

constructed is clear from contemporary accounts of two public performances given in Paris in 1754 and 1755, aimed at demonstrating what must have been the most effective of all the various versions of Castel's harpsichord. Castel, who organized these performances himself, described their impact in a letter dated April 1755. Having decided the previous autumn that his *clavecin* was at last finished, he resolved to show it to a select audience, which he did on 21 December 1754. This, he recalled, was 'the day of St Thomas the patron of the uncredulous and of the Harpsichord', claiming that:

> *there was nothing but acclamation and clapping of hands in consequence for the space of half an hour that I played ... Everyone wanted to see, and see again this novelty. I put them off to New-year's day ... The Harpsichord played, and two hundred persons owned that they had never seen any thing more beautiful, or more brilliant ... I alone assuring them, that this was not even a* sketch, *a* beginning *of it, so far was it from* perfect.'[67]

One remarkable thing about this latest version of Castel's ocular harpsichord was that it evidently involved the use of some sort of box or receptacle containing upwards of a hundred wax candles, their light shining through coloured glass apertures. Castel had been thinking for some time about the possibilities of some kind of luminous projection. From a letter to Montesquieu dated 1739, it is clear that he had been experimenting with lanterns 'tuned by colour degrees [*diapasonnées par les degrés de couleur*] ... with lanterns, wonderful effects can be achieved using glass, horn, netting, taffeta, even oiled or varnished paper, especially when the lanterns are made as mobile as mine are'.[68] And in his 'Journal', which recorded the various stages in his erratic progress towards completion of the harpsichord, he again mentions preparing 'transparent sheets and candles, colours and lights, screens and valves'.[69]

The harpsichord demonstrated in Paris in 1754–5 may still have been only a model or prototype. However, we know that at least one full-scale ocular harpsichord was actually built and publicly exhibited, although not by Castel himself. Evidence of this is

---

67 Ibid., pp. 12–13.
68 *Mémoires de Trévoux*, August 1739, pp. 1676ff.
69 The title Castel gave to his manuscript, in the form of a series of letters addressed to the Comte de Maillebois, was 'Historical and demonstrative journal of the practical execution of the ocular harpsichord'. His text, which remained unpublished, is now in the Royal Library Albert I in Brussels; see Franssen 1991, pp. 30ff.

provided by the anonymous pamphlet, already referred to, entitled *Explanation of the Ocular Harpsichord*, whose author must have been closely associated with Castel, since he repeatedly mentions visits to the inventor's workshop and discussions about how the harpsichord should be constructed. This unidentified friend or colleague also acted as an intermediary between Castel and his English admirers, conveying letters to and from the officers of the Royal Society in London.[70] And it seems that, in 1757, he himself built and exhibited a full-size instrument, corresponding for the most part, although not entirely, to Castel's specifications. His pamphlet describes both its appearance and its dimensions:

This Ocular Harpsichord ... is in the form of a beaufet, *at the height of five feet eight inches, breadth three feet four inches, and in depth two feet, placed perpendicularly upon the fore part of a common Harpsichord ... the Harpsichord is executed in great, and is indeed as great as it can be for a portable Harpsichord. Smaller ones may be made which one single person may manage, but they would only be proper for a chamber, but not to make any figure in an audience-room.*

Elsewhere, the author refers to the light of 'five hundred and odd lamps' and to 'sixty coloured glasses ... The same touch that produces the sound will, at the same time, start the luminous colour ... The coloured glasses are transparent enamels, of an elliptic form, of two inches and a half diameter.' That it was indeed the author of the *Explanation* who built this formidable contraption is betrayed by his use of the first person singular ('I could have given to the apertures ... different forms and different figures ...').[71]

Several interesting things emerge from this description of the instrument. First, its maker had evidently abandoned Castel's triadic red-yellow-blue arrangement, reverting instead to a sequence of seven colours starting with violet: a sequence that, like Newton's, is linked not to a C-major but to a D-minor scale. ('Thus the most refrangible ray, the violet, answers to D ...')[72] Secondly, this version of the harpsichord – which, as far as we know, was exhibited only in London – was not just a curiosity to be shown off in private to a handful of enthusiasts. Instead, it was clearly intended for large-scale public performances, something underlined by the allusion to 'making a figure in an audience room'.

---

70 Castel was a foreign member of the Royal Society; the same pamphlet records with evident satisfaction that 'the Royal Society of London admitted him one of the members that compose that illustrious body' (*Explanation* ..., p. 8).
71 Ibid., pp. 21–2.
72 Ibid., pp. 18–19.

It seems to have comprised two elements in one: an ordinary harp-sichord capable of emitting musical sounds, with a very large vertical box erected on top of it. In the front panel of the box were coloured apertures, through which the light was meant to shine. Whether it shone out into the room, in the direction of the audience, or away from the audience, falling upon a screen of some kind, is not clear.[73] In either case, we can only assume that the five hundred candles required would have produced an astonishing effect, even in a sizeable auditorium. Equally, they might well have started a terrify-ing conflagration. Perhaps this was the reason why this instrument was never actually demonstrated – or so it appears. A handwritten note appended to one copy of the *Explanation*, now in the British Library, indicates that the harpsichord could be seen at the 'Great Concert Room in Soho Square',[74] but the writer adds ruefully that he had been admitted 'to a sight only of the instrument, for nothing was then performed nor afterwards, as ever I heard, neither did I ever know why'.[75] His disappointment notwithstanding, this lack of performances may have been a good thing, given the high incidence of disastrous theatre fires in eighteenth-century London.

Success and failure of Castel's experiments

One of the best recent accounts of the ocular harpsichord, that by Maarten Franssen (1991), emphasizes the extent to which Castel's ambitions remained unfulfilled, his dreams unrealized. Franssen paints a pathetic picture of an old man 'sitting between the remnants of his models, none of which was capable of coming anywhere near what he had in mind for the performance of his instrument', complaining that there was nothing left for him to do but 'adjust and readjust the debris of my harpsichord to the taste of the public'.[76] Castel's unknown collaborator, too, seems to have been painfully conscious of what he saw as the failure of his experiments. In his pamphlet describing the London version of the harpsichord, he writes in self-deprecating tones that the instrument had been 'only made for philosophical eyes ... there can be no

---

73 Mason believed that the 'series of fifty glass shields ... faced back towards the player and viewer.' ('Father Castel ...' p. 115.) The *Explanation*, as already noted, specified sixty coloured glasses.
74 This is probably an allusion to the former residence of the Venetian Ambassador at 21 Dean Street, Soho. The house had been in use as a venue for musical performances since December 1751, when the violinist-composer Felice de Giardini staged the first of a series of twenty concerts there. It would have been an appropriate setting for the display of an innovation such as the ocular harpsichord, being well-provided with all the most modern equipment including a 'German stove' to prevent the audience from catching cold; see Robert Elkin, *The Old Concert Rooms of London*, London (Edward Arnold) 1955, pp. 58ff.; also Forsyth, *Buildings for Music*, p. 28.
75 There are two copies of the *Explanation* in the British Library. The one bearing the handwritten note, presumably added by its original owner, has the shelf mark 104. h. 4 (1).
76 Franssen 1991, pp. 30–1.

pleasure expected to be felt from it, but that which a curiosity for optics and music will give to a mind of philosophical turn.'[77] In a sense, he was right: the *idea* of an art of coloured light that would emulate music was more significant than any success or failure that might have been experienced in attempting to stage some sort of performance. Indeed, Castel's ideas in general exerted far greater influence than his achievements – the more so since those ideas were, in several important respects, very different from the theories advanced by most of his predecessors. Nearly all previous writers who compared colour with musical sound had focused upon the supposed resemblance between music and *painting*. Castel, too, thought it might be possible to arrange colours on a canvas or wall hanging in the same order and in the same combinations as the pitches to which they supposedly corresponded. Thus one could, in theory at least, have a room 'tapestried with rigaudons and minuets, sarabandes and passacaglias, sonatas and cantatas and, if you like, a complete representation of all the music of an opera.'[78]

But, for much of the time, he seemingly held rather a low opinion of painters and of painting, despite the more durable qualities of the latter when contrasted with music. He even thought that his ocular harpsichord might teach 'a lesson to painters ... that they might learn from it, how to speak intelligently about tones, and dissonances, and about the harmony of colours, what they have said about these subjects having hitherto depended upon nothing more than taste and feeling.'[79] What his *clavecin* was meant to produce was not a kind of surrogate painting but what Castel called a 'concert for the eye', resembling the pleasing and seemingly logical succession of tones that were the only essential constituents of music. His letter of April 1755, quoted above, outlines his programme for a new art of colour:

My aim is to make harmony, and almost music, enter in at the eye, as it has hitherto done at the ear. My aim is to make harmony as well seen as heard ... My aim is to represent by colours all that is represented by sounds. My aim is to make sound as it were, be seen at the same time as it is heard, and to make colour be heard at the same time that it is seen.[80]

---

77 *Explanation*, p. 17.
78 'Clavecin pour les yeux', p. 2573.
79 Ibid., pp. 2574–5.
80 *Explanation*, p. 14.

The symphony in the sky

The new art Castel had dreamed of was all the more remarkable for being entirely abstract. Like music, it had no need of images or any kind of narrative in order to convey its meaning. Today, his vision of a soundless music composed solely of abstract colour and light must strike us as surprisingly modern. Not until almost a century had elapsed after his death did Romantic artists, critics and philosophers first point to music on account of its abstract, expressive character – not as the paradigm of an essentially orderly art, as writers had done in the past. But also, Castel's account of the 'musical' effects of colour and light appears to foretell what we might think of as a characteristically Romantic sensibility. A vivid example of how, in the nineteenth century, an artist working in a quite different medium conceived of the affinities between aural and visual experience can be found in a famous essay by Austrian author Adalbert Stifter, entitled *Die Sonnenfinsternis* (1842). Here, Stifter describes a total eclipse of the sun that he, accompanied by several friends, had witnessed in Vienna on 8 July 1842. He was, he recalled, profoundly moved: only listening to music could compare with the power and grandeur of that moment, the impression created by:

that inexpressibly tragic music composed of colours and lights, which pervaded the entire sky – a requiem, a dies irae such as to break one's heart ... Might one not imagine a music for the eye, created out of the simultaneous or successive juxtaposition of lights and colours, in just the same way that sounds create music for the ear ... Should it not be possible for harmony and melody of light to provoke a total effect as powerful and moving as that created by sound? I, at least, could think of no symphony, oratorio or the like composed of such noble music as those few minutes of light and colour in the sky.[81]

Even if Stifter's account of his experiences may strike the reader as little more than a poetic conceit, there is an uncanny resemblance between the language he chooses and Castel's description of the effects of colour he had seen so clearly in his mind's eye.[82] But without the convenient occurrence of a solar eclipse, Castel's scope for

---

81 'Die Sonnenfinsternis am 8. Juli 1842', in Adalbert Stifter, *Wien/Die Sonnenfinsternis*. Mit einem Nachwort von Johannes Urdizil, Stuttgart (Reclam) 1963, pp. 79, 81.

82 Interestingly, Castel referred more than once to the rainbow as God's equivalent of the ocular harpsichord, the latter being destined solely for human eyes; see Karine van Hercke, 'Le journal du clavecin oculaire', in Castel 1995, esp. pp. 20ff.

actually demonstrating how powerful such effects could be was severely limited. It was clear to him that, rather than resorting to half-hearted expedients such as dyed fabrics or tinted paper, it was the motion of coloured light that had the potential for creating by far the greatest impact on the spectator. As already noted, during the last years of his life he turned his attention increasingly to the problem of devising a light source powerful enough to produce precisely this kind of impact. Before the advent of electricity, however, those attempts were, in purely practical terms, doomed to failure. Not until more than a century had elapsed did advances in technology place in the hands of a new generation of enthusiasts an effective means of realizing Castel's vision of an art of mobile colour.

EPILOGUE:
COLOUR-MUSIC — THE ART OF LIGHT

Incessantly we compare painting with music and music with painting, because the emotions we experience reveal to us analogies where cold observation discerns only differences.
Mme de Stael, *De l'Allemagne* (1810)

Castel's legacy

The story told so far might have ended more neatly, had Castel's ambition to create a 'colour keyboard' gone with him to the grave. However, this was very far from being the case. For more than a century after his death, the idea of an instrument capable of displaying colours or projecting coloured lights continued to fascinate not only artists and musicians but also scientists and men of letters. For this reason alone, it seemed important to go beyond the end of the eighteenth century in order to trace, at least in outline, those scientific developments that led ultimately to the invention of the colour organ: a continuous process of innovation and experiment that culminated in the famous 'colour-light' performances that dazzled audiences during the years around 1900.

Soon after Castel died in 1757, a number of people suggested ways in which his 'ocular harpsichord' might be improved. One alternative design, by Johann Gottlob Krüger, author of *De novo musices*, sought to address a frequently voiced criticism of Castel's method: namely, the difficulty of combining several colours simultaneously so as to create a 'chord' as in music. Krüger himself made a detailed drawing (fig. 47) that shows how he proposed to solve this problem by incorporating into his version of the harpsichord a variety of discs, apertures and lenses of different sizes. This drawing is worth studying because it conveys at least some idea of how the instrument he envisaged might have looked. (We do not possess a single design by Castel or any of his collaborators that shows either the overall appearance of his *clavecin oculaire* or the way in which its internal mechanism was meant to function.)

Another device that, although based on Castel's original idea, would have been far easier to construct was illustrated by Guillaume-Germain Guyot in his *Nouvelles récréations physiques et mathématiques* of 1769 under the title *Musique oculaire* (fig. 48). This was a simple optical toy, destined to be placed on a table top, whose mechanism consisted of a rotating cylinder that was turned by hand in time to the music: the forerunner of more complex optical devices for creating the illusion of movement such as the zoëtrope and the zoë-praxinoscope that were popular in the early years of the twentieth century. Guyot himself, however, remained

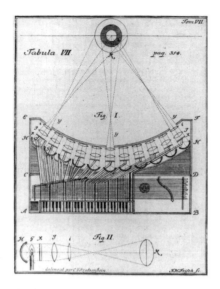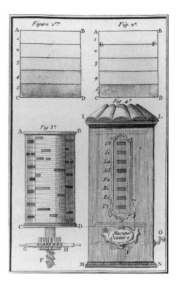

Figure 47. Johann Gottlob Krüger, design for an ocular harpsichord, from *Miscellenea Berolinensia*, 1743, vol. VII, plate viii.

Figure 48. Guillaume-Germain Guyot, toy version of the ocular harpsichord, from *Nouvelles récréations physiques et mathématiques*, 4 vols, Paris, 1769–70, vol. 3 ('Illusions d'optique'), p. 240, pl. 23, figs 1–4

sceptical about the whole notion of an analogy between colours and musical tones, pointing once again to the overriding difficulty already mentioned, namely that colours could provide no equivalent for a chord in music, since two or more colours, when mixed together, created an entirely new colour, whereas the constituent notes of a chord were still perceived as individual pitches.[1]

Other writers found different grounds for criticizing Castel's colour harpsichord and the theory on which it was based. Jean-Jacques Rousseau, in his *Essay on the Origin of Languages*, wrote:

Not knowing how to paint pictures for the ears, people have attempted to sing melodies for the eyes. I myself have seen that famous clavecin on which, it is claimed, one can make music with colours. But it would betray a poor grasp of the ways of nature if one ignored the fact that the effect of colours derives from their constancy whereas that of musical tones depends on their mobility.[2]

---

1 For a more detailed account of eighteenth-century proposals for creating colour-instruments of various kinds see Barbara Kienscherf, *Das Auge hört mit. Die Idee der Farblichtmusik und ihre Problematik*, Frankfurt/M. (Peter Lang) 1996, pp. 38ff.

2 J. J. Rousseau, *Essai sur l'origine des langues*, chapitre xvi: 'Fausse analogie entre les couleurs et les sons' (Rousseau 1970, p. 169).

Goethe, in much the same vein, stressed what he saw as the essential difference between colours and tones, likening them to two rivers, which, although they could be traced to a single source, 'follow quite different directions, so that there is not a single point in the course of one that might be compared with that of the other.'[3] He also sharply criticized the essay *On the History of Pictorial Harmony in General and of the Harmony of Colours in Particular* by his contemporary Johann Leonhard Hoffmann. Hoffmann, too, had devised a system of correspondences between colours and musical tones, although his method is decidedly peculiar, compared with Castel's. Instead of attempting to match the spectrum of colours to the diatonic octave, he arranged his colour scale so as to distinguish between what he termed *Hauptfarben* (principal colours: dark blue, red, lemon yellow, sea green and ultramarine) corresponding to the lines of the treble stave (in ascending order: C–E–G–B–D) and *Tinten des ersten Rangs* (shades of the first order: violet, light red, grass green, sky blue and 'red an octave higher'), which he assigned to the spaces between the lines (D–F–A–C–E).[4] Like Rousseau, Hoffmann was sceptical about the value of Castel's *clavecin oculaire*, which he called 'unrealizable and impractical', dismissing its 'motley assemblage of colour tones' as little better than those found on the rags that painters use to clean their palettes. 'Even if harmony is occasionally to be found therein', he wrote, 'this makes far less impression upon the heart or mind than a simple fantasy played upon an ordinary keyboard, consisting of nothing more than suspensions, resolutions and passages of complex figuration.'[5]

Colour-music

Notwithstanding these criticisms of Castel and the decline in his posthumous reputation,[6] discussion of a new art of colour tones that would rival music continued for at least the next century and a half. Several reasons can be adduced for this enduring interest in what eventually came to be known as 'colour-music'. One was that, as the nineteenth century progressed, critics and writers on visual art came increasingly to disparage the kind of painting that relied primarily

---

3 Johann Wolfgang von Goethe, *Zur Farbenlehre*, vol. 1 (*Entwurf einer Farbenlehre*), *Fünfte Abtheilung* (*Nachbarliche Verhältnisse*), § 748.
4 See Johann Leonhard Hoffmann, *Versuch einer Geschichte der mahlerischen Harmonie überhaupt und der Farbenharmonie insbesondere*, Halle (Johann Christian Hendel) 1786, pp. 103ff.
5 Ibid., pp. 40–1.
6 In his poem *La Peinture* (1769), which provided a description in verse of the ocular harpsichord, the painter Lemierre referred to 'the industrious Castel who today is not known any more'; see Franssen 1991, p. 33. In his *Colour-Music. The Art of Mobile Colour* (see n. [17] below), A. W. Rimington refers in the vaguest terms to earlier ideas about the relationship between colour and music, which 'in the sixteenth century (!) took somewhat more tangible form in the mind of a Jesuit, Lewis Bertrand Castel' (Rimington 1912, p. vii).

on narrative content for its effect. Music, by contrast, appeared self-sufficient, conveying both emotion and meaning without the need for words, stories or representations of any kind. Why, it was asked, could painting not do the same? Or at least, why could there not be a kind of visual art that offered, as one English critic expressed it, 'nothing but its own merchandise'? The critic in question was Philip Gilbert Hamerton who, in his book *Contemporary French Painters* (1868), wrote about the contempt that 'many artists of the present day are beginning to have with regard to literary interest, dramatic interest, historical interest, and all other such extraneous interests in the art of painting'. He continued:

Painting, like journalism, should in their view offer nothing but its own merchandise. And the especial merchandise of painting they hold to be the visible melodies and harmonies – a kind of visible music – meaning as much and narrating as much as the music which is heard in the ears, and nothing whatever more.[7]

Although this sounds like a plea for abstract painting, that is not what Hamerton had in mind. In the next sentence, he writes approvingly about those artists who 'when they paint a woman, do not take the slightest interest in her personally, she is merely, for them, a certain beautiful and fortunate arrangement of forms, an impersonal harmony and melody, melody in harmony, seen instead of being heard.' What evidently concerned him were the formal, abstract qualities to be found even in conventional painting – qualities that he likened to the attributes of music. Just how conventional was his taste in painting is revealed by the names of those artists whose works he illustrated in his book. These included Ingres (now one of the revered figures of nineteenth-century art), Bouguereau, Ary Scheffer, Meissonier and Gérôme, while the above-quoted passage comparing visual art with music is followed by an extended discussion of the achievements of the French realist painter Paul Delaroche (1797–1856). However, from Hamerton's later writings it is clear that, by the 1880s, the more ethereal art of Impressionism had started to capture his interest. In his *Imagination in Landscape Painting* of 1887, for example, he writes about how even accidental combinations of mere pigments [although they may be easily be condemned as a] desertion of nature ... are

---

7 Philip Gilbert Hamerton, *Contemporary French Painters. An Essay*, London (Seeley, Jackson and Halliday) 1868, p. 37.

certainly not a desertion of art, for there may be a colour-music without meaning, invented by the imagination, exactly as there is a sound-music without meaning, or, at least, of which the meaning could not possibly be expressed in any language other than its own. He also describes how, when an artist's mind:

loses the sense of substance, the vision of the world becomes for it what Wordsworth aptly called 'eye music' ... Painting is then no longer a study of tangible things at all, but a dream like the dreams of a musician. Then comes a new exercise of the imagination, which no longer occupies itself with imaginary scenes and things, but only with sequences and relations – in short, it becomes musically creative.[8]

Over and above its ethereal nature, another supposed advantage of music was that, since it incorporated the element of time, it was able more easily to evoke movement and thereby trace the ever-changing patterns of our thoughts and feelings. This mobile character of music was often contrasted with what was widely perceived to be a major shortcoming of painting, namely its essentially static quality. (Castel, among others, had also criticized painting on precisely these grounds.) One of several Victorian authors who thought painting inferior to music in this respect was the Reverend H. R. Haweis. In his book *Music and Morals*, published in 1871, Haweis turned confidently to a comparison between colours and musical tones, whose fleeting character he contrasted with the immobility of pigment:

No method has yet been discovered of arranging colour by itself for the eye, as the musician's art arranges sound for the ear. We have no colour pictures depending solely upon colour as we have symphonies depending solely upon sound. In Turner's works we find the nearest approach; but even he, by the necessary limitation of his art, is without the property of velocity. The canvas does not change to the eye – all that is, is presented simultaneously as in one complex chord, and thus the charm of velocity, which is so great a property in emotion, and which might belong to a colour-art, is denied to the painter ... Had we but a system of colour-notation which would as intensely and

---

8 Philip Gilbert Hamerton, *Imagination in Landscape Painting*, London (Seeley & Co.) 1887, pp. 72–3; on Hamerton himself see also James Kissane, 'P. G. Hamerton, Victorian Art Critic', *Burlington Magazine*, vol. 114, no. 826 (January 1972), pp. 22–8.

instantaneously connect itself with every possible tint, and possess the power of combining colours before the mind's eye, as a page of music combines sounds through the eye to the mind's ear – had we but instruments, or some appropriate art-mechanism for rendering such colour-notation into real waves of colour before the bodily eye, we should then have actually realized a new art, the extent and grandeur of whose developments it is simply impossible to estimate.[9]

In order to illustrate his ideas, Haweis at first mentions only 'exquisite tints painted upon the dark curtain of the night at a display of fireworks', explaining that he had chosen the 'art of pyrotechny' rather than 'painting of any kind, because in it we get the important emotional property of velocity, necessarily absent from fixed colouring'. But from other references it seems clear that he was already dreaming in prophetic fashion of a new art of coloured light. A few sentences further on, we find him describing the 'delicate melodies of single floating lights, changing and melting from one slow intensity to another through the dark'. 'Why', he asks, 'should we not go down to the Palace of the People and assist at a real Colour-prelude or Symphony, as we now go down to hear a work by Mozart or Mendelssohn?' However, Haweis acknowledged that this 'Colour-art', as he called it, had still to be created. Its 'symbols and phraseology' still needed to be discovered, its 'instruments invented and its composers born', if it were to rival music as a 'Art-medium of emotion'.[10]

Nineteenth-century pioneers

Haweis was right in pointing to the lack of instruments capable of realizing the new colour-art he envisaged. For much of the nineteenth century, the question of how to create such instruments continued to exercise the minds of scientists and amateurs alike. As early as 1806, in an article published in a Dresden newspaper under the title 'The Melody of Colours', an unnamed German writer had suggested using the newly invented Argand lamps, which, by comparison with earlier methods, produced a greatly enhanced level of illumination, thanks to more efficient means of combustion.[11] Nevertheless, the difficulty of

---

9 H. R. Haweis, *Music and Morals*, London (Strahan & Co.) 1871, pp. 32–3.

10 Ibid., p. 34. Rimington (see below, pp. 255ff.) later acknowledged Haweis as a 'strong supporter and eloquent champion', whose hopes 'have, to some extent at least' been realized by 'the colour organ and allied mobile colour instruments' (Rimington 1912, p. 155).

11 'Die Melodie der Farben', *Abend-Zeitung*, no. 65 (13 August 1806), p. 258, quoted after Kienscherf 1996, p. 56. According to Kenneth Peacock, Erasmus Darwin in England had made a similar suggestion even earlier; see 'Instruments to Perform Color-Music: Two Centuries of Technological Experimentation', *Leonardo. Journal of the International Society for Arts Sciences and Technology*, vol. 21, no 4 (1988), p. 401.

obtaining a sufficiently powerful light source remained. Some suggested solutions to this problem must strike the modern reader as little more than pipe dreams. One author, D. D. Jameson, in a brochure written in the 1840s described what he termed an 'apparatus for colorific exhibition' and how such an apparatus might be constructed:

A dark chamber, lined with bright tin plates; twelve round apertures in the wall holding glass globes, containing translucent liquids of the prismatic colours, and their semi-tonic intermediates; lamps on the outsides of the bottles, mobile opaque covers on the insides. A pianoforte with its keys connected to these covers; with power to elevate them on percussion of the keys, to heights proportionate to the vibrative extent of their respective octaves. With each note, a strong colour is evolved in the dark room and reflected by its sides; and the duration and extension of this colour are greater or less according to the tune and position of the note which it represents and accompanies.[12]

As for the glass globes, he recommended the 'bottles seen in the windows of druggists' shops' as suitable for the purpose. We do not know whether Jameson ever attempted to demonstrate his ideas publicly. However, he did provide his readers with colour 'translations' of such popular songs as 'See! The Conquering Hero Comes', 'Highland Laddie' and 'Jim Crow', perhaps in the hope of convincing them of the validity of his theories. He thus anticipated by nearly half a century a prediction made by the French writer Louis Favre, who suggested in 1889 that it might be possible to 'translate' into colour 'a piece composed for musical sounds, and practised senses could recognize the piece of music by the colours which represented it and *vice versa*'.[13]

From Jameson's description, it is clear that the problem of providing a sufficiently powerful means of illumination was, for the time being, insuperable. The effect he described could only be achieved in a darkened room, the relatively feeble light from the coloured globes set in the walls being reflected by shiny metal plates. Not until the last years of the nineteenth century, with the advent of the incandescent light bulb and reliable sources of electricity, did the art of coloured light that Castel and others had dreamed about at last become feasible.

---

12 D. D. Jameson, *Colour-Music* (London, 1844), quoted after Adrian Bernard Klein, *Colour-Music. The Art of Light*, London (Crosby Lockwood & Son) 1926, p. 188.
13 Louis Favre, *La Vérité. Pensées* (Marseilles, 1889), quoted after Klein, *Colour-Music*, p. 11.

The advent of electricity

One of the first inventors to rise to this new challenge was the American painter Bainbridge Bishop who, starting in the late 1870s, experimented with an apparatus consisting of coloured glass lenses and shutters that could be fastened to the case of a portative organ. The shutters were raised or lowered by levers attached to the keyboard. In this way, when different notes were played, light was allowed to pass through one or other of the lenses. At first, he simply used daylight as a source of illumination, only later exploiting the possibilities offered by electric light. His invention was, it seems, so effective that it captured the imagination of none other than P. T. Barnum, the famous American showman and self-styled 'Prince of Humbugs', who acquired Bishop's instrument for his collection. According to Thomas Wilfred, inventor of the *clavilux* (another colour-light instrument that enjoyed considerable success in the United States of America during the 1920s and 1930s), Bishop's colour organ was later to be seen among the 'rarities' of the Barnum Museum on New York's Broadway. Wilfred described it, however, as merely a 'more advanced edition of Castel's *clavecin oculaire*', while noting that here 'music and color could be played both together and separately'.[14]

By 1895, improvements in the design of vacuum tubes led another enthusiast, William Schooling, to point to the possibilities these offered for emulating more exactly the ebb and flow, the changing rhythms and character of music by means of coloured light, since:

vacuum-tubes or vacuous chambers ... could be illuminated in succession or combination by the use of a keyboard, on playing the notes on which the electric current would pass through different tubes. Contacts could be made so easily that the most elaborate chords or combinations of colours could be played with the utmost simplicity, and the intensity of the light, corresponding to the loudness of the sound, could be varied, as in a piano, by using a pedal to alter the intensity of the current, so causing the tubes to shine with a brilliant light or to glow in the softest of hues. Such an instrument could be made on any scale; it could be used out of doors and be seen by thousands; it could be placed in the largest hall, or it could be adapted to the most

---

14 Thomas Wilfred, 'Light and the Artist', *Journal of Aesthetics and Art Criticism*, vol. 5, no. 4 (June 1947), p. 249.

modest private requirements; while there would be no fear of annoying our neighbours with our performances.

It requires no great effort of the imagination to picture the beauty of such effects, even with vacuum-tubes as we know them now, when practically no artistic effects are ever aimed at with them; and if to such displays were added the power to appreciate the meaning put into them by a great colour-composer, it seems scarcely too fanciful to imagine that the influence upon our feelings and our thoughts would be, not less but more than any influence of music now.[15]

A. W. Rimington's colour organ

The most important pioneer of colour-music was undoubtedly the English artist Alexander Wallace Rimington. Rimington was Professor of Art at Queen's College London and a gifted painter, etcher and watercolourist. His works were shown at the Paris Salon and in Berlin, where they received an honourable mention. He was also a frequent exhibitor at the Royal Academy, and the Fine Art Society in London devoted a series of seven special exhibitions to his watercolours.[16] At what point he began his researches into music and colour is not clear. In his book *Colour-Music*, published in 1912, he refers only to 'experimental work carried out by me for a good many years past'.[17] What is clear is that, by 1895, he had succeeded in actually building a powerful colour organ comprising fourteen giant arc lamps connected to a power supply of 150 amperes, later described as 'the first serious attempt to construct an instrument for the performance of colour-music'.[18] Rimington's brainchild had its début at St James's Hall in London on 6 June that year before an invited audience that included 'the Duke of Norfolk, Princess Hohenlohe, Cardinal Vaughan, the painter Alma Tadema and many other prominent people'.[19] Wilfred described the scene:

On the stage a large white curtain of heavy silk has been carefully draped in deep folds, and down in the centre aisle towers a huge cabinet with an attached organ-keyboard – the colour organ, with its elaborate mechanism and fourteen arc-lights within.

15 William Schooling, 'Colour-Music. A Suggestion of a New Art', *The Nineteenth Century. A Monthly Review*, edited by James Knowles, vol. 38, no. 221 (July 1895), pp. 127–8. Schooling's article, written not later than 1893 but not published until 1895, was also cited by Rimington in his book *Colour-Music* (see n. [17] below), pp. 155ff.

16 Rimington died on 14 May 1918; these details are taken from his obituary printed in *The Times*, 20 May 1918.

17 A. Wallace Rimington, *Colour-Music. The Art of Mobile Colour*, London (Hutchinson) 1912, p. vi.

18 Klein, *Colour-Music*, p. 190.

19 Wilfred, 'Light and the Artist', p. 249.

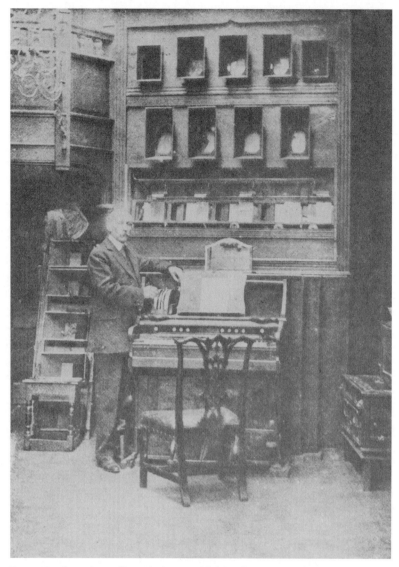

Figure 49. Alexander Wallace Rimington with his colour organ, *c*.1910

The distinguished looking young professor delivers a lecture; then the hall is darkened and the strange performance begins.[20]

It began, apparently, with Wagner's overture to *Rienzi*, in which the colour organ was accompanied by a small orchestra, and

20 Wilfred, loc. cit. (as preceding note). *Distinguished looking young professor*: Rimington (b. 9 October 1854) was then aged 40. His lecture is reprinted in Klein 1926, Appendix V, pp. 256–61.

continued with preludes by Chopin in C minor and A major, a waltz by Dvořák and Gounod's arrangement of Bach's *Ave Maria*. The success of the evening was such that Rimington was prevailed upon to stage more appearances both in London and in the provinces. At the first of these, held on 27 June 1895, again at St James's Hall, *Rienzi* was replaced by Wagner's *Siegfried Idyll* and *Ave Maria* by what the critic of *The Times* called 'Gounod's perversion of Bach's first Prelude'.[21] A further concert in Manchester, held in November that same year, was noticeably less successful. Provincial audiences were, it seems, more sceptical, some members of the public even protesting that they considered themselves the victims of fraud.

Perhaps discouraged by this, after 1895 Rimington (who allegedly 'loathed publicity') seems to have given no more such demonstrations.[22] Even so, his colour organ soon became famous. Its inventor included many photographs of it in his book (fig. 49) and no less a personage than Sir Arthur Sullivan played on it – apparently with closed eyes.[23] It was also frequently described: for example, by the American collector and writer on art Arthur Jerome Eddy, who travelled extensively in Europe during the years before the First World War. While in London, Eddy paid a visit to Rimington's studio at Norwood, where he saw 'a curious instrument with keyboard and stops' and, at the other end of the room, 'a white screen, hung in folds to give greater depth and life to the colors playing upon it'. Eddy described in detail Rimington's attempts to create an art of coloured light in the eighth chapter of his book *Cubists and Post-Impressionism*, entitled 'Color Music'.[24]

In 1926 another author, the Englishman Major Adrian Bernard Klein, published an exhaustive account of the art of colour-music as it had developed up to that date, including biographical information about its most important practitioners and descriptions of various instruments for uniting music and colour.[25] Along with other details, Klein reproduced the patent application Rimington had filed in respect of his invention, which

---

21 *The Times*, 28 June 1895.
22 According to Klein 1926, p. 9.
23 Ibid., p. 7.
24 Arthur Jerome Eddy, *Cubists and Post-Impressionism*, London (Grant Richards, Ltd.) 1915, pp. 140ff. The book had originally been published the year before in Chicago by the firm of A. C. McClurg & Co. Eddy was an important early collector of modern European paintings, among them works by Kandinsky. He also wrote *Delight, the Soul of Art* and *Two Thousand Miles on an Automobile*.
25 *Colour-Music. The Art of Light* (see n. [12] above) went through three editions in the course of a decade and remains an important source of information, containing many documents, reviews and eye-witness accounts pertaining to the early history of the colour organ. Most subsequent discussions of this topic are heavily indebted to Klein's book.

tells us a good deal about the appearance of the instrument and its manner of construction.[26] This application, dated 24 September 1894, refers specifically to 'electric arc lamps or oxyhydrogen lamps' and also makes clear that Rimington's was a species of tracker organ, as distinct from the electrically powered pneumatic organs that would soon come into widespread use.[27]

One detail is of special interest: the way in which Rimington addressed the problem of colour octaves. This had proved a stumbling block for many who had previously occupied themselves with analogies between colours and musical tones. A peculiar feature of the musical scale is the fact that it keeps repeating itself. Having traversed the full gamut of pitches from a to a', for example, we can then reproduce the 'same' notes at a higher or lower octave simply by doubling or halving their original frequencies, as shown in the following table:[28]

a″ = 880 Hz
a′ = 440 Hz
a = 220 Hz

But while scientists had shown that colours, too, could be arranged in a scale, like notes, their frequencies cannot be doubled in similar fashion.[29] Each colour has its own particular frequency and beyond the gamut of frequencies from red to violet no more colours are visible to the eye. Thus, the problem of finding an equivalent in colours for higher or lower octaves in music remained. Jameson, as we saw earlier, thought that apertures in the walls of his darkened chamber might be made larger or smaller, producing circles of coloured light of different sizes in order to represent the 'same'

---

26 Klein, op. cit., pp. 265–73.

27 The caption to one photograph, reproduced between pp. 46 and 47 of Rimington's 1912 monograph, refers specifically to the 'pneumatic "action" of a mobile colour instrument with keyboard'. This may have been a later (or merely different) version of his colour organ, by comparison with the one described in the 1894 patent application; in his book, Rimington refers to having constructed 'several such instruments' (*Colour-Music*, p. 36).

28 'Hz' here denotes hertz or cycles per second. In Western music, standard pitches have been used for more than a century to facilitate tuning. The current standard pitch of a' = 440 Hz was adopted in 1939, a' – the A above middle C (c') – usually being taken as a referent pitch. When an orchestra tunes up, the players adjust their pitch to the a' sounded in advance by the oboe, usually considered the least temperamental of all wind instruments.

29 Rimington thought that measuring the relative rates of vibration of the colours at opposite ends of the spectrum showed that one (violet) had a frequency very nearly twice that of the other (red), from which he concluded that the 'octave of colour is in fact practically complete', even though it 'does not extend to the first note of the octave above it' (Rimington 1912, pp. 19–20). In this respect, his ideas resembled those of Newton who, in 'An Hypothesis hinted at for explicating all the afforesaid properties of light' (1672), had written that one might 'suppose the vibrations causing the deepest scarlet to be to those causing the deepest violet as two to one; for so there would be all that variety in colours which within the compass of an eight [ie octave] is found in sounds'; see Shapiro 1984, n. 28 to p. 546. Note that Newton considers the *magnitude* of red light to be approximately twice that of violet, a ratio that is inversely proportional to their respective *wavelengths*.

notes when sounded in a higher or lower register. Rimington's solution was more like Castel's. Using dyed fabrics or coloured paper, Castel had suggested representing different octaves visually by variations in tone of the same colour: the same tint but in a lighter or darker shade. What Rimington envisaged was, in effect, the same, only using coloured light as a means of 'providing higher and lower octaves in the colour scale of relatively paler and deeper intensity, somewhat analogous, though not strictly corresponding to, the higher and lower octaves of the musical scale, though, of course, in the colour the wavelength remains the same'.[30]

The 'art of mobile colour'

Rimington's instrument, like that described by Schooling, was silent. However, its inventor noted that 'it adds much to the enjoyment of the colour if the music is simultaneously rendered into sound', as was evidently the case at the first 'performance' given in 1895, when the colour organ was accompanied at different times by a piano, an organ and an orchestra. But it is clear that Rimington also considered the play of coloured lights to be pleasurable and entertaining in itself, without needing to be reinforced by music. In his book *Colour-Music*, he describes the effect of just such a performance:

Imagine a darkened concert-room. At one end there is a large screen of white drapery in folds surrounded by black and framed by two bands of pure white light. Upon this ... there appears the faintest possible flush of rose colour ... While it is still lingering upon the screen a rapid series of touches of pale lavender notes of colour begin to flit across it, gradually strengthening into deep violet. This, again becomes shot with amethyst, and afterwards, changing gradually into a broken tint of ruby, gives a return to the warmer tones of the opening passage.

A delicate primrose now appears, and with little runs and flushes of pulsation leads through several passages of indescribable cinnamon colour to deep topaz. Then suddenly interweavings of strange green and peacock blue, with now and then a touch of pure white, make us seem to feel the tremulousness of the Mediterranean on a breezy day, and as the colour deepens there are harmonies of violet and blue-green which recall its waves under a Tramontana sky. More

---

30 Rimington, *Colour-Music*, p. 47.

*and more powerful they grow, and the eye revels in the depth
and magnificence of the colour as the executant strikes
chord after chord amongst the bass notes of the instrument.*

*Then suddenly the screen is again dark, and there is only
a rhythmic and echoing beat of the dying colour upon it. At
last this disappears also, and there is another silent pause,
then one hesitating tint of faded rose as at the opening of
the composition.*[31]

Somewhat oddly, Klein maintained that 'all Rimington's early
researches were directed towards determining whether there was
any natural artistic relationship between sound-music and colours',
citing as evidence the performances given in the summer and
autumn of 1895, when the display of coloured lights had been
accompanied by music. He also remarked that 'on the whole,
Rimington reached the conclusion that sound-music and light-
music might be simultaneously performed, to the mutual
enhancement of their respective emotional effects.'[32] Rimington
himself says something different. Commenting on his own
description of a soundless colour-light performance, quoted above,
he writes that, although it is 'an extremely simple example … it may
suffice to show the kind of effect produced by an unadorned form of
mobile colour not accompanied by music.'[33] Evidently, he was
convinced that the silent play of coloured lights was sufficient in
itself to capture the interest of the spectator and elicit admiration,
just as music was capable of directly affecting the emotions of the
listener without needing the intermediary of words. Elsewhere, he
compares the emotional appeal of music to that of colour,
emphasizing that colour, too, was 'capable of providing almost as
much pleasure and interest as sound' and that it 'has quite as great,
or even greater power of appealing to the emotions'.[34] 'Music', writes
Rimington, 'interests, refreshes, invigorates, saddens, or makes us
glad through its action upon the emotional side of our nature … It
is with the emotional side of the subject that the new art of Colour-
Music is chiefly concerned, and it is especially through such an art
that it is possible to study the influence of colour upon our senses
and upon our minds, and, through them, upon our lives.'[35]

---

31 Ibid., pp. 57–9.
32 Klein 1926, p. 8–9.
33 Rimington, p. 59.
34 Ibid., p. 2.
35 Ibid., pp. 11, 13. More traditional notions of music, regarded as the paradigm of an essentially orderly art
    or as an image of cosmic harmony, were seemingly of little interest to Rimington and others who occupied
    themselves with the topic of colour-music; at least, such notions are scarcely mentioned in their writings.

Another intriguing thing about the lengthy description quoted above is that Rimington specifically associates the effects of coloured light with the impressions produced by such natural phenomena as the 'Mediterranean on a breezy day' or a 'Tramontana sky'. Was he, perhaps, anxious to forestall criticism of the exclusively abstract nature of the visual delights colour-music could offer, ignoring the fact that music itself was, by this date, almost universally admired for its 'abstract' qualities, its freedom from any representational function? Certainly, he is at pains to point out that there are 'few people who cannot admire a sunset' or the 'gradations and interweavings of green and turquoise, deep blue and violet' to be seen in the play of the waves, even while admitting that our main pleasure in observing such phenomena derives from our appreciation solely of colour.[36]

But the most frequent criticism of colour-music had nothing to do with the abstract nature of the effects produced. Rather, its main drawback was the irritation – rather than pleasure – induced by the flickering of the lights. People objected that the eye soon tired of attempting to follow rapidly changing sequences of colour and that fatigue and finally boredom ensued. Wilfred wrote:

The draped screen pulsates with changing colour; there is no form, only a restless flicker, hue after hue, one for each musical note sounded. As the tempo of the music increases, the accompanying colours succeed one another too rapidly to be caught by the eye, while the ear readily accepts and enjoys the most rapid passage in the music.

The eye seeks an anchorage, a scrap of form to focus on, but none appears. Questions are whispered, heads shaken. Is there really a colour for each note? There must be … But it hurts my eyes![37]

The same criticisms were repeatedly voiced in connection with later demonstrations of the 'art of coloured light'. It was claimed that little pleasure could be gained from contemplating colours that succeeded one another with too great a rapidity – by contrast with music, where the ear follows with satisfaction the trills and arabesques of an accomplished vocalist or deftly executed scales and arpeggios on a keyboard instrument such as the piano. There is some force to this objection. Think of the rapid passages of decoration to be found in Mozart's piano concertos – let alone

---

36 Ibid., pp. 87–8.
37 Wilfred, 'Light and the Artist', p. 249.

Beethoven's (the opening flourishes of the 'Emperor' concerto would be an obvious example) – and imagine translating each of these notes into colours, one by one. In fact, Rimington was well aware of this problem, noting that the main obstacle to 'appreciating colour-music at the outset lies in being unable to appreciate rapid changes of colour upon the screen … A spectator to whom mobile colour is new … cannot follow fast changes without considerable difficulty.'[38]

However, even allowing for these and other reservations, there can be no doubting the public's interest in the phenomenon of the colour organ. To judge only by the bibliography printed in Klein's monograph, the first demonstrations of Rimington's 'art of mobile colour' in the summer and autumn of 1895 seem to have produced a crop of at least 150 articles in newspapers and journals – some, admittedly, of a more scholarly nature than others.[39] And it appears that well over a thousand people actually witnessed these early performances of colour-music, thereby fulfilling Schooling's prophecy that colour organs could be made 'on any scale' and that they could be 'placed in the largest hall' and 'seen by thousands'.

'Prometheus: the Poem of Fire' and Skryabin's 'light keyboard'

Rimington's obituary in *The Times* credited him both with the invention of the colour organ and with 'carrying out original researches into the relations between colour and music'.[40] The same brief notice also recorded that his theories had been 'recently adopted and employed by Scriabine, the composer, in his *Prometheus* and other works'. Although flattering to Rimington, this statement is not entirely accurate. 'Prometheus: the Poem of Fire' (op. 60) was the last completed orchestral work by the Russian composer Aleksandr Nikolaevich Skryabin (1872–1915).[41] Among the musical forces required for its performance was a *tastiera per luce* – literally, a 'light keyboard'. (In the score, the uppermost part is marked simply *luce* – 'light'.) Here, the puzzle begins. Klein, whose testimony is generally reliable, claims that Sir Henry Wood, who had already conducted 'Prometheus' in London in 1914 with the composer at the piano, approached Rimington with a view to his supervising the production of the intended light effects in a further performance scheduled to take place at the Queen's Hall the following year – a performance

---

38 Rimington 1912, pp. 68, 94.
39 See Klein 1926, pp. 228ff.
40 See n. [16] above.
41 In the various books and articles about him that have been published in Western languages, Skryabin's name has been transliterated in many different ways. In footnotes and quotations, I have followed the spelling given in the original sources, without regard for consistency. In my own text, however, I have used the transliteration that approximates most closely to the Cyrillic alphabet: Skryabin.

subsequently cancelled because of the outbreak of war.[42] Other writers have maintained that, when the Russian Symphony Orchestra under Modest Altschuler played the work at Carnegie Hall in New York in March 1915 – the first time, in fact, that 'Prometheus' was heard complete with colour-light accompaniment – the part allocated to the 'light keyboard' was executed on Rimington's instrument. This, certainly, is not true. The colour organ (later christened 'Chromola') used in New York was designed by an American engineer named Preston S. Millar, although Millar evidently based his design to some extent on Rimington's ideas.

Skryabin himself was not present in New York and it is hard to judge how far that performance lived up to his intentions, given that he never provided any very precise indication as to exactly what kind of light-producing instrument he had in mind. (At the world première of 'Prometheus', given in Moscow in 1911, which he did attend, the play of coloured lights he had envisaged was simply omitted, perhaps because of the cost or because no suitable instrument was then available.)[43] As far as we know, the composer, who died from blood poisoning in the spring of 1915, never saw the work performed publicly in the way he had intended. However, it seems that, around the time of the Moscow première, he had given several private performances of 'Prometheus' in the music room of his Moscow apartment for the benefit of friends and colleagues. On those occasions the musicologist Leonid Sabaneev, a close friend of Skryabin and a composer in his own right, played a piano reduction of the giant score, while Skryabin himself took charge of the lighting effects.[44] These were produced by means of a simple device designed by Alfred Mozer, another friend of Skryabin's, who taught electronics. It consisted of a circle of light bulbs, painted in various colours and fastened to a wooden board. Pressing different buttons activated a succession of coloured lights that were reflected by the white ceiling of the music room. Surprisingly, whereas more grandiose colour organs have not stood the test of time, this crude contraption survived both war and revolution and can still be seen in the Aleksandr Skryabin Museum in Moscow. Sabaneev recalled

---

42 Klein, op. cit., p. 9. According to James M. Baker, two English performances of 'Prometheus' using Rimington's colour organ were scheduled for early 1915, on 9 February in Liverpool and 13 February in London; see 'Prometheus and the Quest for Color-Music: The World Premiere of Scriabin's Poem of Fire with Lights, New York, March 20, 1915', in James Leggio (ed.), Music and Modern Art, New York/London (Routledge) 2002, p. 78.

43 Klein (p. 44) claims that there was a 'colour projection apparatus' but that it 'failed to function'; Hugh Macdonald, who has made a special study of Skryabin's music, writes that 'a complicated and costly apparatus was planned for the first performance … but was "not ready".' See 'Lighting the Fire: Skryabin and Colour', Musical Times, vol. 124, no. 1688 (October 1983), p. 600.

44 These details derive from a recollection by the music critic Oskar von Riesemann, another friend of Skryabin, who claimed he had 'often' heard and seen 'Prometheus' performed in this way; see Kienscherf 1996, pp. 119–20.

that the effect produced in combination with the music, simple though Mozer's device might have been, was extremely moving. In a discussion of the analogy between colour and music, published in the Moscow periodical *Muzyka*, he wrote:

Anyone who has heard 'Prometheus' performed with its accompanying light effects must acknowledge that the impression created by the music perfectly matches that of the illumination and is twice as effective as a consequence, being thereby intensified to the utmost – and this in spite of the extremely primitive lighting apparatus, which was capable of producing only a vague approximation of the colours.[45]

Apart from later adding colour indications by hand to a copy of the printed score, Skryabin himself revealed next to nothing about his intentions in composing 'Prometheus'.[46] He seems to have left matters of that kind to Sabaneev, who, in an article published in the *Blaue Reiter Almanac* in 1912, provided a detailed analysis of the music together with an interpretation of its meaning. Of greatest use to the intending performer, his article included a table of 'correspondences' between colours and musical tones that showed how the part written for the light keyboard was to be realized. It looked like this:[47]

C	red	F#	bright blue
G	orange-pink	D*b*	violet
D	yellow	A*b*	purple-violet
A	green	E*b*	} steely-metallic sheen
E	pale blue	B*b*	
B	similar to E	F	dark red

45 Reprinted as a footnote to Sabaneev's article 'Prometheus von Skrjabin' (as n. [47]).

46 Skryabin's annotations are dated 16 March 1913. The score itself is now in the Bibliothèque Nationale, Paris; its significance is discussed in Baker, '*Prometheus* and the Quest for Color-Music', p. 80. See also ibid., p. 76 and table 3.1 for a comparison of Skryabin's system of correspondences between colours and musical pitches with that originally published by Sabaneev in 1911 (see following note).

47 L. Sabanejew [sic], 'Prometheus von Skrjabin', in *Der Blaue Reiter. Herausgeber: Kandinsky, Franz Marc*, Munich (R. Piper & Co.) 1912, p. 60. Sabaneev's table is given in a footnote summarizing an earlier article about 'Prometheus' that had appeared in Russian in the Moscow periodical *Muzyka* (no. 9, January 1911).

Prométhée.

A. Scriabine. Op. 60.

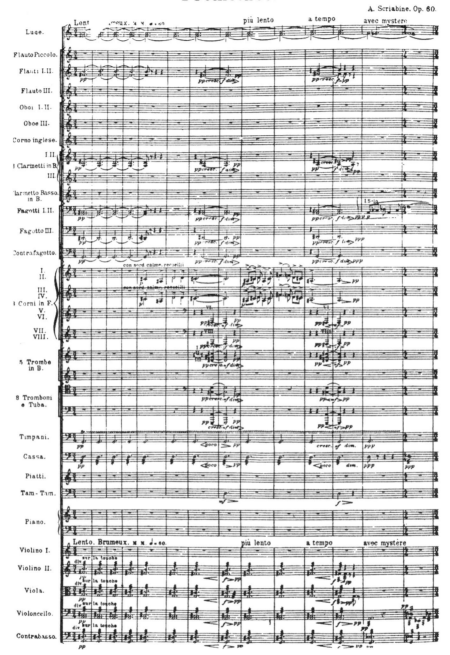

Figure 50. Opening bars of the score of Skryabin's 'Prometheus' showing the part for light keyboard (marked *luce*)

Although Sabaneev's table corresponds closely to Skryabin's subsequent annotations, it is strikingly at odds with the other 'systems' of correspondences between colours and musical tones that we have encountered so far. These were, in most cases, based on the diatonic scale – for example, that of C major. It is evident from Sabaneev's article that, rather than a scale, what Skryabin had in mind was that 'great circle of fifths' mentioned in an earlier chapter, from which (as previously explained) we can generate all twelve semitones of the chromatic scale by repeatedly superimposing one fifth upon another (C–G–D–A–E–B, etc.).[48] However, Sabaneev's table does not propose an equivalent spectral colour for each of these semitones. B-flat and E-flat have no specific colour, only the same, steely-metallic sheen, while B has no colour of its own but 'shares' the same colour (pale blue) as E.

Another distinguishing feature of the *luce* part in 'Prometheus' is not mentioned by Sabaneev but is at once obvious if we turn to the score (fig. 50). There is, throughout virtually the entire piece, a 'right hand' part and a 'left hand' part, both written on a single stave using conventional musical notation, even though the colour keyboard itself was soundless. Thus, these two 'melodic' lines represented only colours, not musical pitches. The lower line (left hand) is slow-moving in the extreme. Progressing very gradually over the course of more than twenty minutes from one long held note to the next, it produced a barely defined background of colour against which the 'action' took place. The upper line moved much more rapidly in response to the shifting tonality of the music, although it is perhaps misleading to speak of 'tonality' at all in discussing 'Prometheus', since Skryabin has by now more or less abandoned traditional keys, whether major or minor. Instead, the music alternates between different 'tonal centres', which ultimately derive from a distinctive and tonally ambiguous six-note chord, based on a sequence of perfect, augmented and diminished fourths – the famous 'Prometheus-chord' – that recurs in different transpositions and inversions throughout the piece. Although the structure of the music is not easily discerned on first hearing, even if following with the score, the progression from one tonal centre to the next is invariably marked by the movement of the right hand of the *luce* part from one note (that is, colour) to another. This means that, if 'Prometheus' were performed as Skryabin intended, complete with colour-light accompaniment, this shifting tonality would be more readily apparent, each change of tonal centre being emphasized by a corresponding change in colour.

---

48 See above, ch. 1, pp. 32–3.

Sabaneev's article likewise draws attention to the way in which changes in colour accompany changes in the music, adding that, according to Skryabin's system of correspondences, particular colours were equated not only with individual notes but also with different keys: 'Every key has its corresponding colour; every change in the harmony has a corresponding change in colour.'[49] But only at the very end of 'Prometheus' do we encounter anything that is really recognizable as a key, when increasingly atonal harmonies unexpectedly resolve on to a radiant chord of F-sharp major, described by a critic of one early performance as 'a triad so long hungered for that it gave little pleasure when reached beyond that which came from relief'.[50] Since, according to Sabaneev, Skryabin associated the key of F-sharp with bright blue, we must assume that, at this point, the auditorium would suddenly have been bathed in an aura of brilliant blue light.[51]

In fact, 'Prometheus' both begins and ends in blue. Sabaneev describes the opening (marked 'slow' and 'misty' by the composer) as taking place in a 'bluish-lilac twilight', although the interval F-sharp–A given to the light keyboard should, strictly speaking, have produced a combination of blue and green – colours that might, on the face of it, seem little suited to a work entitled 'The Poem of Fire'. One possible explanation has to do with the fact that, as Sabaneev suggests in his article, Skryabin did not have any literal or descriptive aim but instead a far-reaching mystical, even cosmic programme in mind. The mythical figure of Prometheus, who stole fire from the gods, symbolizes the struggle undertaken by the creative spirit, from the first vague stirrings of the desire for fulfilment to the final attainment of spiritual wisdom. The importance of this notion of spiritual progress is also stressed by Skryabin's biographer Faubion Bowers, who describes the opening of this musical 'poem' as follows:

The symphony begins with Chaos, the inchoate ooze of the formlessness of the world – blue and green inertia of matter ... Here the orchestra represents the Cosmos as it was before Karma, before lives have been lived and deeds accumulated predestination. Out of this long sustained chord dimly rises

---

49 'Prometheus von Skrjabin', loc. cit. (as n. [47] above).
50 H. E. Krehbiel writing in the *New York Tribune;* the review is reprinted in Klein 1926, pp. 240ff.
51 Skryabin's own handwritten annotations (see n. [46] above) point to a rather different conclusion. Here, referring to the last few pages of the score, he writes of 'threatening flames ... blue lilac ... then fiery, become blinding, *grows white* – conflagration, embracing the world, cataclysm ...' This suggests that the concluding F# major chord was meant to dissolve into blinding white light, displacing colour – something that, as Baker remarks 'could not have been inferred simply from the color-organ part itself' ('*Prometheus* and the Quest for Color-Music', p. 80).

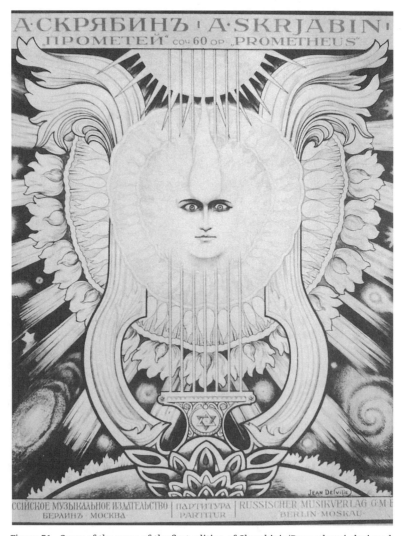

Figure 51. Cover of the score of the first edition of Skryabin's 'Prometheus', designed by Jean Delville, published by Koussevitsky's Russischer Musikverlag, Berlin, 1912

the melody of the Creative Principle. Then, a muted trumpet sends up the Will theme (blue vanishes). Languor ensues, and the 'contemplative' harmonies of the theme of Reason appear. Over this sweetly sings a solo flute – the 'dawn of human consciousness' (green flashes back over blue, and shortly vanishes). The piano (Man) enters imperiously, almost marchlike, and expresses its firm existence (the colour of steel). At the second repetition of the end of the

piano's initial figure, the colour of glowing red envelops
both piano and orchestra.[52]

If this underlying programme seems somehow familiar, it is perhaps because it vividly recalls that on which the Dutch artist Piet Mondrian's almost exactly contemporary painting *Evolution* (1910–11; pl. 14) is based. Mondrian, like Skryabin, was deeply influenced by the prevalent occultism of the early twentieth century. Not only does *Evolution*, like 'Prometheus', represent the path from spiritual darkness to enlightenment, symbolized by the open eyes of the female figure in the central portion of the triptych; it, too, is cast in a relatively sombre colour key, in which blues, violets and purples predominate.[53] Seen in the context of such ideas, the dominant blue tonality of 'Prometheus' seems less surprising, since many mystically inclined thinkers likewise regarded blue as the quintessentially spiritual colour. Skryabin's own interest in mysticism is well documented, as are his links with theosophy, a spiritual movement that attracted many writers and artists during the 1900s. While he was composing 'Prometheus' he was living for much of the time in Belgium, where he is known to have made contact with theosophical groups. He may even have joined a secret cult within theosophy called 'Sons of the Flames of Wisdom', to which the Belgian theosophist Jean Delville also belonged. It was Delville who created the cover design for the first published edition of the score of 'Prometheus', with its many esoteric allusions (fig. 51). Among these is the Star of David, which, according to Skryabin, was really the ancient symbol of Lucifer, encompassing all religions. We also know from the recollections of his brother-in-law, Boris de Schloezer, that Skryabin subscribed to theosophical journals and that he read and re-read Blavatsky's *The Secret Doctrine*, in which the fundamental tenets of theosophy were expounded.[54]

Skryabin's preoccupation with theosophy is important in connection with 'Prometheus' because the theosophists, too, associated colours with musical tones as well as with specific emotional states. (Although writer after writer on music had pointed

---

52 Faubion Bowers, *Scriabin, a Biography*, Mineola, NY (Dover Publications, Inc.) 2nd rev. edn 1996, pp. 207–8.
53 For an excellent analysis of Mondrian's *Evolution* triptych see John Milner, *Mondrian*, London (Phaidon) 1992, pp. 79ff.; on the influence of occultism on modern art more generally, see the catalogue *The Spiritual in Art. Abstract Painting 1890–1985*, Los Angeles (County Museum of Art)/New York (Abbeville Press) 1986.
54 'He read Mme. Blavatsky's *The Secret Doctrine* (in a French translation) many times, marking in pencil the most significant passages'; see Boris de Schloezer, *Scriabin. Artist and Mystic*, Oxford (Oxford U. P.) 1987, p. 71. We also know that Skryabin read Blavatsky's *Key to Theosophy* early in 1905. In a letter dated 8 May that year addressed to Tatyana Schloezer, he described it as a 'remarkable book. You will be surprised how close it is to my thinking'; see James M. Baker, 'Scriabin's Music: Structure as Prism for Mystical Philosophy', in James M. Baker, David W. Beach and Jonathan W. Bernard (eds), *Music Theory in Concept and Practice* (*Eastman Studies in Music*, no. 8), Rochester, NY (University of Rochester Press) 1997, p. 64 and n. 57.

to its direct appeal to the emotions, few had previously equated individual notes – for example, E-flat – with a particular emotion.) In Besant and Leadbeater's *Thought Forms* (1905), one of the most widely read of all theosophical texts, sound is explicitly 'associated with colour ... when, for example, a musical note is sounded, a flash of colour corresponding to it may be seen by those whose finer senses are already to some extent developed.'[55] The theosophists also identified both tones and colours with numbers, metals, planets and days of the week. In this, they resembled the seventeenth-century Jesuit Athanasius Kircher, who is often considered an adherent of the same esoteric tradition. Kircher, as we saw in the previous chapter, believed in a similar system of correspondences between birds and mammals, minerals and gemstones, angels and planets, colours and musical tones.[56] This kind of belief in a far-reaching complex of correspondences and affinities encompassing all forms of sensory experience, all knowledge and systems of classification could scarcely fail to impress Skryabin, who, at the time of composing 'Prometheus', was also sketching (at least in his mind) the 'prefatory action' to what he called his 'Mystery': a grandiose ritual that would embrace not only music and colour but also taste, smell and touch and whose performance was to mark the final accomplishment of the merely material phase of human existence.

Like 'Prometheus', Skryabin's 'Mystery' was intended as a manifestation of what Sabaneev called 'mystical-religious art, expressing all the occult faculties of mankind, whose ultimate goal is the attainment of ecstasy, to which end it has, from the beginning, always employed every means of affecting the human psyche.' Sabaneev compared this new form of art to a religious service, 'the modern-day offshoot of those mystic rituals of antiquity, having preserved – if only to a limited degree – the ideal of the unification of the arts: music (singing, the pealing of bells), physical movement (kneeling, the ritual gestures of the priest), the interplay of perfumes (incense) and light (candles, lighting in general), even painting. All the arts are here united in one harmonious whole and to a single purpose: that of heightening religious experience.'[57]

At one level, both Skryabin's 'Prometheus' and his 'Mystery' are symptomatic of that characteristically *fin-de-siècle* preoccupation with synaesthesia and with breaking down the barriers that had

---

55 Annie Besant and C. W. Leadbeater, *Thought Forms* (London/Benares, 1905), p. 75, quoted after Baker 2002, p. 70. *Thought Forms* particularly influenced artists, perhaps partly because it was well illustrated.
56 See above, ch. 6, pp. 235–6.
57 'Prometheus von Skrjabin' (see n. [47] above), pp. 57–8.

hitherto separated different art forms.[58] They also owe an obvious if perhaps only superficial debt to Wagner, whose conception of 'music-drama' likewise embraced all traditional forms of art including music, poetry, declamation, stage movement and scenic effects, thereby creating an artistic whole supposedly greater than the sum of its parts. Wagner, too, had pointed to antique precedent for his notion of the 'total work of art' (*Gesamtkunstwerk*), although Sabaneev in his article on 'Prometheus' remarked dismissively that 'this idea' had been formulated 'only vaguely' by Wagner and that it had been 'grasped in a much clearer form' by Skryabin. But Skryabin's affinities with occultism and theosophy and his allegiance to the Wagnerian notion of the *Gesamtkunstwerk* should not blind us to the originality of his attempt at fully integrating colour with music, in striking contrast to early demonstrations of Rimington's colour organ. When Rimington's instrument was used to accompany musical performances, the correspondences between the colours it produced and the ebb and flow of the music were, as its inventor admitted, for the most part arbitrary and depended largely upon the whim of the performer. The composer had not dictated them, nor were they written into the score, as they were in the case of 'Prometheus'. In the latter, the *luce* part was, in a sense, essential to a successful rendering of the work – so much so that, as Sabaneev observed, the music was 'virtually inseparable from the harmony of colours'. Although Skryabin himself willingly sanctioned and even participated in performances that made no attempt to provide any form of visual accompaniment, critics sometimes lamented the lack of coloured lights and complained about the unsatisfactory effect created by the music when heard on its own, as happened at the second London performance of 'Prometheus' in 1914. One such critic was John Runciman, who, writing in the respected journal *Music Quarterly*, objected that 'Prometheus' had been heard 'without the accompaniment of the "colour symphony". I wonder what would happen if the colour symphony were tried without an orchestra.'[59]

Reactions to Skryabin's experiments

Even today, the difficulties of performing 'Prometheus' as its composer presumably intended, complete with the full array of coloured light effects, remain daunting. The work is scored for a

---

58 There is an enormous literature on the phenomenon of synaesthesia, a topic not covered in this book. The interested reader may wish to consult the on-line bibliography compiled by the Leonardo Bibliography Project, entitled 'Synesthesia and the Arts', to be found at www.mitpress.mit.edu, which lists several hundred books and articles on this subject.

59 John F. Runciman, 'Noises, Smells and Colours', *Musical Quarterly*, vol. 1, no. 2 (April 1915), p. 151.

very large orchestra (including harp, celesta, chimes and multiple brass) plus solo piano, plus organ, plus wordless chorus, which means that it can only be played in the largest of auditoria. But to fill – really fill – a large concert hall with rapidly changing coloured lights is a task designed to tax the ingenuity of even the most resourceful lighting engineer. And in Skryabin's own day such a project was simply unrealizable. Millar, inventor of the 'Chromola' that was used at the March 1915 performance of 'Prometheus', had spoken of his 'dream to utilize an entire theatrical stage, hanging parallel curtains of thin diaphanous gauze from the proscenium, back to the rear wall of the theater, thus giving the light depth and sufficient space to expand and create atmosphere'.[60] But, in the end, the colours were apparently projected on to a small white screen suspended above and behind the musicians, with disappointing effect. Klein, writing in 1926, likened it to a 'school magic-lantern show', claiming that the audience who witnessed this 'miserable performance' was 'bored' and adding that it was 'no wonder that the beauty of the music was not enhanced, nor that the attention of the audience was actually diverted from it, a result which was the reverse of the composer's intention.'[61] His assertion that the attempt to combine music with colours provoked widespread dissatisfaction is borne out by a review in the *New York Times*, whose critic wrote that the lights:

were continually shifting and melting, but without visible relation to the sounds. In the midst of what seemed to be one phase the lights would change half a dozen times. There was no variation in intensity as the music grew more emphatic; at the height of its proclamation there was the same pleasing variety of yellows, oranges, violets, purples, and emeralds as there was in the beginning. The composer's clue was not entrusted to the lights, and to the first bewildered ben-eficiaries of the new art, it still seemed to be a sealed book.[62]

Part of the problem was that, whereas Skryabin had intended colour as a means of reinforcing and intensifying the meaning of the music, many of those who attended the 1915 Carnegie Hall performance evidently regarded the whole thing as some kind of experiment

---

60 Quoted after Peacock, 'Instruments to Perform Color-Music', p. 403.
61 Klein 1926, pp. 171–2.
62 *New York Times*, 21 March 1915, quoted after ibid., p. 248. One exception among the generally unfavourable reviews is the notice printed in *Illustrated World* (summer 1915), a popular magazine of science and technology, which refers to the play of 'many-colored lights, blending, sweeping onward in overpowering beauty' and calls the event a 'musical triumph'; quoted after Baker 2002, p. 61.

aimed at determining the relationships between colours and musical tones. This, at least, is the impression conveyed by the notice printed in the avant-garde New York magazine *291*, under the heading 'Color Music':

Nothing was proved on the question of the relationship of colour to music in the concert given by the Russian Symphony Orchestra at Carnegie Hall on March 20th. The experiment as it was performed was absolutely unsuccessful. The idea that two sensations of such different character as those produced by the organs of sight and by the organs of hearing could be mingled to form one sensation ... still remains a theory. What has been demon-strated up to the present, is, that of two simultaneous sensations one always predominates to the detriment of the other.[63]

In fact, the greatest difficulty remained one that Rimington had already identified. The obvious differences between our faculties of sight and hearing meant that, whereas the ear delighted in the changing patterns of sounds out of which music – all music – is created, the eye soon tired of a flickering succession of coloured lights, especially when these effects could be produced only on a relatively small scale. This problem was compounded by the fact that the 'art of mobile colour' was, for the most part, formless, lacking any easily identified shapes or patterns on which the eye could focus. This omission was, in part, deliberate, since Rimington had explicitly cautioned against trying to incorporate specific forms into colour light performances, writing that he himself had:

made many experiments with regard to the introduction of form, as the painter understands it ... and come to the con-clusion that if used at all it should be indefinite or merely decorative ... This kind of form introduced into the colour perhaps gives added interest to it in slow compositions, but in rapid ones the eye and the mind have quite enough to do to appreciate and enjoy the colour itself without the addition of form, which would seem to be an unnecessary complication.'[64]

But whereas different colours could be made to follow one another in a pre-determined, even seemingly logical sequence, a mere succession of coloured lights could not produce for the eye any

---

63 'Color Music', *291*, no. 2 (April 1915), n. p.
64 Rimington 1912, pp. 71–2.

equivalent of the distinctive forms and motifs on which music was based – for example, the first and second subjects of a traditional sonata-form movement, the recurring and easily recognized 'voices' of a fugue or the musical *Leitmotifs* so frequently employed by Wagner. For this, what was needed was an entirely new kind of visual art, 'animated' in the same way that music itself was animated – an art that might, at the same time, rival painting in its ability to create what the writer Clive Bell christened 'significant form'.[65]

In fact, such an art lay just around the corner. Or rather, it had already arrived. One reviewer, berating Skryabin's 'extremes of ultra-modern cacophony', thought it 'not likely' that his experiments at combining music and coloured light would be repeated by other composers, adding pointedly that 'moving-picture shows offer much better opportunities'.[66] And indeed, artists were not slow to realize film's potential for liberating visual art from the narrow confines of immobility, thereby making it more like music. By the early 1920s, at the latest, pioneers like Hans Richter and Viking Eggeling had begun experimenting with animated films, some of them hand-coloured, that were based mainly on a repertoire of abstract geometric forms – films such as Richter's *Rhythmus 21* (1921) or Eggeling's *Diagonal Symphony* of 1923–4. Both in their titles and in their visual structure, these films allude constantly to music – especially *Diagonal Symphony*, which is clearly based on the pattern of exposition–development–recapitulation characteristic of a traditional sonata-form movement.

Richter and Eggeling were not, however, the first artists who thought in such terms. A whole decade earlier, when art-film was still in its infancy, the Finnish-French painter Léopold Survage, then working in Paris, had embarked on a lengthy series of watercolours, now recognized as among the earliest studies for abstract animated film, to which he gave the name 'Coloured Rhythms' (pl. 15).[67] Although these experiments were not actually translated into the medium of film, Survage's aim was none the less unequivocal. In a document he submitted in the summer of 1914 to the French Academy of Sciences, he wrote:

I will animate my painting. I will give it movement. I will introduce rhythm into the concrete action of my abstract

65 The phrase occurs in Bell's book *Art*, published in 1914, but it had also been used by Roger Fry in writing about Cézanne; on the relation between Bell and Fry see Frances Spalding, *Roger Fry. Art and Life*, London (Paul Elek) 1980, pp. 123ff. and esp. 163ff.

66 *Nation*, 25 March 1915, quoted after Klein 1926, p. 244.

67 The path that led from abstract painting to the development of abstract animated film – one followed by various artists at this time – has been traced by Sara Selwood in her article 'Farblichtmusik und abstrakter Film', in Maur, *Vom Klang der Bilder*, pp. 414–21.

painting, born of my inner life. My instrument will be the cinematic film, that true symbol of accumulated movement. I will execute the 'scores' of my visions, which correspond to successive phases of my states of mind.

I am in the course of creating out of coloured rhythms and rhythmic colours a new visual art of time.[68]

At first hearing, Survage's statement sounds like a clarion call heralding an entirely new form of art. In fact, his ambition to 'animate' painting does little more than echo Castel's desire to bestow on 'inanimate colours' the characteristic mobility of music. In the same way, the seemingly revolutionary technique, first developed in the 1920s, of adding a soundtrack to a strip of celluloid film enabled artists to fulfil what was, in reality, a very old aspiration: to create a durable form of spectacle in which visual and auditory experiences might be combined, not at random, but in a precisely determined fashion. Seen in this light, the parentage of the 'talking film' – like its close relation, the colour-light performances staged by several artists in the years immediately after the Great War, among them Alexander László and Ludwig Hirschfeld-Mack – can itself be traced back, via Rimington and those other Victorian inventors whose innovations I have already described, to Castel's *clavecin oculaire* and even beyond: to the beginnings of opera and the musical extravaganzas of the late sixteenth century. Arguably, Skryabin's 'Prometheus' and his 'Mystery' as well as the experiments of his compatriot Vladimir Baranoff-Rossiné and the cinematic innovations of pioneer film makers such as Oskar Fischinger and Walter Ruttmann all belong, in the end, to that same tradition of development.

But while modern writers on the visual arts, like their eighteenth-century counterparts, pointed constantly to the example of music, it was usually for reasons that were, philosophically speaking, quite new. Artists and critics, philosophers and theorists from the Romantic era onwards admired music for what was now thought to be its most remarkable attribute: its abstract yet, at the same time, inherently expressive character. Indeed, music, which many eighteenth-century writers had distrusted on account of its alleged inability (except when linked to verbal content) to convey any very precise ideas, soon came to be extolled as the highest form of art: a model or paradigm the other arts would do well to emulate.[69] In this

---

68 Paris, Académie des Sciences, document no. 8182 deposited on 29 June 1914; quoted after ibid., p. 228.
69 For a characteristically eighteenth-century view of music, see Kant, *Critique of Judgement*, section 53, where music is compared unfavourably with poetry, the former being considered as 'more enjoyment than culture'.

sense, there really was a 'change of understanding' that occurred towards the end of the eighteenth century – which is why, in the sequel to this volume, I shall return to those thinkers and writers of the Enlightenment whose deliberations on music's relationship to its 'sister arts' mark, in my opinion, an essential first step on the path that leads to the formulation of a new 'modernist' aesthetic.[70]

I shall not try to summarize here the arguments contained in that further volume. Suffice it to say that, with the dismissal of realism and naturalism, artists at the beginning of the twentieth century found themselves under growing pressure to explain or justify a form of visual art that paid little or no attention to nature or to questions of narrative or representation. Pointing to the undeniably 'abstract' nature of music, through which the composer could communicate readily with the listener without recourse to stories or images of any kind, was one way of attempting to formulate such a justification.

And yet, as late as the eve of the First World War, arguments that highlighted music's abstract, expressive qualities and likened these to the effects produced by colour, line and form – that is, the abstract resources of painting – were still sometimes linked to older ideas that had to do with the intrinsically logical, even mathematical nature of music. For example, at the exhibition of the Allied Artists' Association, held in London in 1913, several works by Kandinsky were shown, among them paintings to which – deliberately, it seemed – the artist had given the musical title *Improvisation*.[71] These were pictures that, lacking any recognizable form of depiction, shocked audiences because of their abstract and therefore seemingly random nature. Reviewing that exhibition, the critic Roger Fry, who had become increasingly interested in the abstract tendency in contemporary European art, singled these paintings out for particular mention. Evidently seeking to counter accusations that non-representational art consisted of nothing other than an arbitrary conglomeration of colours, Fry here writes pithily and very much to the point:

After a time, the Improvisations *become more definite, more logical, more closely knit in structure, more surprisingly beautiful in the colour oppositions, more exact in their equilibrium. They are pure* visual music.[72]

---

70 For details of volume 2 of this study, entitled *Visual Music*, see above, n. [22] on p. 21.
71 Three paintings by Kandinsky were shown at the 1913 AAA exhibition (nos. 285–7), among them *Improvisation 29* and *Improvisation 30*; see 'European works of art exhibited in London between 1910 and 1914', in Anna Gruetzner Robins, *Modern Art in Britain 1910–1914*, London (Merrell Holberton/Barbican Art Gallery) 1997, pp. 186ff., 192.
72 *Nation*, 2 August 1913.

BIBLIOGRAPHY

William R. B. Acker, *Some T'ang and Pre-T'ang Texts on Chinese Painting* (*Sinica Leidensia*, vol. 8), Leiden (E. J. Brill) 1954

—, *Some T'ang and Pre-T'ang Texts on Chinese Painting*, vol. 2, Leiden (E. J. Brill) 1974

James S. Ackermann, *Distance Points. Essays in Theory and Renaissance Art and Architecture*, Cambridge, MA/London (MIT Press) 1991

Leon Battista Alberti, *On the Art of Building in Ten Books*, Joseph Rykwert, Neil Leach and Robert Tavernor (trans.), Cambridge, MA/London (MIT Press) 1988

Paul Alfassa, 'L'origine de la lettre de Poussin sur les modes d'après un travail récent', *Bulletin de la Société de l'Histoire de l'Art Français*, 1933, pp. 125–43

Francis Ames-Lewis, *The Intellectual Life of the Early Renaissance Artist*, New Haven/London (Yale U. P.) 2000

Art in Theory 1648–1815. An Anthology of Changing Ideas, Charles Harrison, Paul Wood and Jason Geiger (eds), Oxford (Blackwell) 2000

Robert W. Bagley, *Shang Ritual Bronzes in the Arthur M. Sackler Collection*, Cambridge, MA (Arthur M. Sackler Museum/Harvard U. P.) 1987

James M. Baker, 'Prometheus and the Quest for Color-Music: The World Premiere of Scriabin's *Poem of Fire with Lights*, New York, March 20, 1915', in James Leggio (ed.), *Music and Modern Art*, New York/London (Routledge) 2002

Nancy Kovaleff Baker and Barbara Russano Hanning (eds), *Musical Humanism and Its Legacy. Essays in Honor of Claude V. Palisca*, Stuyvesant, NY (Pendragon Press) 1992

John Baldwin, *Masters, Princes and Merchants: The Social Views of Peter the Chanter and his Circle*, Princeton, NJ (Princeton U. P.) 1970, 2 vols

André Barbera (ed.), *Music Theory and Its Sources: Antiquity and the Middle Ages*, Notre Dame, IN (University of Notre Dame Press) 1990

Andrew Barker (ed.), *Greek Musical Writings*, vol. 1 (The Musician and his Art), Cambridge (Cambridge U. P.) 1984

—, (ed.), *Greek Musical Writings*, vol. 2 (*Harmonic and Acoustic Theory*), Cambridge (Cambridge U. P.) 1989

Paola Barocchi (ed.), *Trattati d'arte del cinquecento fra Manierismo e Controriforma*, Bari (Laterza) 1960–2, 3 vols

Robert L. Benson and Giles Constable (eds), *Renaissance and Renewal in the Twelfth Century*, Oxford (Clarendon Press) 1982

Jan Bialostocki, 'Das Modusproblem in den bildenden Künsten. Zur Vorgeschichte und zum Nachleben des "Modusbriefes" von Nicolas Poussin', *Zeitschrift für Kunstgeschichte*, vol. 24 (1961), pp. 128–41

Anthony Blunt, *Nicolas Poussin. The A. W. Mellon Lectures in the Fine Arts*, London/New York (Phaidon/Bollingen Series) 1967

Jean Bony, *French Gothic Architecture of the 12th and 13th Centuries*, Berkeley (University of California Press) 1983

Bruce Boucher, *The Sculpture of Jacopo Sansovino*, New Haven/London (Yale U. P.) 1991, 2 vols

Calvin M. Bower, 'Natural and Artificial Music: The Origins and Development of an Aesthetic Concept', *Musica Disciplina*, vol. 25 (1971), pp. 17–33

Thomas Brachert, 'A Musical Canon of Proportion in Leonardo's Last Supper', *Art Bulletin*, vol. 53 (1971), pp. 461–6

Roger Bragard (ed.), *Jacobus of Liège. Speculum Musicae*, Rome (American Institute of Musicology) 1973, 7 vols (Corpus Scriptorum de Musica no. 3)

Robert Branner, *Gothic Architecture*, New York (George Braziller) 1961

David Bryant, 'The "Cori Spezzati" of St Mark's: Myth and Reality', *Early Music History*, I (1981), pp. 165–86

David J. Buch, 'The Coordination of Text, Illustration, and Music in a Seventeenth-Century Lute Manuscript: La Rhétorique des Dieux', *Imago Musicae*, VI (1989), pp. 39–81

Walter Burkert, *Lore and Science in Ancient Pythagoreanism*, Cambridge, MA (Harvard U. P.) 1972

Susan Bush, *The Chinese Literati on Painting. Su Shih (1037–1101) to Tung Ch'i-ch'ang (1555–1636)*, Cambridge, MA (Harvard-Yenching Institute Studies XXVII) 1971

—, 'Tsung Ping's Essay on Painting Landscape and the "Landscape Buddhism" of Mount Lu', in Bush and Murck 1983, pp. 132–64

—, and C. Murck (eds), *Theories of the Arts in China*, Princeton, NJ (Princeton U. P.) 1983

—, and Hsio-yen Shih (eds), *Early Chinese Texts on Painting*, Cambridge, MA (Harvard

U. P./Harvard-Yenching Institute) 1985

Castel 1995, *Études sur le XVIII Siècle, vol. 23: Autour du Père Castel et du clavecin oculaire*, Roland Mortier et Hervé Hasquin (eds), Brussels (Éditions de l'Université de Bruxelles, Groupe d'étude du XVIII Siècle) 1995

Louis-Bertrand Castel, 'Clavecin pour les yeux, avec l'art de Peindre les sons, & toutes sortes de Pièces de Musique', *Mercure de France*, IX (November 1725), pp. 2552–77

Henry Chadwick, *Boethius. The Consolations of Music, Logic, Theology and Philosophy*, Oxford (Clarendon Press) 1981

I. Bernard Cohen and Robert E. Schofield (eds), *Isaac Newton's Papers and Letters on Natural Philosophy and Related Documents*, Cambridge (Cambridge U. P.) 1958

Francesco Colonna, *Hypnerotomachia Poliphili. The Strife of Love in a Dream*, introduction by Joscelyn Godwin, London (Thames & Hudson) 1999

Nicholas Cook, *Music, Imagination and Culture*, Oxford (Clarendon Press) 1990

Francis Macdonald Cornford (trans. and commentary) *Plato's Cosmology. The Timaeus of Plato*, London/New York (Kegan Paul, Trench, Trubner/Harcourt, Brace) 1937

Richard L. Crocker, 'Pythagorean Mathematics and Music (Part I)', *Journal of Aesthetics and Art Criticism*, vol. 22, no. 2 (winter 1963), pp. 189–98; '(Part II)', vol. 22, no. 3 (spring 1964), pp. 325–35

Elizabeth Cropper, *The Ideal of Painting. Pietro Testa's Düsseldorf Notebook*, Princeton, NJ (Princeton U. P.) 1984

Paul Crossley, 'Medieval architecture and meaning: the limits of iconography', *Burlington Magazine* vol. CXXX, no. 109 (February 1988), pp. 116–21

Dante Alighieri, *The Divine Comedy*. John Ciardi (trans.), New York/London (W. W. Norton), 1970

René Descartes, *Compendium of Music* (*Compendium Musicae*). Walter Robert (trans.). Introduction and notes by Charles Kent (Musicological Studies and Documents, 8), Rome (American Institute of Musicology) 1961

Kenneth J. DeWoskin, *A Song for One or Two. Music and the Concept of Art in Early China*, Ann Arbor, MI (Michigan U. P.) 1982

The Dictionary of Art. Jane Turner (ed.), London (Macmillan) 1996, 34 vols

Effetto Arcimboldo. Trasformazioni del volto nel sedicesimo e nel ventesimo secolo, exh. cat. Palazzo Grassi, Venice 1987

Explanation of the Ocular Harpsichord upon Shew to the Public, London (Hooper and Morlay) 1757

Lothar von Falkenhausen, *Suspended Music. Chime-Bells in the Culture of Bronze Age China*, Berkeley (California U. P.) 1993

—, 'Issues in Western Zhou Studies: A Review Article', *Early China*, vol. 18 (1993), pp. 139–226

David Fallows, *Dufay (The Master Musicians)*, London (J. M. Dent), 2nd rev. edn 1987

John Fauvel, Raymond Flood, Michael Shortland and Robin Wilson (eds), *Let Newton be! A New Perspective on his Life and Works*, Oxford (Oxford U. P.) 1988

Iain Fenlon, 'St Mark's before Willaert', *Early Music*, vol. 21, no. 4 (November 1993), pp. 547–63

Michael Forsyth, *Buildings for Music. The Architect, the Musician and the Listener from the Seventeenth Century to the Present Day*, Cambridge (Cambridge U. P.) 1985

Maarten Franssen, 'The Ocular Harpsichord of Louis-Bertrand Castel. The Science and Aesthetics of an Eighteenth-Century Cause Célèbre', *Tractrix. Yearbook for the History of Science*, 3 (1991), pp. 15–77

Franchino Gaffurio, *The Theory of Music*, translated, with Introduction and Notes by Walter Kurt Kreyszig. Claude V. Palisca (ed.), New Haven/London (Yale U. P.) 1993

John Gage, *Colour and Culture. Practice and Meaning from Antiquity to Abstraction*, London (Thames & Hudson) 1993

—, *Colour and Meaning. Art, Science and Symbolism*, London (Thames & Hudson) 1999

Joscelyn Godwin, *Athanasius Kircher. A Renaissance Man and the Quest for Lost Knowledge*, London (Thames & Hudson) 1979

—, *Music, Mysticism and Magic. A Sourcebook*, London (Routledge & Kegan Paul) 1986

Lindy Grant, *Abbot Suger of St-Denis. Church and State in Early Twelfth-Century France*, London/New York (Longman) 1998

The New Grove Dictionary of Music and Musicians. Stanley Sadie (ed.), London (Macmillan) 1980, 20 vols

Penelope Gouk, *Music, Science and Natural Magic in Seventeenth-Century England*, New Haven/London (Yale U. P.) 1999

Hans R. Hahnloser, *Villard de Honnecourt. Kritische Gesamtausgabe des Bauhütten-buches ms. fr 19093 der Pariser National-bibliothek*, Vienna (Schroll & Co.) 1935

Frederick Hammond, *Music and Spectacle in Baroque Rome. Barberini Patronage under*

Urban VIII, New Haven/London (Yale U. P.) 1994

—, 'Poussin et les modes: le point de vue d'un musicien', in Olivier Bonfait *et al* (eds), *Poussin et Rome* (Actes du colloque de l'Académie de France à Rome, 16–18 novembre 1994), Paris (Réunion des musées nationaux) 1996

Alec Harman and Wilfred Mellers, *Man and His Music. The Story of Musical Experience in the West*, London (Barrie and Rockliff) 1962

Charles Homer Haskins, *The Renaissance of the Twelfth Century*, New York (Meridian) new edn 1955

E. A. Havelock, *Preface to Plato*, Oxford (Basil Blackwell) 1963

Isobel Henderson, 'Ancient Greek Music', in Egon Wellesz (ed.), *New Oxford History of Music*, vol. 1 (*Ancient and Oriental Music*), London (Oxford U. P.) 1957

John B. Henderson, *The Development and Decline of Chinese Cosmology*, New York (Columbia U. P.) 1984

S. K. Heninger, Jr., *Touches of Sweet Harmony. Pythagorean Cosmology and Renaissance Poetics*, San Marino, CA (The Huntington Library) 1974

G. L. Hersey, *Pythagorean Palaces, Magic and Architecture in the Italian Renaissance*, Ithaca, NY (Cornell U. P.) 1976

Johann Leonhard Hoffmann, *Versuch einer Geschichte der mahlerischen Harmonie überhaupt und der Farbenharmonie insbesondere, mit Erläuterungen aus der Tonkunst und vielen praktischen Anmerkungen*, Halle (Johann Christian Hendel) 1786

William Hogarth, The Analysis of Beauty, Joseph Burke (ed.), with rejected passages from the manuscript drafts and autobiographical notes, Oxford (Clarendon Press) 1955

John Hollander, *The Untuning of the Sky. Ideas of Music in English Poetry 1500–1700*, Princeton, NJ (Princeton U. P.) 1961

Deborah Howard, *Jacopo Sansovino. Architecture and Patronage in Renaissance Venice*, New Haven/London (Yale U. P.) 1975

—, and Malcolm Longair, 'Harmonic Proportion and Palladio's *Quattro Libri*', *Journal of the Society of Architectural Historians*, vol. 41, no. 2 (May 1982), pp. 116–43

John James, *Chartres. The Masons who Built a Legend*, London (Routledge & Kegan Paul) 1982

Jamie James, *The Music of the Spheres. Music, Science and the Natural Order of the Universe*, London (Little, Brown & Co.) 1994

H. James Jensen, *The Muses' Concord. Literature, Music, and the Visual Arts in the Baroque Age*, Bloomington, IN/London (Indiana U. P.) 1976

Martin Kemp (ed.), *Leonardo on Painting*, New Haven/London (Yale U. P.) 1989

—, *The Science of Art. Optical Themes in Western Art from Brunelleschi to Seurat*, New Haven/London (Yale U. P.) 1990

Dale Kent, *Cosimo de' Medici and the Florentine Renaissance. The Patron's Oeuvre*, New Haven/London (Yale U. P.) 2000

Peter Kidson, 'Panofsky, Suger and St Denis', *Journal of the Warburg and Courtauld Institutes*, vol. 50 (1987), pp. 1–17

Barbara Kienscherf, *Das Auge hört mit. Die Idee der Farblichtmusik und ihre Problematik*, Frankfurt/M. (Peter Lang) 1996

Dieter Kimpel and Robert Suckale, *Die gotische Architektur in Frankreich 1130–1270*, Munich (Hirmer) 1985

Adrian Bernard Klein, *Colour-Music. The Art of Light*, London (Crosby Lockwood & Son) 1926

Arthur Koestler, *The Sleepwalkers. A History of Man's Changing Vision of the Universe*, London (Hutchinson) 1959

Carol Herselle Krinsky, 'Seventy-Eight Vitruvius Manuscripts', *Journal of the Warburg and Courtauld Institutes*, vol. 30 (1967), pp. 36–70

Jan LaRue *et al.* (eds), *Aspects of Medieval and Renaissance Music. A Birthday Offering to Gustave Reese*, London (Oxford U. P.) 1967

Richard Leppert, *The Sight of Sound. Music, Representation and the History of the Body*, Berkeley/Los Angeles/London (California U. P.) 1993

Lionello Levi, 'L'Arcimboldi musicista', in Benno Geiger, *I dipinti ghiribizzosi di Giuseppe Arcimboldi, pittore illusionista del cinquecento (1527–1593)*, Florence (Vallecchi) 1954

Kenneth Levy, *Gregorian Chant and the Carolingians*, Princeton, NJ (Princeton U. P.) 1998

Edward Lockspeiser, *Music and Painting. A Study in Comparative Ideas from Turner to Schoenberg*, London (Cassell) 1973

Gian Paolo Lomazzo, *Scritti sulle arti, a cura di Roberto Paolo Ciardi*, Florence (Marchi & Bertolli) 1973, 2 vols

Lionel March, *Architectonics of Humanism. Essays on Number in Architecture*, Chichester (Academy Editions) 1998

Wilton Mason, 'Father Castel and his Colour Clavecin', *Journal of Aesthetics and Art Criticism*, vol. 17, no. 1 (September 1958), pp. 103–16

Thomas J. Mathiesen, *Apollo's Lyre. Greek Music and Music Theory in Antiquity and the Middle Ages*, Lincoln/London (Nebraska U. P.) 1999

Karin von Maur (ed.), *Vom Klang der Bilder. Die Musik in der Kunst des 20. Jahrhunderts*, Munich (Prestel) 1985

Ernest G. McClain, *The Myth of Invariance. The Origin of the Gods, Mathematics and Music from the Ṛg Veda to Plato*, Boulder, CO/London (Shambhala) 1978

—, *The Pythagorean Plato: Prelude to the Song Itself*, Stony Brook NY (N. Hays) 1978

—, 'The bronze chime bells of the Marquis of Zeng: Babylonian biophysics in Ancient China', *Journal of Social and Biological Structures*, 8 (1985), pp. 147–73

James W. McKinnon, 'Jubal vel Pythagoras, quis sit inventor musicae?' *Musical Quarterly*, vol. 64, no. 1 (January 1978), pp. 1–28

—, *Man and Music: Antiquity and the Middle Ages. From Ancient Greece to the 15th Century*, London (Macmillan) 1990

—, *The Advent Project. The Later-Seventh-Century Creation of the Roman Mass Proper*, Berkeley/Los Angeles/London (California U. P.) 2000

Alain Mérot, *Eustache Le Sueur 1616–1655*, Paris (Arthena) 1987

—, *Nicolas Poussin*, London (Thames & Hudson) 1990

Marin Mersenne, *Harmonie Universelle, contenant la Théorie et la Pratique de la Musique* (Paris, 1636). Édition facsimile ... ed. F. Lesure, Paris (Éditions du CNRS) 1975, 3 vols

Renato Meucci, 'Domenichino "musicologo" e le origini della Sonata a tre', in the catalogue *Domenichino 1581–1641*, Rome (Palazzo Venezia) 1996–7: Milan (Electa) 1996

Kathi Meyer-Baer, *Music of the Spheres and the Dance of Death. Studies in Musical Iconology*, Princeton, NJ (Princeton U. P.) 1970, repr. New York (Da Capo) 1984

Solon Michaelides, *The Music of Ancient Greece. An Encyclopedia*, London (Faber) 1978

A. P. de Mirimonde, 'Poussin et la musique', *Gazette des Beaux-Arts*, VI, vol. lxxix, March 1972, pp. 129–50

Jennifer Montagu, 'The Theory of the Musical Modes in the Académie Royale de Peinture et de Sculpture', *Journal of the Warburg and Courtauld Institutes*, vol. 55 (1992), pp. 233–48

Jennifer Montagu, *The Expression of the Passions. The Origin and Influence of Charles Le Brun's Conférence sur l'expression générale et particulière*, New Haven/London (Yale U. P.) 1994

Kiyohiko Munakata, 'Concepts of *Lei* and *Kanlei* in Early Chinese Art Theory', in Bush and Murck 1983, pp. 105–131

—, *Sacred Mountains in Chinese Art*, Urbana/Chicago (Illinois U. P.) 1991

Stephen Murray, *Building Troyes Cathedral. The Late Gothic Campaigns*, Bloomington and Indianapolis (Indiana U. P.) 1987

A. M. Nagler, *Theatre Festivals of the Medici 1539–1637*, New Haven/London (Yale U. P.) 1964

Paul von Naredi-Rainer, *Architektur und Harmonie. Zahl, Maß und Proportion in der Abendländischen Baukunst*, Cologne (DuMont), rev. edn 1999

Joseph Needham, *Science and Civilisation in China*, vol. 2 (*History of Scientific Thought*), Cambridge (Cambridge U. P.) 1956

—, *Science and Civilisation in China*, vol. 4, *Physics and Physical Technology* (part 1: *Physics*), Cambridge (Cambridge U. P.) 1962

Isaac Newton, *Opticks, or a Treatise on the Reflections, Refractions, Inflections and Colours of Light*, New York (Dover) 1952

Richard Norton, *Tonality in Western Culture. A Critical and Historical Perspective*, University Park and London (Pennsylvania State U. P.) 1984

Robert J. O'Connell, *Art and the Christian Intelligence in St. Augustine*, Oxford (Basil Blackwell) 1978

John Onians, 'The Last Judgement of Renaissance Architecture', *Journal of the Royal Society of Arts*, no. 128 (October 1980), pp. 701–18

—, 'On how to listen to High Renaissance art', *Art History*, vol. 7, no. 4 (December 1984), pp. 411–37

—, *Bearers of Meaning. The Classical Orders in Antiquity, the Middle Ages and the Renaissance*, Cambridge (Cambridge U. P.) 1988

Christopher Page, *The Owl and the Nightingale. Musical Life and Ideas in France 1100–1300*, London (J. M. Dent & Sons) 1989

—, *Discarding Images. Reflections on Music and Culture in Medieval France*, Oxford (Clarendon Press) 1993

—, 'Johannes de Grocheio on secular music: a corrected text and a new translation', in C. Page, *Music and Instruments of the*

Middle Ages: Studies on Texts and Performance, Aldershot (Ashgate/Variorum Collected Studies Series) 1997

Claude V. Palisca, 'G. B. Doni, Musicological Activist and his "Lyra Barberina"', in E. Olleson (ed.), *Modern Musical Scholarship*, Stocksfield/Boston/Henley/London (Oriel Press) 1980, pp. 180–205

Palisca 1985 (a)

Claude V. Palisca, *Humanism in Italian Renaissance Musical Thought*, New Haven/London (Yale U. P.) 1985

Palisca 1985 (b)

Claude V. Palisca, 'The Artusi-Monteverdi Controversy', in Denis Arnold and Nigel Fortune (eds), *The New Monteverdi Companion*, London (Faber) 1985, pp. 127–58

—, *The Florentine Camerata*, New Haven/London (Yale U. P.) 1989

Andrea Palladio, *The Four Books on Architecture*. Translated by Robert Tavernor and Richard Schofield, Cambridge, MA/London (MIT Press) 1997

Erwin Panofsky (ed.), *Abbot Suger on the Abbey Church of St.-Denis and its Art Treasures*. Edited, translated and annotated by Erwin Panofsky, Princeton, NJ (Princeton U. P.) 1946

—, *Gothic Architecture and Scholasticism* (London/New York, 1951) rev. edn Cleveland/New York (Meridian Books) 1957, 1966

Kenneth Peacock, 'Instruments to Perform Color-Music: Two Centuries of Technological Experimentation', *Leonardo. Journal of the International Society for Arts Sciences and Technology*, vol. 21, no. 4 (1988), pp. 397–406

Tom Phillips, *Music in Art through the Ages*, Munich/New York (Prestel) 1997

Nino Pirrotta, *Music and Culture in Italy from the Middle Ages to the Baroque*, Cambridge, MA/London (Harvard U. P.) 1984

J. J. Pollitt, *The Ancient View of Greek Art. Criticism, History and Terminology*, New Haven/London (Yale U. P.) 1974

—, *The Art of Ancient Greece: Sources and Documents*, Cambridge (Cambridge U. P.) 1990

Keith Pratt, 'The Evidence for Music in the Shang Dynasty: a Reappraisal', *Bulletin of the British Association for Chinese Studies*, September 1986, pp. 22–50

Curtis Price (ed.), *Man and Music: The Early Baroque Era. From the Late 16th Century to the 1660s*, Basingstoke (Macmillan) 1993

Thomas Puttfarken, *Roger de Piles' Theory of Art*, New Haven/London (Yale U. P.) 1985

—, 'Poussin's thoughts on painting', in Katie Scott and Genevieve Warwick (eds), *Commemorating Poussin. Reception and Interpretation of the Artist*, Cambridge (Cambridge U. P.) 1999, pp. 53–75

—, *The Discovery of Pictorial Composition. Theories of Visual Order in Painting, 1400–1800*, New Haven/London (Yale U. P.) 2000

Virginia Chieffo Raguin, Kathryn Brush and Peter Draper (eds), *Artistic Integration in Gothic Buildings*, Toronto (University of Toronto Press) 1995

Gustave Reese, *Music in the Middle Ages*, London (J. M. Dent & Sons) 1941

L. D. Reynolds and N. G. Wilson, *Scribes and Scholar. A Guide to the Transmission of Greek and Latin Literature*, Oxford (Clarendon Press) 2nd rev. edn 1974

Jean Paul Richter, *The Literary Works of Leonardo da Vinci* (compiled and edited from the original manuscripts), London (Phaidon) 3rd edn 1970

A. Wallace Rimington, *Colour-Music. The Art of Mobile Colour*, London (Hutchinson) 1912

Jean-Jacques Rousseau, *Essai sur l'origine des langues, où il est parlé de la mélodie et de l'imitation musicale*. Édition critique. Avertissement et notes par Charles Porset, Bordeaux (Guy Ducros) 1970

J. Rykwert and A. Engel, *Leon Battista Alberti* (exh. cat., Palazzo del Te, Mantua): Milan 1994

Howard Saalman, 'Alberti's Letter to Matteo de' Pasti Revisited', in Cecil L. Striker (ed.), *Architectural Studies in Memory of Richard Krautheimer*, Mainz (Philipp von Zabern) 1996, pp. 147–50

L. Sabanejew [sic], 'Prometheus von Skrjabin', in *Der Blaue Reiter. Herausgeber: Kandinsky, Franz Marc*, Munich (R. Piper & Co.) 1912, pp. 57–68

Annemarie Schimmel, *The Mystery of Numbers*, New York/Oxford (Oxford U. P.) 1993

P. H. Scholfield, *The Theory of Proportion in Architecture*, Cambridge (Cambridge U. P.) 1958

Herbert M. Schueller, *The Idea of Music. An Introduction to Musical Aesthetics in Antiquity and the Middle Ages*, Kalamazoo, MI (Western Michigan University Medieval Institute Publications) 1988 (Early Drama, Art, and Music Monograph Series, 9)

Stefan Schuler, *Vitruv im Mittelalter. Die Rezeption*, Cologne-Weimar (Böhlau) 1999

Hans Sedlmayr, *Die Entstehung der*

Kathedrale, Zurich (Atlantis) 1950

Eleanor Selfridge-Field, *Venetian Instrumental Music from Gabrieli to Vivaldi*, Oxford (Blackwell) 1975

Alan E. Shapiro (ed.), *The Optical Papers of Isaac Newton*, vol. 1: *The Optical Lectures 1670–1672*, Cambridge (Cambridge U. P.) 1984

John Shearman, *Mannerism*, Harmondsworth (Penguin) 1967

Lon R. Shelby, 'The geometrical knowledge of mediaeval master masons', in Lynn T. Courtenay (ed.), *The Engineering of Medieval Cathedrals*, Aldershot (Ashgate) 1997, pp. 27–53

Otto von Simson, *The Gothic Cathedral. Origins of Gothic Architecture and the Medieval Concept of Order*, New York (Pantheon Books/Bollingen Series XLVIII) 1956, 2nd rev. edn 1962

F. J. Smith, *Jacobi Leodiensis Speculum Musicae, A Commentary*, III, Henryville-Ottawa-Binningen (Institute of Medieval Music) 1983

Christine Smith, *Architecture in the Culture of Early Humanism. Ethics, Aesthetics and Eloquence 1400–1470*, New York/Oxford (Oxford U. P.) 1992

Jenny F. So (ed.), *Music in the Age of Confucius*, Washington, DC (Smithsonian Institution/Freer Gallery of Art/Arthur M. Sackler Gallery) 2000

R. W. Southern, 'Humanism and the School of Chartres', in *Medieval Humanism and other Studies*, Oxford (Blackwell) 1970, pp. 61–85

R. E. Spear, *Domenichino*, New Haven/London (Yale U. P.) 1982, 2 vols

John R. Spencer, 'Ut Rhetorica Pictura. A Study in Quattrocento Theory of Painting', *Journal of the Warburg and Courtauld Institutes*, vol. 20 (1957), pp. 26–44

Martianus Capella and the Seven Liberal Arts, I: *The Quadrivium of Martianus Capella*, by William Harris Stahl, Richard Johnson, and E. L. Burge, New York/London (Columbia U. P.) 1971 (commentary) and II: *The Marriage of Philology and Mercury*, New York (Columbia U. P.) 1977 (translation)

Bruce Stephenson, *The Music of the Heavens. Kepler's Harmonic Astronomy*, Princeton, NJ (Princeton U. P.) 1994

Oliver Strunk (ed.), *Source Readings in Music History*, rev. edn by Leo Treitler, New York (W. W. Norton) 1998. One-volume edition; contains:

Strunk I
Thomas J. Mathiesen (ed.), *Greek Views of Music*

Strunk II
James McKinnon (ed.), *The Early Christian Period and the Latin Middle Ages*

Strunk III
Gary Tomlinson (ed.), *The Renaissance*

Strunk IV
Margaret Murata (ed.), *The Baroque Era*

Strunk V
Wye J. Allanbrook (ed.), *The Late Eighteenth Century*

Strunk VI
Ruth A. Solie (ed.), *The Nineteenth Century*

Strunk VII
Robert P. Morgan (ed.), *The Twentieth Century*

Robert Suckale, 'La théorie de l'architecture au temps des cathédrales', in Roland Recht (ed.), *Les Batisseurs des Cathédrales Gothiques*, Strasbourg (Éditions les Musées de la Ville de Strasbourg) 1989, pp. 41–50

Michael Sullivan, *The Birth of Landscape Painting in China*, Berkeley (California U. P.) 1962

Robert Tavernor, *On Alberti and the Art of Building*, New Haven/London (Yale U. P.) 1998

Allan Temko, *Notre Dame de Paris*, London (Secker & Warburg) 1956.

André Tessier and Jean Cordey (eds), *La Rhétorique des Dieux et autres pièces de luth de Denis Gaultier*, Paris (Société française de musicologie) 1932

Gary Tomlinson, *Monteverdi and the End of the Renaissance*, Oxford (Clarendon Press) 1987

Tonino Tornitore, 'Musica per occhi', in *Effetto Arcimboldo* (see above), pp. 345–56

R. H. van Gulik, *The Lore of the Chinese Lute. An Essay in Ch'in Ideology*, Tokyo (Sophia University: Monumenta Nipponica) 1940

Vitruvius. Ten Books on Architecture. Translation by Ingrid D. Rowland ..., Cambridge (Cambridge U. P.) 1999

David L. Wagner (ed.), *The Seven Liberal Arts in the Middle Ages*, Bloomington, IN (Indiana U. P.) 1983

D. P. Walker (ed.), *Les Fêtes de Florence (1589). Musique des Intermèdes de 'la Pellegrina'*, Paris (Éditions du Centre National de la Recherche Scientifique) 1963

—, *Studies in Musical Science in the Late Renaissance*, London/Leiden (Warburg

Institute, University of London/E. J. Brill) 1978

Aby Warburg, 'I costumi teatrali per gli intermezzi del 1589', in Gertrud Bing and Fritz Rougemont (eds), *A. Warburg, Gesammelte Schriften, Band I: Die Erneuerung der heidnischen Antike. Kulturwissenschaftliche Beiträge zur Geschichte der europäischen Renaissance*, rev. edn Nendeln/Liechtenstein (Kraus Reprint) 1969

Martin Warnke, *Bau und Überbau. Soziologie der mittelalterlichen Architektur nach den Schriftquellen*, Frankfurt/M. (Syndikat) 1976

Charles W. Warren, 'Brunelleschi's Dome and Dufay's Motet', *Musical Quarterly*, vol. 59, no. 1 (January 1973), pp. 92–105

Albert Wellek, 'Renaissance- und Barocksynästhesie. Die Geschichte des Doppelempfindens im 16. und 17. Jahrhundert', *Deutsche Vierteljahrsschrift für Literaturwissenschaft und Geistesgeschichte*, Halle/S., vol. IX (1931), pp. 534–84

Albert Wellek, 'Das Doppelempfinden in 18. Jahrhundert', *Deutsche Vierteljahrsschrift für Literaturwissenschaft und Geistesgeschichte*, Halle/S., vol. XIV (1936), pp. 75–102

Egon Wellesz (ed.), *The New Oxford History of Music*, vol. 1 (*Ancient and Oriental Music*), London (Oxford U. P.) 1957

M. L. West, *Ancient Greek Music*, Oxford (Clarendon Press) 1992

Roderick Whitfield (ed.), *The Problem of Meaning in Early Chinese Ritual Bronzes* (Colloquies on Art and Archaeology in Asia, no.15), London (Percival David Foundation of Chinese Art) 1993

Elspeth Whitney, 'Paradise Restored. The Mechanical Arts from Antiquity through the Thirteenth Century', *Transactions of the American Philosophical Society*, vol. 80, part 1 (1990), pp. 1–169

Thomas Wilfred, 'Light and the Artist', *Journal of Aesthetics and Art Criticism*, vol. 5, no. 4 (June 1947), pp. 247–55

Christopher Wilson, *The Gothic Cathedral. The Architecture of the Great Church 1130–1530*, London (Thames & Hudson) 1990

Emanuel Winternitz, 'The Role of Music in Leonardo's Paragone', in Maurice Natanson (ed.), *Phenomenology and Social Reality. Essays in Memory of Alfred Schutz*, The Hague (Martinus Nijhoff) 1970

—, 'Leonardo and Music', in Ladislao Reti (ed.), *The Unknown Leonardo*, London (Hutchinson) 1974

—, *Musical Instruments and Their Symbolism in Western Art: Studies in Musical Iconology*, New Haven/London (Yale U. P.) 2nd edn 1979

—, *Leonardo da Vinci as a Musician*, New Haven/London (Yale U. P.) 1982

Rudolf Wittkower, 'Brunelleschi and "Proportion in Perspective"', *Journal of the Warburg and Courtauld Institutes*, vol. 16 (1953), pp. 275–91

—, *Architectural Principles in the Age of Humanism*, London (Alec Tiranti) 3rd rev. edn 1962, repr. 1971

Craig Wright, *Music and Ceremony at Notre Dame of Paris 500–1550*, Cambridge (Cambridge U. P.) 1989

—, 'Dufay's *Nuper rosarum flores*, King Solomon's Temple, and the Veneration of the Virgin', *Journal of the American Musicological Society*, vol. 47 (1994), no. 3, pp. 395–441

Franzsepp Würtenberger, *Malerei und Musik. Die Geschichte des Verhaltens zweier Künste zueinander*, Frankfurt/Bern/Las Vegas (Peter Lang) 1979

Xiaoneng Yang (ed.), *The Golden Age of Chinese Archaeology. Celebrated Discoveries from the People's Republic of China*, New Haven/London (Yale U. P.) 1999

—, *Reflections of Early China. Decor, Pictographs, and Pictorial Inscriptions*, Kansas/Seattle and Washington (Nelson-Atkins Museum of Art/University of Washington Press) 2000

Jeremy Yudkin, *Music in Medieval Europe*, Englewood Cliffs, NJ (Prentice Hall) 1989

De tutte l'opere del R. M. Gioseffo Zarlino ... Il primo volume, contenente l'Istitutioni harmoniche divise in quattro parti ... in Venetia, MDLXXXIX, Apresso Francesco de' Franceschi Senese

Heinrich Zimmermann (ed.), 'Das Inventar der Prager Schatz- u. Kunstkammer vom sechsten Dezember 1621, nach Akten des k. u. k. Reichsfinanzarchivs in Wien', *Jahrbuch der Kunsthistorischen Sammlungen des Allerhöchsten Kaiserhauses*, vol. 25, Vienna/Leipzig (F. Tempsky/G. Freitag) 1905, II. Teil, pp. xiii ff

Giangiorgio Zorzi, *Le chiese e i ponti di Andrea Palladio*, Neri Pozza Editore [Venice] 1967

INDEX

PICTURE CREDITS